A LIFE OF ONE'S OWN

Joan Dash

A LIFE

Three Gifted Women

OF ONE'S OWN

and the Men They Married

HARPER & ROW, PUBLISHERS

NEW YORK, EVANSTON, SAN FRANCISCO, LONDON

Photograph of Margaret Sanger courtesy Sophia Smith Collection, Smith College; Edna St. Vincent Millay, Wide World Photos; Maria Goeppert-Mayer, courtesy Joseph Mayer.

Quotations from *Atoms in the Family*, by Laura Fermi, copyright 1954 by The University of Chicago. Copyright 1954 under the International Copyright Union. Published 1954. Composed and printed by The University of Chicago Press, Chicago, Illinois, U.S.A. Used by permission.

FIRST EDITION

STANDARD BOOK NUMBER: 06-010949-1

LIBRARY OF CONGRESS CATALOG CARD NUMBER: 76-138717

to J. G. D.

Contents

Acknowledgments

I HAVE INCURRED a great many debts in the course
of writing this book: to Genevieve Young, formerly of Harper & Row,
now at Lippincott, who first suggested that I write it and encouraged
me through the early stages; to Ann Harris, of Harper & Row, for the
delicate process of editing; to the many friends who prodded and helped
and advised, especially that most loyal friend, my husband, J. Gregory
Dash; and to several libraries and other learned institutions, the Library
of the University of Washington, Smith College Library and the main
branch of the Seattle Public Library among others. To all those connected with the three gifted women I have written about, those who
allowed me to interview them by mail, by telephone or in person, I wish
to express a general sense of indebtedness, as well as more specific thanks
in the paragraphs that follow.

For the Margaret Sanger section, I am grateful to Smith College for
the use of their Sophia Smith Collection, with its abundance of letters,
journals and papers; the kindness and hospitality of Smith College were
embodied in Elizabeth Duvall, then bibliographer, and always the most
resourceful of librarians. I am grateful also to Dr. Grant Sanger for his
approval and cooperation, and for a brief but illuminating interview; to
Dr. Alan Guttmacher of Planned Parenthood for reading the manuscript; to David Kennedy, History Department, Stanford University,
who read and evaluated it; and to Nathaniel Wagner, Department of
Psychology, University of Washington, for sympathetic criticism.
Planned Parenthood allowed me to use their library and to consult the
taped interviews with birth control pioneers that Martha Stuart had

conducted for them, including interviews with Dr. John Rock, Sir Julian Huxley and Morris Ernst. I am especially grateful to Joan Sanger Hoppe for recollections of her father.

For the section on Edna St. Vincent Millay, I am deeply indebted to Norma Millay for the privilege of a day's visit to Steepletop, and for hours spent discussing her "poet sister" in her natural setting. Miss Millay permitted me to consult the files, at Harper & Row, containing Eugen Boissevain's business letters to his wife's publishers. I am grateful also to Norman A. Brittin and John J. Patton, both Millay scholars, for the time they spent in reading and criticizing this portion of the book. I am especially thankful for the many hours spent by Dr. Charles Mangham and Dr. George Allison, psychoanalysts, in thoughtful conversations about the psychological probing that forms so large a part of this biography; they were most generous with their time. The late Max Eastman allowed me to interview him at Martha's Vineyard, and reminisced about his friend Eugen Boissevain. Leonie Adams recalled a visit to Millay in Greenwich Village. Miriam Burstein was my conscientious research assistant, and Grace H. King's thesis on Millay was extremely helpful.

For the story of Maria Goeppert-Mayer I am chiefly indebted to the late Maria Mayer and to her husband, Joseph Mayer, who made time in their busy lives for many, many hours of interviewing. Their candor and patience, in explaining to a stranger the peculiar joys of the scientific life, were surpassed only by their tactful hospitality. I am grateful also to Lawrence Wilets, of the Department of Physics, University of Washington, for several lengthy discussions of atomic physics; his remarkable gifts as a teacher enabled me to glimpse, however dimly, Maria Mayer's nucleus. The manuscript was read and criticized by Charles Weiner, Director, Center for History and Philosophy of Physics, the American Institute of Physics, and I wish to thank him for his suggestions. The Library of the American Philosophical Society furnished transcripts of several interviews with James Franck and one with Maria Mayer, from their "Sources for the History of Quantum Physics," a project undertaken jointly with the American Physical Society and begun in 1961. Laureen Nussbaum, of the Department of Foreign Languages, Portland

State University, was the able translator of Maria's letters in German to her mother. Innumerable friends and colleagues of the Mayers contributed their recollections: I am especially grateful to Laura Fermi for her lively account of the Leonia years; to Dr. Katherine Rice; to Victor Weisskopf; to Peter Mayer and his sister, Maria Wentzel; to Edward Teller; to Ruth Jacobsohn; to Alice Kimball; to Dr. Maria Stein; to Harris Mayer; to Karl Herzfeld; and to Frieda and Harold Urey.

I wish to express my thanks to those who permitted me to quote from copyrighted material: Laura Fermi, for *Atoms in the Family,* published by the University of Chicago Press; Dr. Grant Sanger, for *My Fight for Birth Control,* published by Farrar & Rinehart, and *Margaret Sanger: An Autobiography,* published by W. W. Norton; and the late Edmund Wilson, for *The Shores of Light,* published by Farrar, Straus. I want to thank as well several informants who shared their recollections with me but who preferred to remain unnamed. I am grateful too for the general interest and encouragement of Patricia Myrer, of McIntosh & Otis; Lynne Harrison, photographer; and Michael, Elizabeth and Tony Dash, critics.

J.D.

Introduction

AN EMPIRE IS CRUMBLING—vast, far-flung, long-entrenched. Faint hearts among us cry out in favor of the status quo, implore extremists to remember the past was not so bad and the darkies sang as they worked and there were loving masters as well as vicious ones. If God did not intend some to be slaves and others free why did He create two kinds of people, one childlike and pliant, one masterful, daring, aggressive? But the foremost of the rebels are champing at the bit; there is no accommodation possible, nothing to be negotiated, exploiter and exploited must henceforth live apart. Babies will be conceived in test tubes—I am speaking, of course, of men and women, of the empire that extends from bedroom to board room—sex will amount to little more than a therapeutic exercise and in the glorious era that follows revolution, androgynes will walk the earth while machines, and a few primitive human types, victims of the slave mentality, will rock the cradle and produce the pellets of food and snips of plastic clothing that once kept millions of women lashed hand and foot to what used to be known as Home.

But the empire that is crumbling now is not as old as the human race; like every other empire it had a beginning as well as a middle and an end, and before that beginning there was another empire, a female one. Therefore what men have been doing to us we once did to them, and I for one find this immensely consoling, balm for the ego as well as reassurance when the future looks barren and sexless. There have been sexual revolutions before, and when the fighting and the fury were over winner and loser, master and slave, went home to bed, where they discovered the war had settled nothing.

Where was this female empire, and when? It was not, strictly speaking, an empire at all, but rather a world view, that women were the superior and more powerful sex, as indeed they were throughout the Near East during all the centuries of neolithic prehistory. Greek myths record a civilization where women were tribal priests and rulers, and deity was the Great Goddess, whose mystery was motherhood, fertility in the flocks and fields and in the human womb. Some humble tasks were delegated to men—hunting, fishing, the care of the herds—and in religious life they played a limited role. According to Robert Graves, at certain times a temporary king "deputized for the Queen at many sacred functions, dressed in her robes, wore false breasts. . . . His ritual death varied greatly in circumstance; he might be torn in pieces by wild women, transfixed with a sting-ray spear, felled with an axe, pricked in the heel with a poisoned arrow, flung over a cliff. . . . But die he must."

The rule of the Great Goddess lasted some five thousand years, succumbing at last to the discovery that her mystery was no mystery at all, that women, who used to conceive at whim or with the help of the wind and coupled solely for their own erotic pleasure, did nothing of the kind. And men, being bigger and stronger and full of pent-up resentment, took suitable vengeance; they have been taking it ever since. Still, there is a considerable amount of wry comfort to be wrung from the knowledge that we women did not enter history as subservient beings —that female sexuality had to be forcibly repressed and reshaped according to the needs of the agricultural revolution, of settled family life and orderly inheritance. Men have been harsh rulers in this empire of theirs, but at least we did not go meekly into servitude. I like that part of it, knowing that it was the awesome strength of female sexuality that required such powerful suppression.

There is something else I like about the recollection of the Great Goddess, and that is the awareness that if women made prehistory while men made history until today, the future may prove to be a collaboration, with God neither male nor female but Janus-faced, female on one side, male on the other. If we can scrape up the wit to keep machines from ruling over both, sex may survive, and even love, and who knows but that marriage will live on, in whatever altered form. It may have to go underground for a while, like the Goddess; but was she ever really dead? Didn't Portnoy describe her as his mother? And do we not see her here and there among the more thoughtful of the current revolutionaries—nails sharpened, blood in her eye and poisoned arrow gripped in her unmanicured hand?

The news this time is that women must become, are on their way to becoming, self-realizing individuals, no longer the objects of men's dreams and desires but free to act out their own desires. Is self-realization for women possible if they continue to live with men? It has been known to happen, and with all the passion currently being expended on the subject, surely we will learn how to make it happen more often. There are no guarantees; even when men had absolute authority over women many, perhaps most men led dreary lives utterly empty of self-realization. After the revolution, sisters, some of us will still lead dreary lives, for the fault is often not in our men but in ourselves that we are underlings.

My own expertise in this matter—of where the fault is, whether in ourselves, our men, the institution of marriage or in the stars that govern history—arises chiefly from belonging to that generation of women, now middle-aged, who first wondered en masse what price we had paid for having been born women. For my generation, as for my mother's, higher education and the fruits thereof were readily available, but it was poisoned fruit, for we had known since infancy that our chief duty was to get a husband. Our success in life would be measured by his rather than our own attainments. Therefore whatever we had been educated for we did, but only briefly; whatever little bastion we had managed to establish, a joblet with a future, a toehold in the door of graduate school, we tore it out when the babies came or our husbands were transferred, for, knowing which side our bread was buttered on, we were determined to Help Him Get Ahead. We did the same for our children—if they succeeded, the boys professionally, the girls at marriage, the credit would be largely our own; everything was to happen to the good American wife through her influence on others.

But my generation was not composed solely of Blondies. It included women like one I recently interviewed; considerably older than I am and married to a Nobel laureate scientist, she raised four talented children including a physicist daughter. She is lively, earthy and smart; she has not, so far as I can tell, manipulated anyone. She sets a good table, envies nobody, certainly no man, and is too old to be liberated. Marriage as we knew it was more diverse than the stereotype.

Perhaps it was this very diversity that so sorely troubled us. For we had a foot in both worlds and, belonging fully to neither, hated both. We hated the women who stayed contentedly at home, the women we suspected we were superior to and who had the effrontery to be happy; as for the few who had made it in a man's world, these we both hated and feared, for they showed us our own folly. It had been made clear to us that we would cease to be women, womanly women with loving husbands and happy children, if we could not suppress our longing for anything else. We did not quite suppress the longing, we only suffered for it and were ashamed that we suffered; our very suffering showed what we were—jealous of men, if not worse than jealous. Perhaps the subterranean memory of the Great Goddess lived on in all of us and we have been serving out our time to prove her power is dead.

But this was marriage in my generation. By the 1960s, with the birth of the pill and the awareness of overpopulation, much that used to be true began to seem doubtful, such as the clear knowledge that a womanly woman yearned for babies. Suddenly it became possible, perhaps even advisable, never to have them, or to have only one. In the case of an unwanted baby—and how they used to haunt us, the babies that might slip past a diaphragm incorrectly inserted, or statistically ineffective, or simply forgotten—abortion became a real, even a legal alternative. And babies were the glue that held it all together; what were we doing, all those centuries, if not breeding infants and placating the masters who fed and clothed them, earning protection by conjugal relations and home cooking? Nowadays young people have been putting off marriage in favor of a phenomenon called "living together"—it used to be called "living in sin," but now the minister or the rabbi visits young couples in their flats or communes and whatever they talk about it is certainly not the sin of an unregistered union. When they do marry, they seem to postpone having babies, perhaps forever. Or, when there is a baby, the air being full of the new freedom, the right kind of man takes it upon himself to share, half and half, in its upbringing. Sex has become far less romantic, thanks to the pill, and much of the emotional energy that was once poured into it flows now into self-realization, into work, and girls speak of their work as they once spoke of men. It is a loss and some would say a sad one, but perhaps sex seemed romantic to us mainly because it removed us from the adult world in which we were doomed forever to second place.

The young today who share their lives and sometimes the care of their infants share everything else—housework, cooking, cleaning—for it is a basic belief of the present sexual revolution that no activity outside the bedroom belongs exclusively to either sex, that no work is "woman's work." This, I think, has never happened before; whatever used to be man's work, even among those rare and exotic primitive people who apportioned the cooking and housework to the men, women did something clearly different. Whether this will blur the differences between the sexes is a troubling question; a psychologist I know insists it will not, that so long as the glands themselves are not tampered with men will be those whose role is penetration, and women, those who are penetrable. Amid all the impassioned discussion of passive vagina and active clitoris, the truth about the clitoris is that it will never go far.

Women today are freer to choose than any who ever lived before. If, for millennia, we were exploited by men it was chiefly because our exploitation served society as a whole; this exploitation is no longer practical, just as it is no longer useful for society that women should be limited by their physiological attributes. Yet neither is it useful to blame the men—would we not have done the same in their position, and did we not do it, once? Nor should we blame the uterus and the much-maligned vagina, or menstruation, or pregnancy. We can live with men and we can learn to live with our own innards, although not without some painful adjustments. No matter how painful, it beats unisex and surrender to the machines.

Which brings me to the subject of this book—three gifted women who did precisely that, learned to live on self-respecting terms with themselves, and with a man. Not, I must add, with unvarying and equal success. Born about a decade apart, they reached adulthood in the early years of this century when the structure of marriage had begun to feel the first serious tremors. While following the lives and unfolding genius of the three women themselves, I have kept a weather eye cocked for those problems of coexistence—how daily life is managed, whose work determines what decision, what sacrifices are made and by whom, at what price—that are the stuff of marriage. What does it mean to be a wife or a husband in a union where the woman has a fully realized life of her own, equaling or eclipsing her husband in worldly success—this is what I have been concerned with, for this, it seems to me, is what we are talking about and will continue to talk and argue and search our souls about, along with the vexed question of whether we want to be husbands and wives at all. To which latter, by the way, each of the three would have answered, emphatically, yes.

None of them was exempt from the self-doubt that plagued my generation and my mother's; none had plain sailing, professionally speaking. Their characters and their careers were deeply marked by the difficulty of being female in a male world, and the conflicting drives to be at once a woman, some man's woman, and one's self. This is partly why I chose to write about them; yet I must confess I chose them for another and more compelling reason, the reason all biographers must ultimately confess to—they were women who intrigued me, whose personalities no less than their accomplishments I longed to know more about.

And, learning about them, I became equally intrigued by the men they had chosen, in one case finding the husband more memorable than his wife. Eugen Jan Boissevain married a brilliant poet, Edna St. Vincent Millay, at the height of her fame; they lived together for twenty-five years, by no means serenely, for she was as troubled as she was gifted, in some ways childlike, certainly unstable. But the history of literature is full of tormented and brilliant poets, while men like Boissevain, noisy and sensitive, impulsive, courageous and tenderly devoted, are hard to come by. I found him a beguiling subject, almost too attractive to write about objectively.

William Sanger, by contrast, was a husband in the traditional style; no villain, he started married life with the best of intentions. The pretty redheaded nurse he married was shy, she wanted "bringing out" and he encouraged her on every hand, to read and study, to enter a more challenging social circle, in a word, to find herself. But Sanger succeeded too well and after fourteen years the marriage dissolved in bitterness. When Margaret Sanger married again it was to an older, wiser man, J. Noah H. Slee, who spent the rest of his life trying to lure her home. It was not a particularly happy marriage; perhaps happiness in marriage was not something for which Margaret Sanger was entirely suited, although she wrote a book by that name.

Joseph and Maria Mayer most closely approached the modern ideal of marriage as a union between two fully realized individuals, both scientists, both eminent, their professional lives almost as closely entwined as their personal lives. But because they were real people rather than fictional, much of what I learned about them was unexpected—that only one was a feminist, namely Joe; that one was gentle and pliant, namely Maria, not in her work, of course, but in her very feminine character. Puzzled by the demands of parenthood, hedged about by the barriers the academic world threw up against members of her sex, Maria Mayer longed at times to call it all off, to stay at home and become a housewife. Fortunately for science, she had other longings as well.

All that they accomplished—the poet Edna Millay, the crusader Margaret Sanger and the scientist Maria Mayer—was done in a time when conventional marriage was the rule. There were exceptions; they were the exceptions. As was Virginia Woolf, who first envisioned "A Room of One's Own." In the waning years of the old empire, each of them, gently or belligerently, consciously or unconsciously, was a revolutionary.

In the biographies that follow I have tried to examine not only three remarkable women and the men they married, but the childhood families, especially the parents; all the influences, early and late, that affected their work, as well as why and how they chose it and why pursuing it was important to them. This has led me to judgments I ought, perhaps, to have avoided; in the case of Edna Millay I became willy-nilly a literary critic, a discipline for which I am not fitted by training and perhaps not by temperament. In the case of the Mayers, it was necessary to sketch in some analysis of the character of scientific research as well as the personalities of scientists insofar as they can be said to have any "typical" personality. I turned to the findings of two well-known psychologists, but much of the picture is my own, the distillation of twenty-five years of living among scientists who are my husband's colleagues and friends, and where I have not cited authority for an opinion, the opinion is mine.

Biography, like beauty, is in the beholder's eye. Omissions as well as the material included form the portrait that is finally put in the reader's hands. The portraits of these three women, their work, their marriages and how all was arranged and divided and eventually integrated, are highly personal ones.

Margaret Sanger

"THAT BEAST OF A MAN William took me away for a drive last Monday and drove me to a minister's residence and married me. I wept with anger and couldn't look at him for it was so unexpected. . . . I had on an old blue dress and looked horrid. . . . I'm very sorry to have the thing occur, but yet I am very, very happy." So Margaret Higgins Sanger described her wedding in a letter to her sister Mary, while to another sister she sent a similar account, adding that Bill was "beastly, insanely jealous."

This strident clash of emotions—the happiness in anger, the "unexpected" marriage to a "beast of a man"—was not confined to Margaret's wedding day, for hers was an altogether puzzling and contradictory nature. Margaret Sanger was to become a rebel-crusader who served the most rational of causes with the mystic dedication of a saint. In the fashion of saints she grew to be a difficult and baffling woman, utterly single-minded, resentful of anyone who contested her authority and vision, vain, combative, intolerant, superstitious. Yet she was also wise, magnetic, daring, demurely charming, an irresistible and tireless leader, a loyal and generous friend.

Her background was by no means irreconcilable with sainthood, for Margaret Higgins came of Irish stock, poor, high-minded and formerly Catholic. That her childhood was an unhappy one we know by her description of her home town—"when I'm passing through Corning at night by train, my body knows I'm there without my seeing it. I actually become sick to my stomach." Born in 1879, the sixth of eleven babies born to Anne Purcell Higgins who died of tuberculosis in her forties,

Margaret could never remember her mother without recalling her racking cough, and how she leaned against the walls while she waited for it to stop. Gentle, patient, forbearing as her mother was, Margaret's father was entirely the opposite, a man of artistic temperament and many talents, dangerously outspoken, self-centered and the chief figure in Margaret's childhood; in many ways Michael Hennessy Higgins resembled Bill Sanger, who was also an idealist and a dreamer, egocentric, romantic, impractical. She felt for her father a somewhat similar mixture of adoration and resentment, as well as a subtle undercurrent of fear, hardly understood yet undeniably present in later accounts of her childhood. But love and admiration were uppermost; Margaret called her father "the spring from which I drank."

He was an Irish immigrant, a freethinking Socialist who earned his living carving headstones and monuments; and in the Catholic town of Corning, New York, inhabited chiefly by immigrant factory workers, much of what he carved were Catholic headstones. Margaret once told a friend that when he worked on a saint's likeness her father muttered, "That son of a bitch!" with each blow of the chisel. Since he never tried to conceal his beliefs and sponsored the appearance in town of iconoclasts like Robert Ingersoll and Henry George, commissions were few, the children often went hungry, and what Higgins earned he too often shared with others who were hungrier.

Even as the family increased, her father's outspoken hatred of Catholicism further narrowed their sources of income, until commissions could only be found outside of Corning. More than poverty, the children suffered from a sense of isolation, from the scorn and rejection of their classmates, who shouted names at them on their way to school, stuck out their tongues, called them "children of the devil." Margaret's mother, a practicing Catholic until the time of her marriage, apparently never tried to alter her husband's views or behavior, any more than she thought of calling a halt to the procession of babies that drained her strength and the family resources. "Though never very strong, Mother was always busy sewing, cleaning, doing this and that for the ever increasing family. I wondered at her patience and her love for him!" Margaret wrote later. And, "not one of us dared to utter a word of criticism or condemnation about her adored and adoring husband."

"Every day, even when going to work," Margaret said of her father, "he put on spotless white shirts with starched collars and attachable cuffs; these were something of a luxury because they had to be laundered at home." Although he was an avowed believer in women's rights, there was nothing in her father's Irish background to suggest that a man might wash a dish; he was an expert in the sickroom, himself delivering each of their eleven babies, but otherwise "paternal duties did not exist." It was his consumptive, everlastingly pregnant wife who had to carry "the responsibilities of feeding and clothing the family as her own, and managed on the combined income of three or four older children to keep the wolf from the door."

Even as a girl Margaret was sharply aware of the contrast between the small families of the rich living on the hillsides, and the crowded homes of the poor huddled on the river flats. "The fathers of the small families owned their homes; the young-looking mothers had time to play croquet with their husbands in the evenings on the smooth lawns. Their clothes had style and charm, and the fragrance of perfume clung about them." For the rest of her life she was to be haunted by a desire to belong to that world of small and happy families, to be herself a woman of style and charm; money, clothes, distinguished friends never assuaged the need, and in her fifties, an international figure with a rich husband and a handsome country estate, she still believed it was beyond her grasp. "We, the children of poorer parents, knew not where we belonged. Everything that we desired most was forbidden. Our childhood was one of longing for things that were always denied. We were made to feel inferior to teachers, to elders, to all."

Yet there were compensations; the family was a close-knit and interdependent one, perhaps because of their very isolation from others, and remained so long after the children were grown and scattered. And for Margaret especially there was the compensation of a close and affectionate tie with her father. She seems to have taken him, rather than her mother, as her model. "My father must have realized a certain quality in me for he often shared and disclosed unusual ideas for my youthful mind to conjure with," she recalled, and a number of the childhood incidents she most cherished were those that showed him singling her out as his own special child, his audience, apprentice and accomplice in adventure. "The one thing I've been able to give you is a free mind. Use it well and give something back to your generation," he had told his children. Of them all, Margaret was the one who most closely shaped her life to fit his lofty standards. To serve, to think freely, to question all orthodoxy and act regardless of consequences was her conscious desire, her inheritance from Michael Higgins.

But there was a darker side to Margaret's love for her father, a subtle yet deeply troubling fear of male sexuality that she came to think of as "blind, imperious and driving. . . . It seeks only its own satisfaction." If she never fully understood the origin of her mature feelings about men and sex, never really saw them as rooted in the tangle of emotions centered about her father, she was nevertheless aware of her childhood fears of him as a sexual being:

The only memory I have of any sex awakening . . . was when I was ill with typhoid fever. I could not have been more than eight or nine years of age. . . . I remember nothing beyond going upstairs to a cold room and a colder bed. . . . It was pitch dark. I felt about me and knew I was in . . . Mother's bed. . . . Then I heard heavy breathing beside me. It was Father. I was terrified. I wanted to scream out to Mother to beg her to come and take him away. I could not move, I dared not move, fearing he might awaken and move toward me. I lived through agonies of fear in a few minutes. Then Father's breathing changed—he was about to awaken. I was petrified; but he only turned over on his other side with his back toward me. . . . I was cold; I began to shiver; blackness and lights flickered in my brain; then I felt I was falling, falling—and knew no more.

It was during this same period, when she was about eight years old, thrown on her own resources much of the time and intensely introspective, that Margaret experienced what she called a "spiritual awakening," the realization that "I was made up of two Me's—one the thinking Me, the other, willful and emotional which sometimes exercised too great a power; there was danger in her leadership and I set myself the task of uniting the two by putting myself through ordeals of various sorts to strengthen the head Me." In her mid-thirties Margaret wrote in her journal in a similar vein: "today the Anglo Saxon has reasoned his impulses out of existence—he has practically lost the soul of an individual—crushed the mighty impulses of his natural self to don the cold cloak of reason and logic." In middle age she was to declare that "all my life I have acted on an inner voice and when that speaks to me it speaks wisely and never fails me. When I disobey it for one reason or another, for any consideration whatever I always *suffer.*" And she spoke in later years of the need to "be alone, absolutely quiet," in order to receive help from "cosmic forces."

In an earlier era Margaret's inner voice, like the voices that spoke to St. Joan, might have been angelic, and she herself might have been deeply religious. The age of faith was long past, yet her character and career were to an exceptional degree shaped by the impulsive and irrational self. And this too may have been an inheritance from Michael Higgins. Broadly read and skeptical as he was, he was nevertheless an Irishman with some of the Celtic fascination for the irrational. He had studied anatomy, medicine and physiology to enhance his skill as a sculptor, but Higgins was also a devout believer in phrenology; he tended every member of his family through major and minor illnesses and was consulted by neighbors in medical crises, yet he insisted the sovereign remedy for everything was always whiskey, "good whiskey." Margaret developed a similar tendency to rely on eccentric remedies of her own choice, some far stranger than whiskey, and she subscribed to a wide range of nonrational sources of knowledge, Rosicrucianism, astrology, phrenology, reincarnation among them. If the original impulse arose from her father's Irish inheritance, in Margaret it found a broader, more powerful and more deeply rooted expression, one that gives her the ambiguous air of belonging to another phase of history even though her actions were often far ahead of her time.

The loneliness and isolation of childhood life in Corning came to an end when Margaret finished elementary school, for the family put its heads together and decided she must be sent to a small private boarding school, Claverack College, that took the place of high school. Her sisters Nan and Mary offered financial help and Margaret waited on table at Claverack; she had become a pretty, coquettish, sociable girl with a talent for fiery speechmaking, often on behalf of feminist causes. She played the lead in many of Claverack's dramatic productions and one of her closest school friends recalled that Margaret had "great appeal for both sexes," becoming something of a student leader. "Anything she touched, she glorified in some mysterious way."

She had been there three years when she was called abruptly home. Her mother was dying, and Margaret was needed to run the household, care for the younger children and nurse her mother through the last stages of tuberculosis. It was a heavy burden for a girl of sixteen, but there was even more to bear, for Michael Higgins, in a sudden reversal of character probably caused by the shock of bereavement, had become a domestic tyrant overnight. He forbade Margaret and her sister Ethel to see any young men, forbade them to leave the house without permission, and finished by locking Margaret out of the house one night. "I did not know this monster father," she wrote later.

Father and daughter were reconciled within months, but the painful interlude must have strengthened and deepened her early fears of him. She said of that period that thoughts of marriage seemed tantamount to suicide; she had already watched her mother die, worn out before her time and the victim, as it must have seemed, of her father's sexual demands. Each of the four Higgins girls was to be marked for life by the contrast between the suffering mother who died too soon and the self-centered, impractical father. The two oldest girls, Nan and Mary, never married at all; the "saint-like" Mary became the paid companion of the daughter of a rich Corning family, remaining with her for the rest of her life, while Nan became a stenographer. Together they devoted most of their earnings to keeping the Higgins family afloat. In later years they were to help the younger brothers through college, and it was to Nan and Mary that Margaret turned for financial help in the early years of her birth control crusade, and for the care of her own children. The only other Higgins daughter, Ethel, was a year younger than Margaret, whom she strongly resembled. Ethel shared with Margaret some of the brunt of their father's outburst of paternal jealousy when their mother died, and shortly thereafter she married secretly, against his wishes and while still in high school. In later years she was to leave her two children in her husband's care in order to enter nurse's training; she was widowed when still young and never remarried.

But if Nan and Mary had learned to escape the dangers of marriage and childbearing by suppressing their sexual natures, Margaret learned a different lesson. Her sexuality was not crippled, although it was strongly colored, by the fears of childhood and adolescence—perhaps because she was tougher than her sisters, perhaps because, as her father's special favorite, she had come to enjoy conflict the way he enjoyed it. The picture of sexual conflict between primitive and dangerous male and Margaret's idealized woman—"a supreme being respected and worshipped"—expressed in her *Happiness in Marriage* helps to explain not only her own enjoyment of sex, but the source of her attraction for Bill Sanger and others. She both feared the primitive male and delighted in conflict with his "ferocious" nature.

During the weeks of nursing her dying mother, caring for household and children and battling her father, Margaret began to dream of a career in medicine. Doctors did not have to sit idly by and watch innocent people die; they had a special power, by no means infallible, yet it was power. In adulthood Margaret revealed a curious ambivalence about the special power of medical men, whom she both revered and attempted to rival with methods of her own, whether as a birth-controller or as a health faddist. Now she began to cast about for some way of achieving a medical education; it was far too costly for the meager means of the Higgins family, and in any case she had neither the temperament of a student nor the intellectual ability. She decided instead to become a nurse. With the help and encouragement of her two eldest sisters, Margaret spent two years in training at White Plains Hospital near Near York; it was there that she was operated on for tubercular glands, a baffling ailment that remained for more than twenty years a continual drain on her vitality. After graduation she spent a few months in "postgraduate" work at Manhattan Eye and Ear; toward the end of her stay there she met and quickly married Bill Sanger, an architect by profession, an artist at heart, a man as talented and improvident as Michael Higgins.

At the time of their marriage in 1902 Margaret was a slim, pretty girl with masses of reddish hair coiled on top of her head and a look of fragility due to incipient tuberculosis. Bill, who was eight years older, was already established in his career as an architect, but he longed to go to Paris and learn to paint, and dreams of Paris had been one of the chief topics of their six-month courtship. Less than a year after they were married Margaret's tuberculosis flared up; they learned she was pregnant, and the money that might have taken them to Europe sent her instead to a small sanatorium near Saranac. She came back to Bill and their Manhattan apartment in time for a long and agonizing labor, but their infant son, whom they named Stuart, was perfectly healthy. Margaret returned with him to the Adirondacks, where she submitted for eight months to the current treatment for tuberculosis, consisting of mountain air, complete rest and quantities of eggs, milk and creosote tablets. But the inactivity depressed her, the creosote killed her appetite, and a conviction that she had been sent away from home to die finally roused her from her bed one morning, to gather up baby and nurse and escape to her husband. She would doctor herself, she told him. "And don't make me eat! Don't even mention food to me!"

Three weeks later, "free from the horrors of invalidism and comforted by love and devotion," she began to regain a normal interest in life. She was not declared completely out of danger for six years more, but as the immediate claims of the disease receded Margaret and Bill began to think of their future. They wanted a home of their own, a country home designed by Bill, with air and space and freedom for the large family they hoped to have, and together they explored Westchester County for a likely building site. In the Columbia Colony at Hastings-on-Hudson a handful of professional families had settled on fifty acres of hillside overlooking the river. Here the Sangers bought an acre of land and rented a cottage so Bill could commute daily to the city to work, and in his spare time design their house, then supervise its building.

This was the start of what Margaret later called her "suburban interlude," a period she came to look back on with condescending amusement. If she was not slavishly domestic, she said, she was certainly slavishly maternal. In photographs taken with Stuart in her arms she appears as a slim, small, delicate person, demure yet with a certain piquant awareness of just how demure and charming and maternal she looks to the camera. As for Bill, "He took care of me in the little ways

—starting for the train and coming back to put his head in the door and call, 'It's awfully cold. Don't go out without your wrap.' " He loved her and he showed it; indeed Bill Sanger tended to live at the top of his emotions altogether. He was extravagant, generously and theatrically so, bringing her embroidered Japanese robes, opera tickets and flowers when he earned a big commission, and ignoring the bills that piled up when funds were low. This did not always sit well with Margaret, who wrote years later in *Happiness in Marriage* an account of a young couple that were surely the Sangers:

I know one charming young man, with poetic and romantic longings, but absolutely irresponsible toward the prosaic matters as rent bills, grocery bills, gas bills and such unpleasant obligations. Constantly hoping to please his young wife, he spent money on orchids, violets and trinkets of all kinds. These are gestures not to be condemned in themselves; yet in this particular case they did not make the wife happy. Finally she told him that . . . the grocery bills must be paid regularly. The poetic husband sulked. He stopped buying flowers but did not begin to pay the household bills. He had failed to realize that to love fully a woman must be freed from petty worries.

Impulsively generous as Bill Sanger was, tender, solicitous, charming, his bride had called him "That beast of a man," and not without reason. According to the only child of Bill's second marriage, Joan Sanger Hoppe, he was "extremely demanding" and "his temper was impossible." Along with the quick temper went an extraordinary vitality: "I think of my father as a fierce man, bright of eye, self-centered, handsome *but* he was an *alive* man!" Mrs. Hoppe wrote, and it was her belief that "he and Margaret must have had a passionate relationship at the beginning." Certainly this is what that early letter to Mary suggests; in later years friends, lovers and acquaintances were to remark on Margaret's capacity for sensual enjoyment, a quality that pervades her own writings about marriage and contraception. One astute observer, who knew Margaret Sanger in middle age, felt "she was looking for a really good tough heel, you see." If Bill Sanger was not a heel in the usual sense, the same intensity that made him so hard to live with, the blazing temper, quick and open display of emotion and downright craving for mastery satisfied, for the time being, Margaret's love of conflict and her youthful desire to be pursued and overpowered.

In his work Bill Sanger was a perfectionist. Mrs. Hoppe spoke of hours spent posing as his model for a group of etchings—"I was not allowed to move a muscle and I came to hate those sessions." He was equally unsparing of himself; rushing home to Westchester County after a day's work in Manhattan to see what the builder had made of his dream house, Bill was often dissatisfied, and "seizing an ax, he chopped out part of it, usually pounding his fingers in the process," so that some portions were entirely done over two or three times. When their son Stuart was about four, and Margaret several months pregnant, they moved into the partly finished house on an icy day in February; in the middle of the night the German maid banged on Margaret's door, crying, "Madam. Come! Fire in the big stove!"

Margaret pulled Stuart, bedclothes and all, out of his crib, ran next door to a neighbor and by brilliant moonlight watched the whole village trying to save their house.

By summer the burnt-out concrete shell was once more livable and they moved back in, but for Margaret the suburban dream had died the night of the fire and she was never again to live contentedly in what her husband called "Margaret's palace." Grant, their second son, was born there in 1908, and their daughter Peggy twenty months later. Margaret said she loved having babies to care for again, and Peggy was "the embodiment of all my hopes for a daughter." Yet she felt restless, expressed a fear of becoming "kitchen-minded," and fastened the children's clothes with safety pins rather than take the time to sew buttons back on. She began to read and write, partly in connection with a ladies' literary circle that followed the reading list of a Columbia University course; at each meeting one member gave a talk on the subject she had worked up. Politics, the rights of women, Havelock Ellis and his daring explorations of human sexuality were her interests now and Bill encouraged her efforts by telling her, " 'You go ahead and finish your writing. I'll get the dinner and wash the dishes.' He thought I should make a career of it instead of limiting myself to small-town interests."

Yet how was she to make a career of it, hidden away in the pretty suburb and protected from the drama and excitement she had felt when she worked at the hospital? A kind of "world-hunger" assailed her, a yearning to do and accomplish, to live at the center of things. If she had longed, as a child in Corning, to wear perfume and walk with her husband and children in the evening, she had other and more powerful desires as well. Bill, for his part, was tired of commuting to the city. One day they had an offer to buy their house; they snapped it up, and in 1912 the Sangers returned to Manhattan.

Margaret went back to nursing, partly out of a desire to pay her own way; moreover, a great deal of money had been spent on her medical bills, the losses of the fire were not entirely covered by insurance, and Paris was a dream she still shared with her husband. And if they were ever to get to Paris it began increasingly to seem as if they could not make it on Bill's earnings alone. He was past forty, yet solid achievement still escaped him and he was troubled by a deep sense of personal unfulfillment. She must have begun to suspect that his resemblance to her father was dangerously close, that like Michael Higgins, Bill was too impetuous and uncertain ever to make good. In her early thirties now, she felt the first stirrings of a desire for personal independence, the first suspicion of a destiny separate from her husband's.

Bill's mother came to live with them, to take care of the children while Margaret worked; her presence also made it possible for the Sangers to spend many of their evenings in Greenwich Village, or at meetings of Local Number 5 of the Socialist party, which had its head-quarters only ten blocks from their home. For Bill, a long-time Socialist, had a number of friends and acquaintances in liberal circles, including Eugene Debs, the famous Socialist leader, as well as radicals of a far more activist nature, like John Reed, the revolutionary who was later buried in the Kremlin, Emma Goldman, anarchist and birth control agitator, and her lover Alexander Berkman, who had spent fourteen years in prison for stabbing Henry Clay Frick.

It was the golden age of American radicalism, the "Adolescence of the Twentieth Century," in the words of Max Eastman, a fervid young revolutionary who was an editor of *The Masses*. Along with the rethinking of economic and political systems, a process that had been going on in America in one form or another since the first half of the nineteenth century, came a fresh examination of the place of women. Anarchists and socialists of varying political hues agreed that woman belonged, like the Negro and the worker, to an oppressed class; free her, and she would become one of the most powerful forces on the side of revolution. This was a possibility Michael Higgins had never suspected when he taught Margaret socialism and rebellion; indeed her father had never even approved of the nursing career, and when Margaret told him "some of the nicest girls were going into it," he said, "Well, they won't be nice long. It's no sort of work for girls to be doing."

But women of the middle and upper classes were in the forefront now of the search for the New Woman, and in the circles Bill and Margaret joined, Mabel Dodge, Emma Goldman and Isadora Duncan were heroines, each in her own way a living exemplar of woman's right to love where she pleased, in marriage or out of it. Margaret and Emma Goldman were friends for a while, and Emma's newspaper *Mother Earth* was the model for a paper Margaret published several years later. And the Sangers went to parties at the Greenwich Village home of Mabel Dodge, a restless heiress and socialite who had become the chief hostess of the Socialist movement, offering splendid suppers served by uniformed butlers to labor agitators from the mining camps as well as to Harvard intellectuals. Max Eastman wrote:

I must pause to tell you what a powerful and peculiar collector of intellectuals Mabel is. . . . For there is something going on, or going around, in Mabel's head or bosom, something that creates a magnetic field in which people become polarized and pulled in and made to behave very queerly. Their passions become exacerbated; they grow argumentative; they have quarrels, difficulties, entanglements, abrupt and violent detachments. . . . And it was no second-rate salon; everybody in the ferment of ideas could be found there, from Walter Lippmann, representing the drift towards respectability, to Alexander Berkman, representing revolt *in excelsis.*

To the worldly Mabel Dodge, Margaret was "the Madonna type of woman with soft brown hair parted over a quiet brow." And according to Margaret's own recollections of that period she was indeed quiet, somewhat dazzled by the wit and learning of her new associates whose discussions she never quite followed, so that she was often out of step —too far right for a left crowd, too far left when the group was right, and so unsure of herself that on those rare occasions when she had something to contribute she would nudge her husband and ask him to say it for her. She had neither the capacity nor the inclination for closely reasoned intellectual argument, and in Mabel Dodge's salon, among women of obviously forceful personality like Emma Goldman and the radical Elizabeth Gurley Flynn, Margaret's reserved manner and delicately feminine appearance must have set her distinctively apart from the others.

If she did not fully understand what she heard in the Dodge circle, Margaret reacted to it nevertheless. Bill, like her father, was satisfied with theoretical socialism, usually a talker rather than a doer, but the anarchists' call to direct action made a deep appeal to Margaret's impulsive nature, arousing both her sympathy for the underdog and her desire "to live, to act, to rebel." In their attacks on capitalism and established institutions the anarchists spoke to the outsider in Margaret, the scorned child, the victim of the Catholic Church. She had both envied the rich families on the hillsides and resented them; for the next few years she was to see them as the enemy.

Soon after their arrival in Manhattan the Sangers became associated with the Ferrer School, an educational experiment founded by a group that included Emma Goldman and Alexander Berkman; Stuart was enrolled there and Margaret attended evening classes for adults. Here she found, according to the historian David Kennedy, not only political activists but proponents of the radical feminist movement, whose visions were "steeped in the traditions of romanticism, saturated with intoxicating notions of the dignity of the human personality and the related need for unfettered self-expression. Their message deeply moved Margaret Sanger. . . . she soon demanded not only political but also aesthetic and especially psychological revolution. And the cutting edge of the new psychological theories the anarchists constantly invoked aimed at one central fact of life: sex."

Freud, Havelock Ellis, the writings of the Swedish feminist Ellen Key, all contributed to Margaret's growing belief that the psychological revolution that would free women could only be accomplished by the removal of all constraints on sexuality. Although in this she misunderstood Freud, who had never advocated an end to sexual restraints, similar misreading of his work was widespread. As for Havelock Ellis, his view of sex as sacred, all-pervasive and spiritualizing made a direct and unforgettable appeal to Margaret, not through her intellect but through that willful, emotional part of her nature that saw irrational impulse as more precious than reason: "Those who restrain desire, do so because the desire is weak enough to be restrained. Reason usurps its place and governs the weak and unwilling and being restrained, it by degrees becomes passive till it is only the shadow of desire," she wrote a few years later in her journal. Havelock Ellis had tried to spiritualize sex in order to raise it above the animal; Margaret came to see sex as spiritual chiefly in the sense that it was more important than anything else, a divine urge, and therefore sacred.

But in 1912, if she had been converted to the ideal of the sexual revolution, Margaret Sanger was apparently not ready for the practice of it. None of her letters to Bill, and only a few of his, have been preserved from that period, so it is difficult to know with certainty what grounds he had for jealousy. Yet jealousy was what he felt, according to a letter in the fall of 1913:

Do you know this last year has impressed me—and my view is entirely dispassionate—that the so-called "Labor Revolutionary Movement" in New York was nothing but a Saturnalia of Sexuality . . . the reaction for you was inevitable as you admitted—your finer sensibilities only escaped its ravages just in time. . . .

I believe you will right yourself loved one—Let me help you—although I still feel the wound you inflict from time to time.

It seems that Bill is referring here to flirtations rather than full-blown love affairs, flirtations from which Margaret, emotional, romantic, but still at heart a small-town girl and the daughter of a man who held traditional views about sex, had drawn back "just in time." Yet she was also a pretty woman, thoroughly aware of her charm. She had fallen in love with a man of virile and passionate temperament, who was "insanely jealous" even before there was anyone to be jealous of; and now her eye had begun to wander. Bill Sanger was to feel the wound for years to come.

Although Margaret was absorbing the revolutionary ideas of the Ferrer School and the Dodge salon, she had not come to Manhattan for ideas and parlor flirtations only; in the daytime she worked at obstetrical nursing, and in between nursing jobs did what she could for the Socialist party. For a while she was a reporter for their paper, *The Call*, and helped recruit new members, mainly Scandinavian housemaids. One day she agreed to substitute for a speaker who was to have addressed a group of ten working women on labor problems; Margaret had done no public speaking since high school and "I was frightened—thoroughly so. I could not eat my supper." At the last moment she decided to talk, not about labor problems, of which she knew little, but about family health. The speech was a great success, more health talks were requested, and at the second meeting her audience had grown to seventy-five. Soon a series of little lectures followed by question-and-answer sessions was under way, and the women's editor of *The Call* asked Margaret to put the answers in the form of a column. Under the title "What Every Mother Should Know," her first published writings, she discussed the "beauty and wonder and sacredness of the sex function."

Beginning in November of 1912, the series continued for twelve weeks; the last article, aimed at adolescent girls, had discussed gonorrhea, the next was to take up syphilis. But the next never appeared. Anthony Comstock, head of the New York Society for the Suppression of Vice, informed *The Call* that their mailing permit would be revoked if they published the promised article on syphilis, and Margaret's column was replaced with the headline: WHAT EVERY GIRL SHOULD KNOW: NOTHING. By order of the POST OFFICE DEPARTMENT.

Later that year Margaret was asked to head a committee to bring to New York the children of striking textile workers in Lawrence, Massachusetts, mostly immigrant Italians who could hold out longer if their children were fed and housed during the strike. New York's Italian colony offered to take them in, and for six weeks Margaret supervised the health and comfort of these children, coming briefly into national prominence when she testified before a congressional committee as to their physical conditions, "their nationalities, their ages, their weights, the number of those without underclothes and without overcoats." And, reporting for *The Call* on the laundry strike, Margaret wrote that at Lawrence, "capitalism shows its fangs of despotism and murder." She had adopted the anarchist style along with its political beliefs.

Margaret had come to Manhattan to live, to act, to rebel; had found in anarchist circles those who were intellectually committed to rebellion and whose world view supported her emotional needs. And these first stirrings of rebellion against society inevitably pulled her away from her family. In her autobiography she recalled a conversation with Grant: where was Mother going that night, he wanted to know. To a Socialist meeting, she told him. And Grant said, "Oh, I hate soshism!"

Bill had complaints of his own as Margaret's time and energies were shifted to the world outside the family. If he accused her of neglecting him, she in turn could accuse him of a selfish desire to cage her in. But when he accused her of neglecting the children she was defenseless. Grant and Stuart, both of whom became doctors, told the writer Emily Taft Douglas half a century later that during a 1912 epidemic Peggy had apparently contracted an unrecognized case of poliomyelitis that left her with a permanent limp. Mrs. Douglas writes: "Grant . . . thought that the illness . . . was a source of dissension between his parents. However unjustly, Bill Sanger felt that his wife's deep preoccupation with her new concern had made her deficient in caring for Peggy." In all she later wrote about this beloved daughter, Margaret never once mentioned the limp, or the epidemic; she remembered instead "three lovely, healthy children . . . full of life, vigor and happiness. They were glorious examples of wanted children, mentally, and physically." And of the three Peggy was the one with whom Margaret most closely identified herself, picturing the child in words that perfectly suited the mother: "Peggy, the most independent child I ever knew . . . was born to *do*, to act, to lead. She had the qualities of a person of power even at the age of five. Peggy was blonde as Grant was dark, daring as he was cautious, leader as he was follower." Yet beginning in 1912 the daring and active little girl had a limp, for which Bill Sanger blamed Margaret, and Margaret must have bitterly blamed herself.

There was always the consolation that if she neglected her own family, she served others who were in far greater need. For Margaret's obstetrical nursing often took her to the Lower East Side, where she worked to repair the results of the most extreme poverty, ignorance and despair:

> Ignorance and neglect go on day by day; children born to breathe but a few hours and pass out of life; pregnant women toiling early and late to give food to four or five children, always hungry; boarders taken into homes where there is not sufficient room for the family; little girls eight and ten years of age sleeping in the same room with dirty, foul smelling, loathsome men; women whose weary, pregnant, shapeless bodies refuse to accommodate themselves to the husband's desires find husbands looking with lustful eyes upon other women, sometimes upon their own little daughters, six and seven years of age.
> In this atmosphere abortions and birth become the main theme of conversation. On Saturday nights I have seen groups of fifty to one hundred women going into questionable offices well known in the community for cheap abortions.

Day after day the women she visited begged Mrs. Sanger for "the secret," the one the rich women had that would keep them from getting pregnant again. In later years she insisted that she explained to them the only two methods she knew, coitus interruptus and the condom, neither of much use to the poor because they "placed the burden of responsibility solely upon the husband—a burden which he seldom assumed."

"They claimed my thoughts night and day. One by one these women, with their worried, sad, pensive and ageing faces would marshal themselves before me in my dreams, sometimes appealingly, sometimes accusingly. I could not escape from the facts of their misery." Margaret's Socialist friends tried to soothe her with assurances that all would be changed once women had the vote, but she felt they were turning their backs on ugly realities that demanded solutions that very moment, not in some distant utopia. She had been told that a hundred thousand women had abortions each year in New York City alone; how many thousands of them would be dead of abortion before social and economic changes brought relief?

One stifling day in mid-July, 1912, Margaret was summoned to a Grand Street tenement. Her patient was a thin, Russian-Jewish Mrs. Sachs, twenty-eight and the mother of three tiny children; her husband,

Jake, a truck driver, had come home to find the babies crying and his wife unconscious after a self-induced abortion. Jake had called the doctor, who sent for Margaret.

She spent three weeks nursing Mrs. Sachs, in midsummer, in a cold-water flat, with every necessity for comfort and sanitation hauled up and down several flights of tenement stairs, before the patient was out of danger. "Another baby will finish me, I suppose?" Mrs. Sachs asked Margaret.

Margaret turned to the doctor, "a kindly man, and he had worked hard to save her, but such incidents had become so familiar to him that he . . . laughed good-naturedly," and told Mrs. Sachs to make her husband sleep on the roof. When the doctor had gone Mrs. Sachs turned to Margaret, "lifted her thin, blue-veined hands and clasped them beseechingly. 'He can't understand. He's only a man. But you do, don't you? Please tell me the secret, and I'll never breathe it to a soul. Please!' "

But there was no secret, Margaret claimed, at least none that she knew. Three months later she was called again to the Sachs home; another abortion, the young mother in a coma, the husband sobbing. It was all over within minutes this time. Margaret pulled a sheet over the pale face and went home:

> As I stood there the darkness faded. The sun came up and threw its reflection over the house tops. It was the dawn of a new day in my life also. The doubt and the questioning, the experimenting and trying, were now to be put behind me. I knew I could not go back merely to keeping people alive.
>
> I went to bed, knowing that no matter what it might cost, I was finished with palliatives and superficial cures; I was resolved to seek out the root of evil, to do something to change the destiny of mothers whose miseries were as vast as the sky.

This account of the death of Sadie Sachs and the resolution that followed it appears in almost identical form in Margaret's early history of her career, *My Fight for Birth Control*, and in her later *Autobiography*. The narratives are dramatic, even melodramatic, highly personal and deeply felt; yet, like Margaret's claim that she knew of no contraceptive other than the condom or coitus interruptus, they leave the reader with some troubling questions. Margaret was emotional and sensitive; perhaps she was hypersensitive in this case, since the women who accused her in her dreams were probably replicas of her mother, bringing vividly to mind her mother's enslavement to her father and childbearing. Yet the death of Sadie Sachs, no matter how traumatic, could not have been the sole cause of Margaret's conversion. Emma Goldman had been preaching birth control since the turn of the century; she and Margaret were friends and Emma must have been at the very least a contributing cause. But there is no mention of her.

Even more troubling is Margaret's claim that she knew of no contraceptives, and that she searched fruitlessly for a year in America, then went abroad in the hope of finding a contraceptive that could be controlled by women. For the evidence, even in Margaret's own writings, shows this cannot be true.

The historian David Kennedy believes "the real significance of her description of Mrs. Sachs's death and the 'vision' that followed lay in Mrs. Sanger's later relation to the birth control movement." She gave that movement "nearly all her productive years. To it she would sacrifice her marriage and, she may have felt, the life of one of her children. But others emerged to challenge her primacy in the movement. . . . What better claim to uniqueness than to base her actions on that most subjective of motives, the command of an emotional impulse? That would enhance her symbolic role, justify the hardships she had suffered in her private life, and legitimize her claim to sole leadership in the birth control movement."

After the death of Sadie Sachs, Margaret wrote, she asked several doctors she knew for useful contraceptive information; they told her that perhaps there was such a thing, somewhere. But the people she was worrying about wouldn't use it if they had it, and in any case there were laws against passing such information on. She said she then began to haunt libraries, "the Astor, the Lenox, the Academy of Medicine, the Library of Congress, and dozens of others," intent upon digging out the knowledge the doctors had told her probably existed:

The pursuit of my quest took me away from home a good deal. The children used to come in after school and at once hunt for me. "Where's mother?" was the usual question. If they found me at my mending basket they all leaped about for joy, took hands and danced, shouting, "Mother's home, mother's home, mother's sewing." Sewing seemed to imply a measure of permanence.

Margaret said she spent about a year buried in libraries with no result whatever; this year would have been the period from the autumn of 1912 to the autumn of 1913. Yet in 1916, when she was preparing to open the first birth control clinic in America in the Brownsville section of Brooklyn, she went through the neighborhood visiting every drugstore and arranging "with the proprietor to prepare himself for supplying the pessaries we were going to recommend." And as she later explained, this pessary, the so-called Mispah cervical cap pessary, was one of the pre-ferred forms of contraceptive among women of the middle and upper classes in America, and had been for many years. And if the cervical cap pessary was so readily available to druggists in a slum district like Browns-ville in 1916, how can we believe she was unable in 1913 to find any trace of a birth control device other than the condom, either in print or by word of mouth? Among the sophisticated society women of the Dodge circle, if from no other source, she could have learned about douches, suppositories and the cervical cap.

This contradiction is apparent from a reading of Margaret's own narrative. Kennedy further points out that the "Index Catalogue of the Library of the Surgeon-General's Office," for 1898 listed nearly two full pages of books and articles on prevention of conception covering such methods as vaginal douching, suppositories, tampons and the Mispah pessary. Therefore whatever she was doing in the year she devoted to her "quest," Margaret could not have been working daily and without result in the libraries she named. Much of that year must actually have been spent in a long-drawn-out self-evaluation. For by the summer of 1913 her marriage had begun to suffer seriously, not only from the continued preoccupation with outside activities, but from Bill's jealousy, his explosive temper, his need to feel he was the absolute focus of his wife's attention. He shared her new interest in contraceptive methods just as he had shared her interest in socialist activities—he initiated them, after all—and before that he had encouraged Margaret to write and study. Joan Sanger Hoppe remembered her father as being "tremendously supportive" of Margaret in later years, and Margaret's own writings always show Bill Sanger as considerate, encouraging. Nevertheless he felt alone and neglected; he needed far more attention and approval than most men, yet he was getting much less. In the summer of 1913 Margaret decided to get out of New York for a while, to remove the children from the summer's heat and retire with them to some isolated spot in the country in order to think things over.

She rented a cottage in Provincetown; her younger sister, Ethel Byrne, who had recently been widowed, came along, Bill visited on occasion, and Margaret spent her time "brooding and playing with the children, mulling over the past, fearful of the future." If she had begun to suspect that future might not include Bill, she was afraid it might also separate her from her children: "I wanted to bind them to me and allow nothing to force us apart. I clutched at them like a drowning woman in a raging current, as if to save myself from its swiftness."

This mood of Margaret's must have been apparent to others outside her intimate circle, for one day Bill Haywood, the anarchist and labor leader, came to visit at the Provincetown cottage and walked with her on the beach while the children played. "Say, girl," he told her, "you're getting ready to kick over the traces!"

Then, taking her hand and pointing to the children, he added, "Don't do anything to spoil their happiness—will you?" It was Haywood who solved, for the time being, the conflict between her new-found interest in contraception and the unity of the family. Why not go to France with her husband and children? There Margaret could see for herself the conditions that resulted from French working-class sponsorship of family limitation since the turn of the century.

Bill Sanger was delighted with the idea; he was sick of New York, sick of architecture, eager for the long-postponed painting career and ready to try anything that might save his marriage. "Dear heart," he wrote to her at the summer's end, "I love you so. I just want to make things easy for you—I think of things only in terms of you."

In October of 1913 the family set sail for Paris, where Bill was to find a studio and paint, and Margaret to meet members of the French workers' movement. The money from the sale of the Hastings house "together with the savings from our combined labor of years which was invested for our children's future education, had now to be drawn upon for . . . this, our first and long-desired trip abroad," Margaret wrote later, and her subsequent letters to Bill suggest that had he achieved the solid success appropriate to his age and talents, such a financial sacrifice would not have been necessary. Bill felt this too; he was determined to succeed now as a painter.

An apartment was found on the Left Bank, the children were sent to school and Margaret toured Paris with Bill Haywood, meeting leaders of the French Syndicalist movement, which was allied with his own IWW, the Industrial Workers of the World, known everywhere as the Wobblies. Margaret learned that French birth control methods included homemade suppositories, soap douches and the cervical pessary, and "every married woman knew all there was to know about contraception as well as the art of love." There were no legal restraints against birth control, and even abortion, which was all too common, was carried out by reputable doctors. The poorest French families were very small, so that each child had his full share of parental love and attention.

"After I had obtained the facts I had come for I was restless and unhappy and wanted to be off. The brooding spirit was upon me and would not give me peace," Margaret wrote in connection with her visit to France. For after two short months she was eager to return home; her own account suggests she had found in France information unobtainable in America and her sole desire was to put it to use. More likely the precipitate return to the States was connected with her longing to begin the free and active life that had been stirring within her ever since the Sangers came to New York. Bill was happy and productive in Paris, had met Matisse and Monet and counted on a long stay and months of leisure to pursue his painting. Margaret craved action, purposeful, rebellious, combative action; to remain in Paris, a bystander to Bill's self-fulfillment, must have seemed like imprisonment to her. She took the children and left without him. A year and a half later she told Bill that his staying on in Paris had been a sacrifice on her part, and hiding that fact from him was another sacrifice, and "I have no regrets, unless that my sacrifices were made for one too childish and unworthy."

Bill did not let her go with an easy heart; he felt that "to be separated by the big pond is serious work—this is something that has never happened to us. . . . I shall never forget the expression on your face when I threw that last kiss—I feel sure I mean something in your life. I feel *now* too that nobody can take you away from me." But only a few days later his confidence had begun to ebb and he was cautioning her about the dangers of sexual freedom: "Most men seem to violate confidences as regards their relations with the opposite sex—and it always ends by the disparaging of the character of the woman. . . . I would not have a finger ever pointed at you. . . . I shall always love you with all the power of my being—whatever you *do.*"

But Margaret, on the voyage home, was preoccupied with thoughts of her future work. "I knew something must be done to rescue those women who were voiceless; someone had to express with white hot intensity the conviction that they must be empowered to decide for themselves when they should fulfill the supreme function of motherhood. They had to be made aware of how they were being shackled, and aroused to mutiny." Bill was right nevertheless. He suspected her of a desire to shake off the galling bonds of marriage; she spoke of mutiny on behalf of others, and this was certainly what dominated her conscious mind. Unconsciously, she was preparing for mutiny herself.

When she reached New York Margaret established herself in a small apartment and placed the children in a local school; withdrawing what money she could from a rapidly decreasing bank account, she took up her position at the barricades. By teaching the women of the slums to throw off the shackles of involuntary motherhood she would defy the "capitalist class" and the obscenity laws and strike a blow for revolution. The weapon she had chosen was to be a monthly paper, called *The Woman Rebel* and inspired in large part by Emma Goldman's *Mother Earth.*

Red Emma was a heavy-set, warmhearted woman, a Jewish mother turned anarchist, who gave her journal a name that might have been her own nickname, and Margaret did the same. She became the Woman

Rebel incarnate, publisher, bookkeeper, editor and circulation manager
of an eight-page publication whose slogan was "No Gods, No Masters,"
spreading the word that every woman's duty was "To look the whole
world in the face with a go-to-hell look in the eyes; to have an ideal; to
speak and act in defiance of Convention," while the rebel woman's
rights were to be lazy, to be an unmarried mother, to destroy, to create,
to live, to love. It was a manifesto directed not only against the establishment but against Bill Sanger and his desire to imprison her within the
bonds of a tame marriage. The first issue carried an extract from Emma's
essay "Love and Marriage," a prose poem in praise of the anarchist's
bomb, and the IWW preamble. "I have no apologies for the publication
of 'The Woman Rebel.' It expressed exactly what I felt and thought at
that time," an older and more cautious Margaret Sanger felt it necessary
to explain, for even Max Eastman had wondered if she wasn't going too
far. But "too far" was precisely the direction she aimed at. Everything
in *The Woman Rebel* expressed an unmistakable desire to shock, to defy
the property laws, marriage, established religion, law and order. Yet if
she advocated contraception, *The Woman Rebel* gave no details or
prescriptions.

Thousands of letters responded to the first, March 1914, issue of
Margaret's journal. Millworkers in the East, miners in the West, trade
unionists and working women everywhere wrote to ask for more copies
and for the birth control information promised in the paper. From
Europe came "extraordinary results, striking vibrations that brought
contacts, messages, inquiries, pamphlets, books. . . . I corresponded with
the leading feminists of Europe—Ellen Key, then at the height of her
fame, Olive Schreiner, Mrs. Pankhurst, Rosa Luxembourg." Another
kind of response came from the New York Post Office. That March
issue, they said, was unmailable.

Since 1873 the post office had had the authority to decide what was
obscene, according to the so-called Comstock law passed at the insistence of Anthony Comstock and his Society for the Suppression of Vice.
Margaret called him an extraordinary man who "had been granted
extraordinary power, alone of all citizens in the United States, to open
any letter or package or pamphlet or book passing through the mails,

and, if he wished, lay his complaint before the Post Office." Within the first ten years of his career Comstock had caused seven hundred arrests, more than three hundred prison sentences and fines of over sixty thousand dollars; thousands of pounds of "obscene books" and "articles for immoral use, of rubber, etc.," had been seized and confiscated, and Comstock himself traveled nearly two hundred thousand miles during those nine years to protect his countrymen from moral decay. When the post office told her their decision about *The Woman Rebel* Margaret suspected it was based on her advocacy of birth control, although the paper was inflammatory on many counts, for obscenity as well as for preaching assassination. She wrote to ask the post office precisely how she had broken the law, but there was no reply.

One night a group of friends and supporters gathered in Margaret's little flat to decide on a name for her new movement. "Malthusianism," "preventception," "voluntary motherhood," "constructive generation" were among the offerings. Someone suggested "birth control," and "We all knew at once that we had found the perfect name for the cause." The same handful of friends, volunteer typists, secretaries and clerks, joined with Margaret in forming a "little society grandly titled the National Birth Control League."

And she continued, in defiance of the post office, to publish *The Woman Rebel*, whose name and spirit Bill Sanger failed to understand; far from realizing that the combative look in the eye of its author was directed partly at him, he praised the paper and sent a steady stream of pamphlets and materials across the ocean to fill its columns. He called on Christobel Pankhurst to see if she would contribute, and presented a copy to one of the editors of the *New Age* in London, reporting to Margaret she "almost collapsed when she read the watchword of No Lords No Masters." In his spare time Bill was working up a series of cartoons that were to be his own contribution to the paper, and all along he had been urging Margaret, almost from the day she left, to find some way of rejoining him abroad, with or without the children, for "your trip has been cut short—I want to do Europe alone with you. . . . If worse comes to worse I'd rather return than lose you!"

Margaret had no intention of returning to tour Europe and she flatly rejected Bill's cartoons. She took objection to the continuing note of jealousy in his letters, for it was, she said, unfounded; the men who surrounded her now were only comrades, fellow workers for a great cause. Early in 1914, for example, a young Englishman who had helped with *The Woman Rebel* sent her a letter beginning: "Margaret Dear, if only you knew how grateful I feel at times to you—grateful for your gentle kindness, your sympathy and your dear comradeship. . . . Some moments in our lives are lifetimes in themselves. I shall always treasure moments, hours, and a day and a night I have spent with you—because somehow I have felt that I am alone with the stars and the sun. . . . I am not making love to you, because I love you too much for that—" She mailed this note to Bill after writing across it: "Ned spent a day and a night working on the typewriter for me on Rebel Woman—I wrote to thank him—Return this to me dear. This is an example of a fine clean feeling which two can have towards each other. Do you object to this Bill?" Apparently she never told him he no longer had the right to object, nor did she speak in clear and unambiguous terms of their future; as for the Englishman's adoring letter, whatever her motives in sending it to him, its effect cannot have been anything but inflammatory. A far less touchy man than Bill Sanger would have been hurt and confused by such treatment.

Yes, he assured her, she was to be free, he had no desire to tie her down. "But you have advanced sexually . . . (perhaps it's advancing I don't know) but this I know I am here where I always was," devoted, waiting and unalterably monogamous. No other women interested him, "for I still hold that intercourse is not to be classed with a square meal." His work had not gone as well as he hoped, Margaret's rejection of his cartoons he found utterly humiliating, "the part of your letter as regards defining our relations on my return unnerved me," but he had decided in any case to return. He was somewhat "mentally fatigued." He did not consider "my art" as important as she seemed to think he did. And, shortly before he left Europe on the brink of war in the summer of 1914, he wrote to her humbly and hopefully: "Dear heart, let me kiss the hem of your mantle."

Meanwhile Margaret had launched another undertaking; even as she continued to publish her paper in spite of continuing warnings from the post office, she was hard at work on a pamphlet called "Family Limitation," into which were crammed all "the material I had brought back from France, complete with formulas and drawings," descriptions of douches, suppositories, sponges and the cervical pessary, which latter she most strongly recommended. Free of the shrill tone and revolutionary ravings of *The Woman Rebel*, the little booklet was straightforward and practical, fulfilling her promise to provide concrete birth control information to the women of the working classes. It is interesting to note in passing the style of "Family Limitation," a prose style that persisted in Margaret's early writings on sex and contraception, before she learned to depend on professional collaborators. Sentimental, fervent, devoid of an atom of humor and often dull, it exalted sexual fulfillment, which she saw as the panacea for all the world's ills. She said, for example, that "a mutual and satisfied sexual act is of great benefit to the average woman, the magnetism of it is health giving, and acts as a beautifier and tonic." Ten years later, in *Happiness in Marriage*, her only attempt at a marriage manual, she wrote: "Upon the complete realization of the love of husband for wife and wife for husband depends not only the enduring happiness of marriage, but also, to a far greater extent than most people realize, success in life and the release and direction of those hidden vital energies that are so essential to the peace and security which create those values so essential for creative living."

If "Family Limitation" was to fulfill Margaret's promise to the working women of America it must first break into print; yet twenty printers refused to have anything to do with the pamphlet. At last Margaret found a Russian-born anarchist who agreed to set the type, but secretly, after hours when the shop was supposedly closed. A hundred thousand copies were produced, addressed by friends and supporters in a storage room, and left there until Margaret could find some way of distributing them. She knew the law too well to keep a single copy in her own home.

Although they knew nothing about the secret printing of "Family Limitation," Margaret's father and sisters in Corning had been following her career as the Woman Rebel with increasing dismay, deciding at last that her flamboyant and possibly illegal behavior showed she must be in the midst of a nervous breakdown. Michael Higgins therefore came to New York to persuade her to enter a sanatorium. He was still there, still baffled by her explanations, for he "despised anyone who could discuss sex, blaming this on my nursing training," when on an August day two men appeared at Margaret's door. They told the editor and publisher of *The Woman Rebel* that she had been indicted by the federal government on nine counts, meaning a possible prison sentence of forty-five years.

Margaret decided these two agents of the Department of Justice seemed "nice and sensible." She invited them to sit down while she explained birth control, presenting "to their imaginations some of the tragic stories of conscript motherhood." After they had gone her father came into the room, embraced her and said, "Everything is with you—logic, common sense and progress. I never saw the truth until this instant."

Margaret's friends were convinced she would have to spend at least a year in jail, but "My faith was still childlike. I trusted that, like father, a judge representing our Government would be convinced. All I had to do was explain." At any rate, this is Margaret's later version of her sentiments; in the six weeks that elapsed before she was to appear in court she had been completely engrossed in "Family Limitation," she said. And when the federal case came up in October she claimed the time had passed so quickly she had been unable to do much about her defense; she then requested an extension and the request, she said, was denied. Yet nothing had happened that she could not have foreseen. She had defied the law in *The Woman Rebel,* not only by preaching birth control but by advocating bomb throwing and assassination. There had been repeated warnings that the law was being broken, and, when arrested, she was allowed to name the length of time she would need to prepare a defense. Margaret asked for six weeks, and six weeks were granted. Yet when that time had elapsed, "I had had no notice and, without a lawyer to keep me posted, did not even know it had been called until the district attorney's office telephoned." If she had no lawyer, she certainly had a calendar; and in claiming that her request for an extension was denied, she is clearly contradicted by the court records, which show that eight more days were allowed her.

The truth is that Margaret was confused, backed into a corner partly of her own making and partly due to events beyond her control; she ended by making an impulsive decision about her trial, one that had important effects on the crusade for birth control, but was also to cost her the deepest personal pain. This is why her own account is unreliable —not because she intended to deceive others, but rather because she needed, later on, to deceive herself.

Margaret was convinced that her conviction for *The Woman Rebel* was already decided upon; she was in serious danger, therefore, of going to jail for having published an obscene paper. Her friends insisted she was sure to get off if she would plead guilty, yet this she steadfastly refused to do. And while she had no fear of prison, the newspapers were packed with war news, her trial would have little publicity, and any reasoned argument she might work up about her motives and the injustice of the obscenity laws would be buried on the back pages and soon forgotten. Moreover, she had lost interest by now in *The Woman Rebel*, which she thought of as a "sass sheet," past history, and not worth being jailed for; her heart was with her pamphlet "Family Limitation," which clearly challenged the laws against birth control information. For this, and not for the shrill revolutionary outcries of *The Woman Rebel*, she would gladly have gone to jail, but she could not choose which crime she was to be tried for and "Family Limitation" was still in packing cases.

She attempted to solve the dilemma by turning her back on it. In October of 1914 Margaret took a train for Canada, then sailed for Europe with a passport that gave her name as Bertha Watson, for the offense was extraditable. She had come to the decision while sitting in a hotel room the night before: "I wanted no one to influence my decision one way or the other. It was like birth and death—that journey had to be taken alone. Gradually, conviction came. About half an hour before train time I knew that I *must* go." Yet Bill's mother had died, so the children could not continue in her care. Bill had been home for months, their relations strained and constantly shifting; Margaret felt she could count on him to some degree as far as the children's care went, yet even with the best intentions, a man alone, with his living to earn, could not devote himself fully to a boy of six and a little girl four years old.

Stuart had already been placed in boarding school when Margaret's sudden decision was made; it was the two younger children whose welfare most deeply concerned her, especially Peggy, whose leg was swollen from a vaccination. Margaret turned to her sister Nan, whose generosity had helped her through Claverack and nursing school, but this time Nan refused to help; she was deeply shocked and would have nothing to do with Margaret's flight. In the end Peggy and Grant had to be left with some of Bill's neighbors on Fifteenth Street, with the understanding that Bill would supervise their care. Margaret hoped to persuade her sister Mary to take them later on.

Having provided in this makeshift fashion for her children, Margaret disposed of one more task before she left; she wrote to the assistant district attorney and to Judge John Hazel, informing them that their denial of her rights had "compelled me to leave my home and my three children until I made ready my case, which dealt with society rather than an individual. I would notify them when I came back," and with both letters she enclosed, "as though to say, 'Make the most of it,' " a copy of "Family Limitation."

When Margaret had been three days at sea she cabled to four associates a code message that was to release thousands of copies of her pamphlet, all wrapped, addressed to sympathetic union leaders throughout the country and awaiting the prearranged signal; now she was doubly an exile. Tormented by fears for the future—the children's care uncertain, the date of her return impossible to guess at, her reception in England dubious, for the country was at war and she had no visa— Margaret appears in her shipboard journal still to be seeking to justify her flight: "Dear Peggy how my love goes out to you—I could weep from loneliness for you—just to touch your soft chubby hands—but work is to be done dear—work to help to make your path easier—and those who come after you. . . . United States—what stupidity controls thy destiny —to drive from your shores those who can contribute to the happiness of its downtrodden people."

And in the midst of her musings about the tyranny of the United States she thought of another tyranny: "Some of us [women] are like a violin, different fingering will bring out different tunes— We are played upon by various sympathies and why not. Are we to be only a washboard —with only one song— The man who shouts loud about his liberal ideas and thinks himself advanced finds the servile submission of his wife charming and womanly—"

Once she reached London Margaret rented a small, unheated room in a dreary lodging house; the grimness of the winter weather further increased her loneliness and sense of desolation. "Could any prison be more isolated. . . . Could one be more alone . . . in solitary than wandering about the world separated from the little ones you love." And the ambiguity of her feelings for Bill were recorded in the same random notes: "I have this day cast the die. I have written Bill a letter ending a relationship of over twelve years." Yet she added, "Only I am very slow in my decisions. I cannot separate myself from my past emotions quickly, all breaches must come gradually to me."

The London lodging house was close to the British Museum, and it was there that Margaret spent her lonely days reading "the yellowed, brittle pages of pamphlets and broadsides" in which were preserved the history of the British birth control movement. It was called neo-Malthusianism, after the curate Malthus whose "Principles of Population" had advanced, as early as 1798, economic arguments for limiting fertility. British birth-controllers had won their legal battles against the obscenity laws in 1877, with the Bradlaugh-Besant trials; all that was behind them now, and even though a faint air of impropriety still clung to the movement, its active workers were not anarchists and rebels as in the States, but doctors, writers and philosophers of substantial reputation.

Foremost among them were the Drysdales. While Margaret sat in the British Museum, acquiring the start of what was to become a solidly based understanding of the economic and political aspects of population theory, she looked forward to meeting this extraordinary family that embodied sixty years of devotion to her cause. She sent a note to Dr. C. V. Drysdale and his wife, Bessie, and was invited to their London flat for tea; according to the Drysdales' secretary, "on the appointed afternoon we awaited with curiosity, and also a little apprehension, the visit of 'The Woman Rebel,' but we were hardly prepared for the surprise given us by the soft-voiced, gentle-mannered, altogether charming 'rebel' who tapped at the door at four o'clock." Margaret said later that afternoon's meeting was one of the most encouraging and delightful of her life, that the warmth of their reception, the laughter, comradeship and sympathetic admiration almost helped her to forget, as Christmas approached with its burden of nostalgia, her longing for children and home.

Through the Drysdales Margaret was offered an introduction to Havelock Ellis, doctor, philosopher, litterateur and pioneer in the study of sex, whose works she had first read in the Hastings days. Ellis' treatise on *Sexual Inversion* had been withdrawn in 1898 under fire from the British censor, and he was an early proponent of birth control for eugenic reasons, so there was much they had in common. She wrote to him in mid-December, saying she had read all seven volumes of *Studies in the Psychology of Sex*, and would appreciate the wise counsel of their author; an invitation to tea followed along with precise instructions for reaching his flat in Brixton.

Years later Margaret described it as "that sordid apartment . . . across from police headquarters," to which she had climbed the stairs, lifted a huge brass knocker and been welcomed inside by the sage of sex himself. "He seemed like a God, with his tall, slender figure, and his great shock of white hair." Margaret was not the first to find his appearance godlike; Havelock Ellis, at fifty-four, was an arrestingly handsome man with a massive head, splendid beard and brooding blue eyes deeply set under a powerful ridge of brow. Yet his voice was high and weak, his movements uncertain, he suffered from pathological shyness and had difficulty looking others in the eye until they were well-established friends. "Even his wife Edith," Margaret wrote, "often said that his conversation seemed to consist of 'Oh!'—and great silences—and 'Ah!' "

In his writings Ellis had explored, with vigor, courage and sensitivity, the as yet almost uncharted world of human sexuality; he believed this to be his lifelong mission, to light up for others the hidden landscape of sex. For himself he asked and expected much less, for Ellis had been convinced since boyhood that his own sexual powers were so limited that the most he could offer a woman was spiritual intimacy, perhaps enhanced by an occasional loving embrace. His marriage of more than twenty years was built on this belief, and his writings insisted on the overriding importance of the spiritual and aesthetic, rather than the physical, in sex. Ellis' biographer Arthur Calder-Marshall called him a man for whom sex was chiefly in the head.

Now Ellis led Margaret into his gaslit sitting room; with his own hands he prepared tea, cakes, bread and butter, "and we sat down before the humming flame and talked and talked; and as we talked we wove into our lives an intangible web of mutual interests."

As for Ellis, in spite of the great gulf between them—he was highly educated, used to the company of England's most eminent men and women, while Margaret was a small-town girl with a spotty education —he was immediately drawn to her. "I had rarely known a more charming and congenial companion and I had never found one so swiftly." Much of the attraction must have been due to her physical presence alone, to the calm voice and the radiantly feminine manner. Serene, gracious, demure, she believed a woman's greatest charm lay in a certain "dignified reserve," so that she offered a striking contrast to Ellis' nervous, aggressive and unpredictable wife. But beneath the quiet bearing of the "little, delicate woman, refined and shrinking," in Emma Goldman's phrase, was a core of emotional energy, a powerhouse of will and determination. She appealed to Ellis as a woman both restful and exciting; she also appealed to him as an idealist who had left her own children and country in the service of a heroic cause.

They parted at seven that evening with the promise of a second visit. A week later Ellis wrote: "I have begun this new year at the stroke of midnight with a new kiss," Margaret's kiss. For the shy philosopher it represented breakneck speed.

His wife, like Margaret's husband, was in America. Edith Lees Ellis was a writer, lecturer and feminist, an enormously enterprising and energetic woman in spite of poor physical health and a mental disorder that plunged her periodically into black depression, then hurled her upward to peaks of passionate enthusiasm. Today this manic depression, sometimes called cyclothalmic or circular madness, is treated with electro-shock therapy, but little was known about it then and when Edith

Lees had a complete breakdown before her marriage she fought her way back to sanity alone. Havelock Ellis, the kindest, most sympathetic of men, seems never to have fully understood the nature and extent of his wife's condition, for he was repeatedly to ignore her when she needed him most, and never more strikingly than during his early acquaintance with Margaret Sanger. Now Edith was in the midst of an American lecture tour, expounding her husband's philosophy, while Havelock and Margaret met with increasing frequency—at the British Museum, where he guided her reading on birth control; at museums and concerts; at Soho restaurants for lunch; for day trips on the Clyde, long walks in London parks, or at the Brixton flat, to eat a meal Ellis had prepared himself. Havelock's faithful correspondence with his wife had nothing to say on the subject. In his autobiography he insisted he had never meant to deceive Edith, with whom he was always entirely open. She knew he was fond of several other women, that there had been physical intimacy of his limited kind with a special few, and she was often jealous but resigned. It was part of a bill of goods Havelock had sold himself and his wife at the time they were married, that he was not made for an ordinary marriage, did not want children, must pursue his own work without the distraction of children or the financial burden of a dependent wife; long and frequent separations were deemed a necessity, so each maintained a separate household in which a room was always kept intact and ready for the other.

Whether or not Edith fully understood the bargain she was making at the time of her marriage, she agreed to it. A few years later, during one of the long and frequent separations supposedly necessary for her development and his, she wrote to tell him she had discovered strong homosexual feelings for an old friend of hers. Havelock replied—"for I had no prejudices and I well knew she could be guilty of nothing ugly or ignoble"—that he was perfectly happy with the news, and as for her newly found beloved, "Give her my sweetest love." This unlikely response was almost certainly not what Edith wanted to hear. The later course of their marriage suggests she had begun to chafe against Havelock's part-time arrangement with its half-baked physical intimacy, and what she really wanted of him was enough full-time love and devotion to pull her past the delayed adolescence of which this homosexual streak was an expression. Havelock either could not or would not understand.

And throughout he insisted that none of this mattered, since the spiritual quality of their marriage was what counted. The other women in his life, the several women in hers, were unimportant because they represented the merely physical. And when he failed to mention Margaret in his letters to Edith during the two months after they met, his reason, Havelock later said, was only that everything happened so fast that he had no way of knowing how lasting or important the new friendship would be.

Edith was in Chicago on February 3, 1915, when she got the first of the twenty-odd letters that did mention Margaret Sanger:

That this new friendship could prove a shock to Edith, who herself was constantly forming vivid new friendships, I innocently failed to recognize even as a possibility. . . . when I once began to write about my new friend, I wrote about her in every letter, so that it seemed to Edith my letters were all full of this new friend. That was the way in which to some degree—to what degree it is not possible to unravel—I innocently contributed to the tragic procession of events which filled the following eighteen months, and beautiful as my new friend was to me . . . I have sometimes been tempted to wish that I had not met her.

Edith Ellis was faced for the first time with a rival who seemed to offer spiritual as well as physical attractions, who was sweet, calm and congenial in contrast to Edith, whose mental disorder made domestic life a succession of tormented crises. And she could not live without Havelock; he was the rock she clung to. Edith got out of bed at dawn the day after her husband's first letter arrived and composed a six-page reply in which Ellis later claimed he found no traces of bitterness, although she wrote "it is a kind of strange realization which makes it still easier for me to die. I *want* to die."

From then on Edith's letters hovered about the themes of illness, loneliness and death. She had an attack of angina; ulcers burst in her throat and an operation was carried out without anaesthesia. She pleaded with Havelock to rush to her side, but he had no desire to cross the ocean and failed to respond to what he later saw as "the acute sudden poignancy of love in emergency." He told her instead to come on home—the ocean voyage would set her to rights.

Edith returned to England in May of 1915, fully expecting to be greeted at the dock by Ellis and Margaret, who would tell her the marriage was over and her husband, her rock, lost to her forever. Ellis was alone when he met her; he took her home to Brixton, but the "tragic procession of events" had already begun. A few days after her return Edith swallowed a bottleful of morphia tablets.

Havelock rushed out and mixed an emetic, which she took without protest. There were later suicide attempts, there was a complete breakdown and the agony of deciding whether or not she must be certified insane by Ellis and forcibly confined, before Edith finally died in September 1916 in a diabetic coma. Ellis was truly devastated by the loss. Twenty-three years later he wrote: "I am never reconciled to the pathos of this little woman . . . tortured by the very make of her nature, and herself a torturer, yet to the end an absolute and adorable child—that I have never been reconciled to. I hold perpetual dialogue with myself. I repeat all the wise reasons why I should be at peace as she is at peace. Yet it never ceases to wring my heart."

Whatever part Margaret Sanger played in the final scenes of this terrible domestic drama, she certainly played it in complete innocence. Perhaps Havelock and Margaret spoke of the possibility of marriage during the first months of their friendship; such a marriage would have been wildly unsuitable, for each had work that was far more important to them than any personal life, and they would have realized it. There was Edith to be considered, and they must have considered her. But there were even greater barriers, for marriage in the usual sense was what Ellis still most wished to avoid. A few years later when he was sixty, he discovered a handsome French woman of thirty who adored him, believed despite his disclaimers that he could be a successful lover, and by the force of her belief transformed him into one. But to work such a miracle, to impart virility to a man of sixty who has never before experienced it, requires more dedication to another than Margaret Sanger was capable of. At the time of their first meeting he was a godlike being, but to the woman who had been thrilled by Bill Sanger and his "beastly" jealousy, Ellis was not a potential husband. If they ever spoke about marriage, they must have realized they were far better off as friends.

And they remained for life close, intimate, mutually adoring friends. Margaret's picture was in Ellis' bedroom until his death, while her own feelings for him amounted to veneration. She said: "Ellis has been called the greatest living English gentleman. But England alone cannot claim him; he belongs to all mankind. I define him as one who radiates truth, energy, beauty. I see him in a realm above and beyond the shouting and the tumult." There are three more paragraphs of eulogy before she concludes: "I have never felt about any other person as I do about Havelock Ellis." Certainly his influence on her character and career were deep and lasting; his desire to dedicate himself to "what Christians called God but what he preferred . . . to call the Not-Self," in the words of Calder-Marshall, tempered her rebellious streak, her anarchist's love of open defiance. Ellis counseled patience, reason and brotherly love rather than class hatred, and Margaret, with varying degrees of success, tried to subdue her passionate nature accordingly. They were to write, with tenderness and regularity, often once a week, for as long as Havelock lived, and in his declining years it was Margaret's gift of an annual income that permitted Havelock and the Frenchwoman, Françoise Cyon, to live together in comfort and dignity.

Even before Edith Ellis returned to England in May, Margaret had begun a series of journeys that took her first to Holland, then briefly back to England, to Paris, and finally to Spain. The trip to Holland had been made chiefly at Havelock's urging, for he wanted her to visit the country with the lowest maternal death rate in Europe, one-third that of the United States, and in its major cities the lowest infant death rate in the world. These remarkable achievements were originally due to a woman physician, Aletta Jacobs, who opened the world's first birth control clinic in Holland in 1878. In 1883 Dr. Jacobs joined forces with the German physician Mensinga to perfect a diaphragm pessary; in later years, and with the help of another Dutchman, Dr. Johannes Rutgers, the single clinic in Amsterdam became many throughout the country, so beneficial to public health that in 1910 Queen Wilhelmina awarded the Dutch Neo-Malthusian League a medal of honor and a royal charter.

With a letter of introduction to Dr. Rutgers from the Drysdales, Margaret crossed the Channel to The Hague in January of 1915 and spent the next two weeks learning from him the specific techniques of choosing from among fifteen contraceptive devices (there were fourteen different sizes of the Mensinga pessary alone) the right one for each patient. She became so proficient that by the end of her stay she had given instruction and fittings to seventy-five patients, and this without a common language. From The Hague Margaret headed out into the Dutch countryside and spent the next two months visiting clinics and independent nurses, and learning that "Although the Dutch League had several thousand members . . . and although fifty-four clinics were in operation, many well-informed people did not know anything about them. More surprising still, the medical profession as a whole appeared to be utterly ignorant of the directed birth control work that was going on. It did not, therefore, seem extraordinary that no inkling of all this —either clinics or contraceptive methods—had ever reached the United States."

Holland changed all of Margaret's previous thinking about birth control; she began to envision a series of clinics staffed or supervised by doctors rather than the nurses and midwives who ran the Dutch clinics. Moreover, a certain coldness, an impersonal and hurried quality in the Dutch models, must be replaced, she felt, by warmth and individual interest in each patient. Detailed case histories must be kept, for the patient's sake as well as the movement's. And it was in Holland that she first came to realize the importance of proper spacing of births.

By spring of 1915 Margaret was in England once more. The Neo-Malthusian League spoke of the possibility of a pioneering birth control clinic, and Margaret offered to instruct British nurses in Dutch techniques. But the clinic idea came to nothing because of the war. She had a long visit in Spain as a guest of Lorenzo Portet, an associate of the Drysdales; there was the chance of a job in Paris with a publishing firm, through the good offices of Portet, and Margaret considered renting a house there and bringing the children over. But in December of 1914, while Havelock Ellis and Margaret were discovering each other in London, Bill Sanger had received a visit that was to put a different coloring on Margaret's exile. He had written to her about it in January:

On December the 18th last a party came into my studio and left his card, a Mr. Halleck [Heller]. He claimed to be a seller of rubber goods and etc. Not seeing me he called the next day about 8 a.m. and said, "I am Mr. Heller." He said he had heard of your books, stated that he was personally acquainted with you and wanted one of the pamphlets. . . . finally to get rid of him, I went to the library table and in it were your English and French pamphlets and your own pamphlet. I gave him the first one that I found. I thought no more of it until the same man called last Tuesday, January the 19th, and wanted to know where your *books* could be bought. I told him. . . . A few minutes after a grey haired, side whiskered, five foot ass presented himself. He said, "I am Mr. Comstock. I have a warrant for your arrest." . . . I had to submit to two searches, one by the pimp and one by the ass.

Bill said Comstock advised him "like a brother" to plead guilty to the charge of distributing obscene literature. "Somebody mentioned that if I would give the whereabouts of you I would be acquitted and I replied not even if hell froze up." A year in jail was a possibility. There had been difficulty getting bail, he had already spent thirty-six hours in jail and "lived a year in thirty-six hours," but nevertheless he advised Margaret to stay in Europe till his case was cleared up.

Their letters, until the time of Bill's arrest, left little ground for hope on his part that the marriage would continue; Margaret had written to him on New Year's Day in such a vein that he believed she was "excommunicating me from your life." Moreover, if the love affair with Havelock was a spiritual one, Margaret was apparently loved and pursued by others during her year abroad, and their attraction was not only to the spirit. The journalist Walter Roberts wrote to her on January 11, 1915: "And then this morning I woke early to a still more poignant and exquisite experience. You were there beside me, warm, white, fragrant. I was permeated with you, lulled by your caresses. . . . Do I make you feel, dear, dear one, a little of what our honeymoon means to me?" There were probably several other fleeting love affairs during her exile, of which no record remains but Bill's frantic jealousy at the time and scattered references in her letters of later years to meetings with former suitors. For Margaret no longer considered herself a married woman. "His year in Paris away from me," she had written to her sister Mary in December, "has sort of prepared us both for a parting of the ways. I suppose now I am here for heaven knows how long—and it is always hard to live together after a long separation." Yet Bill was unprepared for any parting of the ways; he was in acute pain, covering page after page of onionskin with vivid black penmanship that he hurled across the Atlantic, bristling with betrayal and loss. Hadn't they agreed "that the sex relation and desire should be confined to only us two?" Yet the agreement had been rudely shattered, for "that was *not* to *be* you must break all *bonds*—the attachment of years—and a love—the best I was capable of—was to be weighed coolly. . . . You drained me of all my love for women—you took it all."

Margaret replied by offering, in place of the bonds of the past, a spiritual comradeship; to this Bill answered that there was no use harping on the spiritual; you can't have one without the other. He wanted her, he needed her, he could not bear to give her up, and now he had fresh ammunition. Totally innocent of any breach of the Comstock laws, he was willing to go to jail for her sacred cause. Traces of ambiguity in her letters, occasional spurts of warmth, the absence of an outright and repeated demand for divorce, probably encouraged him to believe it might work.

But Bill's new tactic only irritated Margaret, who saw his arrest as emotional blackmail. No doubt this motive played a considerable part in the events that followed, yet Bill had also begun to enjoy the battle for its own sake, for he had been a civil libertarian, a Socialist and a rebel long before they met. "Well dear heart," he wrote, "it will probably work out for the best for this *white* corpuscled town needs a free speech and free press fight. . . . I assumed that these lawyers had principles but all they think of is to get people *out.*"

Meanwhile Bill's accounts of his other troubles—arrangements made and unmade for the care of the children, shortages of money, the kind offer of two women to pay for the children's care and education—irritated Margaret even more than his attempt to win her back. "It is so long between our letters that your plans and mine conflict, almost constantly. . . . you have given the impression that I have deserted my children and have turned people against me. . . . Allow me Bill once and for all time to relieve you of any duty toward me which you might have at one time performed and on the receipt of this letter you may feel privileged to send the three children to me on the first boat and consider your duties to them and to me ended for all time. . . . If you can't write to me in a spirit of comradeship—you will save yourself and me much unhappiness by not writing at all."

Perhaps she exaggerated the extent of his accusations. On the other hand, even the subtlest suggestion on Bill's part that she was not precisely doing her duty by the children would have met with loud cries of protest. For whatever compelling reasons of conscience and prudence, Margaret had indeed deserted them; she knew it, just as she knew about Peggy's limp, and she suppressed the guilt in this case by blaming the United States or by assuming a posture of outraged virtue with regard to Bill. Nevertheless she continued to miss her children most painfully. Throughout the winter of 1914 she had been troubled by such nightmare fears for Peggy that she tried to arrange for Edith Ellis to bring the child to England when she came home in May. "Have you seen the kiddies?" she wrote to her sister Nan around the time of Bill's arrest. "Write me about them Nan, please do."

Friends in the States had been writing to say that public opinion on the birth control issue had changed for the better; an IWW leader in Chicago said that "five hundred short extracts of 'Family Limitation' were published, and one girl told me the women in the stockyards district kissed her hands when she distributed the pamphlets." He urged Margaret to return immediately to the States. Yet she was warned by others that if she returned she would surely go to jail.

After repeated postponements Bill Sanger's case came up for trial in September 1915 before Justices McInerney, Herbert and Salmon. According to the account given in *The New York Times*, Bill's opening statement began: "I admit that I broke the law, and yet I claim that, in every real sense, it is the law, and not I, that is on trial today." Judge McInerney took a different view. He pointed out that Bill had admitted his guilt, the rest of his statement was simply opinion, and any man or woman who would circulate literature like Margaret's pamphlet was a menace to the community. Therefore Bill had a choice between a fine of $150 and thirty days in jail. At this, the *Times* said, Bill Sanger jumped to his feet and declared he would "never pay that fine. I would rather be in jail with my convictions than be free at a loss of my manhood and my self-respect. This court can't intimidate me." The crowded courtroom then broke into a volley of applause mingled with shouts and cries, as men and women stood on the benches waving hats and handkerchiefs.

Margaret was in England when she got Bill's account of his trial. Comfortably lodged in a charming little private house in Hampstead Gardens, next door to Alice Vickery, the mother of Dr. Drysdale, she had almost decided to accept Portet's offer of a three-year contract with the Paris publishers; nothing could have been more unwelcome at this point than the idea of returning to the States. A month or so earlier she had written to Nan to complain that "Bill had to get mixed up in my work after all, and of course make it harder for me and all of us!" David Kennedy believes she even hoped to settle permanently in Europe as "a sort of propagandist in absentia . . . remote and romantic in the glorious glow of martyrdom and exile." Now that possibility no longer remained. For no matter how she felt about Bill, she was unable to turn her back on him and the courageous, if unwanted, gesture he was making for her cause. Moreover, the children needed her more than ever now, since they were to be deprived of their one remaining parent. In late September, "with lights dimmed to avoid attracting the attention of German submarines," she sailed reluctantly for home.

The voyage was as full of foreboding as her trip to Europe a year before. When she wrote about it later Margaret insisted she had been troubled for months by a peculiar and unshakable foreboding of some dreadful happening, in some way connected with the number 6, and with the date November 6 in particular. She had dreamed about Peggy, she said, dreamed that Peggy was calling to her and wanted to know when she would return, and on the ship she seemed to hear Peggy's voice; at night she awoke with a cold sweat—a "queer sense of presentiment of evil was with me almost incessantly."

Stepping off the boat on October 4, Margaret saw on a newsstand a copy of the magazine *Pictorial Review*, and on its cover the title of a lead article devoted to "Birth Control." "It seemed strange to be greeted, not by friends or relatives, but by a phrase of your own carried on a magazine. I purchased it and, singing to myself, went on to a hotel where the children were brought to me." They were well and happy. Her presentiments, then, were surely nonsense; a cover story about birth control in one of the most respected magazines of the day augured well for her trial and her movement.

From the Tombs, Bill wrote: "Peg Dear Soul, Today the glorious news reached me . . . that you had at last come back. . . . all past differences and understandings recede to nothing in the thought that I shall behold your dear presence once again." Released from prison four days later, he looked old, thin and worn. The two of them had no better luck discussing their future face to face than they had with the Atlantic between them, and Margaret vowed she would not see him for the rest of that winter; all their talks, she said, became exchanges of insults, and from then on she would write to him rather than see him.

She had even more pressing concerns than the state of her doomed marriage; she had three children to catch up with after a year's absence, and her impending trial to prepare. As soon as she returned she had written to Judge Hazel and Assistant District Attorney Content, asking for a week or ten days of privacy with the children before the case was called; to this Content agreed. Margaret then cast about for supporters. In her absence, she soon learned, a group of women liberals led by Mary Ware Dennett had reorganized the National Birth Control League, taking over Margaret's files and the list of subscribers to *The Woman Rebel;* when she asked for their help, Mrs. Dennett explained this was not possible, that they were working to change the laws and could not support someone who had broken them. The New York Academy of Medicine was also evasive, even though their new president had supported the principles of birth control in his acceptance speech. Some radical allies, and the Free Speech League, stood by her; Emma Goldman, during Margaret's absence, had thrown herself into birth control activity and was arrested for distributing a pamphlet she had written on the subject, but Margaret had put the Woman Rebel phase behind her and with it much of her sympathy with radicals in general and Emma in particular. Her reasons were partly practical ones, based on a growing conviction that support must come from a broad section of the population and especially from solid and respectable people, if the movement was ever to succeed on a grand scale. Ellis and the Drysdale circle had urged her to focus her energies solely on birth control, to avoid revolutionary activity and work toward changing the laws through skill and knowledge rather than defiance.

But Margaret's subsequent relations with the National Birth Control League, as well as with her former friends among the radicals, were also deeply influenced by her own singular character. She had come to New York a few years earlier as a shy young matron whose demure manner was combined with a romantic "cult of the irrational," the belief in her guidance by inner voices. These voices had sent her abroad, where she captivated England's neo-Malthusians, a learned, intellectually sophisticated group who found her magnetism irresistible. In her mid-thirties now, she had begun to develop that constellation of personal gifts that give one individual the power to lead many. But with it came what Dr. Alan Guttmacher, today's president of Planned Parenthood, called an "inability to work with others unless she was allowed full command." An inspiring leader, she could not follow, had difficulty compromising, and became increasingly reluctant to acknowledge the independent contributions of others.

Emma Goldman, for example, was once more arrested and briefly jailed in February 1916 for circulating some of the birth control pamphlets she had written herself; although Margaret mentioned the arrest in *My Fight for Birth Control*, she ingeniously managed to leave Emma's name out of the account, naming only the three women arrested with her and ignoring entirely the authorship of the pamphlets. In her autobiography she tried to make up for the omission but her heart wasn't in it. "Emma Goldman . . . belatedly advocated birth control, not to further it but strategically to utilize in her own programme of anarchism the publicity value it had achieved." This was deceptive. Margaret first heard of the birth control issue as a revolutionary gambit from Emma herself. In the same way the British Marie Stopes, whom Margaret spoke of with gratitude and affection, was nevertheless described in *My Fight* as a friend and supporter and the author of *Married Love*, with no mention of her founding Britain's first birth control clinic in 1921.

"As I looked over the situation," Margaret wrote afterward, "I realized the hopelessness of expecting support from such groups or sources. Yet . . . I determined to remain and fight the case out in the courts, depending upon the common sense, the intelligence and understanding of public opinion for the support I needed." And a broad segment of the public had been favorably impressed, first by Margaret's dramatic exile and the publication of the practical pamphlet "Family Limitation," then by Bill Sanger's arrest and defiance of the Comstock laws.

Anthony Comstock was by now a public laughingstock whose career as the arbiter of national morals might have come to a natural end if Bill's trial had not put an end to him altogether; for Comstock caught a cold at the trial and died two weeks later. The law did not change with his death, but there was a certain dramatic sense of the old order's passing, and Margaret's own trial would now take place without the presence of an implacable enemy. But mid-October brought a sudden and terrible change in her fortunes, "a crisis of a more intimate nature, a tragedy about which I find myself still unable to write, though so many years have passed." Five-year-old Peggy contracted pneumonia. There were no penicillins and no miracle drugs; when a week had gone by she no longer responded to treatment, only opening her eyes from time to time to ask if her mother was back from London. It was the cry Margaret claimed she had heard abroad when "the same troubled voice rang in my ears, 'Mother, Mother, are you coming back?' " Peggy died on November 6, 1915, and the date seemed to fulfill the awful foreboding she said she had felt about the number 6, and November 6 in particular.

Certainly the tragic loss confirmed and broadened Margaret's mysticism, just as it must inevitably have reawakened the guilt she had suppressed when Bill accused her of neglecting the children. There was no reason to suppose Peggy would have survived pneumonia had Margaret never gone to England, nor was there any rational basis for believing she could have been protected against polio by more faithful care, but the guilt that follows a child's death is rarely rational. Now the need to justify her past acts was stronger than ever, and Margaret turned to her cause for consolation, finding it in activity itself, and in the sense of unity with the thousands who wrote tender and sympathetic letters. "This fresh contact with the source, contact with the motive power which had taken me out of my maternal corner two or three years before, renewed my desire and gave me the strength to carry on."

A postponement of the trial was immediately offered, but this Margaret refused; only three days after Peggy died she was arranging to attend a meeting of her supporters that was to be held on November 20 at the Park Avenue Hotel. Friends, liberal groups, lawyers as well as her personal physician pleaded with her to accept a postponement or try for some sort of legal compromise, but "the far off voices of the poor mothers themselves seemed to shout: Keep on! Stand firm!" and with a single inspired stroke she resolved to dispense with counsel and plead her own case, "as the ideas I have sought to promulgate are not within the range of the psychology of men lawyers." Throughout, she insisted that the case be put on the court calendar as soon as possible.

There were repeated postponements nevertheless, each one the occasion of a fresh blast of national publicity that jostled war news on the front pages. By mid-February the *New York Sun* reported that "Mrs. Margaret H. Sanger appeared . . . yesterday to make her weekly demand that she be placed on trial. . . . The Sanger case presented the anomaly of a prosecutor loath to prosecute and a defendant anxious to be tried." A photograph taken of Margaret with Grant and Stuart for publicity purposes brought her before the public as a wistful little woman, delicately pretty, still young, and tenderly maternal. Liberal newspapers as well as radical ones were prepared to defend her now, and even the august *New York Times*, it was said, might prove sympathetic. And for the first time in the history of the movement a number of socially distinguished women, a Belmont and a Delafield among them, were lending their names to the cause. From England, meanwhile, came a petition written by Dr. Marie Stopes and signed by such luminaries as H. G. Wells, Arnold Bennett and Gilbert Murray, addressed to President Wilson and urging free speech on the birth control issue. At a dinner scheduled for the night before the trial, on January 17, two hundred guests included Walter Lippmann; Herbert Croly, the editor of the *New Republic;* Miss Fola La Follette, the senator's daughter; and an extraordinary array of socially prominent women, Mrs. Ogden Reid and Mrs. Thomas Hepburn, a childhood acquaintance of Margaret's in Corning and the mother of Katharine Hepburn, among them. Even Mary Ware Dennett's National Birth Control League forgot its qualms about women who break the laws and sprang to Margaret's side.

The trial, when it came at last, could only be an anticlimax. On February 18 the charges against Margaret Sanger were simply dismissed. The indictment was two years old, Mrs. Sanger was not a disorderly person, the government therefore considered there was reasonable doubt, according to the memorandum signed by the U.S. District Attorney.

All my friends regarded the quashing of the Federal indictment as a great achievement. There was much rejoicing and congratulation, but they acted as though they were saying, "Now settle down in your domestic corner, take your husband back, care for your children, behave yourself. . . . Your duty is to do the thing you are able to do which is mind your home and not attempt something others can do better than you."

But I was not content to have a Liberty Dinner and jubilate. . . . The Federal law concerned only printed literature. My own pamphlet had given the impression that the printed word was the best way to inform women, but the practical course of contraceptive technique I had taken in the Netherlands had shown me that one woman was so different from another in structure that each needed particular information applied to herself as an individual. . . . It was no longer to be only a free speech movement, and I wanted also if possible to present this new idea of clinics to the country. If I could start them, other organizations and even hospitals might do the same. I had a vision of a "chain"—thousands of them in every center of America.

The *New York Globe* pointed out that nothing had really been settled by the trial and technically they were right. But if the law had not been changed, public opinion had altered considerably. Peggy's death, Margaret's insistence on going through with the trial nevertheless; her dramatic refusal of counsel—one small frail woman against the might of the federal government—the appearance of socially prominent and spotlessly respectable names in her support: all did their part in the transformation of Margaret Sanger into a national figure and a heroine, whereas before she was only a rebel, vaguely mixed up with the obscenity laws. Now "so many invitations to address meetings in various cities and towns were sent to me that I was not able to accept them all but agreed to as many as I could."

Dr. Marie Stopes had written to Margaret in September, wishing her "Goodspeed and God's blessing on your trial." She also suggested, in connection with Margaret's complaint of insomnia, "I believe a marital embrace from your husband would stop your sleeplessness!" But if Bill and Margaret were no longer on terms that permitted embraces, neither had Margaret been able to carry out her resolve not to see him all winter. In mid-October, quite without warning, she had visited him at his studio, and written two letters that Bill had "treasured and taken to my heart. . . . you know whatever have been our misunderstandings I always felt that unsaid voice you spoke of . . . somehow whispers—that too will pass over."

Apparently she could not bring herself even now to break with him entirely; neither married nor divorced, her status was a continuing source of hope to others as well as to Bill. Walter Roberts wrote from England in March of 1916: "You are my lover, my wonderful Margaret. I long passionately, yet with a sense of unworthiness, to have our lives more closely identified." Whatever permanent alliance was to follow the divorce she might or might not get from Bill, Margaret hoped—unrealistically, no doubt—that it would reunite her with her sons, who were at boarding school. "They are both darlings . . . and I look forward to the days when I can have them with me again. I'll have to go west and find a widower with money and settle down for life." The childhood yearning to be a woman of style and charm who strolled in the evenings with her husband and children still tugged at her from time to time; it never died, but it was to be repeatedly drowned out by the excitement and sense of driving purpose generated by her work.

In the spring of 1916 Margaret set out on a three-month national lecture tour, still terrified of public speaking. Wherever she went, headlines followed. Roman Catholic opposition, often of a high-handed nature, won hundreds of new supporters who might have been indifferent at first to birth control but were far from indifferent to the threat of religious censorship. Margaret's standard speech during this tour started on a quiet note—"The first right of every child is to be wanted"

—and then proceeded with the story of Sadie Sachs and her own dedication to the cause of birth control. She called for free discussion of sexual knowledge, for an end to abortion and the proliferation of the defective, and demanded the emancipation of women—"The most important force in the remaking of the world is a free motherhood!" She gave no illegal details of contraception, however. What she did, and to a degree Margaret herself could not have anticipated, was to enthrall her listeners. Following in the paths of Elizabeth Gurley Flynn and Emma Goldman, who had addressed radical audiences in Chicago, St. Louis, Detroit, Portland and Los Angeles in 1915 on the same subject, Margaret was utterly unlike her predecessors, who harangued their audiences at the top of their lungs. Small, pretty, plainly dressed, she was a woman of refinement, yet a fervent and inspired one who "took the audience and lifted it up. . . . She had the power of a saint," according to the Unitarian minister John Haynes Holmes, who heard her some years later.

Where audiences expressed a desire to start local birth control leagues, Margaret laid out a basic plan of organization, then told them to get in touch with Mary Ware Dennett's National Birth Control League. Always a resourceful strategist, when she ran into trouble she capitalized on it; arrested in Portland, she called a protest meeting, distributed copies of "Family Limitation," which were supposedly not illegal in Oregon, and was followed to the city jail by hundreds of local women, until "The police locked the jail doors to keep them out," according to the *San Francisco Call.* There were thousands of letters of protest to the local newspaper, and a flood of requests to Margaret for copies of "Family Limitation." Exhausted and exhilarated, she returned at last to New York.

The National Birth Control League, Mrs. Dennett's group of educated and liberal women, had invited Margaret to join their executive committee, but she persisted in her claim that her own function was to break the law—to alter it through direct action and judicial interpretation—rather than amend it. She thought of the League as a "bourgeois, pink tea, lady-like" organization and wanted no part of it; yet only a few years later she was to arrive at much the same position as Mrs. Dennett and make her own short-lived attempt at changing the New York State laws by amendment, and in the late 1920s she began a long assault on the federal law. But for the time being her chief desire was for bold and dramatic action, unhampered by organization and free from the conflicting claims of others:

I decided to open a clinic in New York City. . . . Section 1142 of the New York statutes was definite: *No one* could give contraceptive information to *anyone* for *any* reason. On the other hand, Section 1145 distinctly stated that physicians could give prescriptions to prevent conception for the cure or prevention of disease. Two attorneys and several doctors assured me this exception referred only to venereal disease. . . . I wanted the interpretation to be broadened into the intent to protect women from ill health as the result of excessive childbearing and, equally important, to have the right to control their own destinies.

To change this interpretation it was necessary to have a test case.

To keep strictly within the letter of the law Margaret would need a doctor to head her clinic, but although several women doctors had promised to help when the time came, in the end there was no one willing to risk the loss of her medical license. Margaret turned instead to the youngest of the Higgins sisters, Ethel Byrne. Like Margaret, Ethel was a registered nurse and far closer in temperament to their battling father than Nan and Mary were; Emily Taft Douglas described Ethel as "a quiet, intense young woman with an astringent wit and a somewhat competitive feeling toward her older sister."

The two of them tramped through the streets of the Bronx, Brooklyn, and lower Manhattan, east and west, in search of a suitable site, and decided at last on number 46 Amboy Street in the Brownsville section of Brooklyn, which Margaret called "a hive of futile industry—dingy, squalid, peopled with hard-working men and women, the home of poverty which was steadily growing worse." They determined to "open a birth control clinic at 46 Amboy Street to disseminate information where it was poignantly required by human beings. Our inspiration was the mothers of the poor; our object, to help them."

A letter was sent to the district attorney of Brooklyn announcing that from that date forward contraceptive information would be given out on Amboy Street. With Ethel and Fania Mindell, a young Yiddish-speaking assistant who had come from Chicago to work with her, Margaret collected chairs, desks, floor coverings, curtains, a stove, and had five thousand announcements printed in English, Italian and Yiddish, to be handed out house-to-house by the three of them. Neighborhood druggists were warned to put in a supply of Mispah pessaries and condoms.

On Amboy Street Margaret was surrounded by the suffering motherhood from whom she drew her deepest inspiration, but she did not neglect the women of wealth who had rallied to the movement during the trial. Among them was Mabel Dodge, whose opulent salon the Sangers used to attend when they first came to Manhattan. But this was a different Margaret from the shy young woman so unsure of her opinions her husband had to announce them for her; now Margaret's voice was worldly and authoritative, and Mabel Dodge listened in rapt fascination:

It was as if she had been more or less arbitrarily chosen by the powers that be to voice a new gospel of not only sex knowledge in regard to conception, but sex knowledge about copulation and its intrinsic importance. . . .

She was the first person I ever knew who was openly an ardent propagandist for the joys of the flesh. This, in those days, was radical indeed. . . . she told us all about the possibilities in the body for "sex expression"; and as she sat there, serene and quiet, and unfolded the mysteries and mightinesses of physical love, it seemed to us we had never known it before as a sacred and at the same time a scientific reality. . . .

Margaret Sanger made it appear as the first duty of men and women. Not just anyhow, anywhere, not promiscuity, for that defeated its own end if pleasure were the goal; not any man and any woman, but the conscious careful selection of a lover that is the mate, if only for an hour—for a lifetime, maybe.

Then she taught us the way to a heightening of pleasure and of prolonging it, and the delimiting of it to the sexual zones, the spreading out and sexualizing of the whole body until it should become sensitive and alive throughout, and complete. She made love into a serious undertaking—with the body so illumined and conscious that it would be able to interpret and express in all its parts the language of the spirit's pleasure.

Much of what Margaret told Mabel Dodge she had learned from Havelock Ellis.

On October 16, 1916, the nation's first birth control clinic was open to the public. "Would the women come? Did they come? Nothing, not even the ghost of Anthony Comstock, could have kept them away. . . . Halfway to the corner they were standing in line, at least one hundred and fifty, some shawled, some hatless, their red hands clasping the cold, chapped, smaller ones of their children."

Nine days after the opening of the clinic a patient "large of build and hard of countenance" returned to reveal herself as Mrs. Margaret Whitehurst of the vice squad; the office was raided, 464 case histories confiscated, and Margaret marched off behind the patrol wagon—she refused to sit inside it—to the Raymond Street jail. Out on bail next day, she returned to her clinic only to be told by the landlord that the police had made him sign ejection papers. Their lawyer, a promising young liberal named Jonah J. Goldstein, did his best to have all three women tried at once, but by January 8, 1917, after many postponements, Ethel stood trial alone.

The case was already in the public eye; the New York Legislative League had debated birth control before a packed audience at the Waldorf-Astoria only days before, and the Women's City Club had turned hundreds of would-be listeners away from a birth control meeting at the Park Avenue Hotel. A group of socially influential women headed by Mrs. Amos Pinchot, Mrs. Delafield and Juliet Barrett Rublee, formed a Committee of 100 to "lead to the repeal of all laws, Federal and State, which make the giving out of information on the subject of Birth Control a criminal offense and which class such information with obscenity and indecency."

Ethel Byrne freely admitted she had given out advice on birth control; she was found guilty and sentenced on January 22 to thirty days in the workhouse on Blackwells Island. Ethel then announced to the press that when in jail she would not eat, would not drink, would not do "one article of work." She made her will, arranged for the care of her two children and said good-bye to Margaret, declaring:

It makes little difference whether I starve or not, so long as this outrageous arrest calls attention to the archaic laws which would prevent our telling the truth about the facts of life. With eight thousand deaths a year in New York State from illegal operations on women, one more death won't make much difference.

The New York Times recorded these decisions of Ethel's on page twenty, its last page. "Mrs. Byrne Starts Lots of Strikes," the headline said. "Won't Eat, Drink, Be Examined or Bathed, and Says She Won't Work, Either!" The following day, January 25, once more on its last page, the *Times* announced that "Frequent temptations to take a drink of water were placed in her way," but she continued to refuse them. After the third day of Ethel's imprisonment, however, the *Times* rescued her from page twenty and put her on the front page, second column from the left, close to the top and surrounded by war news: "Mrs. Byrne Weaker, Still Fasts in Cell."

The prison staff was frightened now and began issuing semidaily bulletins on Ethel's health, although at first the warden had refused to pander to public interest by commenting at all, except to note that most hunger strikers were fakes. By January 28, again firmly planted on page one, the *Times* announced: "Mrs. Byrne Now Being Fed by Force." She had gone without food or water for over a hundred hours; Ethel Byrne was the first woman in America to be forcibly fed while in jail.

On January 29, according to the *Times,* a rally of three thousand women filled Carnegie Hall to cheer every mention of either Ethel Byrne or Margaret Sanger. Margaret herself was in a state of near-panic; she believed Ethel meant what she said, that she was indeed capable of dying for the cause, and the forcible feeding impressed her not at all. Quite the contrary, the news that Ethel had accepted the feeding only meant, to Margaret, that her fighting sister was too weak to fight back. With the help of Mrs. Amos Pinchot, a friend of Governor Whitman and one of the Committee of 100, Margaret obtained a governor's pardon by giving a promise on Ethel's behalf that she would stop all birth control work while the case was being appealed. She found her sister "thin and emaciated, her eyes were sunken and her tongue swollen, high red spots stood out on her cheeks. She could not see me even across the narrow cell. . . ." Margaret said it took a year of convalescence before Ethel could return to normal life.

Meanwhile there was Margaret's own trial, attended by some fifty of her Brownsville clinic patients and a fashionably dressed contingent of society women; Margaret carried an armful of American beauty roses, and rows of limousines lined the streets near the court. Even the judges were sympathetic; they had no choice but to find Margaret guilty, but they really did not want to punish her with anything more than a light fine.

Goldstein—J.J., Margaret called him—had a more difficult time with his client than with the court. The court repeatedly offered "the highest degree of leniency," if Margaret would only promise not to break the law again. She did so promise but she added, in spite of Goldstein's admonitions to the contrary, "I am perfectly willing not to violate Section 1142—pending the appeal."

The appeal, she was told, had nothing to do with the matter; either she promised, or she did not promise. Was it yes or no? "I can't respect the law as it stands today," Margaret replied, meaning: while we appeal for what we hope will be a better interpretation of the law, I will be breaking it as fast as I can.

She was given a thirty-day sentence in the workhouse.

Margaret said later she had no intention of going on a hunger strike, because the United States had just broken off relations with Germany, war was imminent, and a fast would be buried among the war news. And in any case she had expected a heavier sentence; she went off to the workhouse in fairly good spirits to spend a restful month inside, a model prisoner for the most part who used her time "for reflection, for assembling past experiences and preparing for the future," as well as helping her fellow prisoners with their letter writing. She emerged on March 6 to find a group of old cronies singing the Marseillaise on the frozen pavement. "Behind them at the upper windows were my new friends, the women with whom I had spent the month, and they too were singing."

On the twenty-first of that month she wrote to Bill asking what he would do, what he would have her do, "to secure a legal separation for us both? . . . from your insulting attack upon my character last Friday night I realize at last that I must protect myself as well as my friends . . . by the only power left for a woman in my position to use:—the State. . . . I wish to wipe from my memory all thought of connection with you and shall appreciate any effort on your part to further that end." She had been goaded at last into an unequivocal demand for separation.

Bill replied by sending her flowers. He had made an "insulting attack" on her character by way of his "filthy, vile mouth and slanderous onslaught," and now he hoped to erase the memory with flowers. Margaret was not unresponsive to the gesture, for she told him that "needless to say I appreciate their beauty and the spirit in which you sent them." But the spirit as well as the onslaught were familiar stories to her; Bill's fiery temper and his jealousy had been present from the first days of their marriage and were to remain with him to the end of his life. His daughter Joan Sanger Hoppe described him as often throwing crockery "or a whole dinner table, food and all, over," in a blaze of temper. People who knew both her father and her mother, Mrs. Hoppe recalled, would often say to her, "God, he's so difficult!" Intensely self-involved, he had little concern for the desires of others when they conflicted with his own. As for his generosity, he had courted Margaret, as he was to court his second wife, with a lavish outpouring of presents, opera tickets, dinners in elegant restaurants, and this too remained with him for life, for his daughter remembered, "If I ever expressed an interest in something he would always try to get it for me," although they were rarely together. Yet it was all, in the end, the expression of an inflexible will—the unconquerable temper that erupted whenever he was thwarted as well as the drive to exert power by generosity. This was well enough when Margaret was young, her own will to power undeveloped, a powerful male a delicious challenge. But she had learned, partly from Bill, the need to exert power in her own behalf. Perhaps she loved him still, but she was no longer able to submit herself to either his temper or his generosity.

"Just as you say it is impossible to be alone," she replied to the flowers, "so do I say it is impossible to go on like this. My work is piling up and it is impossible to do justice to it . . . in this unsettled state of mind. . . . There is nothing I have to give you in love, there is nothing to be repaired, there is no way that we can go on together. . . . Unless you can settle this matter immediately and to my satisfaction I shall leave the country within the next few weeks and leave everything to those who are carrying on the work."

By August 1917 he was ready to give way. "Let this be the last you shall hear of me. It is best that you go your way and I go mine," he wrote, and in December he suggested not a complete separation, but a divorce, only insisting that Margaret take the initiative, "as certainly I do not wish to hand down a heritage to the children which would indicate that *I* took the initiative that we should pass out of each other's lives." But she did not file for divorce until September of 1918, and even then the first attempt came to nothing.

In January of 1920 she tried again with another lawyer, apparently in earnest this time—yet within months she appeared unexpectedly at Bill's studio "and showed great curiosity (but did not express it) about the model—well, it was *strictly professional*," he assured her afterwards. "When you took steps for your divorce I thought that was the end of everything. . . . I had a right to assume that you knew your own mind . . . we see each other often and I am expected to maintain an attitude of reserve. . . . It is better that I do not see you—for your presence thrills me—and yet there is no outlet."

An uncontested divorce was granted in 1920; yet, judging from the above letter written two years later, Margaret was reluctant even then to put an end to their relationship. Although free herself, she was not entirely willing to give Bill his freedom, for she enjoyed being pursued and worshiped, delighted in being elusive. "Desire is generated in the pursuit," she believed. "The love of the majority of men is deepened and strengthened by resistance. It puts them on their mettle, gives them the necessary obstacles to overcome, and puts them to the test." If Bill was unwilling to remain forever on his mettle there were others to take his place—none of them as attractive as the personal crusade that was her first love, for "where is the man to give me what the movement gives, in joy, in interest, in freedom?" as she wrote some years later to her friend Juliet Rublee.

For Margaret, whose first marriage had been a battle ground, the scene had shifted. Her battles henceforth were to be fought on another terrain, her opponents would be the law, the church, rivals within the movement, society itself. She had found other outlets, and so, in time, did Bill.

Leaving prison in March of 1917, Margaret learned that one "impressive result of our imprisonment was that the idea of birth control had spread into homes and was discussed by individuals and by groups which otherwise would never have known the words." For this she had Ethel Byrne to thank; *The New York Times* had said of Ethel that everything "in her voice and manner suggested gentleness," and the daring hunger strike with its attendant publicity went a long way toward confirming the new picture of the birth-controller as a liberal, a lady and a mother. The public image had changed, so must the reality. Margaret said she had been disappointed in the Brownsville mothers, who stood behind her at her trial but failed to reopen her clinic, indeed failed to take any action in their own behalf. If the women of the working classes, "the mothers of the child laborers . . . the wives of the wage slaves" could not help in her crusade to help them, she must depend instead on "the clubwomen, the women of wealth and intelligence. . . . Together they must bring about a change of laws and convert public opinion."

A major step in this direction was to be her *Birth Control Review*, whose first issue appeared while Margaret was still in prison; much of the time she spent inside had gone into planning this journal, which was to be sober and scientific in tone, factual, authoritative and aimed at leaders of opinion. Dr. Frederick Blossom, a professional social worker who had pledged six months of his time toward building a foundation for a national birth control organization, now joined forces with Margaret to rent an office consisting of two tiny rooms on the upper floor of 104 Fifth Avenue, the rent and furniture paid for with money he lent. Blossom was financial manager of the *Review*, fund raiser and supervisor of the fifteen or twenty volunteers who answered thousands of letters from embattled motherhood throughout the country. A single paid worker, a stenographer named Anna Lifshiz, often had to wait weeks for her minute salary.

For Margaret was deeply in debt. She took no salary from the movement, turning instead to her sisters when all else failed; lectures and magazine articles paid for her living expenses in a dreary studio apartment, shares were sold in a New York Women's Publishing Company to help finance the *Review*, and Juliet Rublee became a generous contributor. Nevertheless, the years "from the termination of my prison sentence in 1917 to 1921 were leaden years; years of constant labor,

financial worry, combatting of opposition." The boys were at boarding
school, supported by Bill Sanger and Margaret's sister, and they spent
their summers at a small house in Truro near Cape Cod with Michael
Hennessy Higgins:

> At times the homesickness for them seemed too much to bear; especially was
> this true in the Fourteenth Street studio. When I came in late at night the fire
> was dead in the grate, the book open on the table, the glove dropped on the
> floor . . . just as I had left them a day, a week, or a month before. That first
> chill of loneliness was always appalling. I wanted, as a child does, to be like other
> people; I wanted to be able to sink gratefully into the warmth and glow of a
> loving family welcome.

In her autobiography Margaret repeats the sensible reasons for keeping the two boys away at school, describing her frequent visits and her
joy at seeing them, followed by the realization that they were, after all,
ready to return to their classmates when the first pleasure of reunion had
passed. To keep them home, she insists, much as she would have loved
it, would only mean long absences and the uncertain supervision of hired
help. All the same Grant missed her far more than she seems willing to
record. Beginning in early childhood all the way through and past late
adolescence, he wrote cheerfully, patiently, uncomplainingly and constantly of his desire to see his mother. He might have missed a busy
clubwoman of a mother just as much; certainly both boys were well
supplied with loving relatives, the aunts, the grandfather, an athletic
uncle to whom Stuart was especially devoted. But they did not have a
normal family life, for that was not within their mother to give. For
Margaret, the movement took precedence over all personal claims. It
was by her own confession her first thought upon waking every morning
and her last thought before she fell asleep at night.

While she was busy launching the *Review*—distributed on Manhattan street corners by a battling suffragette named Kitty Marion, it
became during the twenty-five years of its publication the official voice
of the birth control movement—Margaret also had to deal with insur-
gency within the ranks. For Frederick Blossom no longer saw eye to eye
with her, and decamped one day taking files, business records and all the
spartan furnishings of 104 Fifth Avenue. Yet he had made some valua-

ble contributions; in December 1916, Blossom had organized the New York Birth Control League, so that for a short period there were two parallel organizations, Mary Ware Dennett's, which supported Margaret's drive for clinics but was essentially aimed at reform of the federal law, and the NYBCL, dedicated to the clinic movement and reform of state laws. If the aims of both were similar, there was continual bickering between the two, and an eventual dissolution of the slender bonds between them came in 1919, when Mrs. Dennett's group was reorganized as the Voluntary Parenthood League. With headquarters in Washington, D.C., they fought for free and open access to birth control information. Margaret's position was now directly opposed to theirs; she gave up the assault on state laws, considered free and open access to birth control information dangerous, and believed it must be channeled to the public solely through the medical profession and clinics. Her position was far more conservative than Mrs. Dennett's and a far cry from the stance she had taken as the Woman Rebel.

Meanwhile Jonah J. Goldstein had been winning a valuable legal prize in the New York State Court of Appeals. Margaret's original conviction for the Brownsville clinic was upheld, but Judge Frederick E. Crane's interpretation altered the meaning of Section 1145, which had allowed physicians to give advice for the cure or prevention of disease. Always taken as meaning venereal disease, it was now seen to mean just what the dictionary said, "an alteration in the state of the body, or of some of its organs, interrupting or disturbing the performance of the vital functions, and causing or threatening pain or sickness." Therefore any physician who gave birth control advice to a married woman for the sake of her health acted within the law. It was the first great breach in the wall.

Public sentiment about birth control had been in the process of change since Margaret's exile in 1914, not only because of the publicity gained by her own dramatic and combative methods, but because of an increasing openness in sexual matters; the New Woman was no longer outrageous, and the First World War, by thrusting women into factories, had made their independence a patriotic necessity. War always accelerates social change; whereas before, contraception had been the secret of the educated woman, banned from public mention, barely spoken of in decent society, now there were more than two dozen local birth control leagues in operation throughout the country. And Margaret herself served as a one-woman league; to the thousands who wrote personal letters imploring practical contraceptive advice, she sent the names of nearby physicians who could be counted on for help.

No sooner was the war over than Margaret hurried off to Europe, eager for a reunion with her English friends. There was a brief visit with Havelock Ellis, who had begun, recently and tentatively, the liaison with Françoise Cyon that was to last until his death some twenty years later; Margaret found him in Cornwall, alone. They took a short trip to Ireland together, their romance past history now, but romance was not absent from that English April, for Margaret met H. G. Wells, was invited to his house at Easton Glebe, and "From 1920 on I never went to England without spending part of the time with H.G., and many of the most attractive people I met were at Easton Glebe." She does not mention a flurry of flirtation with H.G., who was addicted to women and to "all the glittering black magic of sex." Margaret deeply admired him; he was an intellectual giant, brilliant, witty and magnetic in spite of his odd shape, short arms and shapeless torso beneath a walrus face. Wells wrote to Margaret soon after they met: "I want to see you as much as possible . . . as much as possible without people about." Unfortunately there is no way of knowing for sure whether Margaret became one of Wells's many conquests. There are only the few notes from H.G., silence from Margaret, and the misleading suggestion in her autobiography that he was a devoted and faithful husband. H.G. was a notorious and successful womanizer, and if Margaret eluded him, she must have been one of the very few attractive women in his circle who did so.

Through Ellis, Margaret met the poet Hugh de Selincourt, who lived with his wife and daughter and the journalist Harold Child in a house at Wantley, Sussex, that had once been Shelley's. Hugh was Havelock Ellis' dear friend and devoted admirer; he was also a self-proclaimed sexual athlete. From Ellis Hugh had learned that sexual jealousy was contemptible, that a man who admired another man would naturally wish to share with him the woman he loved. Thus Hugh's wife, Janet, was also the lover of Harold Child, and as Janet admired a neighboring doctor, perhaps platonically, she and Harold and Hugh went out each day to gather the flowers that Janet then presented to the doctor.

Into this high-minded ménage à trois came Margaret Sanger, who had preached to Mabel Dodge about the "mysteries and mightinesses of physical love." She was forty years old and admitted to thirty-six, still pretty, still radiantly feminine, perhaps more energetic beneath the calm exterior than ever before, for she had had some success as the leader of a national movement. Both Hugh and Harold Child were captivated. "The whole place breathes your sweetness," Hugh de Selincourt wrote soon after. "Every nerve of me continues in tumult. . . . Ah! the glory of you!" Harold Child's effusions were somewhat more moderate, describing Margaret's eyes as "very far apart and so quietly, unaggressively, immorally brave and candid and simple with the simplicity of a spirit." Margaret told her first biographer, Lawrence Lader, that "Wantley was not dedicated to love in the sense of sex. It fused friendship and love as a spiritual unit," but if she meant by this that she avoided sexual entanglements at Wantley, it seems most unlikely. The tone of Hugh's letters is unmistakably intimate; his soppy prose pursued her across the ocean and down the corridors of time, and several years later he wrote: "Your loveliness goes on spreading and spreading, adorable Margaret. Oh you are singing in me such a song. . . . I kiss your every little corner — You are God-inspired you lovely woman." But if Margaret and Hugh were lovers, as this last passage certainly implies, there was no harm done, for she owed allegiance to no one, and Hugh's wife disclaimed all jealousy on principle. Only a few years later de Selincourt's taste for triangular sex was to cause serious mischief, from which Havelock Ellis never really recovered, but at the time of her first postwar visit Wantley was a haven where Margaret could bask in adoration and worship whenever the demands of her work became too exhausting. She once wrote that de Selincourt was the man of her "adolescent dreams," and his letters were better than "a health cure topped by a case of champagne."

Margaret lectured throughout England and Scotland that spring and summer, chiefly to working class audiences under the sponsorship of the Drysdales; she wrote to Juliet Rublee about the "pale-faced, wretched wives. Men beat them. They cringe before their blows, but pick up the baby, dirty and unkempt, and return to serve him." There was also a quick trip to Germany in search of a chemical contraceptive Havelock had told her about in 1915. Although she found it at last in Friedrichshafen—it was to become the basis of several new jellies and creams widely used in the States—the spectacle of postwar Germany, a country Margaret had always admired, depressed and demoralized her, and on her return to England she was worn out and coughing badly.

By December she was back in New York, full of plans for an organization that would eclipse the activities of Mary Ware Dennett and her Voluntary Parenthood League. With her transatlantic ties and her increasing awareness of the worldwide implications of birth control, both political and economic, Margaret was eager to enlarge the movement to one of international scope. She visualized an American birth control conference to which international figures would be invited, and with the help of a number of rich New Yorkers including Juliet Rublee, established a new national organization, the American Birth Control League, with herself as president.

"Plans and announcements were made that the first national birth control conference would be held at the Hotel Plaza November 11–13, 1921." Birth control advocates from Europe and Asia were to be invited, there would be a doctors' meeting on methods and technique, and a mass public gathering complete with clergymen of all denominations was to cap the conference. Margaret had been counting especially on the presence of some illustrious Englishman, perhaps Harold Cox, an editor and member of Parliament, to lend the final stamp of authority, and in May of 1921 she returned to England to capture her Englishman.

There was another purpose to this second postwar trip abroad, for the tubercular glands had been troubling her again, and she was suffering from the years of overwork and tension that had followed her month in prison, in 1917. Mrs. H. G. Wells kept writing from London that she knew a surgeon Margaret really ought to see. In England she went to bed for a week, and when Harold Cox's promise was finally secured she went on to Switzerland, where she spent an entire month in bed while writing "The Pivot of Civilization," a birth control tract for which

Wells was to write a foreword. All was not convalescence and work, however; during the course of that summer Margaret's letters to Juliet Rublee began to include the name J. Noah H. Slee. He was president of the Three-In-One Oil Company, a rich and conservative American businessman of sixty, South African by birth, staunchly Episcopalian and an admirer of Margaret's who had heard her speak the winter before in New York, and now, in Paris and London, continued to admire her by way of expensive presents and flights across the Channel so they might spend a day together. But Juliet was not to take any of this seriously, Margaret insisted. She said she had no desire to surrender her freedom, and it must have been clear that Mr. Slee could not be put off with an affair; his intentions were persistently and relentlessly honorable.

Before she left England that autumn Margaret had surgery on what proved to be chronically infected tonsils. After twenty-three years of holding an ice pack every night to what she thought were tubercular glands, the true cause of her suffering had been guessed at by Mrs. Wells. Now Margaret returned to the States and her conference with renewed energies. Although it represented the most sophisticated and far-reaching approach to birth control yet seen in this country, tackling problems of eugenics, disarmament, world famine, delinquency and labor, there was little interest in the conference until its final session, a debate on "Birth Control, Is It Moral?" that was to be held at the newly opened Town Hall. Arriving there with Mr. Slee, Harold Cox and Juliet Rublee, Margaret found one hundred police reserves posted outside the building; the place had been booked and paid for weeks in advance, but not a word of debate was to be uttered that night. Acting under the orders of a Monsignor Dineen, the secretary of Archbishop Patrick J. Hayes, the police proceeded to close down the hall in order to avoid discussion of an indecent and immoral subject, and once again Margaret Sanger marched off to the police station behind the paddy wagon. According to the *Times*, "the congestion in forty-seventh street had become so great that reserves were placed at Eighth Avenue, half a block from the station, to keep the throng back. When the prisoners left the station they passed through cheering crowds, which followed on a run to the court."

Next morning the assistant district attorney dismissed the case for lack of evidence. But police and church alike were raked over the coals in newspapers from one end of the country to the other in the months that followed. The Catholic Church had used its formidable powers in Manhattan to close down a public meeting without a warrant; further, Monsignor Dineen, in the prolonged newspaper debates that followed, tried to justify his action by explaining "what particularly aroused me . . . was the presence there of four children. I think anyone will admit that a meeting of that character is no place for growing children." The children were found to be sociology students from Barnard College. The archbishop himself, in a public statement, attacked birth control on the grounds that "The seventh child has been regarded traditionally with some peoples as the most favoured by nature. Benjamin Franklin was the fifteenth child, John Wesley the eighteenth. . . . It has been suggested that one of the reasons for the lack of genius in our day is that we are not getting the ends of families." Margaret retorted that Isaac was an only child, Samuel an only child, and so was John the Baptist.

A second mass meeting was held, this time without incident. But public opinion eventually demanded an inquiry into the causes of the raid; the inquiry proved to be a comic opera affair at which neither Monsignor Dineen nor the police captain appeared, although Mr. J. Noah H. Slee was there to speak in Mrs. Sanger's behalf. By February of 1922 they were investigating the investigation of the raid. No final report was ever issued, but the result of that one night's work at Town Hall had been to draw Roman Catholic authorities for the first time into public discussion of the birth control issue. Echoes of it reached Europe; a Cambridge professor cabled congratulations on her arrest and release to Mrs. Sanger and addressed it, "Saint Margaret, New York."

Early in 1922 Margaret took thirteen-year-old Grant out of school and sailed with him for the Orient; in the midst of the Town Hall affair she had been invited by an organization called the Kaizo group to make a lecture tour of Japan, and when Mr. Slee announced he would join her on the ocean voyage in order to continue what was now a two-year courtship, she decided Grant ought to come as well. Mary Ware Dennett wrote several years later of "Mrs. Sanger's extraordinary swing of the pendulum from revolutionary defiance of all law to advocacy of special-privilege class legislation," and although the matter under dispute was whether or not contraceptives should be available only through physicians, there is probably a reference in her words to another swing of the pendulum. In earlier years Margaret had favored an end to the bondage of marriage laws that confined the sexual relationship, and in radical American circles as well as among England's neo-Malthusians her views and actions were completely acceptable; the distinguished economist Beatrice Webb had described H. G. Wells's novel *The Days of a Comet* as urging a kind of education through promiscuity—"if you could have been the beloved of the dozen ablest men you have known it would have greatly extended your knowledge of human nature and human affairs." It was a valid notion, she felt, and one familiar to British intellectuals, but ultimately exhausting. And after several years of sexual freedom on both sides of the ocean, Margaret was about to embark on a voyage in the company of an ardent admirer, and had seen fit to bring her young son as a chaperone. It was indeed a swing of the pendulum. No doubt she had already recognized in the very correct Mr. Slee the rich widower she had promised herself six years earlier, and was acting accordingly.

The trip to the Orient should have provided Mr. Slee with a prophetic vision of what marriage to Margaret Sanger would mean. Margaret had been denied a visa at the last moment by the Japanese consul, therefore she sailed with a Chinese visa, and throughout the voyage a stream of conflicting cable reports from the mainland informed her that she could not land in Japan, that she could land and not speak, that she might speak but not about birth control, that she might speak about birth control but only in private. When the ship reached Yokohama, according to the Japan *Times*:

An army of star writers from Tokyo—the authorities said that they issued seventy passes to these men alone—a dozen regular waterfront reporters, and

a few foreign correspondents swarmed up the gangway of the ship, which bore
nearly three hundred distinguished persons as first cabin passengers, including
two Japanese delegates to the Washington Conference [on disarmament].

The eager news men rushed up the gangway and scurried about in search of
a notable news story. Was it Admiral Baron Kato they sought? It was not.
. . . Mrs. Sanger and the Cause of Birth Control were what the press of Japan
was interested in—the Peace Conference was an old story.

From the time she arrived in Yokohama Margaret gave over five
hundred interviews in Japan alone; she decided to go from Japan to
Korea, from Korea to China, where no lecture tour had been scheduled
—she was the guest there of a young philosopher, Dr. Hu-Shih—but
thousands of copies of "Family Limitation" translated into Chinese and
privately printed were available in Shanghai, Peking, Nanking, Chang-
sha and other cities soon after she left the country, as a result of
impromptu speeches she made.

And everything Margaret saw in the Orient confirmed her original
belief that there was a single underlying flaw in the universe, and for
that flaw one remedy. This belief became so firmly rooted that by
the mid-1920s an observer spoke of her tendency to sell birth control as a magical cure that "makes the eyes shine and hair curl, per-
fumes the breath, prevents the trousers from bagging at the knees."
Mr. Slee, then, had seen in the course of what became a month's-
long journey that the woman he was determined to marry lived a
hyperactive life, centered around a public cause to which she was
passionately devoted, and which filled not only most of her waking
time but her conscious and even her unconscious mind to such a degree that there could not have been room for much else. This mystical preoccupation with her movement is clearly set forth at the start
of Margaret's *My Fight for Birth Control:*

Some lives drift here and there like reeds in a stream, depending on changing
currents for their activity. Others are like swimmers knowing the depth of the
water. Each stroke helps them onward to a definite objective. . . . As I look back
upon my life, I see that every part of it was a preparation for the next. The most
trivial of incidents fits into the larger pattern like a mosaic in a preconceived
design. . . . When once I believed in doing a thing, nothing could prevent my
doing it.

And the work she believed so devoutly in doing brought her fame as well as notoriety, power, authority and the company of the great. Therefore Mr. Slee must have realized that if they were to marry he would have to share his wife with her movement, not half and half, but far more unequally. Nevertheless he was determined to have her; while courting the woman with flowers, he did not forget to court the crusader with a new filing system for her office, a date stamper and a mechanical letter opener. They were married at last, very quietly, in the autumn of 1922 in London, and the press knew nothing about it for two more years.

What had Margaret Sanger hoped to gain from the marriage? Money, for her cause; she could have made several fortunes for her personal use by investing in contraceptives in later years, but this she always refused to do. She never really wanted money for herself, not even in late middle age when she was worn out with overwork and repeated illness, and dependent on creature comforts, even on a certain degree of luxury. She wanted the money just as she wanted Mr. Slee's respectable and conservative image and his considerable business ability, for what it would bring to the movement. She wanted a stepfather to guide her boys through college and early manhood. She wanted, as she always had before, a protective older man; one difference between Mr. Slee and Bill Sanger was that Margaret had the upper hand with him, as she never had with Bill. She was choosing a man who could not hope to make her life over to fit his own, for her life had already taken its final and desired direction and Mr. Slee was not powerful enough to deflect it.

He paled before Havelock. He lacked the stature, the education and high purpose of men like Harold Cox, Dr. Drysdale, or even the silly but cultivated and literate Hugh de Selincourt. Mr. Slee had in addition a mixed bag of eccentricities that might be considered endearing, amusing or unattractive, according to taste. He went in for lordly gestures, champagne, rooms full of roses, expensive gifts—not unlike Bill Sanger, except that Slee could afford them. He was wonderfully generous to the cause, giving more than fifteen thousand dollars in 1925, and some years even more, but he was also a penny-pincher who kept his daily expenses, including carfare, noted down in a little book. The solid and respectable side of him, like membership in the Union League Club and St.

George's Episcopal Church, where he had been superintendent of the Sunday school for years, was often intolerant and narrow. When Stuart Sanger, then a young man in his twenties, charged a tankful of gas for a friend's car to Mr. Slee's account, Noah wrote: "I permit no liberties of this nature, and never have countenanced them with my own sons. That is my rigid rule of life." And the words he chose express very well that part of his nature: "no liberties," "rigid," "countenance." His first marriage had been extremely unhappy, and one of his sons had left his father's firm already; the other two grown children were rarely on good terms with Mr. Slee.

As for the business ability, and especially the organizational efficiency, which he freely offered to the birth control movement and which was often helpful, it could take the form of busybody interference. Margaret was one to whom interference was painful; with time and age and the contraction of his own affairs, her husband's interference came to seem like an insupportable intrusion, a way of feeding off her own interests when he should have been forming interests of his own. And while he gave advice readily, he became prickly and irritable when advice was given to him, was something of a know-it-all in fact, a trait that age naturally exacerbated. But his fine reputation as a businessman was one he deserved; he was thoroughly honest and well-intentioned. He was respectable and a churchgoer because he believed in prudence, respectability, old-fashioned virtue and the tenets of his church; he was charitable, if somewhat eccentrically so, because charity was a virtue to him.

He was also an attractive man in a certain jovial, ruddy style, sexually vigorous in his early sixties and for the next twenty years. With their marriage Margaret entered the world she had glimpsed and yearned after in her childhood, the world of the upper middle class where ease and luxury dwelt in spacious houses. She and Noah set about almost immediately to build such a house in 1923, near Fishkill, New York. But after the first few years of happy ownership the house became a burden; the expensive clothes Margaret could now afford, fur coats, Paris dresses that for a time she enjoyed to the hilt, tended to remain unworn in her closet later on, and the gifts Noah showered her with always made her uneasy. "On their honeymoon," according to Emily Taft Douglas, "strolling down the Rue de la Paix in Paris, he noted whatever caught her eye in the shopwindows. Next day these items, including an ermine wrap and a strand of emeralds, were delivered to her. She protested that they were not appropriate for her and must be returned. Finally, they compromised, keeping only the emeralds which were lovely with her coloring." Some years later Noah learned that even the emeralds had been pawned for some birth control project. Bill Sanger's gifts had been spurned ostensibly because the household bills were unpaid; Noah's were more gently spurned, and with no real explanation. Perhaps it was because Margaret, who worked with the women of wealth and leisure and had always longed to be one of them, remained an outsider at heart; she could not accept what she felt was not rightly hers, although the longing remained, even increasing with time.

During the first two years of their marriage and before its public announcement Margaret lived in a separate apartment side by side with Noah's at 39 Fifth Avenue, maintaining her financial and personal independence, for all their meetings were by appointment and she remained self-supporting. But once the marriage was revealed this pattern of semidetachment, in the style of Havelock and Edith Ellis, gave way to a more conventional one when the Slees moved into their newly completed manor at Fishkill.

The Fishkill house, called Willow Lake, was Noah's wedding gift to Margaret, and while it was originally thought of as a simple cottage like the one at Wantley, reality soon outstripped the vision of a small, romantic dwelling cradled in the Dutchess County hills. As it approached completion Noah wrote to Stuart: "It is a beautiful home. Your Mother is enthusiastic. . . . The cost is beyond all limits." Willow Lake stood on one hundred ten acres of its own land, seventy of forest, thirty of cleared, rolling land, an acre and a half of green lawn. It was indeed English in inspiration but baronially English, a three-story structure with iron gates, slate roof, carved oak staircase and a library with beamed ceiling. A six-room gardener's cottage, stables, a tennis court, a teahouse and a "woodland studio" that was Margaret's study, overlooking an eight-acre lake bordered by willows, were among the outbuildings. When the house was offered for sale in the 1940s the prospectus suggested its suitability for a "small private school, exclusive camp or sanitarium."

Here at last was a setting worthy of the leader of a national movement, a country seat where everyday living would refresh the spirit and official hospitality on an impressive scale could be dispensed. With Easton Glebe as her model Margaret arranged costume parties, dances and midnight swims for visiting dignitaries as well as friends. She started each day by riding horseback with Noah through their own woods, and as often as she could carried on her work at home, writing her marriage manual, *Happiness in Marriage*, or answering mail with the help of her secretary; although she never failed to commute to the New York office at least once each week, it was in hands not only capable but heroically dedicated. The paid staff of the American Birth Control League, almost entirely female, felt for Margaret the most unabashed adoration. She was "our beloved leader," "our guiding light," her eyes revealed a "steadfast dedication to her cause that had never changed nor faltered, nor weakened down the years."

Willow Lake was also a haven for Grant and Stuart, who came there weekends and during summer vacations, often with friends, to swim, ride or play tennis. If Margaret had hoped for Noah's firm paternal hand, as well as his money, to help launch her boys into manhood, she was not disappointed. Noah sent Stuart through Yale, Grant through Princeton and both to medical school, and he was more than willing to act the firm father, a role for which he was unfortunately poorly fitted, being tactless as well as rigid. Noah's money soon became a handy focus for all the bickering, disagreements and strains so natural between two half-grown men and a sixtyish stepfather of stiff, conventional manners. Margaret wrote to him in 1925:

Stuart had a lot on his mind and I think he feels you do not like him. He says you act as if you don't want him around and he thinks you have influenced me, so that I am less sympathetic than I was before I married you. He says all our conversation is what everything costs and both he and Grant are as uncomfortable as they can be since I've married you. He says they had a home before, where they were welcomed and made to feel they were wanted around. That I went places with them, while now any suggestion of doing anything together meets your opposition and criticism. . . . he says you gave him just the barest amount to get into Yale . . . which has scarcely paid his board and tuition; he seems "brooding" about something.

In the offices of the American Birth Control League, where he was treasurer for many years and where his efficiency and eye for detail had already proved valuable, Noah wrote to the bookkeeper early in 1924, in the same tactless but well-intentioned style he used with his stepsons: "My suggestion is that you resign say at the end of next week. Whatever your good qualities are, and they are many, you have not the right sort of mind to grasp figures or do accounting. . . . You get flustered so easily, and I would say, from my viewpoint, to make it even more clear, you lose your head."

From the first, Margaret and Noah wrote almost daily during their periods of separation, usually short letters devoted to daily happenings and to the reiteration of their love for one another: Noah misses Margaret terribly, sometimes admits this is inevitable since they are kept apart by a great cause in which he, too, deeply believes; more often he misses her terribly and is sure she could come home and stay home if she wanted. Margaret usually misses Noah terribly, most of all in the early years, but the inner voice does not permit her to join him forever, not just yet. At times, however, the fact that she misses him does not prevent a note of irritation from creeping in. He has been carping, complaining, interfering; he is better and sweeter than he sometimes appears, and if he tried he could stop carping, complaining and interfering, which he does only from Habit. There are other men in the world, she reminds him. "It's rather festive being alone," while on shipboard, returning from England in 1924, "men hang around and pay attention to lone women—but I miss J.N. terribly." There are other men, but of course she loves him only; should Noah try the same tactic himself, Margaret immediately stops playing the coquette and with a cry half wounded vanity, half real pain, demands to know what he has in mind:

Sweetheart Noah: My darling:

What does your letter mean when you say that if I leave you you will do "something foolish"? That troubles me profoundly. Surely you *could* not go with some other woman without love and respect! Is it possible that your love for me is only a satisfying physical passion? To believe that would kill me. I do not believe that. I know the strain on you is great, but with me no other man could satisfy me anyway. My love for you is so wholly and fully all of me, that no other person could meet that urgent demand of my passion as you do.

The years immediately following her marriage, years when Margaret learned to adapt herself to her new roles as wife, as chatelaine of Willow Lake and mediator between her sons and their stepfather, were also a particularly crucial time for her work. Returning from London in 1923, she was ready to capitalize on the freedom won by the Crane decision by opening a birth control clinic, and two rooms labeled "Clinical Research" were set apart for that purpose in the same building, 104 Fifth Avenue, where the American Birth Control League was housed. They moved two years later to West Fifteenth Street; here a young doctor, Hannah Stone, came to work as medical director without salary. She made the clinic her life's work and with her husband, the distinguished urologist Dr. Abraham Stone, was to write one of the most popular and long-lived books on sexual adjustment, A Marriage Manual, whose first appearance in 1935 was succeeded by fifty-one printings; it remains in print to this day.

In spite of the Crane decision, the medical profession as a whole had remained wary of birth control. Margaret's early radical activities were held against the movement, so closely identified in the public and medical mind with the name of Margaret Sanger, and the sensational publicity that followed her Brownsville clinic and the Town Hall raid were fuel to the fire. Nevertheless, even in that most conservative of professions there were leaders who had come to realize, as early as 1916, the importance of contraception. Suspicious, slow-moving, jealous of the honor and safety of their profession, they had changed just as the general public had changed, and Margaret hoped to accelerate the process by finding someone to act as a sort of missionary to the medical societies, someone they would trust as they were never to trust her. In the mid-twenties and with Noah's help she induced Dr. James F. Cooper, a gynecologist and former medical missionary in China, an ardent convert to birth control and a man of impeccable credentials, to take this post. She wrote out a promissory note to her husband commemorating the event:

If Dr. Cooper's association with us is successful, I feel certain that the medical profession will take up the work. When the medical profession does this in the USA, I shall feel that I have made my contribution to the cause and shall feel that I can withdraw from full-time activity. . . . Even should this not occur in one year, I shall be satisfied having a Committee taking responsibility off my shoulder.

It is estimated that Dr. Cooper will cost about $10,000 salary and expenses for 1 year. His work will be to lecture before Medical Societies and Associations —getting their cooperation and influence to give contraceptive information in clinics, private and public.

If I am able to accomplish this victory with Dr. Cooper's help, I shall bless my adorable husband, JNH Slee, and retire with him to the garden of love.

Sealed, signed and delivered,
Margaret Sanger

Noah carried out his part of the bargain by providing Dr. Cooper's salary and expenses, but Margaret, however sincere her original intention, never managed to retire with him to the garden of love.

The Clinical Research Bureau became both an active clinic and a center for research, through the meticulous records kept for each patient as well as the continued searching out and testing of new contraceptive materials. Until the 1950s, however, nothing replaced the contraceptive Margaret had first seen in Holland, the Mensinga pessary; before the formation of the Holland-Rantos company in the United States in 1925 these pessaries had to be smuggled in from Germany, shipped to Noah's Canadian factory, repacked there in Three-In-One oil drums and transferred to his New Jersey plant. Margaret kept this ingenious and highly illegal system a secret, and since pessaries were not then manufactured in America, nor could they be legally imported or carried through the mails, the source of the hundreds of Mensinga pessaries dispensed each week at her clinic remained an intriguing mystery.

Unlike the American Birth Control League, which was governed by a board of directors of which Margaret was president, the clinic remained under her direct control; it was her creation, her child, and in times of dissension within the movement, her retreat. But it was only a part of the crowded program on which the new Mrs. Slee, in public still Mrs. Sanger, now embarked. From 1923 on she began increasingly to divide her time between New York, often only a headquarters for speaking tours throughout the country, and Europe, where London was home base, for the movement was becoming international, a fact of which the American Birth Control League seemed to remain unaware in spite of Mrs. Sanger's repeated attempts to broaden their vision:

> Side by side with the clinic . . . another project had been stirring for some time in my mind. Internationalism was in the air, and I wanted that outlook brought into the movement in the United States. To this end I made plans for the Sixth International Malthusian and Birth Control Conference, to be held in New York in March, 1925.

The board of the ABCL did not agree; they felt that such a grand undertaking was far beyond their means, but Margaret, obeying her inner voice, insisted the money would come from somewhere and meanwhile she must go to London to secure "an eminent figure to ornament the assemblage," hoping this time for Lord Dawson of Penn, court physician to the English king.

Luck was not with her, for Lord Dawson was off shooting in the north of England, and Margaret, along with Juliet Rublee, who had accompanied her, settled in to wait for his return. According to Margaret's journal they had a mysterious encounter while they waited:

> Met two queer persons named Mr. Wyeth and Mr. Neal—able to read past incarnations—I seem to have been a nun in an Italian convent three hundred years ago. . . . These men are very ordinary Englishmen yet are serious. Its hard to believe they are "fakers." The power of seeing is strong in one—of healing in the other.

Lord Dawson remained in the north; at a superb dinner party H. G. Wells introduced Margaret to Lord Buckmaster, formerly chancellor of the exchequer, who might be prevailed upon to come to New York in Dawson's place. Arnold Bennett was at the party, and George Bernard Shaw, whom Margaret found somewhat disappointing: "He was in a frivolously facetious mood that evening; and there were other ladies present equally anxious to engage his attention and who succeeded in doing so." Lord Buckmaster was forced to decline because the date of the conference conflicted with the opening of Parliament, but Harold Cox promised to come and speak, as did Dr. Drysdale; Arnold Bennett,

John Maynard Keynes, Lytton Strachey and Julian Huxley, among others, lent their names. In later years Huxley remembered Margaret as "a very handsome creature . . . a forcible person . . . full of spiritual vitality . . . and an inner fire that drove her through fifty years of hard work . . . in spite of insults and public abuse."

Next she set off to visit de Selincourt, who had moved with his household from Wantley to Sand Pit, in Sussex; Margaret had been hearing alarming news from Sand Pit recently, for Hugh had fallen in love with Havelock's beloved Françoise, and all three corners of what became a miserably unhappy triangle had sent Margaret frequent and detailed accounts of their ordeal.

When Ellis first introduced Hugh to Françoise the two young people were immediately drawn together by their admiration for the "king," as they called Ellis. "If you could hear the way he speaks of you!" Françoise wrote soon afterward to Havelock. "He knows all the wonder of you with such reality that his words thrilled me almost as deeply as your presence in the flesh." From Havelock Hugh had learned that jealousy was shameful, that sexual love was cumulative; moreover, Hugh was a man who took exceptional pride in his sexual prowess. Françoise said, many years later, that at the time she even failed to realize she "was embarking on having two lovers." As for Havelock, his first response was not too different from his response to Edith under faintly similar circumstances; her behavior was perfectly natural, he said, and of course he was not jealous. Neither could he hope to hold Françoise, for he was too old, Hugh was too skillful. "I know what a poor sort of lover I am, and I want you to have everything you need." Meanwhile he refused to see either Françoise or de Selincourt, who claimed to be completely baffled—what had he done, after all, but act on the philosophy he had learned at Havelock's feet?

This was the atmosphere Margaret found at Sand Pit: Ellis withdrawn, miserable and magnanimous, while Françoise, willing to give up Hugh like a shot, wanted only to have Ellis back. Hugh de Selincourt, exiled from the great man whom he sincerely worshiped, spoke of that period as a "sort of black hell." Eight months later Françoise and Ellis were reunited and Hugh took up his post as disciple once more, although

Ellis never felt the same about him, sprinkling his autobiography with derogatory remarks about sexual athletes. But Margaret's visit to Sand Pit was understandably dimmed; Harold Child took her off on long drives through the countryside as a consolation.

Returning to the States, Margaret faced the task of finding money for her Sixth International Conference, money the League had refused to provide. She began a fund-raising campaign among subscribers to the *Birth Control Review*, buying one-way passages from Europe for her overseas speakers as the money trickled in, and hoping there would be enough left over to send them back home again. The conference attracted delegates from eighteen countries and representatives of seventy-nine religious and social service organizations; at the special session on contraceptives hundreds of physicians overflowed the meeting hall so that a second session had to be arranged. It was through this Sixth International Birth Control Conference that the movement eventually gained one of its most significant allies, the distinguished gynecologist Dr. Robert Latou Dickinson. When he finally joined the advisory board of the Clinical Research Bureau in 1930, he signaled the start of a new era; only thirteen years after the brief career of the Brownsville clinic there were over fifty clinics in the nation, each under a doctor's direction.

Margaret said a few years later that she had spent more than a year organizing the Sixth International Conference:

It had been a great occasion, a splendid achievement. No more imposing nor important conference has since been held nor had been held previously to discuss a subject so practical, bearing so deeply on the foundations of social evolution. . . .

At the conclusion of the conference, we held an organization meeting in my home to plan for a permanent international association and set the date and place for the next conference. . . . It was from this humble beginning that the population conference in Geneva in 1927 was eventually formed, from which the permanent organization, the International Union for the Scientific Investigation of Population Problems, sprang. . . . It took me nearly one year to recover from the strain, physical, nervous and financial, of the Sixth International Conference. But recover I did. Before the year was out I was straining at the leash and impatient of delays in getting the next conference started.

She was past forty-five. For the last ten years she had worked at a bewildering pace, and during the months of preparing the conference rarely slept more than four or five hours a night. After the conference, that spring, Margaret wrote to Noah that she had "spent a whole evening getting my colon washed out with about ten gallons of salt water. The nurse who did it said I had a great deal of mucous in the intestine, which of course is the trouble." But even after two weeks of colonic irrigation Margaret was snappish and irritable. "I wanted to spend the day with you," she wrote to Noah, "because you felt blue and then as soon as we got together the sparks seem to fly."

This health faddism of Margaret's, of which measures for the relief of constipation formed a major part, was not hypochondria, for she ignored her physical welfare as long as possible, and never complained about her health. Yet even in an era when laxatives were widely advertised and her great favorite, Pluto water, declared in all the newspapers that "Good health demands a frequent internal cleansing with Pluto, America's Physic," her fear of constipation seemed to verge on the obsessive. It was one of Margaret's recurring themes that she could not bear interference from others, being fussed over, told to do this and that, in other words, relinquishing control over herself and her actions, her movements, her destiny. Just as she needed to control others, just as she craved the role of leader and found it painful to compromise, impossible to follow, so did she apparently need to control her own body, to command through force of will the functions of the merely physical self. Mrs. Alexander Dick described her at almost seventy, on the way home from Smith College, where she had received an honorary degree; a car door was accidentally slammed on Margaret's hand, she slumped over with pain yet flatly refused to see a doctor and insisted they drive on home but just not talk for a while. In the same memoir Mrs. Dick recalled a doctor who listened to Margaret speak for two hours, then answer questions, while all the time he knew she was suffering "piercing pains" from a sacroiliac strain. These anecdotes portray a woman of exceptional toughness and courage; and, like her preoccupation with the state of her intestines, they also suggest a woman who will never "give way," who must always command. It is by no means unlikely that

Margaret's wholehearted dedication to the search for a contraceptive controlled by women sprang from the same source, her own deeply felt need to run things rather than to be run, to command the life force in its most intimate expression through the force of her own will.

It is instructive to compare Margaret with Noah, a fussy old gentleman who took physics from time to time, and kept his wife carefully informed of those times. While vacationing at a resort one spring in the mid-1920s he wrote: "I do want you so, my angel of love, and I long for the time to come when I can have you close to me, as I love you beyond life itself. . . . P.S. Bring the high enema tube with you." But if he ever submitted to colonic irrigation or massage at the hands of a professional, his letters fail to record it. Certainly he never took constipation seriously enough to spend two weeks on the coddling of his intestines. Noah had a great deal to say about Margaret's health, for the more she suffered physically from overwork the likelier she was to give it all up and settle down with him to a serene and healthful life, but he always chose, and advised, conservative, medically acceptable treatments, while Margaret's were often inventive in the extreme. In spite of her nurse's training, in spite of her easy access to the best in medical advice, when her intuition suggested some exotic course of treatment she followed her intuition. The miracle was that she survived into extreme old age, and that when she took a notion to doctor Stuart in his late twenties he too survived her remarkable course of treatment.

In the fall of 1926 Margaret returned to Europe to organize the World Population Conference, the one she had been "straining at the leash" to begin. It was to prove a long and intricate undertaking, ultimately a masterpiece of planning and organization that established population control as a problem of worldwide scope and urgency. As early as 1917 Margaret had written in the *Birth Control Review* about the connection between population pressures and war; now, especially in the light of the growth of fascism in Italy and Germany, she saw Geneva, the home of international government, as the ideal site for a world conference. The American Birth Control League protested bitterly this time; they believed Mrs. Sanger was rashly, impulsively foiling their attempts to establish a sound financial policy, as well as overextending what ought to be the proper work of their organization. Undismayed, Margaret took a leave of absence from the League, and one of its conservative leaders became president in her place. Noah had recently sold his Three-In-One Oil Company, for he was approaching seventy and retirement seemed appropriate; he planned to spend the year in Europe with Margaret, although their itineraries would not always coincide.

In London Margaret was met by an old friend and ally, the British suffragette Edith How-Martyn. She saw Harold Child soon after her arrival, the de Selincourts, the Drysdales, even Dr. Hu-Shih, the philosopher who had been her host in China, and in Cornwall there was a long and leisurely visit with Havelock. In September, before she sailed, Margaret had written to Françoise Cyon, offering to pay her a yearly salary for acting as Havelock's secretary in order that they might live together, along with Françoise's two sons, as a family, without the need for Françoise to continue teaching school. The tactful details of this plan were worked out by Hugh de Selincourt, the original idea was Margaret's, for she had always wanted to make Havelock a handsome gift on his seventieth birthday, just a year away; the money, however, was Noah's. Noah himself went from Paris to the south of France, where he meant to hire a villa so Margaret could join him when work permitted. "I'm happy my dearest can give me such comforts and happiness," she wrote. "It will be truly lovely to be with you again."

Arranging the conference from temporary headquarters set up in London, Margaret found she was racing against the calendar; she wanted only the first rank of scientists to attend, demographers, biologists, economists of worldwide reputation, and she was repeatedly told she should have begun sooner. "There is much fear on the part of the Scientists that I have come too late. . . . That I should have been getting them started to work on this last October. . . . It makes me almost sick when I think of it," she told Noah. In December when the professors went off on holiday, Margaret did the same, joining her husband for a month at the villa near Cap d'Ail. De Selincourt came there for a visit, H. G. Wells was at Grasse nearby, and they picnicked together. When

Margaret returned to London Noah went to Majorca, where she wrote him in February:

I have been deeply depressed today and yesterday over the affairs here. I know that were I free to work and keep on the job I could put over a conference that would astound the world—BUT— Here I am, interests divided and diverted and I cannot know what to do. The movement now needs one dominating force to drive it to success. . . . No one else can do it, so it seems. It will crown my past efforts and repay my sacrifices to see this Conference a success. Will you help me? Not by money, darling one, but by seeing this thing eye to eye with me and giving me the time I need to work it up properly. I know how hard it is for you to let me be away from you and I shall try to arrange it so there shall be few separations, but there must be some and unless you say you can help me, I will not go on—

. . . I can never believe that you have come into my life to hold me back, you who are so vigorous and glorious in your love and splendid in your ideals and generosity!

"I wonder if you will ever be peaceful!!!" Noah mused. "Remember I am heart and soul in this one big undertaking you have in hand; but let this be your shining and glorious crown to the nations. . . ." If Noah was not precisely heart and soul with Margaret in the conference, he did take an active role as cotreasurer; meanwhile his travels took him to Corsica, Paris, Barcelona, London and Zurich, and everywhere he missed his wife distractedly. Arriving once in London when she had gone on to the Continent, he found no letters from her, and moreover he had read the only book he had with him, the shops were all shut, he missed her far more, he was certain, than she missed him, and at the end of a letter full of yearning and irritability he wrote: "I wish I could be 10 years younger!"

By cable and by mail Margaret coddled him along. She was besieged by headaches, she said, had been told for the second time that her long hair was responsible, and would like to know how he'd feel if she cut it all off. Shuttling from London to Paris to Geneva, struggling to learn French, opening, in April, permanent headquarters in Geneva, where Noah was to join her that summer, and arranging with him by mail for the shutting up of the French villa, she nevertheless felt an upsurge of confidence. "I'm so full of Conference that I'm a new person to Edith

— She never saw me dominating, curt, ordering her about etc., etc.,"
she told Noah. And back in London she ran into an old flame, reporting
that "he has not married again and says he is looking for the duplicate
of the American woman who spurned him 'for a Millionair.' Someday
you will meet him and be very flattered that I loved you *best.* (Perhaps)."

A week before the conference was to open at the end of August, Sir
Bernard Mallet, whom Margaret herself had selected as its president,
came into her office to look at proofs of the official program. According
to her autobiography:

"Well, we'll just cross these off," he said, drawing his pencil through my name
and those of my assistants.
"Why are you doing that?"
"The names of the workers should not be included on scientific programs."
"These people are different," I objected. "In their particular lines they are
as much experts as the scientists."
"It doesn't matter. They can't go on. Out of the question. It's not done."
A long cry of dismay went up from the staff.

Sir Bernard, Margaret believed, must have been warned "that these
distinguished scientists would be the laughing stock of all Europe if it
were known that a woman had brought them together. Hence . . . Sir
Bernard had secretly pledged that I was not to be a party to the Conference and no discussion of birth control or Malthusianism would
be allowed. He had hoped that the whole thing might be muddled
through. . . ." Apparently the issue was further complicated by delegates
from the fascist countries, anxious that no taint of birth control propaganda should sully a scientific population conference.

Margaret's staff threatened to resign; she said later she "spent most
of Sunday convincing the members of the staff that the Conference was
bigger than their own hurt feelings and making them promise to return," although she never managed to convince Edith How-Martyn,
who would not hear of the workers being ignored. Margaret agreed to
Sir Bernard's requirements that her name and her staff's be omitted
from all official materials connected with the conference, and from all
press releases, although Mrs. Sanger might be named later in the final,
published proceedings. If this graceful, almost self-abnegating submis-

sion on Margaret's part was out of character, it must be remembered that she was a practical woman who had put many months of hard work and high aspiration into this conference; to mar it with mass resignations a few days before its opening date would have seemed to her ridiculous as well as wasteful.

On the last day of the conference, at the closing banquet, Sir Bernard finally expressed his debt to Margaret Sanger. "I can say that I have greatly valued her opinion and advice to myself and my colleagues on the choice of papers and of speakers," and, according to Dr. Drysdale, "the whole company rose and thundered in her honor!" The menu card for the banquet had been decorated with caricatures of all the distinguished delegates, J. B. S. Haldane and Julian Huxley among them, in evening dress with champagne glasses hoisted—not to Margaret, who was absent from the menu card as she was from the program, but to a nurse holding an infant in her arms. "Vive le bébé!" was the slogan beneath the menu. At the far right, the only smiling face amid the scientists belonged to J. Noah H. Slee, on his head a curious and dilapidated porkpie hat and on his face a cheerful smirk. Perhaps it was the scientists and their jealously guarded dignity that amused him.

By mid-September Noah was in London while Margaret stayed in Geneva to edit the proceedings of the conference "under great tension and high pressure. What a woman needs is to be alone, absolutely alone with God for a few days or weeks, until she has filled up the reservoir of her soul again. . . . I have been impatient I know and really horrid at times. You have been tired and disappointed . . . but I was too unhappy to be anything but miserable." She suffered again from constipation, was advised to go to a clinic for help with a "collapsed and fallen large colon." Her future usefulness, she said, would be doubled when the colon had been repaired. And on a railway trip, she told Noah, she had met an interesting couple, a woman her own age with a husband of seventy-nine. "He wears a beard, and ye gods what energy! He is all over the train fussing, talking, moving, getting water for his wife. . . . What a nuisance energy can be." The woman told Margaret she wished her husband would leave her alone. "Women need to be let alone. She wants to talk to other people when he is not around. He does not, he on the contrary wants her to be with him all the time. Poor dears."

Settled into the clinic for several weeks of diet, rest and colonic massage, Margaret continued with the Proceedings. "I do hope," she wrote to Noah, "you will not rush back here where it is dull and lonely. But do stay in London and have a good time." They were to meet in Paris, but the tone of Margaret's letters, while affectionate, is also reminiscent of the woman in the railway car and edgy with the desire that he too must not be with her all the time:

And now . . . are you feeling better? Are you thinking about us and our future? I am. It is not all clear sailing yet I'm afraid, because we are so much alike and yet so different. It is our interests that are so wide apart. There are none that you have that I can take up, so as to bring us into closer harmony, and you do not like me to expand my own, yet there is all the attraction between us. . . . It's really complicated.

My heart is troubled to have you lonely and apart from life's activities but I should wither up and die to be shut off from the intellectual currents of my contemporaries. All I want is a little more freedom. That is not much to ask, but I must be able to feel that I can *waste* a whole night or day or week if I feel it good for me to do so without explanation or asking. I'm too grown up and too developed not to be free.

And, a day later, still at the clinic, where it was "very restful and quiet and my nervous reaction is getting under control," she wrote again: "let all the past unhappiness be behind us and get acquainted all over again, talking over *new* feelings, *new* ideas, *new* hopes and desires—*not old ones!* Can you do this, I wonder? It will be a miracle and will work if we want it to."

A week later:

The combination of work accomplished and quiet, and out of door sunshine all day, simple food, no one to fuss about my doings is really a *souls* rest. You can never know how I *hate* being fussed over. It nearly gives me pain—physical pain. . . . When I am not working on the book I am thinking of you . . . and I am happy in the hope that I am preparing to be with you in a happier and healthier state than ever before. I simply cannot live in a state of "bickering" or an atmosphere of "quarreling" about small unimportant things which usually do not matter.

With the help of Anne Kennedy, executive secretary of the American Birth Control League, the Proceedings were at last ready for printing, and Margaret met Noah in Paris, then returned to London to attend to last-minute details of publication. She meant to join her husband now in Germany, but came down with an unexpected fever. If Noah was lonely in Berlin, she wrote, "you are after all a man—and can find your pleasures and interests. . . . as always I am pressed (like a criminal) for time away from you. Sometimes I feel that you have bought my life and begrudge any day of it outside your realm like a prisoner whose 'time' is to be 'served out.' Now darling forgive this outburst—it is not your fault that I feel like that."

But they did meet that December, and spent Christmas at St. Moritz, where Margaret went ice-skating. Grant and Stuart had gone with friends to cruise through Nassau on Christmas vacation, and Margaret wrote to them: "It will soon be time to think of returning. But just now time hangs heavy on my hands. I am no good as a loafer."

"While still at St. Moritz," she wrote later, "I had been getting messages and letters about the disturbing situation in the American Birth Control League. . . . I found on my return after eighteen months that the tone of the movement had altered." The League had become respectable, cautious, settled; what Margaret called the "pioneer days of our initial aggressive activity" were to be superseded now by the more plodding activity of any conventional charity. The new style was absolutely alien to Margaret Sanger:

To me, this cause was a living inspiration and interest. It was not a "hobby." It was no mere "filler" in a busy social life. . . . To the other members of the Board it was only one of many other interests. Their activities were divided, their time had to depend upon what was left from social duties. Husbands, children, dressmakers, servants, charities, church, entertainment, all had claims on those who now began to dictate to me the policy the League was to take.

She felt the League had become rigid, afraid to take chances; they saw her as representing the kind of free-wheeling, one-woman rule that belonged to the past. A prolonged and bitter struggle was the result, and Margaret finally resigned her presidency, although she remained on the board of directors. Mrs. Ellen Dwight Jones, who had been acting as temporary president in Margaret's absence, now succeeded in that position permanently; exhilarated by her triumph, she proposed late in 1928 that the *Birth Control Review* be removed from Margaret's control and placed under professional management. Now Margaret was furious. She left the League and withdrew entirely from the *Review*, cutting the ties that had linked the Clinical Research Bureau to the League, so that now she was entirely adrift except for her clinic. She told a friend, "My leaving the Review and the League was not because I wished to leave but because there was created inside the Board an influence and an atmosphere which caused such pettiness and criticism that one could do nothing but get out." Noah, resigning as treasurer of the League, sent them three hundred dollars and pointed out that he had already given more than sixty-four thousand "for the benefit of the ideal Margaret Sanger had slaved for," but they would never get another cent from him.

"Hail and farewell! Farewell and hail!" Margaret wrote a year or so later about the breach with the ABCL. But her letters to Noah during that period suggest the long months of internecine warfare had been a serious threat to her almost unquenchable spirit:

> The surgeon doctor said I am O.K. no need of an operation, may have been a stone passing from duct into intestines which caused pain. *Not Nerves*. So stop telling people this is my fifth break down of nerves and such drivel and rot that I am ashamed to have you running around out of captivity talking nonsense. Let's get that little speech out of the way. . . .
>
> I am not blaming you, Noah dear. You are you. No one would have you different. But—I am also I. Our values of life differ. I count success by the growth of one's soul; the development of one's spirit.

"I hope you will go up to Willow Lake and stay there!" she wrote another time. "I don't need your help to get home, I'm arranging everything. . . . If you remain in New York I will be nervous and irritated, for no matter how much I love you I have to be strong and in good health to keep my nerves under constant control when you are here." In addition to worries over the League and her health, over Noah's stinginess and his interference between herself and her sons—"You Greeneyed Monster!" she called him once—one more source of concern cropped up when Stuart, in his late twenties and a long-time sufferer from sinus trouble, came down with acute mastoiditis. He had high fevers and persistent, excruciating pain.

Early in April 1929, "the telephone in my apartment rang, startling me. I was pretty nervous, having been up all night with Stuart." It was Anna Lifshiz at the Clinical Research Bureau, where police had descended without warning. Three nurses and two doctors were already under arrest, fifteen women patients frightened into speechlessness, and the entire operation supervised by the Chief of the Policewoman's Bureau, Mrs. Mary Sullivan, whose advance scout proved to be a woman who had presented herself at the clinic nearly a month before as Mrs. Tierney, the wife of a truck driver and the mother of three. Mrs. Tierney had been examined and fitted with a suitable contraceptive by Dr. Hannah Stone, and now she was back as Patrolwoman Anna K. McNamara.

When Margaret reached the clinic she found Mrs. Sullivan, redfaced, directing the removal of everything that could be carried away—books, diagrams, contraceptive materials, and the case histories of patients in filing cabinets, which had always been considered sacrosanct, unavailable even to nurses. It was a glorious, unlooked-for opportunity to win allies among the medical profession, and Margaret seized the moment by telephoning Dr. Robert Latou Dickinson at the Academy of Medicine. Duly horrified by this violation of medical ethics, he told her to get in touch with Morris Ernst, a lawyer who had allied himself with civil rights causes. Then the entire party, nurses, doctors, filing cabinets and wastepaper baskets full of evidence, went off to the West Twentieth Street police station.

Morris Ernst's plan, based on the Crane decision, was to show how the clinic helped prevent disease, but he meant also to push one step further by showing that proper spacing of births was in itself an aid to maternal and infant health. Five of New York's most distinguished physicians, alerted by Dr. Dickinson, offered to testify to this effect, and a favorable verdict was expected from the start, in fact a certain air of carnival filled the courtroom, where spectators lined the walls, prepared for laughter on the slightest provocation, of which there were many. "I think at last the stupid District Attorney sees that prevention of conception is a means to prevent disease," Margaret told Havelock afterward. "His poor mind was so dull that all he could see and say was that the pessary did *not* cure disease. He kept on asking every doctor, 'Do you see this? (pessary in hand) yes— Do you believe this can cure disease? Do you not advise it to prevent conception?' Then he smiled victoriously to the court as if to say I'll get them.''

One doctor in his testimony pointed out that every woman treated at the clinic was a married woman, in accordance with the law; to which the magistrate responded by asking if social workers investigated the truth of a patient's claim that she was married. Morris Ernst inquired then if there was any other situation in which a doctor had to hire detectives to learn if his patients were married. A wave of laughter filled the courtroom, the magistrate ordered the public out, and spectators left, booing, shouting, singing "Sweet land of liberty!" They were readmitted after the next recess. There was even a seriocomic coda to the trial. During the course of the medical testimony the state of Patrolwoman McNamara's innards, when as Mrs. Tierney she had asked the clinic's advice, was said to include prolapsed uterus, erosions of the cervix, cystocele and retroversion, and she turned up at the clinic some months after the trial to offer herself as a bona fide patient.

In the flurry of publicity that accompanied the trial, *The New Yorker* magazine published a profile of Margaret by Helena Huntington Smith, describing her as "one of those harmless, meek-appearing little women whom wise men are wary of arousing. . . . her face in repose looks almost smiling—the expression of one who bites off nails with all the amiability in the world." This side of Margaret's character, the fist beneath the glove, was not too often seen, at least in print, yet it was perhaps the secret of her particular brand of magnetism that she was demure and harmless on the surface, steel beneath.

Margaret told Havelock later that the raid, the trial and the favorable verdict that followed had put the cause ahead ten years. Never again was the movement to be subjected to Catholic-sponsored harassment in New York; the public health value of the spacing of births had been firmly established, thanks to Morris Ernst and the distinguished doctors who had testified at Dickinson's request, and the loyal support of the medical profession was almost within their grasp.

Ever since she left the ABCL and the *Birth Control Review* in the winter of 1928, Margaret had been essentially cut off from the organized movement, an intolerable situation to one who thrived on leadership and the excitement of combat. Now an uncle of Juliet Rublee's offered to back Margaret financially if she was ready "to start some big thing—a broadening out of the work," and she leaped at the chance. She had made a tentative foray three years earlier into the area of federal legislative lobbying, when Anne Kennedy set up an office in Washington; after five months it was closed down. The Voluntary Parenthood League under Mary Ware Dennett had gone out of existence in 1926, unable to make a dent on the consciousness of the Congress. Yet Margaret had set her heart on a legislative campaign, one that would also serve to educate that vast portion of the American public still ignorant of the value of birth control. Thus expanded to national scale, her activities would surpass in importance those of the ABCL, and if she succeeded, remove that final, stubborn barrier to acceptance of the clinic concept, the federal Comstock law. In April of 1929 the National Committee on Federal Legislation for Birth Control was established, with Margaret Sanger as chairman; their goal was the passage of a federal bill that would open the mails and common carriers to contraceptive materials sent by doctors for the care of their patients. It was called the "doctor's bill" to distinguish it from Mrs. Dennett's "open bill" which had tried for free distribution of contraceptive materials and information, based on the freedoms of the First Amendment.

One of Margaret's first acts was to hire a professional consulting firm, the John Price Jones Corporation, to investigate the financial and organizational problems of the campaign she was about to launch. They eventually advised that it would take more money than she could possibly raise, and they further suggested that Congress was too deeply concerned with the depression to spare any interest in so thorny and thankless a subject as birth control; instead of trying to stir up Congress, they said, Mrs. Sanger ought to work for the unification of the birth control movement, preferably under some other, less controversial leader. Margaret was understandably wounded by this suggestion that she surrender "a position which years of study, work and consecration has made unique." She vowed that she would somehow raise the money

—as indeed she did, for during the worst years of the depression, 1932 to 1936, Margaret and Mrs. Ida Timme collected more than $150,000 for the federal campaign; Noah gave tens of thousands, but the rest was the direct result of Margaret's personal magnetism and her heartfelt belief in the importance of the work. As for the advice of the Jones Corporation that a Congress preoccupied with the depression could never be aroused to the birth control issue, Margaret was determined to prove otherwise; with a few close friends she left New York for Washington and set up permanent headquarters at the Hotel Carlton.

For the next seven years the Carlton was her real home; the scene had shifted, the cast of characters was slightly altered, but for Noah the plot had not really changed since his wedding day. His wife was still saying good-bye to him; one major difference was that now he was completely retired from business. "Return . . ." he cabled her in London. "Every Day is like Week. Cruel to Leave Me. Cable Received."

"A most unkind cable," Margaret scribbled across it. "How *can* you send such a selfish message to me when I am so far away? It's unbelievably unkind." She had torn herself away from Washington to organize the Seventh International Birth Control Conference in Zurich, and although she had asked Noah to come with her he preferred to stay at Willow Lake. She missed him, she said:

I think of all the loveliness of your dear self—all the little things . . . you do, bathing, shaving, stomping the water off in your shower and oh dozens of little intimate things which are part of my life because you do them.

But she was busy consulting physicians and clinic directors from all over the world, searching out new techniques of chemical or hormonal contraception to replace the Mensinga pessary, and however much she missed his stomping in the shower there was always pressing business to distract her. Noah, on the other hand, had all the time in the world for missing his wife; at Willow Lake he watched the blue garden she had planted and wondered what in the world to do with himself, for both Stuart and Grant were too deeply engaged in studies now to travel to Fishkill, and for much of the time his only companions were servants. If he was too proud to tag along with her in Europe, he was not proud enough to suffer loneliness in silence, or find some way of occupying his time. He would not tag along, and he would complain, like a small child unsure of what his rights were but vocal about them.

Early in 1932 Noah suffered a series of business reverses, culminating in the loss of his seat on the Stock Exchange as well as all the money he had put up to save it. It was a loss of more than money to a man who always prided himself on his financial ability; if he was touchy before about extravagance, now he had cause to be touchy, and he badgered his wife incessantly to cut down on expenses. Perhaps because she was truly sympathetic with Noah in his temporary setback, Margaret responded with unusual good humor. During a stay at an inferior hotel in New York she wrote to him:

The lobby looks all right of course, but the usual bangabout cheap and sporting or bounders type of people all over, you know the kind? Those who have to make a good showing on nothing.

I took a single room $3.00 got here early enough to go to bed at 9:30. The room is modernly furnished the bathroom old fashioned sort of plumbing, and cold, no heat, one small cheap bath towel like at the $.25 stores. . . . I had one small and thin blanket on the bed, which was enough while the room was warm but after sleeping a few hours I awakened cold and it got colder and colder. I got up and closed the window and turned on the radiator but no heat could be turned on so I spent the rest of the night exercising my feet up and down to keep from freezing. . . . I finally got drowsy and warm enough to fall into a slumber when I was awakened with such a clatter and noise outside my door, that I was certain some old drunk had fallen against it. The clatter left my door and continued all along the corridor until I had to look at my watch to see the time. It was just 4:30!! Nothing to be alarmed about at all just the famous continental breakfast being served to the guests. . . . In a paper box container thrown through a chute at the bottom of the door I found two rolls, one small pot of bitter coffee, cream, marmalade, sugar and a pat of butter and two paper napkins. . . .

Well as I was wide awake and cold I got up and thanked God for the coffee. . . . Perhaps I'm spoiled dear. But if I am it's all your fault for making me fastidious.

Margaret found that the "frantic, worried, harassed, driven Congressmen" were about as receptive to a birth control bill as to a message from Mars. Foreign debts, unemployment relief, reparations, moratoriums, prohibition and the tariff were their principal concerns, for which they needed every possible vote. And however they expressed themselves on birth control, it could only cost them votes. It was for many of them an issue on which their sole feeling was the desire that it would disappear. "The whole subject," one senator said, "is so damn nasty, I can't bear to talk of it or even think of it," and another senator declared, "if I were the Creator and were making the universe all over again I'd leave sex out of it."

But Margaret and the loyal supporters who had followed her to Washington—Mrs. Hepburn, Mrs. Alexander Dick, Hazel Moore, Frances Ackermann, who helped Noah as treasurer of the National Committee, and Ida Timme—were there to remind senators that birth control, like sex, would not secede. The battle in Washington had a different quality from the skirmishes of the past; it was essentially undramatic, a slow and slogging affair of politicking in waiting rooms and corridors, outwitting receptionists, cornering a senator unawares. Fortunately inspiration still came in the form of letters from what Margaret called "maternity's underworld"; thousands were received each month at the New York office, nearly a million had come in the past ten years, and Margaret had recently compiled some of the most moving in a book called *Motherhood in Bondage*. Now she urged the writers to get in touch with their congressman "and tell him how many children you have living, how many that died, how many abortions you have had, and how much your husband earns. Tell him how desperately you need birth control information and want the 'Doctor's Bill' passed."

Margaret's old enemy, the Catholic Church, followed her to Washington; the National Catholic Welfare Conference had provided a formidable opponent in the person of Monsignor John A. Ryan, head of their Social Action Department, an economist of note, a supporter of the New Deal and a man of comparatively liberal views. But to Margaret Sanger the Catholic Church had no liberals in its hierarchy, could not be dealt with, must be defied. In the opinion of David Kennedy, as she "grew older, her childhood obsession with supposed Catholic deviousness became more and more exaggerated," so that she found it "virtually impossible to muster a spirit of conciliation and compromise when she confronted Catholics."

For there had been a subterranean and almost imperceptible change in the thinking of the Catholic establishment since Margaret's first appearance on the birth control scene. The rhythm method had become acceptable under certain narrowly defined conditions, artificial methods were increasingly used by otherwise observant Catholics, and many of Margaret's associates were urging her by the 1930s to modify her anti-Catholic stance in order to work for a softening of the church's outward opposition to the movement. Monsignor Ryan himself suggested to Colonel J. J. Toy of Margaret's National Committee the possibility of finding a Catholic doctor who might help draft a bill acceptable to Catholics. Ryan's own viewpoint was that strict medical supervision of contraceptives would serve at least to cut off indiscriminate drugstore sales.

But Margaret never modified her behavior so as to make conciliation of Catholic forces in the Congress a possiblity and her public statements continued to mock the paradox of celibate clerics dictating the conduct of married couples. As far as she was concerned Catholicism was mono-lithic and unchangeable, and in 1960, a delicate old lady of eighty, she announced her intention of leaving the United States if the Catholic John Kennedy was elected to the presidency. Catholic opposition under Monsignor Ryan was often as irrational, petty and shrill as Margaret's to them; there were wild accusations of Communist influence, for exam-ple. There was also organized opposition on a lesser scale from such groups as the Society for the Suppression of Vice, Comstock's society; from the Purity League and the Patriotic Society and the fascist mav-erick priest Father Charles H. Coughlin, who said, "We know how these contraceptives are bootlegged in the corner drugstores surrounding our high schools. . . . All this bill means is 'how to fornicate and not get caught.' "

But the grass roots work of the National Committee had begun to win support from such impressive organizations as the Federal Council of Churches of Christ and the Central Conference of American Rabbis. By 1934, five tedious years after the establishment of Washington headquarters, the "doctor's bill" was presented in Congress at the conclusion of a year's lecture campaign, masterfully planned and almost frantic in intensity—more than eight hundred speeches by thirty members of the Committee throughout the country:

> For the first time the Senate sub-committee reported out the bill and it was put on the unanimous consent calendar. The last day of the session came, June 13th. Over two hundred were ahead of it, but there was always hope. One after another they were hurried through and then, miracle of miracles, ours passed with no voice raised against it. . . . Twenty minutes went by. Suddenly Senator Pat McCarran from Reno, Nevada, famous divorce lawyer though an outstanding Catholic, came rushing in from the cloak room and asked for unanimous consent to recall our bill. As a matter of senatorial courtesy Senator Hastings granted his request. . . . It was summarily referred back to the committee and there died.

During the Washington years the squabbles that run like a continuing thread through the Slee marriage began to take on a somewhat different tone, a more realistic one, for Margaret gradually stopped deluding herself and Noah with the belief that one day they would retire together to the garden of love. Instead she counseled resignation and positive thinking. "There is no use scolding and nagging me," she told her husband. "Be cheerful, go to your club a few days a week, go to visit your friends, take in the movies. Stop feeling sorry for yourself and be happy over what you have had and still have in the way of love and deep and abiding affection." Apparently this excellent advice was wasted on Noah. After one of their meetings Margaret recalled that "as usual you jumped in the air and shouted and began to abuse me and talk about calendars to keep track of time spent with you and not spent with you and finally ended by telling me to 'go and not come back.' That of course was pure temper."

But if Noah was cantankerous, demanding and childish, not all husbands were, and Margaret took care to remind him of how the ideal husband behaves, in this case the newly acquired husband of an old friend:

> One can see that she is in love and lives in the atmosphere of constant adoration. Robert certainly adores her and in the right way. He is not the kind

of lover who possesses her or has a proprietary right to her in any way. That would make her very unhappy, but he is the kind of lover husband who considers himself in luck and fortunate to sit beside her and feast on her loveliness. Only the Latins know that feeling in love. I wish our fine American men knew something about it. There would be fewer divorces.

What Noah thought when he learned he ought to sit beside his wife and feast on her loveliness is not recorded; certainly the letter suggests Margaret's rather Victorian vision of woman as a creature finer than man, deserving of worship, in some mysterious way ordained to keep her husband and his brutish nature under control. Noah might well have felt sorrow and a sense of personal loss at Margaret's phrase "lover husband," for these were the words with which he signed his letters in the early years of their marriage, when there was little scolding and nagging and a great deal of missing each other.

By 1934 Margaret was full of plans for a visit to Russia "to see for myself what was happening in the greatest social experiment of our age." Grant, who was ready for his final year of medical school, would join her along with Margaret's new secretary, Florence Rose, and Ethel Clyde, an officer of the federal legislative organization. But during the past autumn Stuart had been struck in the face by a squash racket, which fractured the bone over his eye, and that winter he was operated on nine times. Margaret herself suffered from foot trouble, as well as the old constipation, for which "I've taken buttermilk, orange juice, prune juice, lemons, limes, bananas, Plutos, Swiss Kriss . . . citrate of magnesia, enemas, hot and cold, massage and colonic irrigations," as she told Noah. He was busy at Willow Lake, making an inventory of its contents before renting it out; meanwhile he mulled over a plan to visit South Africa, the land of his birth, in connection with Margaret's trip to Russia. She did not encourage him.

"Don't mention South Africa, that's so very far away and you would not be happier than you ever are. I wonder if *any one* or *any place* can give you happiness! God knows I've tried far harder than any thing I've ever had to do and have not succeeded. . . You'd better stick to [Margaret] and be happy to have her when you can get her." It was finally decided that Noah would join his wife in the south of Europe, after the Russian tour. One leg in a cast, the other suffering sympathetic pains, she went with Stuart to the old house at Truro so they could convalesce together. It was a dispiriting interlude; life had not been easy for her elder son, who took a degree in engineering, then embarked on a career in finance that was somehow unsatisfying, and decided at last to enter Cornell medical school, where, shortly after the term began, the accident on the squash court sent him home, once more an invalid. The repeated operations had left a facial scar, and Margaret was disheartened because Stuart was; his fever persisted, she spoke continually about canceling the trip to Russia and, going one day to Willow Lake, she found the house and gardens so sadly neglected by the servant in charge that she burst into tears.

A week before she was ready to sail Stuart's doctor advised yet another operation. "I rushed up from Washington, where the legislative work for that session was just being wound up, and would have abandoned the Russian expedition had not the operation been entirely successful. Since he was in no danger I continued with my plans." She sailed for Southampton in June of 1934, then to Copenhagen, to Oslo, where Grant joined the group, to Stockholm, and to Helsinki, from where they proceeded to Leningrad.

Margaret found Russia in general exasperating, and especially so when it came to the subject closest to her heart. Surgical abortion was available to every woman who wanted it, and thousands did, but birth control had been utterly abandoned, apparently because a rapidly expanding economy demanded more workers, and the buildup of armed forces in Germany demanded more future soldiers. "The demands of history seemed to have conspired against the fulfillment of a once-promising birth control program."

Noah joined Margaret in Naples; they meant to go to Marienbad together for the cure, but almost as soon as they met a cable from the States announced that Stuart was sick again, and Margaret left immediately for home. There she found the doctors planning a radical operation, for which she refused permission; a long stay in Tucson, Arizona, was offered as an alternative, in the hope that a hot, dry climate might eliminate the need for further surgery. Stuart and Margaret then set off for the southwest in Stuart's little Ford coupé and eventually they settled into a small, hot, dusty pink adobe house where Stuart began a strenuous regime, apparently of his own invention, but one Margaret wholeheartedly supported—in fact the program sounds suspiciously like something she thought up herself and wheedled or persuaded her son into trying. A twenty-one-day fast, no food at all but water whenever desired, was preceded by a week of outdoor living, sunbathing, exercise and diet, and followed by another period of outdoor living and special diet, to gain back the weight lost in fasting. Noah was suspicious of the plan. "Yes dear love I look at Stuart's wound every day," Margaret assured him, early in the course of treatment. "Today it is open and running freely," which she attributed to Stuart's taking Pluto water.

"Please don't mention this to anyone as it gets around and hurts a reputation among Doctors," Margaret wrote to Noah a few days later. "I'm here to see how it goes and I'll forcibly feed him if I see it going bad. He has this on his mind and wants to try it out." Several more days and she had to remind Noah, "Stuart's fast is not 'experimenting,' it's definitely a way to cleanse the tissues of their poisons and toxins. It's a hard way, but a quick way." Judging from the nature of the fluids that drained from his wound as well as the appearance of the fecal matter, Margaret pronounced herself satisfied with his progress.

After ten days of fasting the patient was languid and inactive. "Certainly no human being ever tried harder or suffered more privations to get well than Stuart," Margaret told Noah, who was beginning to ask when this successful nonexperiment would draw to a close so that she could come East again. "It will be a great victory and triumph if he succeeds."

By the first week in December Stuart had regained all the weight lost in fasting, but "It was a hard tug at my heart to leave because just the last few mornings Stuart's wound began to ooze. . . . Of course he urged me to go to you and to disregard his ailment." During the long weeks of nursing she had had time to read, to rest and meditate and reinspect her marriage, and she told Noah she was "trying to think out ways for our future happiness."

. . . as to living in Wash. I think you should not try to live there this winter. I'd like a house of course, as I wrote you but you are not happy with any domestic responsibilities these last few years and get no comforts from a home, so why burden you with them. The responsibilities of a small house are the same as a larger and more comfortable one and I don't like dingy places so let's give up all ideas of comfort or homes or domestic comfort and you live in your club and I'll live as best I can. As you rightly say I've accustomed myself to endure privations in Russia and also out here and can continue to do so the rest of my life. It's all right as long as I am free to go and come as I like and live on a glass of milk or an orange but freedom from distraction and nagging is worth privations and I really think I'd prefer my freedom to all the luxuries any man can afford me. . . . It makes no difference to me dear one—I'm going to work night and day in Congress and try to get that bill through this session. . . . I can go to the Woman's Party and live cheaply and be near the Capitol and join you [in Florida] every three or four weeks one week end. Of course I must try "your very soul" very often and you certainly try mine *more.* . . . But at least I have the decency to cover your limitations and keep our private life to myself. I never discuss you or find fault with you to anyone. I wish I knew you did the same.

In Washington after the long domestic interlude with Stuart, Margaret began again to work day and night, as full of fresh hope and confidence as if she had not already given five tedious years to the project. "The demands on us all are beyond our staff and they are all so conscientious that it's hard to stop them from overdoing," she told Noah. "We had such a hard cruel day meeting rebuffs and discouragement that I need a little comfort from someone who loves me so I'll try you." She was in her element again; repeated frustration, and the Washington years were little else, could not dim her pleasure in it and Margaret had finally come to realize she did the work because she loved the work, a truth she had always concealed from herself and Noah by believing she did it solely for the sake of the high goals pursued:

I'm overworked as I was never before even in the old days. I fall into bed at midnight and awaken at four or five and begin to work again.

Of course I like it. I love it and adore it or I would never do it. That's the answer.

Just a few pages to tell you I love you dearly, devotedly, and am happy that you are out in the sunshine living as a human being should live. *Please cease talking about me* get other interests and discuss *them. Please please do.*

The older he got, the more Noah permitted his pride in his wife's achievements to form the chief subject of his conversation. Moreover, up to his elbows in her business, he was sure he knew better than she did how it should be run, yet interference, as she repeatedly told him, was what she hated most, and Margaret too was getting older, less willing to make allowances, less tolerant of Noah's peculiarities. Their reunions in Florida, she told him, were becoming scolding sessions, and "after a week the atmosphere becomes too thick and unhealthy for one of my temperament. . . . Noah darling I just *can't take it*, that's all. . . . It has become unbearable to be scolded like a Parent scolds a child . . . and under the management of a cross old father," but she added, "I do appreciate it is hard on you to have married a wife with a cause."

By springtime her letters to Noah had become curt and impersonal; she was planning a three-month visit to India that fall and the prospect of such a prolonged separation as well as the cooling tone of her letters may have been what prompted Noah to promise to do better, a difficult resolution for a man midway through his seventies, of fixed habits and fussy disposition, yet he made it, and for a time at least he managed to carry it out. "Your sweet letter and agreement," Margaret wrote to him in May, "came at a time when it *worked*. I was happy to know that you want to do the things to make our lives together happy. I will cooperate too and together we will try again. It's not so much criticism as *blaming* that causes irritation." And, sailing in October on the first lap of her journey to India, "It has been a very happy summer since you got a few ideas of harmony into your dear head and carried them out to everyone. Consequently everyone says 'how dear J. N. has grown.' He always was dear but never expressed it to others I say."

The All-India Women's Conference had invited her to India to begin an active and practical birth control program; Birth Control International Information Center in London sponsored the trip, and for Margaret it was the realization of a long-deferred dream, beginning with a bon voyage party so effervescent with promise it might have been her first journey abroad. "It was such an exciting day," she wrote to Noah. "All those old friends . . . and then forty-five packages books, flowers, cigarettes, dates, figs, toilet articles, your fruit. Juliet's basket and $100 from Juliet also for my very own self not for the cause. . . . Nan gave me a lovely loose leaf book for my story my initials in gold. It's a lovely thing just what I wanted." Did she really succeed in spending Juliet's gift of money on her very own self, and not for the cause? Perhaps she did, for on this particular expedition Margaret set off in girlish high spirits expecting to be dazzled; she was not disappointed.

The visit to India eventually came to include ten thousand zigzagging miles, more than sixty lectures, numberless conferences and meetings and state visits of bewildering ceremony and extravagance. She was a guest of the Maharaja of Baroda, an official guest of the state of Mysore, "the people beg me to stay longer and whole processions come to the station to see me off," she told Noah. "It is impossible to tell you all that I have done. I have been keyed up like an electric battery." All the while, of course, that battery was wired to the States, and to Washington in particular, for every detail of the new federal bill in preparation, as well as the fund-raising and birth control activities in general, followed her across the subcontinent. The most impressive part of her visit came at the beginning, in the form of a personal invitation from Gandhi to stay with him in his home in the tiny village of Wardha, and Margaret called it "the greatest honor that India can pay me or anyone."

She had high hopes of this meeting, for Gandhi's endorsement of birth control "would be of tremendous value if I could convince him how necessary it was for Indian women." She found him at once saintly and exasperating, spiritually radiant, wonderfully kind and hospitable, but "after listening to him for a while, I did not believe he had the faintest glimmering of the inner workings of a woman's heart or mind." Gandhi needed no persuasion on the subject of birth control, but according to the journal she kept of her trip, the only form he could endorse was self-restraint. "I have not a shadow of doubt," he told Margaret, "that married people, if they wish well to the country and want to see India become a nation of strong and handsome, well-formed men and women, would practice self-restraint and cease to procreate for the time being." And if the men could not see it, then the women must "learn to say 'No' to their husbands when they approach them carnally."

But if Gandhi failed to approve of Margaret's methods of birth control—"I would devise other methods," he countered, no matter what techniques she named—the medical profession was solidly behind her. "Doctors come from all over the south of India," she wrote home at one point, "asking me to come to their towns and cities to help get things started. I gave demonstrations in my room, in the dressing room, in the car." Some fifty birth control information centers sprang up in her wake, the start of India's present government-sponsored program to limit population, and Margaret told a reporter after returning to the States that she had been "able to accomplish more in the few months that we were in India than we have been able to do in the twenty-two years of our work in the United States."

As soon as she left India Margaret went on to meetings in Burma and Malaya, then arrived in Hong Kong on the eighteenth of February, when the months of being keyed up like an electric battery culminated in an exquisitely painful gall bladder attack. She spent two weeks in Memorial Hospital, Hong Kong, before she was able to limp on to Japan and then to Honolulu, where she gave eight lectures while crawling in and out of bed, constantly under a doctor's care. A gall bladder operation was postponed, but she was thoroughly drained and spent, "a poor old war horse . . . and now here I was to die in Honolulu." Six months had passed since last she saw Noah; he was to meet her in San Francisco, and she sent him a curious letter:

> Yes darling you are right—I have *changed*. It's some physical and spiritual change, but I feel definitely that the door of *sex life* is closed for me. It may be a shock to you to hear this, but I have a queer feeling about it and prefer to keep it closed. . . . It is something that can not be helped and its suicide to violate so sacred a feeling.
>
> It may be that you too have no interest in such activities and if so there will be no problem between us but if you are still interested then God help us to solve our difficulties.

They spent the following summer together at Willow Lake; no further reference to the "door of sex life" appears in any of the letters they exchanged, so there is no way to tell what caused that rush of feeling or precisely what it led to. But a few years later Margaret wrote to

Havelock Ellis, describing Noah's sexual vigor as he approached his eightieth year:

> One thing I always wanted to tell you and will do it now as I feel you will find it of interest. That is although he is nearly eighty years of age . . . his sexual activity has scarcely waned. He is just as alert at the sight of a lovely shape— and just as urgent in his desires as he was when I first knew him at the age of 63. . . . When I am away for weeks or a month I find him old and stooped and reluctant to action. But at sight of me and affection and harmony he awakens, becomes active and happy, thinks clearly, his memory improves . . . sleeps and eats and walks to a different tempo.
>
> It interests me to watch the power of a love as his has been.

So the sacred feeling, no matter how deeply felt at the time, must have been an ephemeral one. As for the note to Havelock, it suggests that the marriage of Margaret and Noah, with all its petty quarrels and repeated separations, perhaps even because of them, was no mere convenience, no part-time housekeeping arrangement; if a man is to remain sexually vigorous as he approaches eighty he must be blessed with splendid health, but he must also have a companion worth stirring himself for. Noah complained with justice that his wife neglected him but he could not complain that she bored him.

The following winter, remembering Arizona from the time she had been there with Stuart, Margaret returned with Noah and rented an adobe house near Tucson. For the long years of work in Washington had come to an unexpected and almost anticlimactic end. Some Japanese pessaries had been sent in 1930 to the Clinical Research Bureau for testing; they were held up at customs, refused entry and eventually destroyed, but another shipment was requested, to be addressed this time to Dr. Hannah Stone in the hope that by sending them to a physician they might prove deliverable. This shipment too was refused entry, and a suit, the United States versus One Package, was begun in Dr. Stone's name. After two years the case came up for trial in the federal courts in New York with Morris Ernst representing Hannah Stone. Judge Moscowitz decided in the clinic's favor, the government immediately appealed the decision, and in the fall of 1936, while Margaret was readying her forces in Washington for one more assault on

Congress, she learned that three judges had upheld the Moscowitz decision "and had added that a doctor was entitled not only to bring articles into this country but, more important, to send them through the mails, and finally, to use them for the patient's well-being—which, for twenty years, had been the object of my earnest endeavor." So there was no need for a doctor's bill; the Moscowitz decision had accomplished the same result by permitting birth control information and equipment the freedom of the mails, within the country and into it. Now Margaret's Washington headquarters were gradually dismantled, and in New York's Town Hall, where sixteen years earlier police had forbidden her to say a word about birth control, she was awarded the annual medal of the Town Hall Club, "For contributing to the enlargement and enrichment of life." Dr. Robert Latou Dickinson, the eminent gynecologist whose long association with Margaret had had many moments of painful frustration because of her inability to share or surrender control, rose splendidly to the occasion in his congratulatory telegram: "Among foremost health measures originating or developing outside medicine like ether under Morton, microbe hunting under Pasteur, nursing under Nightingale, Margaret Sanger's world wide service holds high rank and is destined eventually to fullest medical recognition." A few months later the AMA, at its annual convention, broke a twenty-five-year taboo when its Committee on Contraception announced that physicians must be informed of their legal right to give contraceptives, and recommended that standards be investigated and techniques taught in the medical schools.

Margaret was approaching sixty now, an age when it becomes impossible to look on oneself as still middle aged. Ten years earlier she had returned from a year and a half in Europe to find the American Birth Control League and the *Review* slipping from her hands. She had relinquished them after a costly struggle, and found another battle front to fight on, yet that battle had now come to a victorious end; the clinic no longer needed her, the goal she had set herself in 1915, of putting birth control under the direction of doctors, was fulfilled. Inevitably she had begun to realize that the day when she would be forced, like Noah, into idle, unwanted retirement was uncomfortably close at hand. "Yes dear one," she wrote to him, "old people do talk of the past, of their *selves*, their doings, their food, their dreams when they talk at all. Sometimes they are silent, when they have wisdom and intelligence and learn how tiresome others can be. We will help each other."

Whether or not the clinic still needed her, Margaret needed the clinic, and she decided to transform the nearly four hundred voluntary county and congressional district committees that had worked for the federal bill into the Education Department of the Clinical Research Bureau; their mission would be to bring contraceptive services to the rural poor, especially in the South, through state public health clinics. It was the era of the Farm Security Administration, of Okie camps and migrant farm workers who married young and produced huge families where privacy was unknown. The diaphragm and jelly used in urban clinics were no more suitable for them than for the masses in India, and Margaret dreamed once more of a pill, an injection or spermatoxin, something as cheap and foolproof as vaccination. She called it her "holy grail."

Nevertheless that ominous day when she would be removed from an active role to one chiefly ornamental and inspirational had to be faced. For the past eight years the birth control movement had been fragmented; there were nearly six hundred clinics in the country, some linked to the League, others to Margaret's Clinical Research Bureau, many to both, and inevitably the two organizations competed for the same funds and support. The John Price Jones Corporation had advised in 1930 that the movement be reunited, and many of Margaret's associates continued to hope this sound advice would one day be taken. In fact since early 1936 delicate negotiations between representatives of the two groups had been under way; as for the League, they were eager to cooperate, for they had never really recovered from the loss of Margaret's name and her formidable fund-raising talents. But Margaret, while realizing how damaging the existing situation was, remained intractable. The League, she insisted, was run by "those whose interest it is to take away credit from others and to snatch it for themselves." If a merger ever took place it was clear that the new organization must be run by someone other than Margaret Sanger.

Early in 1939 representatives of the League and the Clinical Research Bureau announced the formation of the Birth Control Federation of America, with Margaret as honorary chairman; it later became the Planned Parenthood Federation of America. The Clinical Research Bureau continued in the four-story brick dwelling at 17 West 16th Street that Noah had bought for her in 1930, and for a time Margaret was able to keep busy by burying herself in the unhappy task of finding a replacement for Hannah Stone, who had died at the age of forty-seven.

"I spiritually left the front and joined the ranks," Margaret wrote later on about the merger with the ABCL. But hers was not the temperament of a foot soldier. She had few interests outside of birth control, no taste for leisure or the arts of relaxation, and had been away from New York for eight long, hard-working years. As Morris Ernst suggested when he reminisced in old age about crusading women:

. . . good people hate to win. And hate to give up enemies. Well, you know the story about polio. I've talked to a couple of top people at polio and they said, "Look, we have a million women who raised money and took care of the patients and now a son-of-a-bitch named Salk has a cure."

Now the privates can be easily shifted to another crusade . . . but the woman who was a lieutenant-commander anywhere, she can never be a private again. . . . So the leaders understandably do not want to win.

Margaret visited Noah in Arizona for weeks at a time, and in New York divided her energies among the activities, mainly social, of the Federation, the demands of her own clinic, and the heart-rending effort to find a tenant for Willow Lake, where everything was "dull, ugly, dark and dirty!!!" Her life, always before guided by the inner voice, pre-planned by the mosaic pattern, seemed diffuse and vague now, as if the pattern had simply petered out.

About a luncheon given in her honor in New York, she wrote to Noah that "Mrs. Vincent Astor is a guest and ten other prominent society people whom I have never met before. The homes I go into are so artistic and elegant with service of two butlers, etc. etc. It's really an upper strata that we have never touched before in the old days of B.C. . . . The group are very sincere and fine and I feel it wonderful to have the movement represented by these people," and she added that, at a large luncheon at which she spoke in Bronxville the other day, the chairman had said "there were few women or men in USA who after twenty-five years still held an audience spellbound by her charm, sincerity and able presentation."

"Mrs. Potter has had two very smart luncheons for me," she told Noah another time. "Mrs. Reinhardt gave a cocktail party where champagne was the main liquid for 30 smart and brilliant people. . . . All these events were so smart and up-to-date I can scarcely believe I've lived in the same world all this time with these people. The women are all beautiful and dressed exquisitely." Yet Margaret herself, as Noah once pointed out, owned a closet full of Paris dresses even though she chose to wear demure black with white collars or lace, for the dramatic effect. And Margaret owned a house where parties, almost as glittering as the ones she was going to in Manhattan, could be given. She had emerged from her lifelong absorption in the movement, looked about her, seen as if for the first time another kind of life, and wondered if she had chosen the wrong path after all. Yet the possibility of entering it now, of becoming exquisitely dressed herself and refurbishing Willow Lake apparently never occurred to her.

At Willow Lake the guest bathroom ceiling was cracked and falling, the plaster around its tub bulged and cracked, and it was "all together a mess." Downstairs the kitchen was dirty, the old stove too filthy for use, a rich prospective renter had "looked into the oven of the gas range and shuddered and said 'such old fashioned things for modern Margaret Sanger.' Then the ice box downstairs was too much for her and she said '*how* can you keep servants with such poor arrangements?' . . . I was shocked to see it today, but we have done nothing to these walls since 1924—*no wonder.*" At last she had to say:

> If it is not rented by June first we had better take it on ourselves—*unless* you are contented to live by yourself, as I believe you must be. It's always peaceful for us both to live apart we must agree. Even though it is lonely at times, we are both too determined and independent and unable to change our ways of life

consequently we should be frank with ourselves and decide if life together gives us what we need or is worth the cost on our nerves and dispositions. I believe it's a good time *now* to make any necessary changes and of course I'll do all I can to avoid any publicity or gossip. . . . Not even our relatives or children should be told anything at present. . . . I know how I feel, for I want you to be happier than I am able to make you, and I want happiness also which can not be had together.

"Now we are at the cross roads you and I," she wrote another time. "Nagging and criticism and constant complaining has driven out the beauty of our love and I'm afraid love has followed it out." Still she wrote to him nearly every day they were apart, impersonal letters usually listing her activities in New York, or referring to the home they might or might not make together in Arizona. On a trip to Mexico with friends she bought rugs for that possible Arizona home, and told Noah she had met a famous naturalist, a man of eighty whose second wife had recently borne him a baby daughter. "So there is no limit to the breeding power of the eternal male. He is a powerful man very handsome and witty." It is a combative note, in Margaret's former jaunty, feminist style, and rather unlike the rest of her letters to Noah during this period of loneliness and indecision.

Havelock Ellis died. Margaret had visited him earlier that year on the occasion of his eightieth birthday, bringing with her three thousand dollars collected from his American friends. Bill Sanger had a serious operation. "The doctor who is a friend of Grant's wanted to know who is to pay the bills etc. . . . So the boys have to assume responsibility." Just before Christmas in 1941, Noah had a slight stroke. He came to Willow Lake that spring, and Margaret joined him, but a second stroke left him partly paralyzed, and they went together to Tucson, where Margaret gave up all outside work and nursed him devotedly. His mind wandered at times, he "not only dreaded pain, but he hated the indignity of helplessness," she said later, and he wanted her always with him. She said he remembered every detail of their first luncheon together, every place they ever went together, everything they did.

On June 21, 1943, according to Margaret:

I was alone in the house—the nurse was on her four-hour leave—the doctor out on calls. My cook and the man who always takes care of J. Noah were escorting Julia, my old colored cook's body back to Memphis. She had died of cancer two days before.

I went into J. Noah's room about three o'clock to rest on the nurse's cot because there is a good cooler there which keeps the room lovely with cool, dry air. I tried to let the bed down to give J. N. a little more comfortable position as he was then asleep. He opened his eyes and waved me to stop. So I turned to let down the venetian blinds to keep the light from his eyes—he waved me away and said "Let them alone. I want to look at the mountains." Those were the last words he ever uttered.

Margaret's sons flew in to be with her in her bereavement, Grant from New Jersey, Stuart from Palm Beach, both in wartime uniform. Noah's will left everything he had to his wife if she survived him, to be divided between her sons if she did not. Margaret said she was "proud that they loved J. N. enough to make that long, sleepless trip," for none of Noah's own children came. His ashes were buried in a plot in the Fishkill cemetery that Noah had bought many years earlier.

Margaret Sanger survived her second husband by twenty-three years, most of them spent in what was for her semiretirement. "J. N. passed away June 21/43 and little sister Nan Jan 6/44," she wrote in her journal shortly after Nan's death. "Two dear graves side by side in Fishkill cemetery—It is lonely—Lots to do. . . . My painting and B.C. all big interests but one gets a loneliness nevertheless." With her grandchildren —Stuart settled in Tucson while Grant raised his large family in New York—Margaret was an affectionate and indulgent playmate; she put on costume plays with Stuart's daughters, and painted murals for the children's dining room in Grant's Mount Kisco home. She entertained constantly, sometimes elaborately, in the early years of her life in Tucson, took up painting with some seriousness, built a starkly modern house and prodded along the local birth control movement. It was the program of a New York society woman translated to Arizona, a carefree life among a wide circle of friends and family, its pleasures heightened by social position and enlivened by newly developed hobbies. Noah might have loved such a life—at any rate he was always urging her to join him in it. Still, he chose to marry her just as she was, a woman directed by mystical forces that gave her scarcely a moment's rest. And Margaret had purposely chosen to marry a man whose professed wishes she could ignore, and to live instead a life whose chief rewards came from hard work in the service of others. The other life never seems to have tempted her at all until the first one, "in the current of life's activities," had run its course.

From time to time, and for a variety of reasons, Margaret Sanger reentered the national consciousness. In 1949 she was given an honorary degree by Smith College, an honor of which she was intensely proud. In 1952, with Lady Rama Rau and other pioneers, she helped to form the International Planned Parenthood Federation. She had been invited to India by its government, the first in the world for which birth control was national policy, and the trip was combined with one to Japan, although Margaret had had a coronary thrombosis the year before, and four Arizona doctors as well as Stuart insisted such a trip must be out of the question. A delegate to New Delhi remembered her as "visibly trembling all over," while on the stage. "She stood there absolutely erect with nothing to hold onto and I thought 'She is going to collapse before this is over.'" But when Margaret spoke, "It was the most marvellous talk you have ever heard. Her voice was clear, lucid, there wasn't a misspoken word; she didn't hesitate. She absolutely brought down the house." She was seventy-two at the time. Four years later, battling with officers of the Federation, of which she was honorary president, about how soon the next international conference should be held, she was found by that same coworker to be "very spirited and very stubborn," with everyone terrified of disagreeing with her openly, and "somehow I couldn't help admiring her spunk."

But the most important contribution Margaret made to birth control during the years of her retirement had to do with the discovery of the pill, the *"pilule d'or,"* the oral contraceptive she used to call her holy grail, and her connection with it barely came into the public consciousness at all. John Rock, its codiscoverer along with Gregory Pincus, recalls a visit during the early fifties from Mrs. Sanger and Mrs. Stanley McCormick, the widow of the youngest son of Cyrus McCormick, who founded the International Harvester Company. Mrs. McCormick had been a friend and supporter of Margaret's since the Brownsville clinic days; she was an educated but eccentric woman who dressed in the style of another era, immensely rich and a serious-minded philanthropist. Dr. Rock recalled that some woman telephoned him asking for an appointment on behalf of Mrs. McCormick, who was interested in his research. He had never heard of Mrs. McCormick and had no way of knowing the woman who telephoned was Margaret Sanger.

The two women appeared, one of them tall and dressed in a collection of outmoded and showy clothes, the other small, thin, quietly dressed. He concluded that the "more presentable one," who hardly spoke at all, must be Mrs. McCormick, and the tall, eccentric-looking person must therefore be her secretary:

I thought that she was the secretary and that Mrs. McCormick, herself, who wanted to . . . help in some research was merely resting quietly and listening and, you know, playing cozy. Well, on the contrary, it was Mrs. Sanger who was playing cozy, and Mrs. McCormick who was giving me the world.

As for the research that led to the pill, Dr. Rock adds, "there was no government support, no foundation support. There was nothing. There was nothing but Margaret Sanger's influence on a sympathetic lady with charity and plenty of money."

Margaret was eighty-seven when she died of arteriosclerosis in a Tucson nursing home. *Time* magazine said in September 1966: "Half a century ago, when she raised the banners of her lonely crusade, she was lacerated from the pulpits as a 'lascivious monster.' . . . Yet when she died last week . . . her vision had been realized beyond her dreams." She was buried in Fishkill next to Noah.

With or without Margaret Sanger birth control would surely have come to the United States, although probably later and perhaps in a different form; under the sponsorship of the labor unions, for example, as in France, its major impact would have been on working people. As it is, the American movement bears throughout its history the unmistakable imprint of Margaret's personality. The use of the condom as a birth control measure never appealed to her, since she saw men as opponents rather than partners; her goal was a contraceptive that could be controlled exclusively by women, therefore she never thought of mounting a campaign to popularize the condom among the poor. Yet the Mensinga pessary, like the pill, was a middle-class contraceptive; the effort, the money and the missionary fervor that eventually made the Mensinga pessary legally acceptable might have served instead to make the condom acceptable to those who needed birth control most—had Margaret been someone else.

But whether or not a level-headed, thoroughly rational person could have accomplished what Margaret did is another matter; guided by inner voices, aided by cosmic forces, she became an irresistible leader through a contagion of faith. She was of course a fanatic, a brave and selfless one; and only a fanatic would have persisted as she did in the early years, when the church, the organized medical profession and the law were united in their stubborn refusal to give birth control a hearing.

The same "spiritual vitality" and "inner fire" that Julian Huxley spoke of, that caught up and inspired the audiences she addressed in so many parts of the world, affected friends and lovers and family. Bill Sanger, in spite of the tortured history of their marriage, never ceased to love Margaret during the years of separation that preceded their divorce. As for Noah, who complained that she turned her back on him over and over again when the movement needed her, he died remembering only the happiness they had shared. Margaret believed in "the absolute, elemental, inner urge of womanhood," which she thought of as vaguely connected with the maternal impulse, yet her own maternal impulses were pushed to the sidelines of her life along with her children. Grant and Stuart grew to successful manhood, in their choice of medical careers probably emulating their mother, yet they may have succeeded in spite of Margaret rather than because of her.

Surely in Margaret Sanger's case a happy marriage with a sympathetic and congenial husband is unimaginable; given her character she simply could not have remained content in what she thought of as a "tame marriage." She became a rebel to escape from the temptation of such a marriage, and only then found a cause to enlist in; once she was joined to it, her second marriage posed no threat to the full-blown crusader and rebel who had emerged. Marriage was by no means the central fact of her life, nor was sex, in spite of her passionate belief to that effect; her life was dominated by the will to power, and it was humanity's good fortune that she put her craving for power at the service of others.

Edna St. Vincent Millay

O<small>N A SUMMER DAY</small> in 1912 a redheaded girl of twenty, small-boned and delicate although she called herself by a boy's name, Vincent, came back from picking blueberries in a meadow near her home. She found her mother waiting on the doorstep, holding a letter from the sponsor of a nationwide poetry contest; when it was opened they learned he considered her poem "Renaissance" so remarkable he was sure she would win the first prize of five hundred dollars. It was an almost unimaginable fortune to the Millay family, who could hardly picture a hundred dollars all in one lump. But the prize was far more than money; to Vincent it meant that her work would be published, that an escape route from the small town in Maine where she felt stifled and imprisoned was unexpectedly open. And to Cora Millay it was the fulfillment of a dream toward which she had been working for years with tireless, bone-wearying devotion, the dream that her three daughters would someday have "their chance" in the world.

In a sense the writing of the poem and its entry in the contest were the joint accomplishment of mother and daughter, for Cora Millay was chiefly responsible, either consciously or unconsciously, for most of the elements of Vincent's upbringing, those that brought to fruition her singular poetic talent as well as those that determined her stormy emotional life in later years, her physical suffering, her so-called nervous breakdowns, her many loves, and her extraordinary marriage to an extraordinary man.

Cora Buzzelle Millay had been born of old New England stock, part Irish, and was the oldest of six children; her own mother died early so that Cora had to bear much of the responsibility for the younger brothers and sisters. She found neither time nor money to pursue her own musical and literary interests, and when she married a handsome, sandy-haired schoolteacher named Henry Tolman Millay, there was still no money. They had their three girls within four years of one another. Edna St. Vincent Millay was born in 1892, her middle name supposedly chosen because her mother's young sailor brother was injured at sea just before the birth; he was sent to St. Vincent's Hospital, where he was so well cared for that Cora Millay gave her firstborn the name of the hospital in gratitude.

Norma was a year younger than Edna, Kathleen two and a half years younger than Norma. With three children so close in age even a woman as capable and determined as Cora Millay had little creative energy to spare for herself. They lived in a series of small Maine towns, usually on the seacoast, where Henry Millay taught school and later became super-intendent of schools; unfortunately the marriage did not prosper. There was apparently no bitterness, only differences in viewpoint and temperament between husband and wife, and in particular they disagreed about Henry Millay's fondness for poker playing at higher stakes than they could afford. Years later Edna wrote that she remembered a swamp of cranberries, when she was seven years old, and her father's walking "down across that swamp . . . when my mother told him to go & not come back.

"(Or maybe she said he might come back if he would do better—but who ever does better)?" A year after that, still without bitterness, the Millays were divorced.

There followed several years of visiting around among relatives, after which Cora Millay brought her girls to the town of Camden, Maine; it was here they were raised, almost entirely on her own earnings and in accordance with her long-cherished wish that they were to have all that life had cheated her of—every opportunity to develop their creative talents, to lead rich and independent and fulfilling lives, cost what it might.

"My frustration was their chance," was the way she put it. Cora Millay had studied music as a girl; she sang, played piano, copied out orchestral parts for the Camden orchestra; she read omnivorously, wrote both poetry and prose and contributed to many New England periodicals, all in the time stolen from the dead-serious business of earning a living. Her girls were to have everything: "I cannot say why I had it, but so strong in me was the belief in them and their future that, no matter how hard it was, I had to have music books—I had the best private library in Camden—everything that would contribute to their development."

This she managed by going out as a district nurse. At first Cora did her nursing only at night, so as to be home with the children by day; but by the time Edna was eleven or twelve she was away with "live-in" cases for days, even weeks, at a time. The children were on their own then, with Edna in charge. They cooked, cleaned, went off to school and returned from school; they did their homework, went for long walks in the woods or the hills near home, coming and going as they wished, answerable to no one; they sang, played on the old-fashioned pump organ that was later replaced by an upright piano, composed songs, put on impromptu plays; they read, wrote, ate curious meals consisting sometimes of a pan of fudge for supper; they let a week's worth of dishes pile up in the rusty sink and went to bed when they were sleepy.

When their mother returned she pitched right in with the housework. Another woman might have welcomed the chance to rest, to unwind and recoup her forces, but Cora Millay never gave in to the temptation to relax, if indeed she was ever tempted; brisk, active and immensely capable as she was, she might have found relaxation more tiring than work. She gardened and cooked, put up fruits and vegetables in summertime, baked a week's supply of bread on a Saturday night, mended old clothes or ran up new ones, for "We did keep up appearances, and it made the struggle inside themselves all the keener." Her children were as well dressed as any girls in town, supplied with all the luxuries if not the necessities, the magazine subscriptions, the tickets to concerts and plays, but they had no illusions about the price their mother paid. "I let the girls realize their poverty. I let them realize what every advantage cost me in the efforts to live."

And life in the Millays' little unpainted clapboard house, where base-

ment floorboards rested on bare earth, where the bedrooms were unheated and even in the living rooms a precarious fuel supply occasionally
failed, so that a sudden flood in the kitchen provided an impromptu
skating rink, served to weld the family into a tight little corps. "The
hardships that bound the children together made them stronger, and
banded them together in self-defense against the world. If you touched
one you touched the whole of us. That was our safety."

If it was their safety, it was also, judging from Edna's later life, the
source of her greatest danger. Just as Cora Millay said, the goal of her
existence was to give her girls what she had not had herself—independence, creativity, the opportunity to excel. Because in those days such
qualities were almost exclusively the province of men and boys, she
tended to think of the self-fulfilling person as male; and her eldest in
particular she saw as the boy of the family. According to Floyd Dell, who
was Edna's lover in the 1920s, "Her mother had expected a son, and
when the child was a girl, she brought her up, she told me, like a son
—to be self-reliant and fearless and ambitious." Edna, like her sisters,
adored her mother and saw life to a certain extent through her mother's
eyes; accordingly she called herself by the boy's name that was her
middle name and became what her mother wanted her to be, the boy
of the family. It was a tendency only strengthened by there being, in
Henry Millay's absence, no other male in it. There was no one with
whom to contest the role, no one to act out for her the differences
between male and female, neither was there a model of womanliness in
the more conventional style, a woman who took pride and pleasure in
being female, who was gentle and accepting rather than determined and
fiercely ambitious.

When Cora Millay said she meant for her girls to have their chance,
cost what it might, she could not have supposed the cost would be borne
by anyone but herself. Yet in pushing the girls, especially Edna, toward
the independence she herself longed for, Cora Millay must have pushed
too soon and too hard. Consumed as she was with the desire to see
accomplishment, excellence, performance, she seems not to have shown
them that it is possible to be loved for oneself alone, to be loved apart
from success and excellence, to be loved for no other reason than that
one exists.

If there are some children capable of full independence at the age of eleven or twelve, Edna was apparently not one of them. Longing to be free and on her own during adolescence and adulthood, she felt herself still tied hand and foot to that tight little band of four. It was as if, cheated of a part of her childhood, of the tenderness and unambitious love a less determined mother might have felt free to show, she clung tenaciously to childhood, as if she refused to break free because life still owed her a portion of childhood that must one day, surely, be paid.

Thus she was haunted by homesickness for her family until she was past thirty and married; she brought her mother to New York, then to Europe, as soon as she possibly could, and wrote baby talk almost ad nauseam to mother and sisters when she was a grown woman, a poet of considerable reputation. Clinging to childhood was a valuable trait for the poet, serving to keep her vision fresh and childlike, but for the woman it was a damaging and at times an incapacitating need. Seeing herself as a sort of extension of her mother—the one who was to fulfill on her mother's behalf the frustrated ambitions Cora Millay had buried within her—was equally damaging; and so was the lifelong tendency to see herself as the son her mother never had.

As children all three of the girls had boyish nicknames. Edna was Sefe, short for Josephus, Norma was Hunk and Kathleen Wump; Edna wrote to Kathleen when she was past thirty: "Sefe sends you bad picture of hisself, just for fun, cause he wanted to send youse picture of hisself, and good ones ain't forthcomin'." Some years earlier she had written to Norma: "I'm as crazy to see you as if I were going to be married to you." How was such a girl, uncertain of her sexual role, overvaluing her boyish traits because that seemed the surest path to love and approval, to get along with men, to fall in love, to marry? How indeed? It was especially troubling since she had never really seen a marriage at work, never seen husband and wife as friends, lovers, parents, for yet another deeply disturbing element in Vincent's childhood was the loss of her father. She knew her mother had sent him away and must have wondered why he agreed to be sent away, must have felt on some level that his leaving amounted to desertion since he had not loved her and her sisters enough to stay at home. In this desertion was rooted a deep distrust of men and of intimate relations with them, for what happens when you give your love to a man? He packs up and leaves; she had seen it herself at the age of seven.

There is an old saying that the same fire that melts the butter hardens the iron. This childhood that was to cause Edna Millay so much suffering in maturity, both physical suffering subtly rooted in the emotions and more obviously emotional travail, was the childhood that made of her an original poet—"one of the sole surviving masters of English verse," according to the eminent literary critic Edmund Wilson—and a passionately dedicated one. If Cora Millay unwittingly caused the suffering, the creation of the poet was her conscious act.

She provided her girls with what her eldest daughter always remembered as an extraordinarily happy childhood: "Meseems it never rained in those days." Perhaps Edna shut out the unhappy memories, considering them traitorous in view of all the sacrifices her mother had made; perhaps they were buried so deeply out of self-protection that she never felt them at all. In any case she always spoke of her childhood as untroubled, happy, secure, and recalled with tender affection the "simple and marvellous events" of childhood and adolescence when she picked mayflowers on the rocky hillsides and steamed clams in seaweed on the spruce-wooded islands off the coast of Penobscot Bay. If the little wooden house in Camden was meager, grim, drafty, it was set in a lovely hollow just outside the town, surrounded by meadows where tall timothy grass and goldenrod, burdock and Queen Anne's lace flourished, while behind the house the Megunticook River, some fourteen feet wide where it passed the meadow, was a sheltered swimming hole for children too young for the sea. Camden itself, a town of about 3,000 poised between mountains and the steep, rocky seacoast, was known as the "Jewel of the Penobscot," a favored resort for rich summer visitors who chose it as much for the splendid situation as for the New England simplicity and grace of its tree-shaded streets.

Camden was rural yet lively. It made its living from shipbuilding, fabric mills and summer visitors; shipyards, sailmakers, motorboat mechanics and the comings and goings of the active little port, in which ships from India and the Far East docked, were daily reminders of the larger world. There were concerts in summer, local theatricals as well as traveling professional companies, and impromptu entertainments gotten up for the summer people. And at its feet was Penobscot Bay, which has been described as ideal poet's country, like the Lake District in England. Cora Millay had not chosen Camden for that reason, but she could not have chosen better.

In the black dirt garden by their house the Millays planted onions, lettuces, radishes, herbs of every kind for winter use as well as marigolds, nasturtiums and zinnias, for Cora Millay was a dedicated gardener; it was the beginning of what the poet came to call her "Earth-Passion." She seemed to have spent her childhood learning the names of every flower around her, wild or cultivated, every weed, fruit, tree, bird, sea shell, sea grass, sea creature. She wrote to her mother from France in the twenties: "One of the men who were here told me the names of fifty-four wildflowers which I did not know at all, except, in the case of some like vetches and broom, which I had come upon in poems. Such names as milk-wort, willow-herb, campion, hound's-tongue, flea-bane, ladies'-bed-straw, sweet-agrimony . . ." And into her poetry she wove all the growing things of her childhood, details of meadow and garden, of sea's edge and the sea itself, of mountains, wild places, wild creatures, all precisely and lovingly named, as cannily observed as only a born countrywoman could observe them.

If Cora Millay had given her daughter the setting and the example upon which her Earth-Passion was built, she also set the tone of the household, a distinctly bohemian tone, where freedom of expression was valued and every cultural interest lovingly nurtured. There was always music; each of the girls sang and played, sometimes whole operas, sometimes their own compositions, and Edna made an opera of Little Boy Blue when she was about fourteen. Cora said, "I even had a dream once that they might form an orchestra, Vincent at the piano, Norma playing the cornet . . . and Kathleen the harp." Norma became an accomplished operatic singer as well as an actress, Edna almost decided on a career as a concert pianist but gave it up, perhaps because her hands were too small; she remained a music lover for the rest of her life and continued to play for her own pleasure or with talented friends, practicing assiduously, although in spurts. "Indeed, without music I should wish to die. Even poetry, sweet patron Muse forgive me the words, is not what music is," she wrote in her late twenties. And from the ample library at home Edna read precociously and voraciously: Milton, Shelley, Wordsworth; all of Shakespeare when she was eight; Caesar's Gallic wars in Latin the summer she was fourteen; by the time she was twenty she could describe herself as well acquainted with Dickens, Eliot, Scott, Arnold Bennett, Hawthorne, Browning, Kipling, Twain. But the bohemian atmosphere of the Millay household sprang from more than the cultivation of the intellect and the arts; it was the subtle emanation of Cora's own freewheeling spirit, the spirit of a woman who had braved small-town opinion by divorcing her husband and running her own life at the turn of the century, when rare courage and tenacity were required for such an undertaking.

The writer Edmund Wilson, who loved Edna in the 1920s, found her elderly mother most extraordinary; in *The Shores of Light* he described her as "a little old woman with spectacles who, although she had evidently been through a good deal, had managed to remain very brisk and bright. She sat up straight and smoked cigarettes and quizzically followed the conversation. She looked not unlike a New England schoolteacher, yet there was something almost raffish about her. She had anticipated the Bohemianism of her daughters; and she sometimes made remarks that were startling from the lips of a little old lady. But there was nothing sordid about her: you felt even more than with Edna that she had passed beyond good and evil." This freethinker's belief in doing what one wished quite apart from society's view of right and wrong set the stage for Edna's posture as the standard-bearer of youthful freedom in the 1920s and '30s. She was a bohemian before she ever came to Greenwich Village; she had learned it at her mother's knee.

A girlhood friend of the Millays remembered that Cora was "always making witty remarks and would often say something that could be taken two ways. Vincent was that way too, and quick at repartee. It was this constant sharpening of the wits with those with whom she came in contact that developed Vincent's agility of mind so early." Not only did she think on her feet, she even thought in epigram or verse, for the same friend described Edna as tossing off a quatrain, impromptu, to win an argument with Norma. The girls apparently argued, even fought, a good deal, perhaps not a surprising result of their closeness and affection. Edmund Wilson remarked on this closeness later, noting that Edna, aside from her mother and sisters, found people and even lovers interesting mainly as subjects for her poetry. Her emotions about them mattered more than the people themselves, not because she was cold, heartless, manipulating, but because that was where the deepest drama lay— among the tight little band of four, or else within herself, transmuted into poetry.

She was raised in an era when no one need be ashamed of loving poetry, when children took elocution lessons and recited before company, and even adults wrote poems for their own pleasure. Edna, like her sisters, devoured the *St. Nicholas* magazine with its stories, pictures, poetry and articles intended solely for children. *St. Nicholas* had a section written by children, and here, at the age of fourteen, she saw her first poetry published; she had been writing poetry since she was four. Edna won several *St. Nicholas* prizes, had half a dozen of her poems printed there, and in high school wrote for the literary magazine and later edited it. And she told her mother years later: "the reason I am a poet is entirely because you wanted me to be and intended I should be even from the very first. You brought me up in the tradition of poetry, and everything I did you encouraged. I can not remember once in my life when you were not interested in what I was working on, or even suggested that I should put it aside for something else."

Edna also wrote, when she was thirty, "The Ballad of the Harp-Weaver," a poem dedicated to her mother. It is the story of a poor young woman who has neither food nor clothing for her only child—significantly a son. "All that was left us/Was a chair we couldn't break,/And the harp with a woman's head/Nobody would take." And from the music of her magical harp the mother weaves, all through one winter night, a pile of princely clothing for her son. The morning finds "A smile about her lips,/And a light about her head,/And her hands in the harp-strings/Frozen dead." Cora Millay had given her daughter a princely heritage, the will and the need to be a poet; that Edna felt her mother would have paid with her life's blood for her daughter's chance was part of the burden she had to bear.

At seventeen Edna graduated from high school. By her eighteenth birthday she wrote *St. Nicholas* a letter of farewell, for eighteen was the age limit; apparently she felt there was no other outlet for her poetry. Yet there were other publications for young people; there were all the adult New England periodicals to which her mother contributed, as did Vincent's friend the Camden poet Abbie Huston Evans. Nevertheless from the time she left high school Edna stayed at home and did very little; she wrote, she cooked for the family, she took occasional odd jobs typing for summer visitors, she acted in local plays as all the Millay girls had been doing for years. She paid a visit to her mother's people in Massachusetts, joined several girls' clubs whose members had literary readings or teas, but she also went for long and solitary walks and was moody and depressed much of the time. Although the house was full of her sisters' suitors, Edna herself showed little interest in boys, or perhaps they took no interest in her. According to Lawrence Langner, who knew her in the twenties in New York, she was "elfin-like and delicate as a flower"; five feet tall, weighing about a hundred pounds and crowned by a pile of splendid red hair, she must have been as pretty as any girl in Camden. Yet depression and anxiety could turn her colorless, mousy; she could be "bossy" too, high-handed, temperamental, hard to get on with. In the years after high school graduation when she was obsessed with the riddle of her own future, there might have been much in her manner to scare off the boys who flocked around Norma and Kathleen.

Apparently Edna never thought of leaving home and Camden and trying her luck in the world, whether in the theater, in music or in writing; there is no hint that she ever considered full-time work in Camden with the eventual goal of saving her money for college. Perhaps it was because her mother had a poor opinion of college: "I don't think collegiate life is especially good for genius. Might it not have taken the originality and naive quality out of her work?" More likely Edna stayed passively, moodily at home because she was tied to home, to family, mother and childhood. Yet she longed, constantly and without hope, to break free.

"And before she had finally gone to college . . . she had almost, she told me, abandoned the hope of ever sloughing off that life of the small American town, which she put on when she woke every morning like some cursed indestructible dress of girlhood, too worn, too soiled, too small." So Edmund Wilson recalled the Vincent of those late adolescent years in his novel, *I Thought of Daisy.*

It was in this mood that Edna began at eighteen the long poem she called "Renaissance." She worked at it off and on during the next few years, but it was still unfinished in the spring of 1912 when word reached them that Henry Millay, who had settled in the town of Kingman, Maine, was ill with pneumonia. He had asthma and heart trouble as well. Edna took the poem with her and went to Kingman to nurse her father.

Henry Millay had followed the development of his daughters with friendly interest, sending letters and gifts of money from time to time; in spite of Cora's early belief in his instability he was now superintendent of schools in Kingman and chairman of the board of selectmen. Edna sent home an account of her visit that showed she took great pride in him and enjoyed his company: "I see Papa twice a day. We can't talk very much but he loves to have me with him. . . . I never in my life heard so many people inquire for one man. All festivities here are postponed until he recovers. An M.D. and an L.L.D. from somewhere around here came in on the train today just to see him a minute—great friends of his."

Cora was away from home at the time on a nursing job. Reading through magazines during the night, she came across the announcement of a poetry contest in *The Lyric Year;* an anthology was to be published of the hundred best poems written in the United States that year. Three money prizes were offered, the first of five hundred, the others of two hundred and fifty dollars each. She wrote immediately to Edna urging her to cut short her visit and return home, finish the poems she was working on and submit them.

Among the several poems Edna polished up and sent to the contest was "Renaissance." Ferdinand Earle, the editor of *The Lyric Year* and one of three judges of the contest, came across it while working his way through what he later described as more than ten thousand "mediocre manuscripts, most of them insipid and drivelling nonsense," and he was immediately struck by its strength, freshness and originality. He wrote off in high enthusiasm to E. St. Vincent Millay, Esq., whom he naturally addressed as "Dear Sir." A correspondence sprang up, Edna confessed her sex and Earle persuaded her to alter the title to "Renascence."

It was, just as he felt, an astonishing poem quite apart from the fact that the writer was only twenty years old:

> All I could see from where I stood
> Was three long mountains and a wood;
> I turned and looked another way,
> And saw three islands in a bay.
> So with my eyes I traced the line
> Of the horizon, thin and fine,
> Straight around till I was come
> Back to where I'd started from;
> And all I saw from where I stood
> Was three long mountains and a wood.
>
> Over these things I could not see:
> These were the things that bounded me.
> And I could touch them with my hand,
> Almost, I thought, from where I stand!
> And all at once things seemed so small
> My breath came short, and scarce at all.

The poet is enclosed by her childhood landscape, bounded by it, able to touch it with her hand, almost unable to breathe for being closed in by it. Soon she realizes even the sky is so close she can touch it.

> Ah, awful weight! Infinity
> Pressed down upon the finite Me!
> My anguished spirit, like a bird,
> Beating against my lips I heard;
> Yet lay the weight so close about
> There was no room for it without.
> And so beneath the weight lay I
> And suffered death, but could not die.

At last the earth gives way beneath her, crushing her till she sinks six feet under the ground, at peace at last but dead. Overhead she hears the comforting rain, and longs to escape—"I would I were alive again/To kiss the fingers of the rain"—for the grave has become a second prison, even more confining than the one above ground.

She prays for release: "And the big rain in one black wave/Fell from the sky and struck my grave." She springs up, embraces the trees, laughs into the sky and sobs out her gratitude to God, aware at last that "The soul can split the sky in two,/And let the face of God shine through."

"This poem gives the central theme of Edna Millay's whole work," said Edmund Wilson, who calls it "a study of claustrophobia (as well as, of course, a great affirmation of the stature of the human spirit)." And while the poem has been loved, quoted and anthologized for the second quality he names, as an affirmation of the unconquerable human spirit, its power is rooted in the passionate struggle within the poet's mind between the two forces of claustrophobia. She is afraid of being buried alive, that is, of staying at home, sheltered, enclosed and protected by her mother as she is sheltered and enclosed, first by the hills and woods and later by the grave itself. But what she most deeply fears she also most deeply desires, for such is the nature of claustrophobia, as of any phobia. Childhood and maternal protection are what she desperately craves— yet if she permits herself to imagine them she realizes they will crush her to death and cut her off forever from God's sweet world. The price is more than she can bear to pay; the final choice is for freedom.

In style "Renascence" is simple, earthy, homely yet intense. And since the theme of the poem is nothing less than her own survival, it is not amazing that she felt it with the most piercing intensity; what is amazing is her youthful ability to put it into simple words that grip the reader with something of the same terror and relief she must have felt during the two years she wrote and rewrote it, debating between life and figurative death and choosing life at last.

In reality, the immediate effect of "Renascence" was as liberating as the final stanzas of the poem itself, since it brought the small-town girl to the attention of the world. Yet in spite of Ferdinand Earle's assurances, she did not win the first prize of five hundred dollars. Earle did his best to convince the other two judges of the remarkable quality of the poem, but with little success. They agreed at last to give it fourth place, publishing it in the anthology but without any prize, and with that Earle and the Millays had to be content.

The anthology appeared in November of 1912, near the end of a year that had been marked by an extraordinary outburst of poetic activity in America—Amy Lowell, Robert Frost, Ezra Pound, Carl Sandburg, Edgar Lee Masters, Robinson Jeffers were published, some for the first time, that year or very soon after. Anthologies of poetry flowered, magazine and newspaper editors who had shrugged off contributions of poetry in the past began to welcome them, would even pay for them; the magazine *Poetry* was established by Harriet Monroe, and new schools of poetry seemed to leap into being wherever two poets rubbed together. "The fiddles are tuning . . . all over America," said John Butler Yeats. Indeed it seemed as if a poetic renaissance, built upon the dying embers of Victorianism and seeking to express all the forces of modernism set in motion by Freud, Marx, Darwin, by industrial expansion and the growing movement for social reform, had made of 1912 a truly lyric year.

It was against this background of sudden and widespread interest in poetry that the appearance of "Renascence" created a literary sensation bordering on scandal. Readers and critics wrote to complain that "Renascence" was the best piece in the book; the first-prize winner, Orrick Johns, felt "The outstanding poem in that book was 'Renascence' by Edna St. Vincent Millay, immediately acknowledged by every authoritative critic as such. The award was as much an embarrassment to me as a triumph." Edna got letters from all over the country, and one critic called her the young girl from Camden, Maine, who "became famous through *not* receiving the prize." One of the second-prize winners told her she could have his $250 any time she asked for it.

But even before *The Lyric Year* was published "Renascence" had made a major change in Edna's life; that summer at the Whitehall Inn in Camden, she had recited the poem before an audience of summer visitors and caught the attention of Caroline Dow, head of the National Training School of the YWCA. Miss Dow convinced the young poet she ought to go to college, promising to find the necessary scholarship money, and after some months of indecision Edna decided to apply to Vassar.

Before she could undertake the stiff entrance examination required by Vassar, certain gaps in her education would have to be filled, and a semester at Barnard College, to be followed by a summer of intensive study at home, seemed the wisest course. Miss Dow offered to find the money for Barnard as well, and Edna went to New York early in 1913, to live at the National Training School, to study at Barnard and to make the break with her childhood that she had been unable to make on her own. Fate, in the form of the generous Miss Dow, had made it for her; she was now twenty-one years old, an age when many girls were already finishing college, and Edna stood out from her fellow students in other ways. She was already a person of considerable interest to New York literary circles, and invited to luncheons, teas, meetings; in the words of Jessie Rittenhouse, secretary of the Poetry Society, everyone was "on the qui vive to meet her. Pretty, petite, not yet over the wonder of her sudden entry upon the literary scene, she was altogether natural and charming."

"Renascence" worked yet another long-lasting effect; its publication put Edna in touch with two established poets whose work had also appeared in *The Lyric Year*, Witter Bynner and Arthur Davison Ficke, who wrote her a joint letter of praise and admiration in care of Ferdinand Earle. Ficke, a lawyer in Iowa, decided Earle had been taken in, that the writer of "Renascence" could not possibly be a twenty-year-old girl, since no "sweet young thing of twenty ever ended a poem precisely where this one ends; it takes a brawny male of forty-five to do that." Earle told Edna she must write to Ficke herself and disabuse him. She did so; her letters to Bynner and Ficke, especially the latter, were marked by such a spirit of arch, mischievous, even provocative femininity that they could no longer doubt her sex. She simply would not be called a "brawny male," she told them. "Not that I have an aversion to brawny males; *au contraire, au contraire*. But I cling to my femininity!" Ficke, ten years older than Edna, married and the father of a little boy, sent her his photograph; they exchanged poems, discussed the writing of poetry, and the tone of Edna's letters became increasingly flirtatious: "I am enclosing two or three manuscripts that I happened to have on hand. Don't hesitate to tell me you don't like them. . . . I shall bear up wonderfully well under the shock. That word is 'shock'—mercy, I can't write it. . . . Shock; shock; an electric thrill. There. . . ." And she spoke several times of slapping his face. In New York Edna met Bynner at a literary party, but although Ficke came to New York they somehow failed to meet.

After the semester at Barnard Edna returned to Camden to bone up for the Vassar entrance examinations with special attention to history and mathematics, and to Latin prose, in which the Vassar professor of Latin, Elizabeth Haight, had offered to tutor her by mail. They became close friends, and were soon on a first-name basis. By fall of that year Edna had passed the awesome examinations and was duly enrolled in Vassar's class of 1917; but her first impressions of the college were more than a little disappointing. It was a school for young ladies, after all, governed by the strictest notions of propriety, with men resolutely banned from the campus except for closely chaperoned Sunday visits. Edna wrote to Ficke:

> Go to!— Would you have me write you an *im*proper letter?—
> Upon my soul I half believe you would! And I am not yet so Vassarized but that such a thing is still possible. . . .
> I hate this pink-and-gray college. If there had been a college in *Alice in Wonderland* it would be this college. Every morning when I awake I swear, I say, "Damn this pink-and-gray college!" . . .
> They treat us like an orphan asylum. They impose on us in a hundred ways and then bring on ice-cream.—And I hate ice-cream.
> They trust us with everything but men,—and they let us see it, so that it's worse than not trusting us at all. We can go into the candy-kitchen & take what we like and pay or not, and nobody is there to know. But a man is forbidden as if he were an apple.

Yet only a few months later she told her family she was crazy about the college; and indeed Edna's four years at Vassar proved to be productive and memorable ones, for herself as well as for the school, although a persistent thread of rebellion, impish, mocking, sometimes downright disruptive, can be seen throughout her college career. Smoking was forbidden; Edna smoked in a nearby cemetery. Rules about classroom attendance were rigid, but Edna continually cut classes, sometimes cutting more often than she appeared. In one freshman history class she habitually arrived when the session was two-thirds over; chapel she tended to ignore although weekly attendance was required, and the excuses she offered were often outrageous. Several of her teachers became infuriated and complained to President Henry MacCracken, who called her one day to his office and said that no matter what she did, he would not expel her: "I know all about poets at college, and I don't want a banished Shelley on my doorstep." As if her teachers hadn't enough to madden them in Edna's spotty attendance and offhand manner, there was the further outrage of her writing excellent examination papers, for she was a disciplined crammer and blessed with a remarkable memory.

But there were many classes to which Edna gave her wholehearted attention. English literature formed the mainstay of her college studies, along with languages, both ancient and modern—Latin and French, Greek, Italian, Spanish and German. She told her German professor three weeks after the opening of school in the fall of 1913, "I know my work has not been very good yet, but it is going to be. By Christmas I shall be the best in the class." She was, easily, according to Professor Jenney, and by Thanksgiving, not Christmas. Vassar's academic standards were high; President MacCracken, a young and liberal-minded humanist who came there a year after Edna did, claimed he was amazed to find the level of instruction superior to that of Yale and Harvard. And where Edna's interest was aroused she proved to be an apt and sometimes brilliant scholar; "when present," said Elizabeth Haight, "she could stir a teacher and electrify a class."

Although Edna had chosen Vassar because there were more foreign students there than at any of the other first-rate colleges for women, she had unwittingly chosen the school best suited for the training of a creative artist, for Vassar was in those days a hotbed of the performing arts—"a singing college," according to MacCracken. "Marching songs were heard nightly as some group went by. Serenades under dorm windows echoed through the quads. A song contest at Founder's Day gave prizes for the best Alma Mater, the best comic song, and the best choral singing of some chosen classic. . . . New songs sprang up from nowhere, and spread round campus almost daily." To a girl who had been singing and composing since early childhood, this outburst of song proved a delicious challenge and she rose eagerly to meet it.

There was an equal or greater excitement about the theater. "Vassar has always been stagestruck," MacCracken wrote. "In the heyday of the theater Vassar had at least a play a week." And by the end of her second year, Vincent Millay—she was always Vincent at college, the name Edna Millay being virtually unknown in Vassar annals—was one of the most conspicuously successful actresses on campus; in her senior year a one-act play of her own creation, *The Princess Marries the Page*, was produced with the playwright in the starring role. By then she had acquired an adoring following of younger students, who often brought her flowers when she appeared in a play. Vassar's theatrical activities had begun to interest drama critics from nearby Poughkeepsie, even critics from the New York newspapers, and Edna's success in leading roles eventually led her to consider finding work in the theater when she left school.

If she was an erratic but occasionally brilliant scholar, a singer and composer of songs, a hard-working actress and playwright, Edna remained a poet; poetry was her excuse whenever she was late for class or absent from class or chapel. "A poem is like a child, you know; when it is time for it to be born it has to have attention," she told the head warden once. Her poems appeared in several leading magazines and anthologies, as well as in Vassar publications, and one, "The Suicide," received an intercollegiate literary prize.

She made many friends, who found her exciting, original and great fun to be with. As Elizabeth Haight recalled, "A classmate of Vincent told me that one day when they were going out to dinner, she turned on the hot water in two adjoining cubicles to reserve them, but when she got back in her kimono, one was occupied. She rushed into Vincent's room crying: 'Someone has snitched one of our tubs. We haven't a minute to spare, so hurry. We'll have to do social tubbing.' Vincent replied calmly: 'Then I shall wear my new hat!' The other girl told me she would never forget the little thing sitting at the other end of the long tub in the soapsuds, her red head crowned with a purple velvet hat with plumes!'"

She was not universally beloved, however; there were some girls who resented her occasional inconsiderateness to teachers, or her cool withdrawal when she found a conversation or a person boring. Perhaps there was some jealousy mingled with their understandable resentment, since Edna was so conspicuously successful both on campus and off. To her family she remained as close and attentive as ever—homesick, but never desperately so, eager for news of home and always longing for vacations and reunion: "O, I'm so crazy to get home!— Seems to me I can't wait, tho I'm crazy about the college & everything—" She had arranged for Kathleen's entrance to Vassar in 1917 with appropriate scholarship help, and hoped that Norma could come to New York and study clothing design.

Edna's senior year at Vassar was a blaze of glory; she had written the words and music for the Baccalaureate Hymn, the words of the Tree Ceremonies and of the Marching Song, yet it looked for a while as if the graduation ceremonies would have to take place without her. For now that she had fulfilled all the requirements for the degree, her rebellious streak flared up and threatened serious consequences; she had been "campused," forbidden to spend a night away from college, as a result of several minor infractions of the rules. "One May day," Elizabeth Haight recalls, "she went automobiling to the mountains with a college friend and her mother. They went so far that the shades of night fell on them and a defective car made it impossible to drive back that night. Of course, Vincent should have telephoned to the Warden of her Hall. . . . Instead she took a chance that no one would ever know. She was the only one of the three who signed the hotel register." Yet she was also the only one who had been "campused," and when one of the college wardens happened to lunch next day at the same hotel, she saw "Vincent's name written '*after a man's*' on the register, and thought the worst. . . . The faculty voted to suspend her indefinitely. . . . This meant the loss of her degree."

A petition signed by 108 members of the senior class was circulated among the faculty, imploring them to show leniency and nullify "false rumors regarding her reputation." Edna, meanwhile, was living in the home of the college physician, where Dr. Haight found her "very unhappy and quiet, sunk over the fact that she had not heard her hymn sung." All was saved in the end; President MacCracken lifted the suspension and allowed her to return for graduation, claiming that there were few students who had done more for their college than this young poet. And Edna wrote home that commencement went off beautifully, signing the letter "Edna St. Vincent Millay A.B.!"

Although she remained for the rest of her life "Vincent" to many of her intimates, she was now at twenty-five a published poet, with the beginnings of a literary following who knew her, as *St. Nicholas* magazine had not, to be female, and Vincent became increasingly a name reserved for those who were close to her. Among more formal acquaintances and to all her readers her first name was Edna, and sometimes she was Edna to family as well.

The summer of 1917 Edna spent mostly in Camden, "because it's only at home that one can work & iron & mend & sew on buttons & run in ribbons & make window curtains into hats," but she planned to return to New York as soon as she had something decent to wear, for she realized, and the family realized, that her future lay in New York, not Maine. By autumn she was back in Manhattan, once again living at the National Training School of the YWCA and looking for work as an actress, not because she meant to give up poetry forever but because she needed something to live on—"the disgusting money—the dirty necessary money!" She had been haunted throughout her senior year by the awareness that she must earn a living in some palatable fashion and with the assurance that there would still be time for writing; as for poetry itself, apparently there wasn't much to be earned from it. Mitchell Kennerley, publisher of *The Lyric Year*, brought out Edna's first book, *Renascence and Other Poems*, and the long poem that had been her escape route from small-town life enjoyed a fresh spurt of public attention that autumn, but there never seemed to be any royalties from it in spite of Kennerley's promises.

Edna had spent part of the summer after graduation visiting the distinguished British actress Edith Wynne Matthison and her husband, the playwright Charles Rann Kennedy, whom she knew through their connection with Vassar; they gave her letters of introduction to stage people and arranged for her to do poetry readings of her work, lavishly paid for, the young poet thought, at fifty dollars apiece. But her feelings toward the older woman were deeper and more complex than gratitude. Faced with the prospect of making her own way in the world, where she would be cut off from the protection as well as the constraints of Vassar, Edna had been casting about for some practical way of bringing her entire family to New York, as if to reestablish as soon as possible the protection of childhood. With Kathleen already enrolled at Vassar and Norma hoping to come to New York and have "her chance" at a career, surely Mother would follow. "Don't you suppose," she wrote to Norma, "mother could get a job editing some dum page in some newspaper?"

There is no reason to believe this idea originated with Cora Millay, that with her daughters established in New York she feared loneliness in Maine and proposed to follow them; for eventually, when all her girls including Edna were married, Cora Millay apparently chose to remain in Maine, in familiar surroundings and close to her relatives. It was Edna who wanted her mother, and while she waited for her she seems to have turned to Edith Wynne Matthison as to a second mother, a charming, talented, generous figure to whom she could bind herself by the same silver cords of romantic and filial emotion: "You wrote me a beautiful letter,—I wonder if you meant it to be as beautiful as it was.— I think you did; for somehow I know that your feeling for me, however slight it is, is of the nature of love." And, "Love me, please; I love you; I can bear to be your friend. So,ask of me anything, and hurt me whenever you must; but never be 'tolerant,' or 'kind.' And never say to me again —don't dare to say to me again—'Anyway, you can make a trial' of being friends with you! Because I can't do things in that way. . . . Whatever I do, I give up my whole self to it. . . . I am conscious only of doing the thing that I love to do,—that I *have* to do—and I *have* to be your friend.' " And "when you tell me to come, I will come, by the next train, just as I am. This is not meekness, be assured; I do not come naturally by meekness; know that it is a proud surrender to You." She was twenty-five years old and Mrs. Kennedy past forty, yet these words are full of the romantic yearning of a schoolgirl with a passionate crush, or of Eugene Marchbanks (whom she had acted in college) throwing himself at Candida's feet.

In mid-September Edna began making the rounds of New York's theatrical producers. Norma joined her in November; Norma made hats for a while and sold them, but America had entered the European war that spring and she soon found work in an airplane factory. In January they left the National Training School for a tiny apartment on Waverly Place in Greenwich Village, a one-and-a-half-room cold-water flat "hardly large enough for a bed and a typewriter and some cups and saucers; a room, however, with the luxury of a fireplace, for which Joe the Italian brought, every few days . . . a load of firewood at ten cents a precious stick." Here Edna hugged the fire, drank tea, smoked cigarettes and worked at the poems that seemed to earn nothing but rejection slips; meanwhile she continued her efforts to find work on the stage.

The little apartment on Waverly Place was in the very heart of Greenwich Village, only a few doors from the house where Poe had written "Ligeia." Just as Penobscot Bay had been ideal poet's country, so was the Village in those days an ideal setting for the kind of poet Edna Millay was to become in the next few years. Greenwich Village, the section of New York centered around Washington Square, had always been a village within the metropolis, a quiet neighborhood of crooked streets and winding alleys and handsome old red-brick houses, charming, intimate, run down, a haven for the artists and writers who had settled there since Revolutionary times, partly because the rent was cheap, partly because its very physical irregularity seemed to symbolize freedom from conventional American town and city life, from bourgeois standards and money-grubbing.

In the years before the war, poets, painters, college professors, political radicals and theater people came there to create new ways of living the civilized life, often leaving behind them former wives and former families along with the bourgeois strictures they hoped to escape. High-minded, idealistic, they were tolerant of a wide variety of human conduct, especially of sexual freedom; individualists, they were also believers. They believed in Freud, in Marx, in art, poetry, in hard work and mutual cooperation. But in the years directly following the war what had been the attitudes of a special few became, in diluted form, far more widespread; early Villagers like Carl Van Doren, Sinclair Lewis, Upton

Sinclair, Lincoln Steffens, Max Eastman and Vachel Lindsay found their little enclave increasingly crowded by the disillusioned young who were eager to cast off the bonds of the past without any clear idea of what they wanted to replace them with.

It was the second generation of Villagers, the postwar generation, who were the true bohemians. As Malcolm Cowley recalled in his *Exile's Return*: "We had lost our ideals at a very early age, and painlessly. If any of them survived the war, they had disappeared in the midst of the bickerings at Versailles, or later with the steel strike, the Palmer Raids, the Centralia massacre. But they did not leave us bitter. We believed we had fought for an empty cause, that the Germans were no worse than the Allies, no better, that the world consisted of fools and scoundrels ruled by scoundrels and fools, that everybody was selfish and could be bought for a price." Uprooted by the war, cut off from the past while the future seemed to hold no more promise than what could be bought on the installment plan, they drifted to Manhattan, then to the Village, where a furnished hall bedroom could be rented for two or three dollars a week, and the whole top floor of a rickety house for thirty dollars a month.

The prewar Village had for its social center the Liberal Club, by no means exclusively political in its interests yet to a certain degree, as the name suggests, a market place for ideas. Postwar Villagers met in more colorful surroundings. Cowley writes:

. . . the social centers of the Village were two saloons: the Hell Hole, on Sixth Avenue at the corner of West Fourth Street, and the Working Girls' Home, at Greenwich Avenue and Christopher Street. The Hell Hole was tough and dirty; the proprietor kept a pig in the cellar and fed it scraps from the free-lunch counter. The boys in the back room were small-time gamblers and petty thieves, but the saloon was also patronized by actors and writers from the Provincetown Playhouse, which was just around the corner. Sometimes the two groups mingled. . . . The Hell Hole stayed in business during the first two or three years of prohibition, but then it was closed and I don't know where the gangsters met after that. The actors and playwrights moved on to the Working Girls' Home, where the front door was locked, but where a side door on Christopher Street still led into a room where Luke O'Connor served Old Fashioneds and the best beer and stout he could buy from the wildcat breweries.

But Greenwich Village had become more than a physical locale; it was a state of mind, pleasure-loving, partying, sexually free. All across the country young people absorbed and interpreted this state of mind, the girls by bobbing their hair, smoking, giving up corsets, taking lovers; apartments were furnished like the studios of Village artists and writers, tearooms sprang up, dim basement restaurants recreated the bohemian atmosphere in Seattle and Duluth, Peoria and Minneapolis, and Prohibition made liquor glamorous. Flaming youth was flinging off the restraints of prewar America, but for Edna and Norma, living from hand to mouth on Waverly Place, there were no restraints to be flung off, for they had been brought up in an atmosphere of freedom of behavior that made them in a sense Greenwich Villagers by right of birth. Nevertheless the people Edna met in the Village—especially political radicals like Floyd Dell, Max Eastman and Jack Reed—helped to confirm and broaden ideas of social justice she had learned from Shelley, Wordsworth and Milton. They also put her in touch with all that was new and exciting in the arts, for her friends and acquaintances during the next seven years read like a roll call of American artistic achievement: Theodore Dreiser, Upton Sinclair, Paul Robeson, Hart Crane, Jane Heap, Djuna Barnes, Sherwood Anderson, Malcolm Cowley, Lawrence Langner, Susan Glaspell, Eugene O'Neill.

Late in the winter of 1917 Edna applied for a job with the Provincetown Players, where an ingenue lead was wanted for a play called *The Angel Intrudes*. The Provincetown was one of several little theater groups in the Village, all of them recently formed and expressing whatever was fresh, radical, challenging and noncommercial in dramatic art. Born in Cape Cod, the Provincetown was now in its second New York season, in a remodeled private dwelling on Macdougal Street where the dining room was the stage and the audience sat in the drawing room. The entire theater was fifteen feet wide and forty-four feet deep, with about a hundred seats; in spirit it was an amateur's theater in the finest sense, for those who worked in it did so purely for love; they made their livings as painters, novelists, journalists, teachers, sculptors, and the theater was their avocation, their recreation. But their theatrical instincts were sound, for they discovered a "shy, dark boy" with a trunkful of plays; his name was Eugene O'Neill, and the Provincetowners helped to launch him.

If they had no money to offer, they had already begun to attract the uptown critics, and a job with the Provincetown Playhouse must have seemed a promising start to Edna. She was auditioned by Floyd Dell, the author of *The Angel Intrudes*, a tall, slim, very aesthetic young man of thirty, recently divorced, living in the Village and working for *The Masses*, a radical magazine. He decided the "slender little girl with red-gold hair" was perfect for his play; it was only after the audition that he realized Edna Millay, the name she had given, was "the author of that beautiful and astonishing poem 'Renascence.' "

Rehearsals went well, Dell recalled. "When the play opened, she performed her part beautifully. My other play, *Sweet-and-Twenty*, was to be on the next bill, and there was a good part for her if she wanted it. I asked her if she would like to read the script. She said she would rather hear me read it. So I made a date with her for that purpose. I had sold something to 'Vanity Fair' and been paid for it, so I could afford to splurge a little. I took her to dinner in the basement of the Brevoort, a place much frequented by the intelligentsia, and then we went to her room." The night before Dell had dreamed he kissed Edna Millay; he had never consciously wanted to, he said, because she "seemed remote . . . an enchanting fairy-tale princess." But once they were alone in her cold little room they were in each other's arms in short order. She told him she had had a similar dream; that night they became lovers.

Apparently Floyd Dell was her first lover; there had been a number of admirers during the Barnard semester several years before, especially the Nicaraguan poet Salomon de la Selva, but for one reason or another, perhaps only the lack of privacy, Edna Millay's legendary romantic career began on Waverly Place. If Floyd Dell was her first lover, he was not the last. Rather it was as if a new form of escape from the bonds of childhood had been made available to her, a new way of battering at the too-close walls of the shelter she both dreaded and required; indeed Edmund Wilson saw as much in "Renascence," where he found the storm a metaphor for sexual love, and it was the storm, remember, that signaled the poet's release from her grave. Having discovered in Floyd

Dell's arms the freedom that was sexual love, she was to run from lover to lover, from freedom to enclosure to freedom, all the while proclaiming in the poetry of those early years a woman's right to love as willfully and capriciously as a man:

> And if I loved you Wednesday,
> Well, what is that to you?
> I do not love you Thursday—
> So much is true.

This was the philosophy she declared in print, one that sounded like paganism, like the cry of the hedonist in hot pursuit of pleasure. But according to some of the men who were her lovers or observant friends —Dell, Ficke, Wilson—it seems she found little pleasure in the swift succession of lovers that began with Floyd Dell. "Her real sexual experience, which came rather late . . . always leaves her alone again, alone and afraid of death. Withdrawal is her natural condition," Edmund Wilson felt.

For a while at least Floyd Dell was the lover she returned to in between other loves. "There began for us a romance that was haunted by her sense of the inevitable impermanence of love. She refused to marry me. We parted several times. She fell in love with other men and then came back to me. We always forgave each other the hurts of love." Whenever Dell spoke of marriage, she would take the extreme feminist position that it was an attempt to confine women to their traditional feminine role of cooking and baby tending; she would have no part of it. And when Dell, who was in the midst of psychoanalysis, tried to lure her into undergoing analysis herself with a view to curing her "sapphic tendencies"—by which he meant her succession of frantic and compulsive love affairs—she resolutely refused. For any attempt to invade the innermost chambers of the mind, whether by Dell or by a psychiatrist, must have seemed a terrifying prospect, and her defense against it, against anyone's coming too close or looking too deeply, was withdrawal. According to a poem Arthur Ficke wrote, she said of Dell that his "infinite curiosity" pried too deeply into the "darkness" that was hers alone—that there were times when she had found herself wishing she had died before she let Floyd Dell believe she was "his own."

"I am nobody's own"—this is the theme that occurs throughout her early poetry, the ringing declaration of feminist independence. Yet, as Floyd Dell claimed, it was also a cry of rebellion against sex and being a woman. Only alone and with her poetry was she safe from the dangerous claims that might lead to marriage, to cooking and baby tending and the loss of Vincent. For if she married and assumed the role of a woman —no matter how emancipated a woman—Vincent the boy poet, her mother's longed-for son, would surely disappear; this at any rate is what she must have felt, for she saw many marriages in Greenwich Village that included talented women free to exercise their talents. She spoke of poetry as her "soul's chastity," implying not that poetry meant giving up sex, only giving up the womanly role in sex. The woman's role was doubly dangerous because of her childhood realization that to love a man long enough meant to expose herself to the pain of his leaving, as her father had left. But if she could not allow herself to play the woman's part she could play the boy's—could run from one love to the next as boys do, never giving her heart for long and always more committed to poetry than to her lover.

Her subsequent love affairs took much the same pattern as the affair with Dell—a quick and passionate onset was followed by a period of idyllic companionship, followed by bickering and quarreling and an increasingly frantic fear on Edna's part that somehow she was being hemmed in and pinned down. And this in turn would be followed by a roving eye and a new love even before the old one had decently cooled off. "It nearly kills her but she can't help it," said a friend of Edmund Wilson.

Elizabeth Haight, her Vassar professor of Latin, paid a visit to Waverly Place and "asked if, living dangerously, she might not be undermining her genius. Flaming youth answered: 'I always know just what I am doing, Elizabeth; I take no risks. Don't worry about me.'" But Miss Haight did worry, and perhaps the poet worried too: "My candle burns at both ends;/ It will not last the night;/ But ah, my foes, and oh, my friends—/ It gives a lovely light!" she wrote in a quatrain that was to become the rallying cry of spiritual Villagers throughout the country. It does not sound like the voice of a prudent young woman who knows exactly what she is doing, but rather like one who wonders how much of her will be burned out by morning.

From at least one of her lovers she never wholly succeeded in escaping. She wrote years later to Arthur Davison Ficke: "I shall love you till the day I die.— Though I shan't always be thinking about it, thank God." They had been corresponding for five years, ever since his first admiring letter when he read "Renascence." In February of 1918 Major Ficke came to New York, on his way to France with dispatches for General Pershing, and he stopped long enough to visit his old friend from Davenport, Iowa, Floyd Dell. In his mid-thirties now, Ficke was blue-eyed, with thick, wavy hair and an elegant, aristocrat's face; done up in Sam Browne belt and puttees, he must have been a ravishing figure of a man. Dell brought him to Waverly Place to meet the girl he was in love with, the girl everyone in the Village was speaking of that year as "the beautiful young actress at the Provincetown"—by happy coincidence the same talented poet Ficke had been writing to and advising, and who, judging from the tone of her letters, had been half in love with him all along. Norma was there, and so was her beau, the painter Charles Ellis. The five sat on the floor to eat a delicatessen supper; a great pickle was passed from hand to hand, and Norma said it reminded her of a loving cup, whereupon Ficke took up a pencil to compose a sonnet on that theme, writing it out on the top of a pastry box. The sonnet suggests, as some of his other poems to Edna suggest, that he felt she was challenging him to fall in love; it speaks of her hair as a "little cage of lies," bringing to mind Max Eastman's impression that there was something arch, affected, a little actressy in Edna Millay. But he saw as well "a promise in your eyes," and that promise was utterly real and heartfelt. She had fallen deeply, painfully, irrevocably in love, and during the next two nights and a day—all the time Ficke had before he left for France—they were inseparable.

As soon as he had gone she tried to drown herself in the "golden vessel of great song," as if to cling to the lover by recreating him in sonnets. These sonnets celebrate several of the themes that recur in her serious love poetry—that love is almost too painful, too powerful, that she longs to be free of it and in control of herself once more: ". . . that I would be/ From your too poignant lovelinesses free!"; that for no man will she give up her "soul's chastity," the writing of poetry; that all love dies and so will this.

"In me no lenten wicks watch out the night," she says. "I am the booth where Folly holds her fair." Like some of the short and flippant poems that were to appear in *A Few Figs from Thistles*, the outburst of sonnets to and about Arthur Ficke is in a voice poetry-writing women had never used before, a pagan voice with the pagan acceptance that since there is no tomorrow, we must make the best use of today, for it is surely better to be exhausted and finally devoured by love than to live and grow old intact, unused. Reckless and gallant and lonely, these accents were just what emancipated and would-be emancipated young people in America directly after the war were longing to hear.

But for Edna Millay, many of the poems that later appeared in *Second April* were an attempt to write her way out of a devastating experience. "My time, in those awful days after you went away to France, was a mist of thinking about you & writing sonnets to you.— You were spending your time in the same way, I believe." He was; Arthur Ficke was composing the sonnet sequence *Beauty in Exile*, polished, highly literary, and far less intense in feeling than what Edna was writing to him at the time. Perhaps he had already realized he was one who could not live with her passionate intensities.

By July of 1918 the poet had finally succeeded in bringing her entire family to a Village flat at 25 Charlton Street that was roomy enough for four, her mother coming down from Maine and Kathleen from Vassar. Now all the Millays became involved in the Provincetown Playhouse, the girls onstage and Cora Millay helping with costumes. Lawrence Langner remembered their household as something of a Village institution where each evening "swarms of young painters, writers and poets made pilgrimages to their apartment on the top floor," and the young ladies were chaperoned by their mother from Maine, "a bright little birdlike lady." But daytimes were reserved for writing, and Edna locked herself in her room every day with several packs of cigarettes, to work on sonnets.

She was also writing stories and sketches for a popular magazine under the pseudonym of Nancy Boyd; her sisters and mother often helped on the Nancy Boyd pieces, which the poet never took very seriously, considering them chiefly potboilers. And she had embarked on a one-act play, *Aria da Capo*, that perfectly expressed the sense of bitterness and loss, the cynicism, the belief that nothing will ever be any better because history is a treadmill, characteristic of idealistic young people immediately after the war. It was produced by the Provincetown in December of 1919, with Edna directing and Norma in the female lead. *Aria da Capo* proved to be one of the most exciting theatrical events of the season. "I find myself suddenly famous," she wrote to a friend, " . . . and in this unlooked-for excitement I find a stimulant that almost takes the place of booze! . . . There is scarcely a little theatre or literary club in the country . . . that isn't going to produce it or give a reading of it."

It was indeed a brilliant play, instantly successful when it first appeared and still in demand by little theater groups for its biting and outrageous wit. With *Aria da Capo* and with the publication of her first sonnet sequence in the magazine *Reedy's Mirror*, Edna became one of the outstanding Village figures. Surrounded by her family—they moved toward the end of the year to a larger flat on West Nineteenth Street —warmed by the recognition she had worked for so long and earning a small but steady income from the Nancy Boyd stories, she was in the first flush of power and hard-bought success. Yet in the two years since she had come to the Village, working by day at what she was to call the hardest work in the world, the writing of poetry, and by night feverishly pursued and pursuing, she had been burning as dangerously as her candle. Delicately built as she was, with a lifelong habit of eating random meals, drinking too much, sleeping too little, she was piling physical pressures on top of the serious emotional pressures of her love affairs, each of them as deeply felt for a while as if it were to last forever, and ending in the passionate need to escape so that it could not possibly last forever. Jessie Rittenhouse, who remembered Edna from her first visit to New York in 1913, was saddened by the change in her appearance. A party was given by Edna's friend Salomon de la Selva, in honor of a Peruvian poet. "Our youthful host was one of the many admirers of

Edna, who received more attention than the guest of honor. She was at that time . . . with the Provincetown Players and had to leave the dinner early. One could see upon her face the marks of New York and its struggle, also its sophistication, but these made her the more interesting. Rarely does one see a face more mobile and expressive. Even when she was gayest there seemed to be a certain element of tragedy looking out of her eyes."

Early in 1920 Edna met a promising young writer, Edmund Wilson, who worked for *Vanity Fair.* She was then at the height of her Village reputation, publishing steadily both the poems and the Nancy Boyd stories, with three books of poetry ready for publication. Wilson had been attracted to her even before they met—he had read a sonnet of hers that enchanted him, then seen *Aria da Capo,* and "I was thrilled and troubled by this little play: it was the first time I had felt Edna's peculiar power." They met at a party after the theater, to which Edna wore "some bright batik, and her face lit up with a flush that seemed to burn also in the bronze reflections of her not yet bobbed reddish hair. She was one of those women whose features are not perfect and who in their moments of dimness may not seem even pretty, but who, excited by the blood or the spirit, become almost supernaturally beautiful." Admiring her poetry, intrigued by her romantic reputation, Wilson fell "irretrievably" in love with her, as he told Max Eastman later on, adding that it was a common experience, an "almost inevitable consequence of knowing her."

Yet he also found "she was sometimes rather a strain, because nothing could be casual for her; I do not think I ever saw her relaxed, even when she was tired or ill. I used to suppose that this . . . must be due to my own anxieties, but I later discovered that others who had never been emotionally involved with her were affected in the same way. . . . She was not at all a social person. She did not like gossip; did not like to talk current events; did not like to talk personalities. It was partly that she was really noble, partly that she was rather neurotic. . . . She was either like the most condensed literature or music, the demands of which one cannot meet protractedly, or like a serious nervous case—though this side of her was more in evidence later—whom one feels that one cannot soothe."

It was this very intensity Wilson found so magnetic. Coming to call for her in a cab at the house on Nineteenth Street, he saw the children who played in the street run up and crowd round her, not only because she gave them pennies or took them for taxi rides, but also because she simply had that effect on people. "There was something of awful drama about everything one did with Edna." And he also noticed her moods of colorless withdrawal. Years later she was to write to a friend: "It is painfully difficult for me to write a letter . . . the real anguish, the knowing that I must write a letter, and that I want seriously to communicate with somebody; and that I cannot bear even to think of writing a letter." For though she drew people to her, was surrounded in the Village by friends, admirers, adoring children and importunate lovers among whom Wilson felt himself to be only one of a vast swarm, the old claustrophobia had begun to close in, perhaps even more threateningly than in childhood. Village life was dense and intimate; everyone knew everyone else, borrowed ideas and money, sought to impress or hero-worship. Literary people seemed to her like leeches in the druggist's jar, dependent for nourishment on blood, reduced to the desperate extremity of preying on one another—and "I'm the druggist when he puts his hand in the jar!"

Wilson was able to do Edna Millay a considerable service by getting her work published in *Vanity Fair*, a far more prestigious magazine than those that had published her until then, and one that could pay well. Although she liked him, respected and admired him and enjoyed their discussions of poetry, she never returned the love that only increased with her elusiveness. There were too many others competing for her attention, Wilson felt; and the city itself had begun to frighten her, the tall buildings seeming to close in about her so that she was even afraid to cross the street alone. Surrounded as she was by people, they always seemed to be the wrong people; Arthur Ficke had never kept his promise of returning to the Village. "It is a pity you are so far away," she wrote. "There are so few people in the world to whom one has a word to say, Arthur!" And in April she wrote to a friend: "I'm having a sort of nervous break-down."

Overwork, inadequate food and her everlasting worries about money must also have contributed to this emotional crisis, whatever its exact nature, and she was becoming increasingly aware that the kind of life she was leading could not go on forever. Pursued by men like Wilson who begged her to marry, she was afraid to marry; importuned by friends and lovers, she felt painfully alone. Not yet thirty years old, she was preoccupied with a fear of death. She had begun exploring her feelings about death while still in college, in one of her early poems, "The Suicide." Yet Wilson felt "it was not the deaths of the body that she suffered: it was the deaths of all those human relations—it was her rejection, day after day and year after year, of all the natural bonds and understandings which make up the greater part of human life—comfort, security, children, the protection and devotion of a husband, even simple comradeship and affection—so that she was still . . . an outlaw living from hand to mouth, always poor and often ill, bedevilled day and night by all the persons she no longer had the energy to excite to her own pitch of incandescence."

In the summer of 1920 Wilson visited the Millay family at a cottage near Cape Cod that had been lent them by George Cram Cook, who organized the Provincetown. Here he finally got up the courage to propose to Edna Millay. He had a private income and she was sick of being hungry all the time; he thought he heard her say under her breath that marrying him might be the solution. But apparently he was not the solution, nor were any of the other would-be husbands. She decided instead to accept an offer made by *Vanity Fair*, and go to Europe. She would leave the Village, cut free of all emotional ties, even leave her family behind and make a fresh start by spending a year or so abroad.

Everyone went to Europe, and especially to Paris, after the war—Fitzgerald, Hemingway, Sherwood Anderson—for living was cheap there, it was possible to do, think, write, paint as one pleased, and the Continent was a living museum. *Vanity Fair* had arranged for Edna to continue writing the Nancy Boyd pieces from abroad, on a regular salary that would take care of expenses. She would also have the earnings of her second book, *A Few Figs from Thistles*, which came out that year, the slimmest of volumes and a stunning success. Vincent Sheean was to write of it:

The "First Fig" . . . became a sort of motto or epigraph for the whole decade that followed: it is the quatrain which begins "My candle burns at both ends." These lines were caught up and quoted, or more usually misquoted, by every jejune hedonist of the rebellious era, every girl or boy who wanted to experiment with the recently discovered benefits of alcohol, sexual experience, or simply late hours and wild talk. Everyone who was alive during the 1920's must remember how rapidly all customs, manners, and ideas in American life altered during that decade of careless wealth, crumbling standards, and deliberate revolt against society. . . . Edna's four flippant lines in 1920 were the *Marseillaise* of that particular revolution.

A third book, *Second April*, although written during much the same period, was delayed for some time, and it was not yet clear whether Mitchell Kennerley, the publisher, was honestly in trouble or dishonestly evading her. Shortly before she left for Europe, Wilson paid Edna Millay several visits, resigned to having lost her yet stubbornly hopeful. "I remarked that her ex-admirers ought to organize an alumni association—to which she answered with promptness and point: 'On en parle toujours, mais on ne le fait jamais.' " "They talk about it all the time, but they never do it"; they had been practicing French in preparation for her trip.

Arthur Ficke was with Bynner in the Orient; in the fall of 1920 Edna wrote to him, as solemn and sad as an exiled queen: "I love you too, my dear, and shall always, just as I did the first moment I saw you. . . . It is very dear to me to know that you love me, Arthur—just as I love you, quietly, quietly, yet with all your strength, & with a strength greater than your own that drives you towards me like a wind." Nevertheless, he was on the other side of the world when he could have been with her; she told Bynner she missed them both, for they had left a big hole in her world that she walked around warily by day and was afraid of falling into at night. Yet she told her mother late in December that she was going abroad "as a free woman, a business woman, & because I want to travel," not because of any love affair past or present; she had had bronchitis, she added, and another small nervous breakdown. In January of 1921 she was aboard the steamer *Rochambeau* bound for France, having had a week-long stomachache from pure excitement.

Edna walked all over Paris, bought some beautiful French clothes only slightly secondhand, visited the cafés where all the expatriate writers and artists were, and went out dancing to jazz bands; but she was also working long hours in her little room on the Left Bank with Norma's picture in front of her, as she told her "Dearest Darling Baby Sister 'Loved Hunk.' " She had come abroad with the intention of writing no poetry, so that when she went home again she could return to it with fresh perceptions; she was to write the prose pieces for *Vanity Fair*, and she had promised Vassar College a play for its fiftieth anniversary. It was this play, *The Lamp and the Bell*, that she worked on the first two or three months of her stay in Paris.

By summertime, *Second April* was finally published in the States, where it won loud and nearly unqualified applause from the literary critics. For the young, it confirmed and broadened the Millay legend; the love sonnets to Ficke were an extension of the madcap rebel who created *Figs*, but they were balanced in *Second April* by the serious, contemplative pieces: "Ode to Silence," "Memorial to D.C." She was spoken of now as one of America's finest lyric poets, perhaps even more glamorous to the general public for having revealed a darker side, especially the gnawing fears about death. There were many death poems in the new volume, one of the most noteworthy being "The Poet and his Book," in which the poet implores her readers to keep her alive by reading her work:

> Stranger, pause and look;
> From the dust of ages
> Lift this little book,
> Turn the tattered pages,
> Read me, do not let me die!
> Search the fading letters, finding
> Steadfast in the broken binding
> All that once was I!

If death is the ultimate separation—the utter loneliness of separation that was her overriding fear—perhaps it could be conquered through poetry, through the intimacy between the poet and her readers, who could hold her in their hands and give her life even after she had died. She pictures them as homely people—boys and girls whispering in the hedges, farmers at their raking, shepherds on the hills—and cries out to one and all: "Read me, margin me with scrawling,/ Do not let me die!" And in the particular turn of phrase she has chosen, "margin me with scrawling," is the echo of an almost physical intimacy, as if it were her very body she offers up to be scrawled upon. *Second April* is sad, reflective, bittersweet; unlike Edna Millay's two previous volumes it is clearly the work of an adult and maturing poet rather than an astonishing girl. Other events in her life, personal as well as literary, took place in the States that year: three plays were published separately, *The Lamp and the Bell*, *Aria da Capo*, and a one-acter written when she was at Vassar, *Two Slatterns and a King*, and there were new editions of *Figs*. Norma and Charlie Ellis were married at last and Kathleen had married too, a playwright named Howard Irving Young.

"Now I have two bruvvers! And two such nice bruvvers. I couldn't have picked me nicer ones. . . . Well, both my little sisters are young married women, and me, I am just about three months from being an old maid." She had told Edmund Wilson before she left for France, "I'll be thirty in a minute." Even the excitement of Europe could not keep her mind from the dilemma that had tormented her in New York—she was alone, she was living from hand to mouth, emotionally speaking, she longed to marry yet marriage seemed impossible. And during those first months in Paris this debate over how to be at once a boy named Vincent —independent, heart-free, a poet—and a woman, protected and secure in a husband's love, took the form of *The Lamp and the Bell*, the play she had promised to Vassar.

The play is precisely that—a debate, a tug-of-war whose two sides are taken by the two chief characters, both of them aspects of Edna Millay. In form the play is Elizabethan, a pageant with many characters and brilliant costumes and musical interludes, eminently suited to production outdoors. Its theme is friendship and loyalty between women; its plot has to do with a pair of girls who are adopted sisters and friends, one a princess, a proud, chaste, self-reliant Amazon named Beatrice, while the other, Bianca, is gentle, biddable, a clinging vine. Both fall in love with the same man and the gentle Bianca marries him; a series of misunderstandings keeps the two friends apart until Beatrice accidentally kills Bianca's husband while hunting. Bianca dies of sorrow, forgiving her friend and sister on her deathbed, where the two are reunited, and Beatrice returns to rule her kingdom and to raise Bianca's orphan children as her own.

Throughout the play the two girls are repeatedly described as opposites: the one who is Vincent rides her horse astride, the other sits "sidewise aslant your pretty palfrey." To Beatrice-Vincent her lover declares that she rides like a boy, whistles like a boy, and is the only girl he ever saw who played at jousting without holding her sword like a needle: "Which of us, think you, when we are married, will be king?"

And this same Mario, who loves both girls but marries Bianca, finds it wonderful that gentle Bianca should cling to him, should "let me shelter her." Beatrice, he realizes, stands alone; she needs no shelter. It seems inevitable that such a play should also express the muted homosexual elements in Edna Millay's character, bred of her sexual ambiguity and her fear of being a woman. Beatrice's stepmother says, "young girls should not be left alone too much together. They grow too much attached. They grow to feel they cannot breathe apart. It is unhealthy." When the king, Beatrice's father, dies on Bianca's wedding day, Bianca refuses to leave Beatrice alone that night—much as she loves her new husband, her greater loyalty is to Beatrice.

And when a villainous duke, in love with Beatrice, learns Bianca is dying of heartbreak and calling Beatrice's name, he will only let her go to her beloved friend if she will go to bed with him when she returns. And she agrees, for the bond between the two girls is more important than the relationship between man and woman. Perhaps the thread of homosexuality that runs through *The Lamp and the Bell* is less significant than the more obvious theme of debate between two opposite parts of the self, just as it was, in Edna Millay's character, a subordinate theme, apparently well suppressed and well controlled; yet in view of her long and passionate history as a *femme galante* it cannot be ignored. Like Don Juan's, like Casanova's, Edna's compulsive love affairs were to some degree an indication of doubts as to which sex she belonged to, as well as an attempt to bury amid frantic erotic activity the haunting fear that by belonging to any one man she would surrender the man within herself.

Through an act of creative will, then, she solved the problem on paper, killing off Bianca and leaving Beatrice in possession of her freedom, her kingdom, her virginity and the orphan children; if the solution was satisfying to the artist, it left the woman as lonely as before.

One possible remedy for the deepening sense of loneliness was an extravagant plan she had formed to bring her mother to Europe. Edna's letters home, almost from the very beginning of her stay abroad, had been filled with yearning for her family and especially for her mother. That spring she had written to Cora: "I am all the time talking about you. I am like the Ancient Mariner, who had a tale in his heart he must unfold to all. I am always button-holing somebody and saying, 'Someday you must meet my mother.' Mother, do you know, almost all people love their mothers, but I have never met anybody in my life, I think, who loved his mother as much as I love you. . . . If I didn't keep calling you mother, anybody reading this would think I was writing to my sweetheart. And he would be quite right." Since she thought of herself as her mother's longed-for son perhaps it is not surprising that Edna should have compounded confusion by seeing herself as the gallant and adoring son, Marchbanks to Candida, for when she spoke of bringing her mother to Europe she said ". . . and then, my Best Beloved, you and I will just have ourselves a little honey-moon." And, "Do you suppose, when you & I are dead, dear, they will publish the *Love Letters of Edna St. Vincent Millay & her Mother?*"

By autumn of 1921 she had been away from her mother for nine months, longer, she said, than they had ever been separated before, and she fully intended now to scrape up enough money so that Cora could "play around Europe with Vincent a little. . . . I wrote you such a booful letter about this, mothie," she said, referring to her first mention of the plan in a letter that was lost.

Meanwhile Arthur Ficke and Bynner had returned to the States. Edna went from Paris to the north of France, to Hertfordshire in England, to Italy, then on to a brief excursion in Albania, from where she wrote to Ficke: "But when I start to write you all I can think of to say to you is—Why aren't you here?" If her letters home were filmed over by the continuing loneliness, to which a rising note of desperation was added—she had begun to suffer physically from some vague stomach complaint, from the wretched food and from too little money—the letters to Ficke expressed even more than low spirits and the sense of exile: "Arthur, it is wicked & useless,—all these months & months apart from you, all these years with only a glimpse of you in the face of everybody.— I tell you I must see you again."

From Rome she went to Vienna, the cheapest capital in Europe; she was broke but Ficke was not to breathe a word of this to anyone. "It seems a long time," she told him, "since I have seen anybody I cared anything about." Some ten days later she had a letter from Ficke, mentioning a letter from Bynner that she never received; it was the opening scene of a comedy of errors, with a cast of three and marriage for its theme. Bynner had asked Edna to marry him in the letter she never got. "Do you really want me to marry you?" Edna wrote back. "Because if you really want me to, I will." But she added that "all this may not be true at all." He wrote to assure her it was certainly true, he had indeed proposed.

She wrote again: if he had changed his mind, or if he was drunk when he asked her to marry him, he was to write and tell her so and she would understand and they would be friends once more. Otherwise, she was glad he was planning on coming to Europe, so they could talk things over. And of course he was right about her loving Arthur. She had always loved Arthur, had never concealed it, but was it not possible to love several people? "For surely, one must be either undiscerning, or frightened, to love only one person, when the world is so full of gracious and noble spirits." Even if Arthur were not still married she would not wish to marry him, she said, perhaps because she had felt all along that Arthur, like her father, was beyond her grasp, that he was one man who would always elude her. For she absorbed with curious calm the news that he was finally free to marry, having divorced his first wife, and she remained strangely calm when she learned he had fallen in love with someone else: "My dear, I knew all about the girl in New York," long before he told her; knew nothing precisely but suspected everything from the tone of his letters. It didn't matter how often he fell in love, nor with whom, she assured him, "nor how sweetly. All that has nothing to do with what we are to each other."

Edna had written to her mother to postpone the trip to Europe because of the likelihood of her marrying Bynner; now the realization that her mother had been dazed and disappointed hit her hard. She cabled home as much money as she could spare from an advance on a projected novel, and urged her mother to come as soon as she could— for anyone could get married, as she explained to Norma, but not everyone, after the life they had had, could bring her mother to Europe. Meanwhile three-cornered discussion of the possible marriage continued. Both Ficke and Bynner were convinced it was ill-advised, for Bynner believed Edna loved Ficke better than himself, and Ficke, who probably believed it too, said they were too confused to marry for a while. Edna told Arthur it was all a "hicktown meller-drammer," full of outworn jokes; and after that she was able to assure him the marriage was off in any case, for Bynner had jilted her.

Mrs. Millay got to Europe at last, and for a while they tramped all over Paris, to cafés and all-night jazz parties, to cathedrals, museums and churches, doing twelve miles in an afternoon and "having the most beautiful time together," according to a letter to Norma. But that summer they went to England, where Mrs. Millay tried to do something about her daughter's health. Edna had been suffering for months now from some kind of intestinal complaint whose precise nature is never made clear; apparently it involved her "old chronically petrified intestine," as she told "Dear lickle Normie," and she said she came within an ace of having peritonitis. Even the novel she was planning to write suggests a preoccupation with her health, for the book was to be called "Hardigut," and the gut was the seat of her trouble; the novel was supposed to describe a mythical country in which food, eating and all digestive processes were private and shame-ridden, and the intention was to satirize American taboos about sex, in the style of Nancy Boyd.

Whatever was wrong with Edna's gastrointestinal tract, it was almost certainly psychosomatic in origin; after the tension of Greenwich Village, the two "nervous breakdowns," the homesickness of Europe added to her everlasting poverty and the cheap, repellent food, such an out-come is hardly surprising. In the quiet Dorset countryside Cora Millay set about trying to doctor her with simple, wholesome food and plenty of rest. Edna was lodged in a little whitewashed hut in the midst of a newly mowed field, in order to be free of all distractions and disturbances for most of the day, and here her mother brought good plain food of her own making, bread pudding, baked potatoes and plenty of cream and milk—"anything to get the cream into me." She worked and rested and exercised, took long walks with her mother and went horseback riding with a neighbor, none other than Gladys Brown, the girl Arthur Ficke had fallen in love with in New York and who now lived just down the road from the Millays. Edna claimed to like her very much, but she also wrote to Arthur, "Oh, how ridiculous everything is!"

In the solitude of the little thatched hut she worked on "Hardigut," but as the weeks went by she worked less and less; she told Ficke she was so sick she could just about drag herself around. And in early 1923, far sooner than they had originally planned, mother and daughter re-turned to the States. Cora Millay went on to Maine, and Edna settled into a small apartment on Waverly Place in the same building as Tess Root, a friend she had met abroad. Here Franklin P. Adams, the colum-nist FPA, visited one day and was pained to see her strange fragility and a certain high, bright gaiety he said he had never seen in anyone else.

Months went by when she was so tired and sick she never put pen to paper, and she was finally forced to abandon all hope of writing "Hardigut." But while she was still abroad Edna had written a few pieces of poetry, including the long poem "The Ballad of the Harp-Weaver." For this, for eight new sonnets and an enlarged edition of *Figs*, she was awarded the 1922 Pulitzer Prize for poetry, the first woman so honored. The prize made her so immensely proud and happy she resolved to keep the thousand dollars of prize money intact, and to open a bank account with it; she would not break into it, she said, for god or hero, not even for her mother, although the goal of paying her mother's bills and expenses was uppermost in her mind. The Pulitzer Prize was proof of solid critical acclaim; combined with the popular acclaim she had en-joyed ever since the first publication of *Figs*, it put Edna Millay in a singular position. To most young people, according to *Time* magazine, "poetry meant simply Edna St. Vincent Millay," and she was read, quoted, copied, imitated, satirized, her comings and goings reported in gossip columns like a movie star's. Yet she was also recognized as one of the most significant of American poets by those who took poetry seriously; in England, Thomas Hardy said there were two great things to be found in the States, one of them the new American architecture and the other the poetry of Edna St. Vincent Millay. Except for Byron, it is hard to think of another poet with a public as large, as diverse and as personally adoring as hers.

In that same year, 1922, the experimental literary monthly *The Dial* published a long poem by T. S. Eliot called "The Waste Land." When he was first published in America seven years earlier, in *Poetry* magazine, the critic Louis Untermeyer called Eliot's "Love Song of J. Alfred Prufrock" "the first piece of the English language that utterly stumped me. . . . The muse in a psychopathic ward drinking the stale dregs of revolt." He had read it, he said, to a group of friends, no one of whom could keep a straight face except for a psychoanalyst, who declared, "I think a lot could be done for him." Untermeyer's scorn and distaste for Eliot's early poem was almost universally echoed; dense, intricate, obscure, mirroring the fragmentation of modern life and almost as experimental in technique as James Joyce's *Ulysses*, the work of Eliot was addressed to the intellectual few. But in 1922 he found a larger and more sympathetic audience, and Untermeyer became an ardent admirer. Eliot was to become by the end of the 1920s the single most influential voice in American poetry and criticism. And it was this "new criticism" that came to judge the work of Edna Millay with an increasingly jaundiced eye; she was a lyric poet who spoke, and continued to speak, simply, straightforwardly, to the boys and girls, the housewives and farmers and plain people addressed in "The Poet and his Book." Her themes were always herself and her feelings; her techniques—although they became increasingly more sophisticated and supple—were to remain, like her chosen forms, traditional. The sonnet was her most beloved métier, yet in 1912 the sonnet had been considered all but dead. She wrote more and better sonnets; she was to publish in the 1930s an entire book of sonnets. And in 1922, when "The Waste Land" was a cloud no bigger than a man's hand upon the literary horizon, American poetry had begun almost imperceptibly to head off in the opposite direction from Edna Millay. She never made a serious effort to catch up with it.

Some years before, when Norma and Edna lived on Waverly Place, Floyd Dell had taken them one evening to visit his colleague on *The Masses* Max Eastman, and Eastman's friend, Eugen Jan Boissevain. As Dell remembered it, the evening was a stiff, dull failure, and Eastman had much the same impression; the Millay girls seemed to him "a little schoolgirlish, almost simpering." It was something both Dell and Edmund Wilson had noticed in connection with Edna, that she seemed so often to be playacting, being now the Greenwich Village gamine, now a New England schoolteacher, now a Vassar bluestocking, like some perpetual adolescent forever trying out new roles. Eastman had seen Edna from time to time in the intervening years. Eugen Boissevain, a prosperous businessman, had not seen her since that night in Greenwich Village, but they met again in 1923 at another party.

Tess Root, the friend Edna met in Europe, had been wheedling her for weeks to go to Croton-on-Hudson for a weekend in the country. Sick and dispirited, she refused; then one day in April she gave in. Many old-time Villagers had country places at Croton, and it was to a house party in a Village-style household belonging to Dudley Malone and Doris Stevens that they went. Floyd Dell was there with his wife, Arthur Ficke and Gladys came, and so did Boissevain. He was a tall, handsome, ruggedly built Dutchman whose boisterous laughter seemed to fill the rooms with the joy of living. Athletic, powerful, reckless as a pirate, he was also a singularly warmhearted man in whom strength was coupled with extraordinary sensitivity.

According to one biographer's account, Ficke was the life of the party. The group had been discussing a current Broadway hit about a country boy who comes to the big city, where he is pounced upon by city slickers and ultimately ruined; Ficke proposed a charade that would reverse the situation, an innocent city couple spending a weekend among corrupt country people who pull them down to ruin. Dell and Edna Millay had written many impromptu scenes for the Provincetown, and with Ficke's

help they sketched out a playlet along the lines he proposed, with Edna
and Boissevain as the city innocents. Gladys Brown was a homosexual
boy intent on seducing Eugen, Ficke directed his attentions to Edna,
Floyd Dell became a con man. And the city couple, Floyd Dell said,
"acted their parts wonderfully, so remarkably, indeed, that it was apparent to us all that it wasn't just acting. We were having the unusual
privilege of seeing a man and a girl fall in love with each other violently
and in public, and telling each other so, and doing it very beautifully."
When the party was over, when the high bright gaiety was dimmed by
exhaustion, Eugen must have realized how sick Edna really was, for he
took her to his home nearby, called the doctor and "nursed her like a
mother. His care at this time perhaps saved her life," Dell believed, "for
her condition, as shown by a subsequent operation, was very serious."
Eugen called in specialist after specialist until the illness was traced to
its source, meanwhile exercising such strict supervision over her daily
activities that she worked no more than an hour each day and saw no
one at all but the doctors and Eugen.

About a month later Edna wrote to her mother in Maine:

. . . you will like him very much when you know him, which will be soon. And
it is important that you should like him,—because I love him very much, & am
going to marry him.

There!!!!

Will you forgive me?— My mind has been pretty much taken up with all
this, & I have neglected my mummie. . . . Anyhow, we are coming up to Maine
to visit you. . . . We are going to motor up. Gene has a beautiful big Mercer,
—at least he had, but now he has given it to me, so I have one. Won't that be
fun?

If she was certain Cora Millay would "like him very much," she had
more reason for it than the natural bias of a woman in love, for Eugen
Boissevain was immensely attractive, to men as well as to women, even
to Edna's swarm of former lovers. Yet he bore little resemblance to the
men she had fallen in and out of love with before, most of them writers,
musicians, actors, artists or intellectuals of one sort or another. Eugen
was by profession a businessman and by temperament an adventurer, a
man of action, impulsive and spontaneous, who never chose his words

but said whatever popped into his head; he had none of the intellectual's need to hold the center of the stage or the artist's craving for applause; quite the contrary, Eugen Boissevain loved having talented people around him and was eager to do the applauding and appreciating himself. He was discriminating, nevertheless, and his appreciations were judicious and cultivated; he had a deep streak of practicality as well, was painstaking, thrifty, an excellent manager. He seemed to combine a Gallic love of life, a vast appetite for many kinds of pleasure both of the mind and of the flesh, with Dutch solidity, and it was a combination almost everyone found appealing.

Eugen's people were originally French Huguenots who had emigrated to Holland in the time of Louis XIV, where they built their fortunes on banking, publishing, shipbuilding and the East Indies trade; his grandfather had started the first regular shipping line between Amsterdam and Java, his father was a journalist of international eminence, for some forty years the head of the leading Dutch newspaper, and his mother a daughter of the provost of Trinity College, Dublin. In this large, successful and hard-working clan, Eugen, as a young man, was something of a maverick, for instead of entering the business world he seemed to prefer to act the playboy. Traveling all over the world, he went in for big-game hunting and rowed in the Henley regatta; at one point psychoanalysis intrigued him, and he was analyzed in Zurich by Jung himself. In his early thirties, just before the outbreak of the first war, he went to work as a business associate of Marconi in the United States; whatever his precise position, it was not an especially glorious one. While crossing the Atlantic on Marconi's business in 1913, he met an extraordinary young woman, a beautiful American lawyer named Inez Milholland. They fell in love, were married quickly and secretly, and when the secret was out it was considered so spectacular as to require a conspicuous place on the front page of *The New York Times* for July 16, 1913: "Inez Milholland Wedded in Secret," to be followed two days later by another front-page story describing the chagrin of Inez Milholland's father, who said he had never heard of Boissevain—which was not very strange; no one had heard of him, whereas everyone in America who could read a newspaper had been hearing about Inez Milholland for years.

She was a Vassar graduate, the daughter of the editor of the *New York Tribune;* already the heroine of a popular novel, *An American Suffragette,* whose author praised her "wealth of dusky hair, a complexion of roses and cream and a mouth at once strong and sensitive," Inez had been arrested in London for suffrage activities, had led a parade of women demonstrators down Pennsylvania Avenue in the nation's capital while mounted on a white horse, and taken an active role in a strike of women shirtwaist makers, for which she was twice jailed. She was said to be the most beautiful girl who ever bit a policeman's hand, and the columnist FPA called her "some bear-cat."

When Eugen and Inez returned from their European honeymoon to settle in the States, Inez was working for the law firm of Osborne, Lamb & Garvan, and they lived in a luxurious rented house in Harmon-on-Hudson; it was here, in 1914, that Inez brought her old friend the writer Max Eastman. They had happened to meet one day in New York and she told him to "Come on along and meet Eugen, you'll love him."

I did love him—as much as any man I have known since college days. He is handsome and muscular and bold, boisterous in conversation, noisy in laughter. . . . We talked all that evening and far into the night, the three of us. . . . We talked about love, and I truly think that, had the record been made, our conversation might rival in poignancy of interest the most famous discussions of this subject. Inez and Eugen, to insure each to the other the whole wealth of experience, had taken a vow of unpossessive love. Not a vow either, for it was the natural motion of love in the heart of each to wish thus to protect the freedom of the other. I suppose only two very young people, full blooded and confident of their charms, could have undertaken this, much less achieved it.

Apparently Inez was a somewhat humorless woman, utterly sincere, hard-working, effective and idealistic, but incapable of laughing at herself. She took herself most seriously, then, and Eugen took her seriously too. Her work, her professional commitments and the charitable activities to which she gave her time were the chief focus of both their lives, although Eugen retained for a while his business connection with Marconi. He was a devout feminist, a lifelong believer in the causes Inez supported, and whenever her name appeared in the newspapers it was with the additional mention of the "devoted husband," who had accompanied or chauffeured her. Guardian, secretary, manager, indulgent parent figure, he seemed to have chosen the role of one who stands just beyond the spotlights, welcoming reflected glory, holding in one hand his hat and in the other the coat, gloves, purse and papers of his extraordinary wife.

In the autumn of 1916 Inez was hard at work on what had become a *cause célèbre*, the attempt to commute to life imprisonment the death sentence of a farmhand convicted of murder; a number of distinguished women lawyers uncovered fresh evidence to support their claims, and Inez Milholland Boissevain was driven into Manhattan by her "devoted husband" in a last-minute attempt to change Governor Whitman's mind. But Inez had also promised to make a lecture tour of twelve western states, campaigning for votes for women. She was unaccountably tired, she was also reluctant to leave New York without learning the outcome of her appeal to the governor, but she had promised, and she went—accompanied, as always, by Eugen. While on the lecture platform in Los Angeles she suddenly collapsed. Eugen carried her to their hotel room, where doctors were summoned, and it was discovered that twenty-eight-year-old Inez had pernicious anemia. In spite of a series of transfusions she died in the hotel room, with Eugen at her side. He told Eastman about the last words they exchanged. "Shall I come with you?" he asked, sitting by the bed.

And she whispered, "No. You go ahead and live another life."

In the months that followed Eugen plunged into a business venture, perhaps the first he had ever taken seriously; he went after the Dutch East Indies trade that was formerly brought to the States by way of Europe, from which it was cut off now by the German blockade. Meanwhile he moved from the house he had shared with Inez to an apartment on East Eighth Street in the Village, with an extra room in it that he offered to Eastman. The two young men had become fast friends; Eugen liked talented people involved in the arts, and Eastman found Eugen a wonderful companion, tolerant, uninhibited, unconventional, especially when it came to matters of sex. As for Eugen's new business venture, it was apparently destined for success; perhaps his daring spirit, mercantile ancestry and connections with the Indies were an irresistible combination, perhaps it was only his working day and night in an attempt to forget the loss of his young wife. In any case, after three years at it Eugen Boissevain owned a twelve-story building downtown with his name carved across the granite front, and managed a whole fleet of merchant ships, most of them full of coffee. He never took his success in business seriously; according to Eastman, Eugen found it all "a laughable adventure, and his tales of the deals he was putting over, told with Gargantuan laughter at the self-importance of the business class, were a source of delight and instruction." Surely the cream of the jest had to do with Eugen's previous role as the prodigal son of rich and important people. He had spent his youth "bumming around," as he called it, in the pursuit of pleasure, while snapping his fingers at the achievements of his elders. And when he decided to go into business for himself, he continued snapping his fingers, for Eugen used to boast to Eastman about the way he "gypped" his competitors.

The two men lived together off and on for several years, first in the small apartment on Eighth Street, later in a house on Washington Place shared with some friends, and after that in an apartment on St. Luke's Place; it was always Eugen who managed the household when there were no women around. Supervising servants, filling in for servants who disappeared or took sick, planning menus, all these "quotidian matters," as Eugen called them, were his natural domain. Eastman believed Eugen had in him "a strain of something feminine that most men except the creative geniuses lack," and Edmund Wilson, who knew Eugen in middle age, had a somewhat similar impression: "With no particular talent or bent of his own, it was possible for him only vicariously to express this imaginative or sensitive side."

Seven years passed between Inez' death and the house party at Croton where Eugen met Edna Millay; she was a tiny woman, whereas Inez had been tall and commanding, she was shy and withdrawn where Inez had been vigorously self-assertive. But she was also famous, beautiful and talented, as Inez had been; moreover, she was very sick. Eugen must have recognized in her the woman he needed, and who desperately needed him; apparently the moment had come to go on and lead another life.

No date was set for the marriage until the doctors announced that Edna Millay had to have an intestinal operation; then and there Eugen decided she must enter the hospital as his wife, and a wedding party was gathered at the house at Croton. Ficke was there with Gladys Brown, and Norma with Charlie Ellis, and the marriage took place out of doors with the bride in a hastily gotten up white dress and veil. That afternoon she was rushed to the hospital in New York.

As soon as his wife was permitted to leave the hospital Eugen took her back to Croton to convalesce; she was weak and tired throughout most of that summer, and Arthur Ficke came to help prepare *The Harp-Weaver and Other Poems* for publication, not by the unsatisfactory Mitchell Kennerley, who had gone out of business anyhow, but by Harper and Brothers, her publisher from then on. One day when Ficke was going over proofs for the book, Edna amazed him by reciting a poem she had composed during the course of that summer, a funereal sonnet, not a word of which had been put on paper until he wrote it down that day. Apparently she often composed entirely in her head; she was also in the habit of committing to memory great quantities of poetry by poets she admired, Gerard Manley Hopkins, Keats, Elinor Wylie and Arthur Davison Ficke among them.

When *The Harp-Weaver* proofs had been sent back to Harper in the autumn, Eugen took his wife to stay at the Holley Hotel in Washington Square until a house on Bedford Street, also in Greenwich Village, could be made ready for them. The poet told her mother in November she was thrilled to hear the Camden-Rockland bills were all paid; it made quite a hole in her bank account but she meant to fill it up. "I suppose it is a mean pride in me, but oh, I wish I could have done this before I got married!" for everyone thought, she said, that her rich husband had paid those bills when in fact she did it herself, every penny of it, with the money she made by writing. For this the new book was in part responsible; it had been received with great enthusiasm, both critical and popular, and had already begun to make money. Filled with the themes of Edna's past two years—that love does not last, which she had always known but never before regretted, that summer gives way to autumn and autumn to winter and death—its prevailing moods were illness, resignation, despair: "I see so clearly now my similar years/ Repeat each other, shod in rusty black,/ Like one hack following another hack/ In meaningless procession, dry of tears."

Her language at its best is earthy and pungent, sometimes, as in the title poem, bringing to mind old folk ballads. Sometimes—"What lips my lips have kissed, and where, and why,/ I have forgotten, and what arms have lain/ Under my head till morning; but the rain/ Is full of ghosts tonight . . ."—she achieves the mood that is uniquely her own, romantic, feminine, self-centered, toughly sad. There are more sonnets in this volume than in any of her other collections.

That autumn she went to Washington, D.C., at the invitation of the National Women's Party; there on November 17 a deputation called on the president and the day after, in the Crypt of the Capitol, a statue was unveiled in honor of three pioneer suffragettes. After the unveiling Edna Millay, introduced by her friend Doris Stevens as the "foremost woman poet of America," read a sonnet she had written for the occasion, which she later dedicated "To Inez Milholland." The poem was of course a delicate compliment to Eugen, but it also expressed genuine admiration for Inez, who had been, when Edna was at Vassar, an almost legendary heroine. Years before in Greenwich Village, Floyd Dell had given Edna a bronze button such as were awarded to women like Inez who were arrested as militant suffragettes, and she told him with tears in her eyes, "I would rather have the right to wear this than anything I can think of!"

They were settled in their new house at 75½ Bedford Street, a narrow, three-story brick dwelling 9½ feet wide and 30 feet deep, by January of 1924; but hardly were they moved in than Edna had to leave on a poetry-reading tour of the Midwest that had been planned for months. She expected to clear nearly two thousand dollars by it, and was to travel alone, the first and only time she ever made such a tour without Eugen. He planned all her poetry readings after that, making all the arrangements with business people and hotels and going along to supervise her comfort himself. Max Eastman once said Eugen raised his wife's fees for a single reading from one hundred to six hundred dollars, and spoke of it as gleefully as he spoke of his dealings in the import business —he was "gypping" people, and it was a delicious game.

During the course of her western tour Edna wrote a long letter to Eugen while she waited for her train to pull out of the railway station in Chicago; her hands were so dirty, she told him, it was almost theatrical, and everyone who looked at her wondered why such a nice girl, with such expensive cufflinks and such a refined and elegant addressbook, had dirty hands. She herself no longer cared. She had gotten through yesterday's two readings well enough, and some of the people were sweet and real and intelligent, but she had the general impression that a bunch of wealthy people had come together to see what she looked like, and placed bets about how many of her naughty poems she would read. In sum, she said, she felt like a prostitute. "It's amusing to think how entirely, *totally,* ABSOLUTELY different everything would be if you were in this chair beside me," she wrote. "It makes me laugh." Another thought brightened the reading tour. Eugen had promised to take her around the world as a wedding present, that spring; he especially wanted her to see Java and Indonesia.

They left San Francisco in mid-April, on a Japanese ship bound for Honolulu; the poet told Norma that Honolulu was the most *beautiful* place, and that they nearly decided to leave the ship and spend the rest of their lives on the beach eating mangoes. They visited Japan, China, Hong Kong, Java, Singapore, India, Marseilles and Paris, and were gone for most of that year. Leaving Shanghai, bound for Singapore, Edna told her mother "the spray of the ship was full of beautiful bright rainbows!" and at night the phosphorus turned the edges of the waves all green, as if lit by electric lights. She had called to her husband, "Oh, Eugen, rainbows by day and phosphorus by night,—I can hardly bear it!" For some reason, few traces of this long and apparently enchanted journey are to be found in her poems, hardly more than a phrase here and there, but the Boissevains collected things for the home they hoped to have, and some of the brilliance of their wedding trip found its way to Steepletop when they moved there the following year.

Early in 1925 Eugen and Edna were back on Bedford Street. On May

Day a group of young women who had known each other at Barnard, and who called themselves the Ashcan Cats—among them Margaret Mead, a graduate student in anthropology, and a poet named Léonie Adams—got together to make may baskets, a custom of their college days; they would go to Bronx Park for moss and willow twigs, marsh marigolds and other wild things. Léonie Adams recalled that in the late afternoon one of the girls said what they really ought to do was bring a may basket to Edna St. Vincent Millay.

Towards evening the Ashcan Cats arrived at the door of 75½ Bedford Street, placed their basket on the doorstep and knocked. The custom then was to run away, but instead they watched while Eugen opened the door in the moonlight and took it in. When the door had closed behind him one of the girls began to call, "We want Edna!" A window opened above, Edna Millay put her head out, thanked them and asked who they were. "Just some Barnard girls," someone answered—Miss Adams believed it was Margaret Mead. To their delight Edna then appeared at the front door in a long dressing gown, and shook hands with each of them, asking her name, which she repeated carefully. The poet was gracious and subdued, saying little, but the girls had the feeling she was touched by their offering. Léonie Adams learned later from Edmund Wilson that Millay had been despondent that evening, and was so pleased with their visit that she had the may basket photographed.

Franklin P. Adams also visited Edna in Bedford Street that spring— his visits eventually led to his marrying her friend Tess Root—and she showed him through the "burlesque park she had made, her landlord having promised her a garden but having done nought about it." The poet had laid out a miniature park with absurd signs about the grass and flowers and shrubbery that were not there, for she wanted badly to be living in the country. The Bedford Street house was too small for a large and boisterous man like Eugen, but more important was the fact that life in the city had become increasingly uncomfortable for Edna, who hated crowds and tall buildings and longed for solitude. She wanted a house in the country; moreover she wanted, as she had always wanted, to live withdrawn and sheltered and protected there, holding fast to the security of childhood. It was an old story and an old problem, to which marriage brought the possibility of new solutions.

In the early spring of 1925, the Boissevains found their place in the country, seven hundred acres on the slopes of the Berkshires ringed by mountains, three miles from the tiny village of Austerlitz, New York. There were berries and meadows and a brook flowing through a little valley, and it was "one of the loveliest places in the world." They called it Steepletop. Here Edna Millay was to work in perfect solitude, and Eugen, who sold his importing business to move there, was to become a full-time professional farmer, not because it was the career of his choice but because it was best for his wife. "When we got married," he told a reporter a few years later, "I gave up my business. It seemed advisable to arrange our lives to suit Vincent. . . . It is so obvious to anyone that Vincent is more important than I am. Anyone can buy and sell coffee." He was determined, just as Cora Millay had been, that the poet was to have her chance, cost what it might.

"She must not . . . have too many of those other mundane moments in a woman's life—no matter how many servants are around—the moments when her world is filled with the making out of lists, with housekeeping matters, ordering, overseeing. . . . She must not be dulled by routine acts; she must ever remain open to fresh contact with life's intensities." For he had learned "that she does not keep regular working hours; that she is irregular in most quotidian matters. If I let her struggle with problems of order . . . she doesn't write. . . . So I solve it quite simply: I look after everything." At Steepletop Eugen managed not only the farm and the daily life of the household, but all his wife's business affairs as well; he was the guardian of her working time, her health and her peace of mind—in short, he undertook the role of a devoted parent.

Floyd Dell spoke of the way Eugen had nursed Edna "like a mother," and Max Eastman felt his attitude toward her was that of a nursemaid toward a child of whom she was enamored; Eastman said another time that what Eugen most wanted was to be the wife of a brilliant woman. But it was not a wife he wanted to be, since that suggests submissiveness, and certainly Edna did not want to be a husband; what she apparently wanted was to be a child, attached yet free, and under the protection of a powerful, indulgent mother. In Eugen she had finally found a man who needed to be just that, a powerful and protective parent—for in his first marriage Eugen had chosen a gifted woman whom he chauffeured, protected and applauded, and he did not marry again until he met another badly in need of these same services.

Yet if marriage to Eugen, and life in the country isolation of Steepletop, offered withdrawal and shelter, there remained the dilemma expressed in "Renascence," that the powerful parent might protect her so well she would be stifled to death. How was Edna to keep her freedom; what was to become of Vincent, the boy poet, the performer? What about her earlier fear that in order to be a wife she would have to resemble Bianca, the mild and clinging girl who rode sidesaddle?

She had come to believe that to love too long and faithfully meant to suffer desertion. And she must also have believed—her poetry suggests it, as do the frantic love affairs and the fear of marriage she expressed to Floyd Dell—that to love too long meant to become "unmanned," that total surrender to love would mean the loss of control, the loss of power:

> Cherish you then the hope I shall forget
> At length, my lord, Pieria?—put away
> For your so passing sake, this mouth of clay,
> These mortal bones against my body set,
> For all the puny fever and frail sweat
> Of human love,—renounce for these, I say,
> The Singing Mountain's memory, and betray
> The silent lyre that hangs upon me yet?

Love was a threat, and what it threatened was the loss of poetry, since poetry was written by Vincent; in the intimacy of love she feared she might betray Vincent, just as a man, in surrendering himself totally to love, is nevertheless aware that he can be conquered, dominated and finally "unmanned" by the very act of love from which he emerges spent, limp, unmanly. Without Vincent, the boy poet, she would be unlovable—without poetry she would lose the most precious part of life as well as the only way she knew of holding at bay the ghosts that haunted her.

But Eugen, who had the remarkable "feminine" traits Eastman and others had noticed, who enjoyed cooking and running the house—in later years he scrubbed, cleaned, washed his wife's long hair and probably did the laundry as well, all with the grace and dash and noisy pleasure of a pirate king putting his ship in order—Eugen admired Vincent. Just as he admired Inez for her professional performance and considered it in no way a threat to his virility, so did he find in Vincent the proper complement to the feminine traits that were a part of him. Vincent, in fact, was what he most loved in his wife. As for the claustrophobic fears that she might be smothered to death by a personality more powerful than her own, Edna had found in Eugen a man who appreciated her need for freedom. He and Inez had promised each other to avoid possessiveness; each was to remain free to love wherever they wished. When Edna and Eugen married they must have made a similar vow, for in the mid-thirties Elizabeth Atkins, Millay's first biographer, was told by Eugen that his wife was by no means confined to one man; he sent back Miss Atkins' manuscript with the "deeply bitten marginal comment" that to suggest she was so confined was a lie. And Eugen told Alan Ross Macdougall in the mid-thirties, "To be in love is a terrific and continuous excitement. I want to keep that excitement, never being quite sure, never knowing, so that I can ask myself: Does she love me? And have the answer: I don't know." A marriage in which each mate is tied exclusively to the other is "like an ice-box with always some cold chicken in it." So there was always a means of escape for Edna Millay —escape from the dangers of love, of too cozy and close a shelter. When the walls threatened to close in about her she could always fall in love with someone else.

There remained the escape into poetry. Like every creative artist, Edna found in art a way of becoming intimate with what was most terrifying. Just as children tell ghost stories so that the horrors of the night, by repetition, seem less scary, so that they gain in the end the healing illusion that the horrors have been their own creation, so the poet eventually gains the illusion of mastery over her own ghosts. Over and over she tells the story of love followed by desertion, her own desertion of the lover, until desertion itself is an old story. She repeats from late adolescence onward her fear of death, and by her mid-thirties has begun to think of resignation: "Down, down, down into the darkness of the grave/ Gently they go, the beautiful, the tender, the kind/ . . . . I know. But I do not approve. And I am not resigned." By late middle age, although still not resigned to the idea of death, she was trying to see it as another part of life, interwoven with all that is healthy and beautiful: " 'Dust to dust!'—oh, happier far/ The ashes of my body are,/ Since all that's mortal of me goes/ The deathless way of dew and rose!/ Year by year the wasted plain/ Eats its death and lives again. . . ." It might of course be pointed out that one doesn't have to be a poet to come to some understanding of death; quite true, but some people reach understanding through living, others—poets—through writing.

If Edna Millay had been only a neurotic woman, death-haunted, claustrophobic and sexually ambiguous, she might have found considerable satisfaction as well as worthwhile therapy in whatever art form she took up in her spare time, whether painting, writing, the dance or music. But she had also been born with the peculiar genetic equipment that can become high talent, perhaps even genius, and in her earliest years had acquired the habit of hard and precise observation of the world around her, as well as the discipline that leads to transmuting experience into something more than therapeutic art. Her fears of death became everyman's fear of death, her longing for love and her denial of it became the universal cry of the spirit to be part of something greater than the single self. Just as the poetry transcended her own individual nightmares, so did the poet herself, in the very act of writing, push back the cage of self to join humanity at large.

In one of her most famous sonnets she wrote, "I will put Chaos into fourteen lines/ And keep him there." Here is the artist's need for art proclaimed in its purest form: Chaos, night fears, all that is terrifying, will be polished, worked over, carved and recarved until it is finally contained within the sonnet—compressed into fourteen lines, and conquered. This was especially true for the work of Edna Millay, who was the most painstaking of poets, utterly dedicated to her poetry and its perfection, working sometimes ten years off and on at a single poem, and wrenching from her publishers the promise that even after her death not so much as a single comma would ever be altered. Chaos, when put into fourteen lines, ceased to be chaos and became art, and for as long as she was able to write, and to write her best, she stood a chance of remaining in control of chaos.

The Boissevains, then, made their home at Steepletop, where Edna was to write her poetry undisturbed and Eugen's chief tasks were the farm, the household, and Edna. It must have seemed at the time the ideal solution, the perfect balance for the claustrophobe between too much protection and too little. "I have a curious feeling that someday I shall marry, and have a son; and that my husband will die; and that you and I and my little boy will all live together on a farm," she had written to her mother in 1921. And in a sense what she foresaw had come about; she was married, she was living on the farm, if not with her mother, with Eugen, who mothered her; and the son was there too. His name was Vincent.

Before any writing could be done at Steepletop the neglected old white farmhouse they found there had to be expanded, modernized and transformed, a task in which the poet joined with such abandon that "I hardly know if I am writing with a pen or with a screwdriver." New heating and plumbing were installed, walls removed to enlarge rooms, so that an oversize living room could hold two grand pianos, a new wing and a garage added; the place was a hive of masons, carpenters, plumbers, along with more than a dozen children Eugen had hired to help pick and market the berries that grew in great abundance, berries of every kind, both wild and "tame," as Eugen called the cultivated ones. His nephew Fred, a professional landscape gardener, was helping to lay out orchards and gardens; there were working horses and Edna's own riding horse, Rob Roy; there were milking cows, sheep, a pig, several dogs, an occasional kitten, and in the wild forests surrounding Steepletop there were deer, great handsome animals the hunters came and killed in the two-week open season of autumn, to carry them home slung across their cars. Birds were everywhere, and one of the windows of the long living room became the "bird-window," where Edna put food out on the windowsill and the ground outside it, often rising before dawn to do so. Eugen told a visitor, "She runs a hotel for birds."

From the very beginning the Boissevains had trouble keeping servants, perhaps because of the isolation. Visitors came and went, and so, often without warning, did the servants; Eugen took it in his stride:

One day his house would be that of a citizen of the world, with a French butler to wait on the table, and everything done with the greatest *bienséance*, and the next the servants would have as mysteriously disappeared as bees from a deserted hive, and he would be out in the kitchen washing the dishes and whistling a haunting Slavic melody, as light-hearted as a troubadour. He had the gift of the aristocrat and could adapt himself to all circumstances; be at one moment hawking huckleberries in the street . . . and at the next travelling like the Grand Turk up to his chin in pomp.

So Eugen was described by the wife of the British writer Llewelyn Powys, a few years later. If he carried out his household chores with the nonchalance of royalty, Eugen had nevertheless the deeply rooted sense of property that belongs to the bourgeois. That first summer he got lost one afternoon while trying to collect fifty cents apiece from the "dozens of people who come in motor cars and camp on our land and steal our berries," Edna said. And Eastman remembered Eugen's going into the bathroom at Steepletop and finding a slit in one of the little white guest towels, which someone must have used to wipe the blade of a safety razor. He assumed the careless one was Eastman, and gave him a calling down with "excessive intensity." The Eastmans thought of buying a place nearby, then decided against it, and went instead to Martha's Vineyard, but the Fickes fell in love with the Berkshire hills and bought a neighboring farm a few years later.

Another visitor that first summer was the American composer Deems Taylor. He had been commissioned by the Metropolitan to create an entirely American opera with a libretto in English, and he turned to his friend Edna Millay, who was at once a distinguished poet, the author of that fine play *Aria da Capo*, and a musician, who played and composed, had written operas as a child and choral pieces in college. She agreed to share the commission with Taylor, but the task must have awed her, for she seems to have fretted a good deal over whether or not she was really equal to it; she had started something based on the story of Snow White and the Seven Dwarfs, and brought the uncompleted work with her to Steepletop.

At first the alterations were too fascinating to be put aside for the libretto. "Ugin will be back from Albany with presents for Ediner,— paint-brushes and loaves of bread and empty blueberry crates, and maybe if I'm very very good some white lead and linseed oil!" she wrote to her mother. There was also the question of where to work. A study was being built on the second floor of the house, to be fitted out as a library and workroom with an impressive collection of reference books, volumes of poetry in several modern languages as well as Latin and Greek, two sailing charts of Penobscot Bay, and a large sign demanding SILENCE; meanwhile there was a little shack out in the fields, far from the furor of masons and plumbers, and she decided to use it as a makeshift study. Deems Taylor visited the farm about four times, but the rest of the collaboration had to be carried out by mail, and this must have added to the strain the poet was under. For beginning in early summer she had a headache that never let up, and a veil of dark spots dancing before her eyes. Doctors assured her there was nothing the matter with heart, lungs, kidneys, liver, etcetera, nor was there anything wrong with her eyes.

That winter they were snowed in for weeks at a time. Edna worked away in her little outdoor study with a scorching fire at her back "in the funniest little stove," and Eugen walked five miles on snowshoes to fetch the mail. The thermometer was at zero, there was no road to the house at all and they had no telephone. They preferred being without one whenever possible, for the sake of Edna and her poetry:

> What chores these churls do put upon the great,
> What chains, what harness; . . .
> Oh, how the speaking pen has been impeded,
> To its own cost and to the cost of speech,
> By specious hands that for some thinly-needed
> Answer or autograph, would claw a breach
> In perfect thought.

So anxious was Eugen to spare his wife the interruption of "perfect thought" that during those intervals when they did have a phone, it was his practice to run and answer it by the first ring; when they lived for a long spell in a New York apartment, he rigged up a system of flashing lights in order to spare her the sound of the doorbell.

While Eugen went five miles and back to fetch the mail, not knowing, since there was no telephone, whether or not they had mail, the poet worked at her libretto and tried to ignore the headache and spots. She told FPA "it's so beautiful here, even looking at everything through a dotted veil, that I should worry." And Steepletop in the depths of winter had a rare and wonderful beauty; in late afternoon the setting sun was reflected on the all-embracing snow, turning it pink—"that deepest rose-pink that you get once in a while . . . with bright blue shadows" —and she would jump up from her typewriter to stand by the window of her little shack and watch the sunset. When the sun went down beyond the wintry trees it looked like a red ruby. And the quiet of those snowy woods, undisturbed except for the two weeks of the hunting season, must have been balm to the spirit of one who had found the city dirty, noisy, ugly, even menacing. Yet in spite of the beauties of Steepletop, the headache was cause for alarm, especially when her eyes hurt so badly Eugen had to read to her.

He had a pronounced Dutch accent that most of their friends found charming, but his wife apparently chided him about it from time to time, and felt sorry later when he said things like, "Oh, don't scold poor Uge—he does so his best." The accent, and the annoyance of having to be read to, seem to have found their way into one of the death poems in *The Buck in the Snow*, published in 1928, where she speaks of "The books of the wise,/ Badly read/ By other eyes,/ Lewdly bawled/ At my closing ear . . ." This headache coupled with dancing dots lasted about a year; for the rest of her life Edna Millay had headaches when she worked, but the dots never returned. It was probably during that first summer at Steepletop, when the paired symptoms were still something of a novelty that sent her from doctor to doctor without result, that a curious little incident took place at a party. Everyone knew about the headaches, everyone had remedies to suggest, and according to Max Eastman a young doctor came up to the poet at a cocktail party and said he might be able to help if she would allow it. They went into the library, where, after several false starts, the doctor confessed he was a psychoanalyst, and suggested that perhaps without being aware of it she might "have an occasional erotic impulse towards a person of your own sex?"

According to Eastman, Edna's answer to the young doctor—and he must have beeen a very young doctor indeed to offer advice to a woman he barely knew on the basis of observation at a cocktail party—was, "Oh, you mean I'm homosexual! Of course I am, and heterosexual too, but what's that got to do with my headache?" It is hard to tell what she meant, whether she was really aware of the homosexual elements in her character and accepted them with such serenity, or whether, by wise-cracking and the pretense of superior knowledge she meant to put the analyst in his place. In either case, the tone of the incident and the way she described it to Eastman help to explain why she never tried the only possible remedy for headaches that have no physical cause: she had not altered her opinion about analysis since the Village days, when she saw it as a dangerous invasion of her privacy. She preferred to suffer.

Around Christmas, the poet scrapped her idea of a libretto based on Snow White and turned instead to the Anglo-Saxon Chronicle and a half-legendary, half-historical story of pre-Norman England, for which she intended to use only those words that might really have been in use at the time. The new libretto seemed to go well from the first. By March it was nearly finished, and the completed portions were being mailed off to Deems Taylor in Paris; they had decided to call it *The King's Hench-man*. It was completed during the summer, and so were most of the alterations to the farmhouse, so that Cora Millay was able to make her first long visit, putting up dozens of jars of jellies and jams she had made from Steepletop fruit. In the large, old-fashioned kitchen Edna did her share of preserving, using plums and tomatoes from their own gardens, of which she was extremely proud. She took a touching delight in seeing their pantries filled with home-grown produce, and showed off rare flowers that had been grown from seed like a true countrywoman. There was "a riot of sweet-peas until a fortnight ago, and . . . I have potted all my geraniums, and a fuchsia and some rather special petunias, two ice-plants, and millions of carnations. . . . We took some snapshots of a garden we made with the ruined wall of an old barn as a background," she told her aunt. Eugen was marketing berries and fruit, a certified cow gave the finest milk and cream—in short, the farm prospered and was beautiful, the long and awesome task of writing her libretto was behind her, and by autumn of that year her general health had begun to improve considerably, although headache and spots refused to budge.

In October, the Boissevains went to Santa Fe at the invitation of the Fickes, who had been living there for a year because of Arthur's recently discovered tuberculosis; Edna's old friend and "spiritual advisor" helped prepare proofs of *The King's Henchman*. Back at Steepletop in time for Christmas, the poet was in a state of high excitement about the opera; so was the general public, for Taylor had tried to keep everything secret in order to heighten the ultimate effect, and nothing is more exciting than a secret when wisps have leaked out, as they inevitably did. Therefore "attendance at the rehearsal rivaled a regular audience, and all seats were sold for the premiere and the repetition of the following Monday," according to *The Musical Observer*.

Opening night was to be February 17; in mid-January Edna wrote to Deems: "Listen,—listen, Deems: if you hear any more news—good or bad—out with it, see?— I'm a big girl now. Do they still like it?— Did you hear the rehearsal? Was it rotten?— How 'bout it? Semme a pos' card." But she had chosen the wrong person to ask for encouraging news, for on the night of the premiere, according to *The Musical Observer*, "Mr. Deems Taylor himself could be observed cowering, pale and wretched, in corners of the corridor during intermissions, looking ill and embarrassed."

It was a splendid opening, one that attracted crowds of celebrities and filled the opera house; Cora Millay was there, and Kathleen, who had already published a novel and was about to publish her first collection of poetry, came with her playwright husband. Even Norma's absence was an occasion for familial pride, for Norma was singing the leading role in *La Finta Giardiniera*, a Mozart opera produced by the Intimate Opera Company. Despite Deems Taylor's wretchedness in the corridors, *The King's Henchman* went beautifully from the beginning, and when the final curtain went down the audience applauded for twenty unbroken minutes, then shouted for composer and librettist. Taylor and Millay stood alone on the stage, "the scholarly musician and the girlish, frail young poetess," as one newspaper had it. And in the silence that followed Edna Millay told the audience, "I thank you. I love you all." Taylor waited a moment, then added, "That's just what I was going to say."

The King's Henchman was said to have earned about ten thousand dollars for Edna Millay. It made fourteen appearances during three Metropolitan seasons, a record for an American opera, toured the country with similar success and sold out three editions of the libretto, in book form, within twenty days. The critics were not entirely happy with it, however, for some found a lack of inspiration in the music; approving the fine orchestration and perfect craftsmanship, they maintained "the vein of true melody is low." Others claimed Millay had been pedantic in her insistence on historically correct vocabulary, and why was a native American opera, they wanted to know, written about Anglo-Saxons? Was opera in English a necessity at all? "But if we must have opera in our native tongue . . . by all means let Miss Millay write the text and Mr. Taylor accompany it."

Nearly five years had now elapsed since *The Harp-Weaver and Other Poems.* Overall, Edna Millay was an unusually productive poet, for a fairly high output seemed essential to her well-being; how could it be otherwise when, as Wilson observed, her work was the most important thing in life, what she put above everything and everybody? The libretto, the exciting alterations to Steepletop and the unceasing headaches had eaten away at the time she spent writing poetry, but by 1927 she had enough for another volume, and Wilson remembered being summoned by Edna to the Vanderbilt Hotel, early that year, to talk about one of the poems that would appear in it, a poem he didn't much care for. Eugen accompanied his wife, and Wilson was struck by his "protective attitude." As for Millay, "She looked quite beautiful, very high pink flush, and brown dress that brought out her color."

The discussion turned to some of her earlier work. "I said . . . that, when she had written 'Second April,' she had been under so many kinds of pressure that the people who read her poems hardly thought of them as literature at all: there had been an element of panic about them." Edna replied, "Yes, and I still want to knock 'em cold." They seem to be talking about two different things: the personal, confessional quality of much of the love poetry in *Second April*, devoured by readers for what it told about the poet's love life—and her desire to dazzle; she had wanted then to knock 'em cold and she still did.

At this point, according to Wilson, Eugen explained that the new work was different, it was more objective. And when the book appeared, late in 1927, as *The Buck in the Snow*, Wilson decided Eugen was right, that it seemed less desperate, more contemplative. Deems Taylor had a similarly high opinion of Eugen's insight. He said Eugen "had an uncanny sense of English poetry, and was as merciless a critic" of Edna's work as the poet herself. Although no one else has so strong a claim to make on Eugen's behalf, there are suggestions here and there in Edna's letters as well as in some of the business correspondence Eugen wrote on her behalf, that he was no silent spectator to her career, that he prodded her at times, nudged her toward projects he approved of and discouraged her from others. He was always alert to the reactions of critics, and his sound Dutch business sense suggested interesting, even audacious ways of publicizing her work.

A few months after the meeting at the Vanderbilt, Wilson went to Steepletop for a weekend:

> Gene Boissevain, when I arrived, was planting a border of pansies with a gardener's intent application; but his attention seemed soon to flag, for he began singing cockney songs at the top of his voice. Then he addressed himself to oiling the lawn-mower; then suddenly dropped it and proposed a drink. There was a comfortable living room, in which, as one first came into it, one was startled at being confronted by a dark human head staring fixedly . . . from eyes that had black irises . . . a bronze bust of Sappho, painted black. . . . There were also hangings from India, golden birds on a background of green. . . . Edna was interesting herself in the local animals and birds and trees, which were beginning to turn up in "The Buck in the Snow;" but we decided not to go for a walk, as it had been earlier proposed to do. They had a sensitive German police-dog, who, when Boissevain had given her a scolding, would drag herself into the room, bumping against the chairs, as if her hind legs were paralyzed. They thought she was a case for Freud.

The next morning, Wilson asked Edna to play the piano for him. "She had now, she told me, taken up music again and was trying to work regularly at it. She was studying a sonata of Beethoven and played parts of it with her bright alive touch, dropping them, however, with impatience at the raggedness of her own performance." Then she got out a batch of her new poems, and as they went over them together all her old intensity returned. "She was desperately, feverishly anxious not to let her standard down. She sometimes kept a poem for decades before she got it into satisfactory form." Wilson tried to relieve the strain that seemed inevitably to arise between them by describing a comic stage routine he had once seen; she thought it was terribly funny, yet even as she laughed Wilson felt the moment had in it an "awful seriousness." A year later he went to Steepletop again, and found a number of visitors there, the conversation general, the living room serene, and "I had a curious and touching impression, as Edna sat quiet in a big chair, that —torn and distracted by winds that had swept her through many seas—she had been towed into harbor and moored, that she was floating at anchor there."

Among the poems Wilson saw on that first summer visit in 1927 was one she kept and worked over for ten more years, until it appeared in the 1937 volume *Huntsman, What Quarry?* under the title "Menses." An unusual piece of work on many counts, the rhyme scheme irregular, the versifying fairly free for Millay, it is written as if by a man, a husband —in short, Eugen. The theme is a woman's peevish nastiness during menstruation, and how her husband perceives and transcends it: "Go to. You are unwell," he says, when she lets fly at him a stream of insults: "Lord, the shame,/ The crying shame of seeing a man no wiser than the beasts he feeds—/ His skull as empty as a shell!"

But the poem reveals more than a woman's tension during menstruation; the writer suggests she is by nature harsh, peevish and nasty at times, and physiology is only an excuse. "Yet coil; yet strike again./ You cannot riddle the stout mail I wove/ Long since, of wit and love." So he replies in his thoughts to her venom. And in the end the woman succumbs to her husband's limitless patience and his skill at distracting her, and tells him, while sobbing, "You are very patient. You are very kind./ I shall be better soon. Just Heaven consign and damn/ To tedious Hell this body with its muddy feet in my mind!"

This was the safe harbor Wilson had rejoiced to see her in, that she was moored to a man ready in advance to forgive her everything. For Edna could be harsh and nasty at times and at others quiveringly, explosively angry, at Eugen, at herself, at friends or relatives. According to the poem she felt she had little control over her temper, and it was Eugen who had to have control enough for both. For it seems clear that Millay was not gratuitously, cold-bloodedly cruel to Eugen or indeed to anyone. She admired magnanimity and gallant good behavior and tried whenever possible to be magnanimous and gallant herself, especially in the conduct of love affairs. Wilson praised her for it, and Arthur Ficke, in a poem entitled "Epitaph for a Bad Girl," spoke of her as eager, generous and just; a score of former lovers, according to Ficke, agreed with him. If Eugen had more to put up with in twenty-five years of married life than any lover in the brief interlude she allotted each of them, still there is every reason to think Edna wanted to be generous and just with him as well. When she was not, it was because a process as inexorable as menses took over her mind. It is clear from the poem that she understood and valued Eugen's rare forbearance, realized how sorely she provoked him, and was able to see them both with some objectivity.

Nevertheless the marriage was based on a precarious balance, whereby one gave all and the other accepted all. "Miss Millay comes first," Eugen had told Alan Ross Macdougall. "If it is necessary for her work to take a trip round the world, we drop everything and take that trip. . . . If your wife is interested in a certain subject, then seek to know a lot about it. . . . If your wife is interested in the stars, why then, study the stars; keep up with her. I may know more about a language than Vincent does. She will study it and in a while she knows more than I do. I just can't wait then, I must do something about it. I must start something else—invite dangerous, stimulating people here; make things happen." Like Cora Millay, he had put Edna, with her wholehearted agreement, in a most difficult position and with the added complication that she was no longer a child, able to see the parent through a child's eyes as infinitely strong, just and perfect. This parent was human, had needs, faults, sufferings of his own, could fall sick, could even, on the rarest of occasions, so far forget himself that he struck back, perhaps unconsciously. "Edna had now been led back to something like the rural isolation of her girlhood, and in her retreat she had no children to occupy her, to compel her to outgrow her girlhood," as Wilson pointed out. Norma believed their childlessness was Eugen's choice, but whether because of his wife's emotional problems or his own needs, there is no way to tell.

Tucked away in their rural isolation, the Boissevains nevertheless, until the 1940s, came out frequently for travel, for regular and extended vacations—they spent some twenty percent of their lives traveling and visited every state in the Union, according to Eugen—for long descents on New York to shop and go to the theater and visit friends, and for the much-applauded poetry readings. There were guests, spirited house parties with literary friends like the Fickes and the Benéts; there were musical evenings when the large living room echoed with Mozart and Brahms or the impromptu singing of Norma and Edna. There were elegant meals, home-brewed wine, argument, mischief, the unrecorded love affairs, the serious work of writing poetry—and with it all, it was as if the walls she had chosen to shelter in still threatened at times to close in and stifle her. Edmund Wilson remembered her telling him on one occasion "when she had apparently spent weeks in bed, that she had done nothing but weep all the time; and on another, she startled me by saying, in the midst of showing me her poetry: 'I'm *not* a pathetic character!' "

Absorbed as she was with the needs of her own troubled spirit, it is hardly amazing that Edna found neither time nor inclination for an active interest in politics. But in the summer of 1927 something happened to pull her briefly away from Steepletop and onto the national political scene, with Eugen in her wake. It was her first, although not her last such foray, and each time what propelled her outward was not the intellectual insight but the emotional one. Although Edna had an intellectual turn of mind, in the sense that she learned readily and enjoyed intellectual tasks to a marked degree, she never did any original thinking on political subjects; indeed her later political pronouncements as well as most of her social and political poetry (with the possible exception of "Epitaph for the Race of Man") are dreary and derivative.

But she felt intensely. Her feelings for others were necessarily muffled, since she was so preoccupied with her own emotional self-preservation, but once they were aroused she could become a noble and tireless partisan.

Nicola Sacco and Bartolomeo Vanzetti, two immigrant workingmen, had been arrested in May of 1920 for the murders of the paymaster and guard of a Massachusetts shoe factory; they spoke little English, were self-avowed anarchists and pacifists, and the temper of the country in the postwar years was such that a pair of foreign-born radicals were considered capable of anything. It became increasingly clear as time went by that there was no solid evidence against them, that Sacco and Vanzetti were guilty not because of anything they had done but because of who they were. The peculiar structure of Massachusetts law at that time permitted the trial judge himself to rule on appeals from his own verdicts. Therefore Judge Webster Thayer, who had been singularly unsympathetic to Sacco and Vanzetti when they were first tried in his court, was able to refuse their demand for a new trial, and repeatedly refused similar demands for the next seven years. By 1927 the injustice of the Massachusetts legal system, as well as the personal qualities of the two accused—rather than dangerous radicals, they were mild, unworldly believers in universal brotherhood—were displayed before the entire western world; a hundred French lawyers drew up a protest against the death sentence, George Bernard Shaw, Albert Einstein and a small army of American writers, artists and intellectuals demanded a reversal. Nevertheless in April of 1927 Judge Thayer officially sentenced the pair to death, and that August the governor of Massachusetts finally rejected an appeal for clemency. The execution was to take place that month.

On August 20 a group of Boston sympathizers sent out a wire: "Picketers urgently needed to picket State House beginning Saturday morning until the execution of Sacco and Vanzetti. It is all we can do now. Will you come and bring anyone you can for that service." Edna and Eugen went to Boston, Edna to march with the picketers in a group of thirteen artists and writers including John Dos Passos, and Eugen well supplied with bail money.

About a hundred and fifty demonstrators were arrested that day on charges of loitering, and Edna Millay was one of them, bailed out by her husband for twenty-five dollars; he stood by to put up bail money for a number of their friends. Later that day the poet had an interview with Governor Fuller of Massachusetts, and she tried to convince him of the fallacy of death sentences by telling him how two men had been convicted and hanged for murder in Maine, their appeal to the governor ignored; later someone confessed to the murder. That evening Edna read a poem, "Justice Is Dead," to a crowd of sympathizers in Salem Street before the Old North Church, and about twenty minutes before midnight she sent the governor a final appeal, reminding him of the mistake that was made in Maine: "Let fall from your harassed mind, all, all save this: which way would He have turned, this Jesus of your faith?" A few minutes after midnight Sacco and Vanzetti were executed.

The Boissevains went back to Steepletop then, because Edna was not well enough to take part in the "death march" of Sacco-Vanzetti sympathizers three days after the execution. She had refused to pay a fine for loitering, and expected to spend a fortnight in jail along with several fellow demonstrators, including Dos Passos, but they were finally acquitted in early December. Meanwhile her letter to the governor, including her account of the Maine affair, was released to the newspapers, and on August 25 the *New York World* printed a letter pointing out a number of errors in her story. At this Edna wrote to her mother, asking for as much material as she could gather about the hanging in Maine; then she assembled a reply that was published in the *World* in October. All these mistakes, she pointed out, only served to show how fallible people are, even those with the best intentions like the governor of Massachusetts. She also published an article, "Fear," later that month in *The Outlook*, castigating the American public for its indifference to justice, and speaking of "the ugliness of man, his cruelty, his greed, his lying face." These themes were to appear again in the mid-thirties, in "Epitaph for the Race of Man."

At home at Steepletop, the money earned by *The King's Henchman* was plowed back into the farm and its outbuildings. The workhouse out in the meadow became an attractive little guest house with a bar; a tennis court was installed as well as a swimming pool. The Fickes bought their home, Hardhack, fourteen miles off, and while it was being made ready they stayed with the Boissevains; Ficke liked Eugen immensely, and dedicated a volume of poetry to him, but between the two women there seems to have been something less than perfect sympathy. The ebb and flow of servants continued: "Anna and Conrad left without giving notice; for a while Freida and her sister worked for us, but they had to go because Freida had to get ready to teach school. Then we got a Swedish couple from an agency in New York, very nice; they have just given notice. In the meantime I have been working very hard on my new book of poems, trying to get it ready in time." This was *The Buck in the Snow*, several of its poems concerned with Edna's recent experiences in Boston and expressing an interest in social issues she had barely whispered of in her previous work; many, like the title poem, had to do with life at Steepletop, with nature and the countryside.

The English writer Llewelyn Powys and his wife, Alyse Gregory, stayed with the Boissevains during the winter of 1930–31, living in the remodeled guest house; Powys was tuberculous, and the dry mountain air was expected to do him good. Some years later his wife wrote the following description of Eugen:

Handsome, reckless, mettlesome as a stallion breathing the first morning air, he would laugh at himself, indeed laugh at everything, with a laugh that scattered melancholy as the wind scatters the petals of the fading poppy. . . . When we stayed in a house which they lent us opposite them in the Berkshire Mountains, I had an opportunity of studying this Dutch gentleman with a French name and a Castilian heart. I would see him in his scarlet coat going out over the freshly fallen snow to count his poultry or to visit his stables, his head as haughty as an Indian chieftain's . . . or standing watch at his gate, as formidable as his Russian wolfhound Allair, lest someone disturb the delicate poet whom it had fallen his lot to protect. . . . He could . . . devote himself with a sustained frenzy to some haphazard business speculation that was to secure leisure for an indigent artist friend; he could retire into the utter stillness of his remote hills, or riot through the midnight hours with the young fops who owned property near him. He could go racing down the precipitous mountain roads in his high-powered motor-car as fast as a meteor, or spend days putting up preserves in his back kitchen. His blood was testy, adventurous, quixotic, and he faced life as an eagle faces its flight. . . . His kindness to Llewelyn and to me in hours of unusual calamity was such as only a great gentleman and a man of heart could have shown, and Llewelyn always felt for him, combined with his gratitude, a singular affinity of temperament.

Judging from her prose Alyse Gregory was an enthusiast, but nevertheless about Eugen she says what everyone says—that he was a man with an appetite for life, ready to taste and experience whatever came his way. But he was not a mere boyish adventurer, carefree out of prolonged youthfulness. He had earned his success as an importer; having taken upon himself the task of handling his wife's business affairs, he proved to be the most practical and hardheaded of managers, alert to details of every kind—hardly anything escaped him, especially ways of saving money—yet he remained touchingly sensitive to the feelings of others.

To his wife he was the perfect audience, for he had no interests of his own that even approached in intensity his absorption with her. "Vincent and I may get into an interesting discussion at six in the morning and at noon we are still not dressed, still talking, still tremendously excited by ideas. We read books together; we tramp about; she talks over a new poem with me. . . . Any day I may have an hour of extraordinary beauty in my life. . . . In marriage a man must seek adventure; he must use his brain."

But Max Eastman felt the Boissevains were trying too hard to retain the excitement of the early years of marriage. "What Eugen and Edna did was to stimulate their hearts and dull their cerebral cortices with alcohol," he said, for Eastman felt that romantic solitude at Steepletop was damned dull once the first bloom had worn off, and because the Boissevains could not face this realization, they drank. There seems little doubt that at times they really did drink too much—Edna certainly did —but whether or not it was to escape boredom is debatable. More likely alcohol was a way of enabling her to live with a psyche that broke down from time to time, and Eugen to support the process of worrying and watching and coping.

"I must start something else—invite dangerous, stimulating people here; make things happen," Eugen had said. And once the tennis court was laid down he arranged for periodic tournaments followed by dinners-with-champagne, at which he handed out loving cups to the winners like a jovial master of ceremonies, for Edna loved the game and played well when her health permitted. A great house party in the summer of 1930 lasted three days, and must have brought dangerous and stimulating people in plenty to Steepletop and to the homes of three of their neighbors. "On the evening of July 22nd we are having the Jitney Players here to give a show for us: Gilbert's 'Haste to the Wedding,' I believe it will be. . . . In any case it will be something silly and amusing and very well presented and a hell of a lot of fun," Edna told Mr. and Mrs. Deems Taylor, when she invited them. Fourteen house guests were to stay at Steepletop, and the Fickes' house would be filled as well as the new homes of their friends the Branns and the La Branches; fifty or sixty souls in all. The players pitched their stage in a natural amphitheater near the farmhouse at Steepletop, and there were flares, a little band, a hot dog stand and lemonade, and not a servant in the house. Nevertheless Edna told the Deems Taylors they could come before the house party if they liked; she must have had boundless confidence in Eugen's ability to cope with domestic crises.

When she was interviewed on the subject of their unconventional household, in the early thirties, Edna said she could like nothing better than this novel arrangement of her husband's running everything. It was her unconcern with daily matters, she said, that protected her from the things that ordinarily eat up a woman's time and interest. "But I haven't made the decision to ignore my household as easily as it sounds. I care an awful lot that things be done right. . . . But if I had to live in a mess, or live in a neat room and give up writing, I prefer the mess."

All the same she never really forgot her girlhood training in housekeeping, and at times, directed either by whim or by sudden necessity, she could become formidably domestic for a while. Returning in 1931 from a long trip to find the house in chaos: "I spend half the day cleaning house, and the rest out of doors. It will be some time before I get the house clean and in order, after three months of that French slut, but I adore to do it. I adore to send everything in the house to the cleaner, and then scrub the house and hang up the clean curtains and lay down the clean rugs. We have no servants and we're going to keep going without them just as long as we can stick it." There were other times when quite without warning the poet appeared in her kitchen wearing old clothes and a cloth wrapped round her head; grabbing mop and pail, she would scrub for half a day. She was also known to shoo the cook out of the kitchen so she could prepare a dinner and serve it herself, while singing sonnets. These were exceptional events; in general what she liked most, she said, was to come into her dining room as a guest to a restaurant and be presented with a charming dinner. Nevertheless it is impossible not to speculate about whether Eugen's desire to take charge of all "quotidian matters," to play the nurturing female role in his own uniquely noisy, exuberant style, had tended to stifle his wife's domestic interests—whether he might not have taken over a part of their lives that, with encouragement, she could have handled herself, or shared with him. He said she needed protection from life's realities; perhaps he had deprived her of their bracing effect.

In the autumn of 1930 Edna had written to "Dearest Artie," Arthur Davison Ficke, that it was not true that life is one damn thing after another—it was one damn thing over and over; first you got sick, then you got sicker, then you were not quite so sick, then you were hardly sick at all, then you got a little sicker. The constant headache that tormented her for over a year after they first came to Steepletop is no longer mentioned, but she had a headache all the same, one that stayed with her whenever she was writing. And she had been, after the long hiatus that followed *The Harp-Weaver*, extremely productive. *The Buck in the Snow*, published in 1928, was not too well received in the States although it met with great enthusiasm in England; Max Eastman thought perhaps this was because Millay had been silent for so long she was thought of as a legend rather than a living poet, and expectations were impossibly high. Some of those who thought well of the new volume were especially interested in the few poems connected with the Sacco-Vanzetti trial, hoping they meant Edna Millay would soon give up her unending preoccupation with the state of her own emotions and pay attention to the world. Their expectations were unjustified. She did turn in later years to political matters, but inferior poetry was almost invariably the result; in the vein of contemplative, philosophical reflection she was occasionally rather successful, but it was never her forte, for she remained, as she began, deeply interested in herself, her loves, her perceptions, her fears. In spite of its mixed reception by American critics, *The Buck in the Snow* was not the same old thing warmed over, for there was a great deal of technical inventiveness in it; not technical facility, which suggests a soulless use of tried-and-true forms, but delicate and accomplished play with rhyme and rhythm that often gives the effect of free verse.

One of the most striking poems in the volume, "Moriturus," treats once more the claustrophobic theme of "Renascence," but here the poetic fabric is bone-simple, without ornament or affectation; the poet meets Death face to face like a child and with a child's direct and homely reactions:

> If I could have
> Two things in one:
> The peace of the grave,
> And the light of the sun;
>
> My hands across
> My thin breast-bone,
> But aware of the moss
> Invading the stone,
>
> . . . .
>
> If I might be
> Insensate matter
> With sensate me
>
> Sitting within,
> Harking and prying,
> I might begin
> To dicker with dying.

Buried alive, then, but with the guarantee that she would remain alive, she can bear to contemplate her dilemma, the contradictory desire to be dependent and independent. But there are no guarantees, as she comes to realize by the end of the poem; whereas in "Renascence" she chose life of her own accord and sprang from the grave to meet the sunlight, here she seems unable to choose, and can only put up a doomed and helpless resistance when Death comes to fetch her:

> I shall bolt my door
> With a bolt and a cable;
> I shall block my door
> With a bureau and a table;
>
> . . . .
>
> With his hand on my mouth
> He shall drag me forth,
> Shrieking to the south
> And clutching at the north.

To write with such simplicity demands great literary courage, especially in the face of the changing fashions in poetry. In the many nature poems in *The Buck in the Snow,* the world-I-cannot-hold-thee-close-enough sort of girlish swooning is less in evidence than before, and in its place we find a strong, sure, highly pictorial affirmation, if not of hope and joy, then of courage and gallantry. With middle age only minutes away, the poet had begun to look backward, remembering childhood, regretting the loss of sharp sensation; she has achieved a certain objectivity about her self and her emotions, and in comparing "Moriturus" with "Renascence" we can even find a degree of ironic amusement in the attempt to keep Death from the room by blocking the doorway with a bureau.

Some thirteen years later the poet Rolfe Humphries wrote a critical essay in connection with Millay's *Collected Sonnets* that probably explains the cool reception of *The Buck in the Snow:* ". . . the fact that the direction of her progress has been from legend to success somewhat confuses discussion of her merit as an artist. If she is not taken quite seriously in this role today, it may be that she was taken too seriously twenty years ago." There is praise as well: "She was very good to begin with . . . the manner remains original, the contrivance adroit, the epithet nice, the music clear." But in the 1920s she had been read and quoted more than any other living American poet; anything less than that necessarily represented decline, therefore decline was inevitable. She had merely published, in *The Buck in the Snow*, another volume containing some fine poems and many interesting ones, therefore she had amazed and astonished no one.

In the spring of 1931 Edna Millay published a sequence of fifty-two love sonnets entitled *Fatal Interview*, and if critical judgment was mixed —a lengthy discussion of love, at the height of the Great Depression and in sonnet form, of all things, seemed curiously precious to many— popular reaction was enthusiastic indeed. Here there could be no mistaking the personal note, the sense of intimate revelation. *Fatal Interview* follows a woman through a single love affair from its first beginnings, to her pursuit of the beloved, to his capitulation—when she had "ravished to my bitter smart/Your kiss from the stern moment"—to the joyous and triumphal consummation; this is followed by the man's increasing restiveness, their breaking up, her final resignation to loss. For unlike any of the love poetry Edna Millay had written before, *Fatal Interview* ends when the man has tired of the woman; she was past forty when the sonnet sequence was published, therefore it was written at an age when her amorous career must have begun to suffer from the encroachments of time. But the fear of desertion had been with her from the beginning, from early childhood when her father walked across the cranberry field; it had haunted all her love affairs. In *Fatal Interview* she met her fears and grappled with them and survived: "How simple 'tis, and what a little sound/ It makes in breaking, let the world attest:/ It struggles, and it fails; the world goes round,/ And the moon follows it."

A contemporary critic said of *Fatal Interview* that "all her references are everywhere traditional. Book-lore is her reality. . . . High-syllabled words from books . . . traditional conceptions and old stories are Miss Millay's materials. . . . She does not write to tell the world what it does not know already, but to announce a truth that poets have voiced for ages." And it is unfortunately true that Edna Millay's habitual delight in mythological references—Venus, golden Jove, forsworn Aeneas, mortal Endymion in the Latmian cave, as well as antique props like the winged helmet, winged heel, sword belt and bridge-chain—seems to flower forth in this volume so that passion is everywhere presented in lofty and bookish terms redolent of libraries and the midnight oil and Vassar College. Nevertheless the reader is persuaded, given the least desire to be so persuaded, that here is a woman experiencing before his eyes a whole range of deeply felt emotions. The poems are uneven in quality; there is no one sonnet as good, all the way through, as the best six- or eight-line sequences. And yet it is extremely moving, the trappings and properties are lifted from books but the feelings come from the blood and the spirit. Like the love sonnets of Elizabeth Barrett Browning they surmount fashion, leap over the boundaries of literary criticism and pierce the heart of the common reader.

Surely it is impossible to read *Fatal Interview* without wondering how real were the events it describes; Edmund Wilson, who called it "certainly one of her most successful works and one of the great poems of our day," took it to be a true account of a single love affair, representing "her old pattern of escape by breaking away from her domestic arrangements." Elizabeth Atkins, the biographer, was told as much by Eugen, when he read through her manuscript and corrected her statement that the poem must be a work of the imagination since the poet "was living quietly with a husband of eight years' standing" at the time this passionate love affair was supposed to have taken place. Eugen had already made clear his beliefs about monogamous marriage: "Unless you are a fool and so conceited as to think you are the greatest, the most wonderful man in the world, how can you expect a woman to love only you. And if you could know for a certainty that never, never would the personality of another appeal to her, you would be bored."

But how did such a complex adventure take place, practically speaking? "Along my body, waking while I sleep,/ Sharp to the kiss, cold to the hand as snow,/ The scar of this encounter like a sword/ Will lie between me and my troubled lord" implies some degree of concealment. If Max Eastman invited his potential lovers home so that his Russian wife, Eliena, might inspect them, Edna Millay almost certainly did not.

"How shall I leave your side, how shall I go?" she asks later on, for she must rise and wring her hands and steal away. Some of the later poetry suggests meetings in the city, in the lover's apartment, and some, like "The Fitting," suggest a European background; she and Eugen were not always together on their trips to Europe as they were at Steepletop.

Such conjectures are almost as hard to resist today as they were when *Fatal Interview* first appeared, revealing no clue at all as to the identity of the lover, nor has any clue yet turned up; Edna Millay was then and for the rest of her life entirely discreet and reticent about her personal life, which was never intended as a public entertainment. When Harper, many years later, suggested she assemble a collection of her love poems with a mellow foreword saying how each of them came to be written, she went to great pains to explain she might need money, but not that much.

In the library at Steepletop where the poet did most of her writing, sailing charts of Penobscot Bay decorated the walls; although no newspapers were delivered to the house, the Boissevains subscribed to a couple of gardening magazines and to one about yachting that they read together, cover to cover, with intense interest. As long ago as *Second April*, in her twenties, Edna had been writing about her longing to be near the sea—"Screaming to God for death by drowning"—and in another poem she declared, "Mine is a body that should die at sea!" She was living in New York then, "Sick of the city, wanting the sea," but the desire remained with her all through the years at Steepletop. "More sea than land am I . . ." and "In these cool waves/ What can be lost?—/ Only the sorry cost/ Of the lovely thing, ah, never the thing itself!"

Edmund Wilson recalled that when he visited Steepletop Edna told him "the only bad feature of Austerlitz was its not being near the sea, of which she had a permanent need, that the hills and the woods walled her in and sometimes made her feel imprisoned (this was, as I now can see, one of the phases of her recurrent claustrophobia)." It seems strange that she could feel imprisoned among the hundreds of solitary acres that were Steepletop, where for days, even weeks at a time she might not see an unfamiliar face—there were the servants, there was the farmer John Pinnie who helped Eugen run the farm, there was Eugen, who had posted a sign warning uninvited visitors to leave. What is still more curious is that her longing for the sea so often includes the desire to die at sea.

That these feelings had to do with claustrophobia seems beyond argument, but there is more involved than a craving for unboundedness, since she wants not only to escape from hills and woods that make her feel imprisoned, but to become one with the sea, to dissolve in it. And the sea is in all western languages a female, just as ships are female; it is the maternal element, by poetic extension (and by biological truth) akin to the amniotic fluid in which the embryo dwells. Man descends from the creatures that lived in the sea and in his personal history repeats the journey, growing within the nourishing, protective maternal sea until he is propelled with a sharp cry into the air, and begins the long, slow adaptation to life on his own.

To swim in the ocean is to be surrounded by the ocean's power, at once endangered by that power and supported by it, held aloft by its buoyancy; and to die there, to dissolve and become one with the ocean, can be seen as the ultimate expression of the need to join what is powerful, supportive and all-encompassing. Edna Millay had such a craving; perhaps it can be interpreted as one more aspect of the lifelong clinging to childhood and maternal shelter, a craving so deep-seated she could write about it as ending in death.

She was a splendid swimmer, as was Eugen, although two previous accidents had somewhat dimmed his pleasure in ocean bathing. And in 1933 the two of them saw an island, solitary and beautifully wild; Edna fell in love with it and Eugen bought it for her.

They had been visiting Tess Root Adams at her vacation home on Bailey's Island, Maine; waking at dawn to watch the sunrise, they saw nothing at first but sea and sky. Soon an island appeared on the horizon, rocky, remote and, to the poet, utterly enchanting. It was Ragged Island, one of the least accessible of many small islands in lower Casco Bay, a pile of rocks surrounding some fifty acres of scrub forest with one small harbor and an old house. By late summer, Eugen was writing to Eugene Saxton at Harper: "We have bought an 85 acre island off the coast of Maine. Three miles out at sea. Inaccessible, inhospitable and all together too wonderful and beautiful for words. . . . If she gets a writing fit there you'll have a book for spring, otherwise doubtless fall. Voilà la dope intérieure." Once they owned Ragged the Boissevains did as little as possible to it, coming there regularly every summer and at odd times the rest of the year, almost always alone. Tess Adams, who had helped Eugen with the details of the purchase and whose house on Bailey's Island was in plain sight of Ragged, was not to be invited there for another twelve years, and many intimate friends of the Boissevains were never invited at all. It became a sea-girt cloister where Edna could spend hours at a time immersed, mother naked, in the water, where she and Eugen could be "entirely alone in our little house and entirely alone on the island, to gather driftwood, and haul our lobster-traps, and make fish-chowders, and sail, and read, and sit on the rocks."

That autumn Eugen asked if Harper would be able to sell some of his wife's manuscripts to collectors, and the following February she wrote herself to request an advance of five thousand dollars, to be taken out of her royalties as they accrued. The year before Edna had written, again by herself, for a modest advance, adding, "Hardened as I am, I feel sorry for you when you get this letter, I know you're going to burst into tears." The purchase of Ragged Island, the extensive alterations to Steepletop, and the need—increasingly pressing—for her to recoup her forces each winter in southern climates, whether the Caribbean, Florida or the Mediterranean, probably account for the shortage of money. For the Boissevain-Millay household was doing extremely well financially. In addition to their usual sources of income, the farm, Eugen's Java property and Edna's books, she had been reading her poetry over the nation-wide WJZ Blue Network since December of 1932, the first literary figure of national stature to be so recognized by radio. As for the poetry-reading tours, although Eugen had been able to command higher fees after the publication of *Fatal Interview*, the Boissevains insisted they made little profit from them, since the poet had to travel so expensively. The readings themselves were emotionally exhausting, and the constant travel, even with Eugen's close attendance, was a serious drain on her health.

Eugen tried getting his wife to cut down on the poetry tours, and she agreed at least once to make no further commitments for a while, then bought an expensive painting and had to arrange for readings right away, to pay for it. For in spite of all her complaints, her claims that the audience came in search of scandal and she felt like a prostitute, in spite of the very real pain and tension that accompanied her public appearances, Edna must have got at least as much as she gave to her audiences during her memorable readings. "Public appearances were cruelly exhausting to her, as her husband . . . told us," according to Florence Jenney, the Vassar professor of German. "She dreaded especially the initial plunge into the reading; it was almost impossible for her to begin. Let this enlighten as best it can those members of the audience to whom she seemed, in the opening moments of her readings, incredibly hesitant, coy, arty. Her behavior was not a pose; it was a last-minute struggle to defer the inevitable agony of beginning." Once she started the tension seemed to melt away, the deep voice, vibrant and dramatic, lonely yet intimate, held the audience in a close embrace and they listened as people do to music. Yet the moment the reading was over Eugen rose as if from nowhere and whisked her away so fast "the disappointed and curious crowd . . . in ignorance of the real reason for her headlong flight, ascribed it to wilful arrogance. This was not true. She told us that . . . for many weeks her head had ached constantly."

Sick with apprehension before the recital, whisked away by her protective genie the moment it was finished, to the angry murmurs of a packed house that had been sitting like enchanted children while she read and wanted afterward only to shake her hand and hear her say an informal word or two—why had she come, since it was not for the money? Why had she not remained comfortably at Steepletop and forgone the headache and the ensuing exhaustion altogether? The answer can only lie in those moments when she and the audience were one: "Boys and girls that lie/ Whispering in the hedges,/ Do not let me die,/ Mix me with your pledges." Her poetry, whether in print or in the auditorium, was the siren call of a lonely woman longing for love and admiration and intimacy, yet once she had it, it was as if she had thrust her hand into the jar of leeches—they could suck her blood and drain her dry.

Everyone who knew her spoke of Edna as being "frail"; she was especially subject to respiratory infections, which account for the annual trips to warmer climates. The summer they bought Ragged Island, hoping to spend all of August there, she had a long bout of flu and was sick for weeks, barely able to stagger about and confined to bed for days on end. The flu was further complicated by a severe attack of poetry, so that sick as she was, she persisted in working "twenty-four hours a day." But that winter they were able to sail to the south of Europe, where the poet hoped to get warm at last, with all her energies kept intact for work. As for Eugen, she told Alan Ross Macdougall that he hoped to make a fortune at Monte Carlo; in any case, he certainly couldn't lose one.

The book she worked on twenty-four hours a day, and took with her to the house at Antibes rented from Eugen's brother, was to be *Wine from These Grapes,* the first volume of poetry she ever published without a single love poem. Its main feature was a sequence of eighteen sonnets, "Epitaph for the Race of Man," reflective and philosophic in character and concerned with man's seemingly inborn need to destroy himself. Wilson said she had been working on a long poem with a similar theme as far back as 1920. And in 1941 she told Grace King, who was writing a doctoral thesis about Millay, that she never intended "Epitaph" as a gloomy prediction—considering how few years were to elapse before the discovery of atomic fission, the aptness of the prediction is extraordinary—but rather as a challenge; it was, she said then, a heartfelt tribute to the magnificence of man. But "Epitaph" does not sound like a tribute, it sounds like an epitaph.

By the mid-thirties critical opinion of Millay had become increasingly harsh. When she wrote love poems it was said that her concerns were too narrow, that she had not grown, and when, as in "Epitaph," she turned to larger issues, she did not do so in the approved style, intellectual, dense, symbolic and obscure. Both the poet and her husband were aware of this drift in critical opinion, and Eugen's letters to Eugene Saxton, Edna Millay's editor at Harper, when *Wine from These Grapes* appeared were full of anxiety about the forthcoming reviews; would it not be possible to choose the reviewers, to choose interviewers for some of the papers or magazines who could be depended upon for sympathetic treatment? "I think the people who are reviewing the book now are waiting an opportunity to slam her," he said. In spite of their fears and in spite of a number of unfavorable reviews, the book sold well at a time when money was especially desirable.

For Llewelyn Powys and his wife were in trouble; his tuberculosis was worse and he had been having serious financial worries as well. Along with three friends and neighbors Powys had circulated a petition protesting the cruel treatment of delinquent girls in a home in his neighborhood in England, and British libel law permitted the four to be sued and fined for this petition. Powys' share of the fines, along with court costs, came in the end to nearly three thousand dollars, a staggering sum for a dying man who had always lived precariously. All the same, Lulu, as Edna called him, insisted he wanted help from no one. She sent him a thousand dollars in March of 1935, largely due to *Wine from These Grapes*, promising two thousand more within weeks and more after that if he needed it—and if he persisted in refusing her help, she said he would "wound me with a hurt I shall never recover from."

In *Wine from These Grapes* three poems mourn the death of Cora Millay, in February of 1931. She had been buried at Steepletop, and during the next twenty years the memory of her devotion and rare courage was to appear and reappear in Millay's poetry, although never so poignantly as in "Childhood is the Kingdom Where Nobody Dies":

But you do not wake up a month from then, two months,
A year from then, two years, in the middle of the night
And weep, with your knuckles in your mouth, and say Oh, God! Oh, God!
Childhood is the kingdom where nobody dies that matters,— mothers and
fathers don't die.

And if you have said, "For heaven's sake, must you always be kissing a person?"
Or, "I do wish to gracious you'd stop tapping on the window with your thimble!"
Tomorrow, or even the day after tomorrow if you're busy having fun,
Is plenty of time to say, "I'm sorry, mother."

If *Wine from These Grapes* was her first departure from love poetry, her first foray into the philosophical, an even more unusual venture was to follow. In the late twenties Edna had met a young American poet, George Dillon. A few years later, when he began translating Baudelaire for his own pleasure, she urged him to publish his translations. Soon she found herself drawn into Dillon's project, partly out of a love for Baudelaire and the French language, partly out of a fascination with the seemingly infinite subtleties of translation, and by the mid-thirties Millay and Dillon had embarked upon a joint volume, an English version of *Les Fleurs du Mal* that was to be published by Harper. Dillon spent part of one summer at Steepletop, then went on to Maine with the Boissevains to continue work on the book. In September Eugen took his wife to Europe, where she wanted to consult French experts about Baudelaire. They were back at Steepletop a month later with the poet in a state of exhaustion, for this first and only attempt at translation had become a tense and feverish business, in which no detail was too trivial to merit her passionate attention.

As soon as Baudelaire was safely in the hands of the publisher, Eugen became anxious to get his wife away from deep winter at Steepletop, so anxious that for once he left her at home and went on ahead to Florida by himself, in order to select and rent a furnished house; and even as he hunted one he kept up a barrage of wires to Steepletop, urging her to get on the next train and join him. But in his absence all the chores connected with leaving home and usually managed by Eugen—closing up the farmhouse, directing the servants as they packed—seemed to drain what little strength she had left. She was "simply exhausted after getting the Baudelaire off to Harpers," yet once she had settled into the rented house at Delray Beach Edna proceeded to send letter after letter to Dillon about their book, and this in spite of the neurotic fear of letter writing that had plagued her during much of the past winter—a fear that troubled her off and on during much of her adult life, and for which she had coined the name "epistophobia." Title page, book jacket, table of contents, all were weighed and discussed with Dillon or with Saxton; once the corrected proofs had been returned to the publisher, and a promise secured not to bring the book out on April Fool's Day, Edna wrote to Arthur Ficke that she would "probably sell what is left of my honour, in order to buy up the whole edition." There was nothing left to do after that but wait, and wait she did, jittery with hope and fear. Eugen wrote to Saxton around mid-March: "Miss Millay says that whereas she for a moment saw you as through the smoke of battle darkly, she now once more beholds you face to face. She wishes me to say that she is drugging herself to sleep every night and reading detective stories all day long, in order to make the moments pass, until the advance copy of THE BOOK arrives."

When it did, she proclaimed herself "entranced . . . it is beautiful . . . am weak with excitement." But she did not forget to worry and fidget that Dillon's feelings might be hurt by some lack of attention to him; accordingly Eugen sent a telegram to Harper urging, with his usual careful politeness, that an advance copy be sent to Dillon, for somehow this courtesy had been overlooked in the excitement of getting the book to press. After that both Eugen and Edna kept up a flow of useful suggestions about how to promote the book. Eugen said: "It might be good business for you to send a copy to the French Ambassador in Washington and one to the American Ambassador in Paris. . . . These babies have nothing to talk about at their official dinners and receptions and this book would give them something to say to their neighbours at table, and more or less, in line with their job."

Their excitement about the book died down; they could not have sustained such tensions for long, certainly Edna could not, and her husband's interest was of course more moderate. The book was received for the most part quite coolly. A few reviewers were enthusiastic, more were able to praise it here and there, but there were many who complained of the freedom the translators used. There was more Millay than Baudelaire, someone said, and they had been altogether too "easygoing." The Dillon-Millay Baudelaire is of little interest today, and we can only wonder why Edna was so gripped by her self-imposed task: in what way had it fired her imagination? Was it her long-standing affection for French language and culture, or the intellectual challenge of translation with its assorted rigors and exactnesses and nuances appealing to the schoolteacher in her? Whatever she dreamed of finding among *The Flowers of Evil*, Edna paid a high price in eight months of wear and tear on her nerves, for she wrote to "My Darling Lulu" that she had "never worked so hard on anything in my life."

Early in May, after months of fog, wind, clouds and pouring rain, the Boissevains left Delray Beach for Sanibel Island off the west coast of Florida. Here they registered at the Palms Hotel about an hour before sunset. Instead of going up to their room, Edna went out to the beach to gather shells, for which the island is famous—in the corner cabinets of the dining room at Steepletop, open shelves designed to show pieces of china were used instead to display her favorite seashells—and "Looking back up the beach a few minutes later, I saw the hotel in flames." All the Boissevains' luggage was destroyed in the fire, every bit of clothing they had with them including even Edna's hat and coat, the old battered copy of Catullus she never traveled without, and the entire manuscript of a nearly finished dramatic poem, "Conversation at Midnight."

They drove north after that, unable to visit the great showplace Magnolia, near Charleston, where they had been expected "because by the time we got near Charleston I was such a complete mess and such a sight," as she explained later to the owners of Magnolia. They were traveling north at thirty-five, thirty, twenty-five, then twenty miles an hour, she wrote, in a car with a loose bearing, "to the accompaniment of an increasingly interested populace," and she was "swathed in something which once had been a white linen suit, and wrapped in a rug in lieu of a coat. . . . We were so painfully unpresentable that we slunk into hotels late at night with our arms over our faces, and sneaked out before daybreak."

Edna said the only "truly *emotional* loss" in the hotel fire was her seventeenth-century copy of Catullus; the lost poem could be reconstructed, since she had an excellent memory for finished work, although the partly finished sections gave her an "exhausting and nerve-wracking time." But for years she had not traveled anywhere without a book of Latin poetry in her suitcase, and the old leather-bound Catullus was usually on her night table when she went to bed, as trusty and familiar a companion as her toothbrush. Now it was gone; there were other copies of Catullus to be bought and the dramatic poem could be reconstructed, yet in neither case was the replacement to prove as satisfactory as the beloved original. And other misfortunes followed.

Just a few months after the hotel fire Eugen was driving his wife in their new station wagon, near Steepletop; going round a sharp turn, "the door flew open and Edna was thrown out and rolled down the embankment," he told Alyse Gregory. "She had a big bump on her little red-head, scratches and bruises all over, and her right arm was all bunged up so that she cannot play the piano or use the typewriter. She's getting better now. But we are not pleased with God, although he might have done worse." That autumn the poet wrote to her young friend Dante Bergonzi, a student at a nearby music school who had lived one summer in the guest house at Steepletop, and who often came to play chamber music with the Boissevains and a few of their friends, that she was suffering from bursitis, and Eugen had strained his shoulder practicing hard serves on the tennis court, so he too was out of commission. "Isn't it too hateful, after so longing to have a tennis court, finally to get one, and such a beautiful one, and then to be laid up for three months or so with bursitis? For it takes about three months, they say, and by that time it will be too cold to play until next summer." But it was not bursitis that troubled her, it was a serious injury to the nerves of her back, caused by the fall from the car, and it was to prove exquisitely painful for long stretches of time; unlike bursitis, it lasted for years rather than months.

The fire on Sanibel Island and the injury to her back, had they happened to a fictional character rather than a real one, might have been inserted into the plot to mark a change of fortune, a shift in the prevailing winds. Certainly Edna Millay's life up till then had not been one of unadulterated happiness; she had earned a dazzling success as a poet, a success both popular and critical, national and to a certain extent international. Her popularity was not what it once was—the fantastic adulation of the early 1920s was quite gone, and the critics were lukewarm—yet her poetry continued to sell; at her death in 1950, more than twenty of her books were still in print. For fifteen years, then, she had been a published and much-loved poet; since 1923 she had also been a wife who lived in safe harbor with the most devoted of husbands, a man who protected her not only from the world but from herself, calming her quivering temper tantrums, soothing her bouts of depression or self-doubt. Yet if he was the priest who guarded the sacred flame, Eugen was also a man of flesh and blood, who got sick from time to time, injured himself practicing tennis serves and drove a car from which his wife was somehow ejected and seriously injured. He must have had other moments, unrecorded though they remain, of less than perfect love and strength. In the late thirties his wife wrote: "I'm in a vile temper this morning. Ugin's gone and contracted the flu, or something; and we can't go to Cass Canfield's to dinner tonight. . . . I don't know whether to be sorry for poor Ugin, or furious with him." Surely the very price "poor Ugin" paid in making over his life to the service of Vincent and poetry suggests occasional spurts of irritation toward the object of so much care, especially since she chafed under that care. Eugen must surely have wondered, however well he hid it from himself and from his wife, whether or not his life of self-sacrifice was worthwhile.

In the late thirties, then, when a change seems to become apparent in the texture of Edna's life, it is not a total change by any means, but rather as if the darker threads in a woven fabric start to crowd out the lighter ones until the fabric seems dark all over—yet light threads remain, and dark ones have been there all along. Her always precarious health was to sustain blow after blow, physical, mental, and combinations of the two, starting with the injury to her back. And all the while the events that led to World War II were preparing for Edna and Eugen both, a hypersensitive poet and an expatriate Dutchman, such a series of alterations in the quality of life that the few years after the fire were also the last few years of relative comfort and plenty and peace of mind that remained to them.

In December of 1936 Edna left Steepletop for a stay in a New York hotel, partly in order to buy clothes, for much of her wardrobe had been packed in the half-dozen pieces of luggage that were lost on Sanibel Island. A few weeks after her arrival she came down with flu, and by the following May: "I am still here. I have been working all winter and all spring on my new book—not like a dog, not like a slave; dogs and slaves must be relieved and rested"—but working, she said, like a poet. The new book was *Conversation at Midnight*, the dramatic poem that had burned and was being salvaged; but she also took time that spring to translate a Spanish poem that was to be included in an anthology, *And Spain Sings*, the proceeds of which would benefit the Spanish Loyalists.

Edna had been a pacifist until the early thirties, "a true conscientious objector. My thought and opinion were that it was wrong to go to arms," but now her pacifist faith was buffeted by the Spanish Civil War, and by the rise of rightist dictatorships in Italy and Germany. The state of American political belief, the comparative values of communism, fascism, capitalism as well as traditional religion, were discussed and debated in *Conversation at Midnight*, which reflects doubts, fears and dissatisfactions the poet seems to have been mulling over since the mid-twenties. She told a reporter shortly before *Conversation* was published that communism was repugnant to her, for she was intensely an individualist. She hated fascism, had deep and long-standing reservations about capitalism, and felt that another war was inevitable; to confront such a war, one that might write an epitaph for the race of man, must have seemed unthinkable without some faith, however vague or ill-defined, whether in mankind or in democracy. And in the new poem she had done her best to examine the state of belief in America, as if to come to some understanding of her own altered values.

Once again Millay had done what so many critics, favorable and otherwise, were always imploring her to do—she was contemplating the world instead of her own navel. Nevertheless the reception of *Conversation* was anything but cordial, some critics suggesting she should have taken the hotel fire as a sign from heaven and left the manuscript in the ashes; a friendly critic said it contained some of the worst lines Millay had ever written. The passage of time has failed to uncover fresh virtues in *Conversation*; the word "mishmash" comes inevitably to mind since it is a melange of many poetic styles, some of them almost prose, and of many points of view, the whole unsatisfying, inconclusive and frequently dull. It is a rare reader nowadays who can get through the poem without skimming. Yet it must have taken courage for Edna to write something so different in form and content from all her previous work, and the poem has a certain interest as an expression of her increasing involvement with the objective world and the ideas of ordinary people in the thirties. In that sense, at least, she had come a long way since the years when Wilson found her uninterested in politics and uninterested in other people.

In *Conversation* seven men of different backgrounds meet for an evening of fellowship, talk and drink, each personifying a different view of the world, one a priest, another a communist, another a rich business-man, and so forth. The central and most attractive figure is the host, Ricardo, whom the poet thought of as holding ideas closest to her own. He seems rather more like a combination of herself and Eugen, with a few flecks here and there of Arthur Ficke, to whom the book is dedi-cated. Ricardo is described as "the son of an Italian petty nobleman and an American woman," who had inherited a fortune, a house in town, a handsome estate in the country, and a gentle, affectionate nature. Blessed with striking physical beauty and an aristocratic and subtle mind, he is a liberal and an agnostic. It is an apt picture of Eugen Boissevain and a loving one—in fact the entire work is carried out with a certain affectionate touch that suggests all the men in it were modeled on real men Edna knew, and the conversation at midnight modeled on real evenings of good talk, perhaps including the dangerous and exciting people Eugen said he brought to Steepletop for her entertainment. Yet there were no women in Ricardo's house that night.

During the very period when Edna had been rewriting *Conversation*, holed up in a New York hotel and working harder than a slave, she had been offered an honorary degree by New York University; the chancel-lor's wife invited her to be guest of honor at a dinner for a small group of women the evening before commencement and Edna had accepted with pleasure. But she learned a week later that a separate dinner was to be given that same night for male recipients of honorary degrees, and she composed a scorching letter begging that she might be the last woman "to swallow from the very cup of this honour, the gall of this humiliation." Apparently it never occurred to her that in *Conversation* she had done just what the university did—assembled a company of the choicest spirits and left the women out; it was one more expression of her lifelong ambivalence about the female role.

The Boissevains' neighbor George La Branche, it was generally

agreed, had been the model for Merton, the worldly stockbroker and
hunter of *Conversation at Midnight*, and it was at his house in the
autumn of 1937 that a dramatic real-life conversation took place. In the
La Branches' gun room, one night, Arthur Ficke found Edna relaxed
and unguarded after six cocktails and he came at her, she said, like a
prosecuting attorney. "To whom did you write that sonnet, Vince?" he
demanded, meaning one of the love poems in *Second April*, the one
beginning, "And you as well must die, beloved dust . . ."

She replied that the sonnet was written to him, by no means a
startling revelation, for many of the poems in *Second April* celebrated
their brief love affair and she had already told him so, although apparently she never told him just which ones. All the same, when the six
cocktails had worn off Edna had second thoughts about her admission,
and she wrote to Ficke saying the sonnet had not been intended for him
at all. She scolded him, affectionately and gently, for his indiscretion,
reminding him that she had always been reticent about her personal
affairs and those of other people. He had done the same thing once
before, she remembered, when he asked in half-serious fashion whether
or not Llewelyn Powys had ever been her lover. And it was wrong of him
to do so, wrong then and wrong now, and she was truly sorry if she hurt
his feelings by pointing it out.

But she really had written that sonnet to Darling Artie, and was to
confess as much in 1945, shortly before he died. Perhaps, she said then,
she concealed it earlier because she didn't want him to know for sure
how terribly, how sickeningly in love with him she had been when the
poem was written; and perhaps she was still in love with him in 1937,
in the gun room, she said. She was forty-five then, and Ficke about ten
years older, and the love poems she was writing at the time show a
quality of dry, amused resignation to the fact that passion, especially
extramarital passion, is hardly at its best in middle age. Some of the
poems in *Huntsman, What Quarry?* describe the aftertaste of such
overripe love affairs; in "Rendezvous" a woman meets her young lover
in his overdecorated apartment and wishes she did not feel like his
mother. In "Theme and Variations" an impatient lover who is eager to
be finished and away is seen as an inferior article, an unworthy successor

to her previous partners. Her tone is ironic, faintly self-mocking, but the emotions seem real and painful all the same, for time was slowly closing off one means of escape from what Edmund Wilson had called "her domestic arrangements."

It was during this period, in the years just before 1940, that Max Eastman lost sight of his friend Eugen and of Edna Millay. "She seemed to be mysteriously sick a great deal of the time," Eastman recalled. "She cultivated for all it was worth the privilege of being sick. She lived largely upstairs in her bedroom, and would fly up there from the slightest annoyance—a noisy guest, an untimely call from a neighbor or a passing friend." He said that Edna babied herself, and Eugen·babied her, and "one felt on entering Steepletop that some very fragile piece of china, inestimable in value, was in unstable equilibrium upstairs, and that even the air-waves, if too much agitated, might unbalance it. Eugen, to be sure, could disturb the air-waves all he pleased, and being an obstreperous, athletic, noisy-laughing person, he disturbed them a plenty, but he did stand guard over his frail treasure, his 'child,' as he sometimes called her. . . . I doubt very much whether that state of affairs increased the output of poetry."

It was also during this period that Max and Eliena began to feel they ought to say something about the Boissevains' drinking; Max wrote to Eugen, and Eugen wrote back saying it was true, they did drink too much, and they meant to do something about it very soon. But Eastman said they never did. The writer Upton Sinclair, an old friend of Edna's from Greenwich Village days, met her in Pasadena in 1940 on one of the poetry-reading tours, and was as distressed as Eastman about her drinking. Sinclair wrote: "I greeted her in a dressing room of the Pasadena Community Theatre, and we sat down to chat. With her was her husband, . . . a charming, kind fellow. . . . When it came time for Edna to go on stage and speak, Eugen drew a flask from his back pocket and handed it to his wife. She took a heavy swig. . . . evidently this was routine."

"I went out and listened," Sinclair continued, "while she read a dozen or more of her poems to an audience of ladies; then when it was over, I went behind the scenes again; and there Eugen produced the flask again, and I watched Edna empty it."

Many of her actions during this period—the drinking, the living upstairs in her bedroom—must have stemmed from the injury to her back, and there seems no doubt she was in real and prolonged pain. But Eastman felt she had decided as a child "that she was a specially delicate-fibered, somewhat supernal being, and this did not help her when she was called upon to triumph over pain." Neither did Eugen help her. His protectiveness had done nothing to encourage her to face hard realities; he had always faced them for her, yet pain was a burden she had to bear alone. Eugen failed her in more practical ways: knowing she drank too much—if not "too much" for most people, it would nevertheless have been too much for a woman with a history of gastrointestinal illness—he had promised to put a stop to it and never did. Aware of the emotional strain that came with the poetry readings, he permitted them to continue, and what was more striking, he himself, the protecting parent, carried the flask of liquor that his wife emptied. But if the two of them were working hand in glove to keep her a child, Edna was really ill all the same, physically as well as emotionally, and becoming demoralized by pain. She withdrew increasingly into the isolation of Steepletop, cut herself off from most of her old friends and turned to gardening, to music, and more and more to Eugen.

In *Huntsman, What Quarry?* along with the love poems that inspect extramarital passion with the dimmed eyes of forty-five, a poem called "Thanksgiving Dinner" celebrates conjugal love. The poet says her garden has been broken by frost, the tomatoes, grapes and peppers all frozen, yet she walks among them smiling. "I can live on the woody fibres of the overgrown/ Kohl-rabi, on the spongy radish coarse and hot,/ I can live on what the squirrels may have left of the beechnuts and the acorns . . ./ For pride in my love, who might well have died, and did not." She will cook for him a banquet of beets, cabbages, leeks, potatoes, turnips—"We will laugh like spring above the steaming, stolid winter roots."

The personal poems in *Huntsman* are resigned and wryly mature, almost contemporary in feeling, but it is the political poems that mark the new paths Edna Millay had begun to take. "Say that We Saw Spain Die" is a memorial to defeated Loyalist Spain, and five sonnets, "From a Town in a State of Siege," probably are also concerned with the

Spanish war. The title poem indirectly expresses her long-standing pacifist convictions and could have been written today by a radical member of the women's liberation movement. It contrasts a hunter, pursuing the fox, and a girl who invites him to spend the night with her and "let the fox run free." He hesitates, the fox breaks cover, and off the man rides —"Hoick! Hoick!" cries he. Although the ballad has been interpreted in a number of ways, its meaning is surely the most obvious one, that women love life and living creatures and lovemaking, while men can never really resist the chance to show off, hunt glory and make a killing instead.

Edna thought the best poem in the book was the sonnet "Czecho-Slovakia," written almost immediately after the German invasion of March 1939. Another of the political pieces, "Underground System," expresses the poet's fears for the United States, where "moles have built their palace beneath us: we have not far to fall," meaning that home-grown fascists and communists, who would betray us from within, might also join forces with one another—"they have tunnelled the sub-soil/ With separate chambers; which at an appointed knock/ Could be as one, could intersect and interlock." The poet read "Underground System" in October of 1939 when she took part in a forum put on by the *New York Herald Tribune,* at which Mrs. Franklin D. Roosevelt and George Washington Carver also spoke. "Miss Millay, who has been ill, was assisted to the platform, and left it immediately after the conclusion of her talk." It was her first public appearance as a political figure since the execution of Sacco and Vanzetti; her speech urged repeal of the Embargo Act of 1937, which kept the United States from selling arms to England and France and fostered an atmosphere of neutrality, when there was every reason, she said, for us to speak out in favor of those two countries "whose concepts of civilized living are so closely akin to our own." Americans had taken up this neutral, pacifist position not because they hated war but for selfish, personal reasons—"because it is more comfortable to live in a country which is not at war." This shrill and bitter tone, like that of a schoolteacher reprimanding students too dull or lazy to care about their duties, pervades much of the poetry she was to write for the next seven or eight years.

In May 1940, when Germany invaded Denmark, Norway and the Low Countries, all of Eugen's large family in Holland were in immediate danger; from that time until the end of the war he seemed to live with one ear pressed against the radio. As for Edna, she had long since stopped questioning the rights and wrongs of war—when Hitler had finished with the Low Countries and attended to England and France, he would turn to America, no longer protected by the oceans because "There Are No Islands Any More," the title of one of the first of her propaganda poems. To avoid invasion, she maintained, America must be armed to the teeth, and if invasion proved unavoidable at least we would be prepared for it. "After I am dead and gone, I want there to be alive in the world a true democratic ideal . . . to continue in this country, in this crisis," she told an interviewer.

Another and more personal result of the occupation of Holland was the loss of all Eugen's income from Java; now Edna would have to support them both. The still mysterious pain in her right arm had become continuous, and "the outrage of unalleviated pain has been coupled with the infuriating obligation of laying one sweet luscious grand after another between the self-complacent and condescending teeth of one officious and inefficient hospital after another." Nevertheless "it does not matter because I have been able to work." Her work was now the writing of propaganda poems—"not poems, posters," she called them, meaning they were not to be considered as art at all, but as vivid journalism.

In the autumn of 1940 Harper brought out her poster poems as a book, *Make Bright the Arrows.* Apparently the mysterious pain had been diagnosed at last, only a few months before the book appeared, and whatever its name, a course of treatment consisting of "tons of calcium gluconate and assorted minerals and vitamins-sometimes-w-and-y which I have been patiently swallowing and often managing to keep from chucking up again" began slowly, and over many months, to show results. "One whole day I was almost entirely without pain," she wrote to her editor at Harper in March of 1941. There were relapses, however, caused by certain positions or tasks, or by anxiety, which tightened up the nerves and caused excruciating pain, and sometimes the morphine, which "poor Ugin" had learned to inject although he "naturally hates like hell to have to give it me," seemed to take forever to bring relief.

Although her physical health showed promise of improving now, there were other sorrows to be endured. Llewelyn Powys had died in 1939, and after sending his widow a brief but heartfelt note of condolence, Edna had let the months slip by without another word, "and oh, how often we have spoken of you, and always with deep love for you and deep anger and scornful reproach for ourselves," she wrote, a year and a half later. "But, Alyse, I have been very ill, and Eugen has been desperate about me. Day & night he has nursed me. He has written no word to any one. His face has been gray with anxiety."

And the critical reception of *Make Bright the Arrows* was a source of pain, all the more piercing because there seemed to be no one, even among her loyal friends, who appreciated her motives in writing it; some of the reviews, she said later, were insolent to the point of being "actionable." The poetry of *Make Bright the Arrows* certainly can be described as hysterical in tone, and in workmanship so inadequately slapdash it is hard to believe Edna Millay really wrote it. Edmund Wilson had said years earlier that she was incapable of writing badly, even when she wrote under a pen name and solely to make money; now he learned she could write very badly indeed. He was astonished and worried by her propaganda poetry "on a level of war-time journalism of which I had not imagined her capable. I tried to explain it as partly due to the natural anxieties of Eugen when Holland was seized by Hitler," but he ended by deciding she was in the grip of a feverish obsession, to which women of genius were sometimes prone.

What did Edna Millay have to say for herself in connection with this poetry, of which friends and literary critics were scornful to the point of libel? She said that *Make Bright the Arrows* was her contribution to her country, in what she felt to be a time of great need. She believed it was important to rouse the nation and her fellow citizens, both to the national danger and to the possibility that democracy might die all over the world, and her beliefs were shared by many thoughtful Americans.

Whether or not she was acting on them hysterically and obsessively is another question. It must be remembered that in the late thirties and early forties, when she had been increasingly isolated at Steepletop, critical assessment of her poetry had gone from tepid to cool; even Max Eastman, one of her staunchest admirers, felt she wrote nothing of consequence after *Conversation at Midnight,* although *Huntsman,* a fine book, was published shortly thereafter. Eugen was aware of the change in literary taste, and tried to procure her a sympathetic hearing, as we have seen; the poet herself was fully and poignantly aware of it. She wrote to George Dillon in 1938 that she had been for a long time "without anybody to talk with about my poetry, no other poet I mean. Most of the other poets who are my friends or good acquaintances dislike my new stuff." And during the late forties she poured her pent-up feelings about the high priest of poetry and criticism, T. S. Eliot, into a collection of poems, never published, that satirized him unmercifully: "There is, I think, in these poems of mine against Eliot nothing which could be considered abusive: they are merely murderous." It seems apparent then that to isolation and physical pain had been added the worst of all sufferings for Edna Millay, the knowledge that her poetry, her reaching out to others, was somehow failing her, for the others had become unreachable. Increasingly she began to turn her efforts toward the nation as a whole, reaching out to her countrymen whom she must at all costs save from a danger they refused to see.

To a dear friend of Vassar days Edna had sent *Make Bright the Arrows* as a Christmas gift in 1940, and the friend, the mother of three draft-age boys, took this volume of poems that had been intended, according to the poet, as a call for military preparedness, to mean a call for American entry into the war. She was understandably hurt and angry, and Edna wrote back to her: "Is it not unjust of you, my dear friend, to accuse me of trying to incite this country to send an army to fight on foreign soil just because my idea as to how best to keep this country out of war differs radically from yours?" And "though I have no sons to be caught in this war, if we are caught in it, I have one thing to give in the service of my country—my reputation as a poet. How many more books of propaganda poetry containing as much bad verse as this one does, that reputation can withstand . . . I do not know—probably not more than one. But I have enlisted for the duration. Have you the slightest conception of what this reputation means to me, who have been building it carefully for more than twenty years. . . . Thus, you see, the dearest thing in life I possess which might possibly be of help to my country, has already gone over the top, in the hope that your sons need never go to war."

Certainly it was the dearest thing she possessed—the central core of selfhood, the one part of herself she knew to be real; and instead of taking a job in a munitions factory as her sister Kathleen did, Edna was using this most precious part of herself as a love offering. Yet it was persistently spurned. Her poetic voice grew increasingly frantic and shrill, her audience seemed ever more exclusive and the critics, instead of being merely cool, began to pan her mercilessly. In 1940 she wrote a poem for the *New York Herald Tribune,* excoriating Franklin Roosevelt and his try for a third term in words that suggest a woman at the end of her tether; she said he had the diseased ambition of Macbeth, Napoleon and Julius Caesar rolled into one. That same year the journalist Vincent Sheean met her at a benefit dinner for China Relief, and found the poet "in her smallest and most frightened mood. She had been very ill and she had worried immeasurably over Hitler's victories in Europe . . . I thought she looked like a stricken deer." Edna went to the chair that had been assigned to her, and found she was to sit among strangers; in an agonized whisper she told Sheean, "Please, I must have Eugen sitting beside me. Believe me, it's true. I don't know what will happen if he isn't here. Please, please—otherwise I'll have to go home." Sheean said he could tell she was not exaggerating in the slightest.

By December of 1941 the U.S. had finally entered the war, which Edna took as proof that her poetry "did no good at all. The Americans who read it didn't even know why I had written the verses, or why, having written them, I should be in such haste to publish them." In spite of her efforts, she said, and those of others like her, Pearl Harbor had been permitted to happen—and it is only further proof of the fragile and feverish state of her emotional being that so intelligent a woman should have allowed herself to believe her poems capable of altering the course of history. If her fears for her country and for democracy were rational ones, her actions—the poetry, the speechmaking, as well as the agonized manner—were apparently as obsessive and hysterical as Wilson believed.

By Christmas she was already hard at work, as she told Witter Bynner, on more verses "for my poor, foolish, bewildered, beloved country"— and the pain under her shoulder was gone, really gone, at long last. The following June the Nazis razed the town of Lidice in Czechoslovakia, and the Writers' War Board, which Edna had joined as soon as war was declared, asked her to write a memorial poem for broadcasting, a task she said looked difficult at first—she had never been able to "write tailor-made verse before"—but she consented because "I knew I should not be able to draw one contented breath unless I tried." A long verse narrative was the result, as shrill and unpolished as everything else she wrote during that period, but with some lovely passages reminiscent of the old Millay style, describing country life in Lidice before the tragedy.

On October 19, 1942, a distinguished cast headed by the actor Paul Muni dramatized *The Murder of Lidice* over NBC; it was transmitted by shortwave radio to England and other countries, and Eduard Beneš, the President of the Republic of Czechoslovakia, wrote later to tell Edna Millay how moving he found the poem. Jean Starr Untermeyer, a poet herself and the wife of a poet, both old friends of Edna's, were among the many celebrities in the studio audience that night, and Mrs. Untermeyer had not seen her for years. Like Sheean, she was amazed and pained at this public appearance of a woman who seemed to be sick, frightened and completely unlike the legendary Edna Millay: "She was a travesty of the girl I had known. Her hair, which she wore in a long pageboy cut, was now shades lighter than the red-gold locks of her girlhood. It seems to me now . . . that she was attired in a long, straight gown of dark red velvet, but the face under the yellow thatch of hair had changed, almost unbelievably: it had aged but not ripened. With its flushed cheeks it reminded me of a wizened winter apple."

Early in 1943 Kathleen, the youngest of the Millay sisters, died quite suddenly and unexpectedly, shortly after applying for admission to the Women's Army Corps; and Gene Saxton died during the course of that summer. "Of course I can't write about him or even think about him without crying," she said in a letter to his secretary; she was crying while she wrote it, and meanwhile she was stone broke. "If I don't get some money I can't go on writing, can't go on doing anything." Could Harper help? For the poetry readings, even had she been in good health and able to continue them, had to stop with the war. Much of what she earned by writing now she gave away, many of her wartime activities were unpaid in any case, and Steepletop, which had long been mortgaged, was hard to operate at a profit under wartime conditions. A younger Eugen Boissevain might perhaps have reveled in the chance to gyp people, but now Eugen was close to sixty, one of his cousins had been tortured and killed in Holland, others of his family were in constant danger because of their links to the Dutch underground; Eugen was no longer an adventurer, he could not consider rationing and the other restrictions on daily life imposed by the war as a joke or an opportunity to gyp people. Instead he took every restriction with the utmost seriousness, even to using a horse and buggy for driving to market, rather than consume the fuel to which Steepletop, as a working farm, was entitled. With the loyal help of John Pinnie, the farmer who had been employed at Steepletop from the beginning and who was to remain there after Eugen's death, and with whatever occasional hired hands he could scrape up, Eugen labored out of doors, his skin as dark as old leather, his massive frame bent, although he remained commandingly hand- some. He worked indoors as well, did the cooking and cleaning, even washed his wife's hair, for he was "the only thing in the house," as he put it. In the great, old-fashioned kitchen at Steepletop, with its ancient cooking range and icebox and laundry sink, there were no modern conveniences whatever—only the bells that used to summon servants, long since vanished into war work.

In 1944 the Writers' War Board called once more on Edna Millay, this time for a contribution to a continuous twenty-four-hour program to be broadcast on D day over NBC; two million British and American soldiers were to invade the beaches of Normandy, and she composed "Poem and Prayer for an Invading Army," whose emotional burden must have been felt with passionate sincerity by Eugen as well as by the poet herself. "Let them come home! Oh, let the battle, Lord, be brief,/ and let our boys come home!" The prayer was read by the actor Ronald Colman.

Shortly after the broadcast, Edna Millay suffered what she later called "a very handsome—and, as I afterwards was told an all but life-size—

nervous breakdown," spending months in Doctors' Hospital in New York. When she finally emerged she was weak, trembling and thoroughly frightened because she seemed unable to write a single line of poetry.

She told Edmund Wilson the reason for her breaking down was the cumulative strain of five years spent writing nothing but propaganda poems—"And I can tell you from my own experience, that there is nothing on this earth which can so much get on the nerves of a good poet, as the writing of bad poetry." Coming from anyone else such an explanation might be hard to accept—yet for years she had been immured at Steepletop with all the old escape routes cut off, her reputation dwindled, her frantic propaganda posters rejected, so that they became more frantic still. She was gradually being deprived of her one sure defense against nightmare—the working and reworking into poetry, assured and splendidly crafted poetry, of the fears that for over two decades she had held precariously at bay. When she was no longer able to transcend the nightmare through poetry, she was engulfed by it.

In the summer of 1945 Vincent Sheean went with the Boissevains' old friend Tess Root Adams to her summer place on Bailey's Island, Maine; Edna and Eugen stopped there too, on the way to Ragged, turning up late one afternoon in a car loaded with pots and pans:

Our conversation was lively, but Edna took very little part in it. . . . She was rather silent and looked very frightened, small, and withdrawn. At this time she had been going through the most painful crisis any writer, and, I suppose more particularly, any poet, can experience in life, which is the inability to compose anything at all. She could not write. . . . Miss Millay was, to put it bluntly, a frightening apparition to many of us. Her temperament was so variable that it was impossible to tell what mood might overwhelm her next; and she was obviously so painfully sensitive that any untoward phrase or sudden noise could thrust her into a private hell from which she might not emerge for days. . . . Her terror communicated itself and created terror. I hardly dared to look at her more than once or twice that evening.

And throughout, Eugen was jovial, talkative, constantly forestalling whatever might give her pain, and talking so that she would not have to talk.

The war ended that summer, and in the fall of the year Arthur Ficke died after much suffering; he was buried at Hardhack, and Edna Millay read the much-discussed sonnet "And you as well must die, beloved dust," over his grave. Ordinary, normal life was supposed to resume now, and to some degree the stirrings of ordinary, healthy life had begun for Edna, if slowly and tentatively. She had started at last to write poetry again, and in the summer of 1946 was able to send Edmund Wilson three new poems. But the long-standing "epistophobia," her hatred and fear of letter writing, amounted now to "desperation and pure panic," suggesting that she was by no means fully returned to normal; longing to reach out to old friends, the act of reaching out seemed to terrify her.

There was still no money; perhaps Eugen's Java properties might be reclaimed but for the time being the Boissevains were up against it, although the poet repeatedly rejected moneymaking schemes her publishers thought up, inspired in large part by their desire to see her condition improve. At least she was willing to joke about it: "for one year more may it be said of me by Harper & Brothers, that although I reject their proposals, I welcome their advances," she wrote to Cass Canfield, her new editor at Harper. They had suggested a collection of her dramatic works, but Edna felt that all but *Aria da Capo* were insubstantial; they suggested a collection of love poems, but she thought it unseemly. If Harper would leave off letter writing, she said, she might have enough leisure in which to continue with the poetry she was already working on, and soon there would be enough for a book. She was working slowly and carefully now, "lest I be caught again in that paralyzing nightmare of writing against time, which I so often experienced when writing for the radio during war."

One September day at Ragged Island she wrote a note to Eugen: "Darling, come up from the harbour. . . . Don't go out, please. We have everything here," for the sea was too rough, she felt, for him to leave the island. And yet he had gone back down to the harbor again, although they had come up together only a short while ago—"you drenched to the skin, I shining and excited. . . ." She finished off with a tiny poem in Dutch that translates as: "Dearest: I'm going topside,/ Maybe I'll sleep./ Maybe not./ You are never home." The last four words, suggesting that Eugen is the wanderer and she the patient homebody waiting for him to finish adventuring, are echoed in a poem that was probably written during this same period; "Truck-Garden Market-Day" describes a woman moving happily and slowly about the house, "For the men are in town, and their noise gone with 'em." She recalls her girlhood room at night, and the cool empty bed, moonlit and virginal. Then:

> More than my heart to him I gave,
> When I gave my heart in soft surrender—
> Who am now the timid, laughed-at slave
> Of a man unaware of this, and tender.
>
> Never must he know how I feel,
> Or how, at times, too loud his voice is—
> When, just at the creak of his wagon-wheel
> Cramped for the barn, my life rejoices!

It is possible to detect, in this poem and in the brief bit of a note on Ragged, a quality of compliant, even submissive love, in which there is real awareness of how much she depends on Eugen, and not only on his abilities as a sick-nurse. Certainly they were closer than ever before, the enforced isolation of the war years during which Eugen was maid, cook and sole companion having culminated in the long-drawn-out convalescence when every ounce of his energy must have been focused on her well-being. Old friends, some of them returning to Steepletop for brief visits for the first time in many years, tried to assess the changes there.

Vincent Sheean, once more accompanied by Tess Adams, came in 1948 to celebrate Mrs. Adams' birthday; he found Edna in good temper and good health this time, talkative and argumentative and displaying at the dinner table an appetite that impressed him. Tess Adams told him later that Edna had been " 'just like the old days,' without the agonized shyness and multiple terrors of recent years." But Edmund Wilson and his wife went to Steepletop almost on impulse a few months later, and Wilson, who had not seen her for nearly twenty years, "felt, as I had not done before, that Edna was buried there."

Eugen "came out in his working-clothes. He shuffled in his leather moccasins, he had aged: he was graying and stooped. It seemed to me that he was low in morale. 'I'll go and get my child,' he said. I did not realize at first that this meant Edna." In the living room Wilson found most of the things that had been there in 1929, all badly worn now, shabby and dim. "One saw, standing outside the window, three rusty old tin oil-barrels, on which Edna could put food for birds without having it stolen by the squirrels. In one corner, a litter of copy-books covered table, couch, chair and floor." When the poet herself came in, "It was a moment before I recognized her. She had changed so in the nineteen years that, if I had met her unexpectedly somewhere, I am sure I should not have known her. She had become somewhat heavy and dumpy, and her cheeks were a little florid. . . . She was terribly nervous; her hands shook; there was a look of fright in her bright green eyes."

Eugen came in with martinis. "Very quietly he watched her and managed her. At moments he would baby her in a way that I had not seen him use before but that had evidently become habitual, when she showed signs of bursting into tears over not being able to find a poem or something of the kind. My wife said afterwards that Gene gave the impression of shaking me at her as if I had been a new toy with which he hoped to divert her."

Edna showed Wilson some of the poetry she was working on, much of it unfinished, and he described it as "of an almost un-relieved blackness." There were times, however, when she seemed like "a good-natured, healthily laughing elderly woman." Yet the Boissevains never seemed to go anywhere or to see anyone, and when Wilson asked if they wouldn't like to go to the music festival at Tanglewood, an hour's drive from Austerlitz, he was astonished that Edna, who loved music so, had not gone for years, and knew nothing about what the Tanglewood concerts had become; she could not be persuaded to go.

The journalist Dorothy Thompson had an equally depressing visit to Steepletop; she came there late one afternoon, having been more or less invited by Edna, to find Eugen pruning bushes. He asked if she had an appointment and seemed reluctant to let her in, but finally said he would see if his wife felt equal to company. After a long interval—

. . . he returned bringing Edna by the hand, as if she were a recently invalided small child. She was wearing a Chinese Mandarin coat of once-brilliant blue, slightly faded though still handsome. . . . Eugen fussed over her, speaking in language just short of baby talk; and she answered him like a little girl getting over a mild case of the measles and wanting to be babied. When he saw that she was properly settled, Eugen went out and closed the door. As soon as he was gone, Edna's whole manner changed; she began talking in the customary hearty way Dorothy remembered, and the two friends gossiped like a pair of old cronies. . . . Dorothy was thinking about leaving when the door opened and Eugen entered carrying a table tray, which he set on the floor by the fireplace, arranging a large pillow beside it, and announcing that his child must have her supper now. Edna instantly reverted to her earlier role, allowing herself to be docilely led over to the low table and seated cross-legged on the pillow . . . while Eugen spread a napkin across her knees, murmuring over her like a fond nurse.

This anecdote appears in a recently published biography by Jean Gould, and the author believes it may have been exaggerated in the telling; if we take it at face value, coupled with Wilson's impression, we must conclude that Eugen, who had always babied his wife, carried it to bizarre extremes in the years that followed her all but "life-size nervous breakdown." But Edna's reaction seems to have been one of passive acceptance; having been deprived for a number of years of the nourishment she found in the writing of excellent poetry, she was able to pour herself once more into her work, and nothing else really mattered. She told Cass Canfield of Harper that she was "so tired out from writing poetry that I am nearly killed," but a book would soon be ready. She wrote to Edmund Wilson in early August that she had so often longed to talk with him, yet she had to say he had better not come to Steepletop, for "I can't see anybody on earth just now; I am working seventy-two hours a day; and I don't dare run the risk of being deflected." One of the reasons she was working so hard, all day long and often into the night, was that Eugen urged her to; he had regretted the wartime poetry, just as she did, and must have felt not only the need for her to reclaim her reputation, but even more important the value to his wife's mental health and stability of work she could be proud of.

When Wilson had been at Steepletop one year earlier he had asked Edna to read, so his wife could hear her; but when she started "the room became so charged with emotion that I began to find it difficult to bear." The Wilsons left, although Mrs. Wilson felt they ought to have stayed. "What had desolated and frightened me there was death," he said later, "to which Eugen was wearily resigned but against which Edna, when I saw her, with the draughts of her unfinished . . . poems, was making her last fierce struggle."

Late in August 1949 Eugen went to see a doctor because of a persistent cough. He was just short of seventy and seemed to be in good health —he had attended to the haying that month, with what he called "insufficient help"—but the cough was diagnosed as a cancer of the right lung, and Eugen went to Deaconess Hospital in Boston, where the lung was removed. He seemed to be recovering, but then suffered a stroke, and died on the thirtieth of August, 1949.

Edna Millay drank recklessly, and had a complete breakdown after the funeral; she was in Doctors' Hospital for several weeks. According to Cass Canfield:

The question then arose as to whether or not she should be allowed to return to her home in Austerlitz, New York, as she wished to do. Her doctor sidestepped making a decision since there was a danger that in her melancholy condition she might commit suicide. So the decision was left to a few intimate friends, who were divided in their opinions, with the result that it was finally put up to her editor. I decided that she should be allowed to do what she wished and took her back to Austerlitz. On this rather long motor ride we confined our conversation to what we saw and observed on the way; when I left her in her lonely house I remember that she thanked me for my detachment and said, "I'm not going to kill myself. Don't worry."

A month later she was working again, going over an introduction William Benét had written for some of her early poems that were to be reissued. In a letter to Canfield about Benét's introduction she sounded brisk and tart, quite businesslike; and a month after that, with Christmas approaching, she wrote a long letter to a pair of friends who wanted to give her a gift, full of what sounded like girlish high spirits. She wanted typewriter ribbons, she said, and had no idea what they cost nowadays, but "I should feel so rich, so reinforced, so sassy!—with a new ribbon on each of my three typewriters." If the epistophobia had abated for the time being, she remained cut off and withdrawn from sociability in other ways; the telephone wires were taken down in January, because their humming bothered her; spring was "six weeks later than usual," and even in April the roads were impassable, so that John Pinnie had to walk to the farm each day; to her old friend Tess Adams she wrote in August: "No, I can't visit you, darling; and even if I could, I would not— thanking you very much, however." Even the following October her message to Tess was singularly inhospitable: "I should love to see you; but (and this is one hell of an invitation, as I know) can you arrange to come after lunch and leave before dinner? (!!!)"

With vitamin capsules, oranges and thick steaks, Edna had under-taken to mother herself, now that there was no longer a Eugen to do it. She told Norma she managed this by inventing a nurse for herself, whom she named Mrs. Somebody-Anybody, and half the time she was the nurse, and the rest of the time herself, being nursed. Thus the vitamins, oranges and steaks were inserted into the anemic Miss Millay, who loathed them, by the devoted and insistent Mrs. Somebody-Any-body, who knew how good they were for her. She managed Thanksgiv-ing Day by ignoring it, and Christmas by sitting at the piano and playing carols, and celebrated New Year's Eve by telephoning Eugen's people in Holland.

She had endured the winter successfully, entirely alone, just as she wished to be, but the coming of spring was another matter; she was afraid of spring—"Shrinking from being hurt too much." She told Mary Herron, the postmistress at Austerlitz, "I have already encountered the first dandelion. I stood and stared at it with a kind of horror. And then I felt ashamed of myself. . . . And suddenly, without my doing anything about it at all, my face just crumpled up and cried. How excited he always was when he saw the first dandelion! And long before the plants got big enough for even a rabbit to find them, he had dug a fine mess, for greens. He used to say 'pick dandelions'; and I would say, 'Not pick, —dig.' . . . Alas, alas, and alas."

Perhaps the reason she had resolved to stay at Steepletop alone was to realize the full extent of her loss, just as she had crossed the ocean almost thirty years before without seasick pills, to get the complete experience, undiluted. Now she was feeling everything, or close to it; she had the phone taken out again—it was always in and out before, but the reason she gave now was that when she heard it ring she seemed to hear Eugen's footsteps running to answer it. Norma believed she had "insisted upon staying alone at Steepletop, to attempt in her own way to adjust to life without him. The hired man came as usual each day to do the chores and what errands were needed, and during that stark winter she trained her mind to her work. Soon there would be a book."

By summer of 1950 she was working on a Thanksgiving Day poem, to appear in the *Saturday Evening Post,* a task to which she devoted much more research and effort, she felt, than it was worth, but she was grateful for the assignment. Ten days before the deadline she scrapped it, realizing "as things got worse and worse in Korea . . . a few Indian war-whoops . . . and a neighborly little scalping party" were meaningless to a nation in terror of the atom bomb. Then she set about rewriting in the spirit of the times, and passed her summer alone, not yet equal to Ragged Island, writing more of the bubbly, faintly hysterical letters to friends.

She had given the living room at Steepletop a complete spring cleaning in the course of the year, waxing the floor, polishing the furniture, recovering couches and chairs in fresh bright fabrics; she thought of it as a sort of memorial to Eugen, because he had remarked not long before he died on how shabby things had become. One night in October, working late in the shining living room over some proofs of Rolfe Humphries' translation of the *Aeneid,* she started upstairs carrying a glass of wine. John Pinnie came there the next afternoon and found her dead of a heart attack, halfway up the stairs with the glass of wine still beside her.

Her ashes were buried at Steepletop beside Eugen's; Norma Millay and Alan Ross Macdougall read her poems at a small private service there, and Tess Root Adams played the Beethoven "Appassionata." About a month later the distinguished American poet and critic John Ciardi, writing in the *Saturday Review of Literature,* expressed, perhaps a bit harshly, the then current assessment of Edna Millay and her work:

"At its slightest her passion made her the mother of the O-God-the-pain! girls. . . . And even at its best it is not likely that her work can be popular so long as poetry continues its present development toward the ambivalent consciousness and the pessimistic intellect. Perhaps her poems must be forgotten. Or perhaps they will become like 'The Rubaiyat' and 'Sonnets from the Portuguese,' poems that generation after generation of the young will be swept away by, gorgeously, overwhelmingly swept away by, and then outgrow."

Four years later the book of poems she had been working on was finally published, with Norma's help, as *Mine the Harvest*, a thoughtful and varied collection, sometimes looking back to her childhood, sometimes occupied with nature at Steepletop, sometimes in a psychologizing mood, a rarity for Edna Millay. Many of her old themes recur in *Mine the Harvest*—misanthropy, the pain inflicted by beauty, the need of women to be individuals. There is a short poem in free verse—"At least, my dear,/ You did not have to live to see me die . . ."—describing the way she felt that last year, living among the relics of her life with Eugen. "I find in the pocket of a coat I could not bring myself to give away/ A knotted handkerchief, containing columbine-seeds."

The poem is reminiscent of "Menses." She speaks of the many things she did that caused her husband pain, of which he kept no record, no memory: "O, love inflexible, O militant forgiveness, I know/ You kept no books against me!" Clearly this is the same man who, in the earlier poem, absorbed whatever punishment her nasty temper let loose upon him—as if a bad-tempered child were to pound with small fists on an inflexible adult bosom. As long as the adult remains inflexible—militantly forgiving—the relationship is unequal; should the adult respond in kind, with anger if not with nastiness, they may be able to negotiate as equals. "The most I ever did for you," the poem says toward the end, "was to outlive you."

It is impossible to assess how much of the feeling in this poem and "Menses" represented the main current of Edna and Eugen's life together—whether she was always the child, sometimes capricious, mischievous or nasty, cared for by a great hulk of a parent whom she occasionally mocked; and Eugen always the self-controlled adult. At least some of the Boissevains' friends suspected that Eugen's mothering kept his wife partially helpless, during the last decade or so of their lives, and if they were right, if Eugen needed her dependence and helplessness, then the two of them may have been gripped together in a destructive union, destructive certainly for Edna. But there were many signs that the marriage was not an inflexible arrangement but a fluid one; certainly there were times when Eugen pushed and tugged his wife toward the outer world, toward health and comparative independence. Perhaps it was only when Edna was at her worst, going utterly to pieces for emotional reasons rooted in her childhood and largely unconnected with Eugen, that he babied her, even dragged out the process of recovery in order to have her dependent on him longer; yet when comparative good health returned he was able to find satisfactions in that too. He was maternal, he was probably overmaternal, but he does not seem to have been the kind of parent who rejoices in the total helplessness of the child.

In a poem called "Hospital" Arthur Ficke wrote, in the thirties, that the voice of Eugen Boissevain had whispered to him about the many modes of being—all one had to do was "choose which level you prefer," and remain there. And this sounds characteristic of Eugen, to choose the way he wanted to live and then live that way. In his mid-thirties he had chosen: the way he wanted to live was as the guardian of a brilliant woman, and having found such a woman in Inez Milholland, he married her. She died only three years later, and for some seven years Eugen occupied himself with business and pleasure until he had the good fortune to meet another brilliant woman in need of a guardian. Once more he had found the level at which he preferred to live, and he stayed there for the rest of his life. It was a demanding job, and sometimes no doubt a frightening one, but it must have had many rewards, and, in any case, it was just what he wanted, precisely what he felt himself cut out for.

But Edna Millay did not choose the level at which she preferred to live. Hers was a life of necessity, not choice; her mother had decided she must be a poet, or at any rate an accomplished artist, therefore she became one. Her mother longed for independence and self-fulfillment, therefore Vincent, on her behalf, became as independent and self-fulfilling as she possibly could, hiding within her innermost being the child who craved shelter and maternal protection. Lonely and dependent as she was, she nevertheless found through poetry the power to balance herself, however precariously, between the two extremes that pulled at her. We can imagine Edna Millay unmarried, we can imagine her married to someone else or successively to several men, we can even see her as the mother of one or two children, but we cannot think of her without her poetry, any more than she could think of herself that way. Poetry made sense out of her existence, almost all of the time; now and then it failed, and she simply fell apart. Surely those terrible times would have happened more often if she had not married Eugen Jan Boissevain.

Maria Goeppert-Mayer

LATE IN THE AFTERNOON of December 10, 1963, eight men and a woman in evening clothes met in a backstage room at the Concert Hall, Stockholm; the king of Sweden and the royal family were gathered in a private parlor nearby. When the audience of two thousand had filled the Concert Hall, king, queen and royal grandchildren entered to take their places in the front row. The audience rose before the king entered and sat down only after he sat, but when the doors to the backstage room were opened and a fanfare of trumpets announced the appearance onstage of the year's nine Nobel laureates, it was the king, tall, aged, hawk-faced and spectrally thin, who first arose to greet them, in an act of homage that becomes for many the most memorable part of the seven days of Nobel week. Then everyone was seated, laureates to one side of the stage, Nobel Committee members on the other. Dr. Maria Goeppert-Mayer, a short, plump woman of fifty-seven with blue eyes and a fine-grained complexion, found the blazing lights set up for the television cameras almost painfully hot. She couldn't see her husband, wondered how she was to endure several hours without cigarettes, and fretted over certain details of the ceremony that lay ahead; but she was also elated, euphoric, sharply aware of being the only woman in the group onstage, the only living woman with a Nobel Prize in science, and the first woman ever to win it for theoretical physics. Excited and apprehensive as she was, she nevertheless wondered why she was not more excited still, why there was a faint taste of anticlimax to the evening.

Of the four categories in which Nobel Prizes are awarded in Stock-

holm—physics, chemistry, physiology or medicine, and literature—
physics has always been honored first because it was mentioned first in
Nobel's will; therefore the three physicists, Eugene Wigner, who had
won half the prize, and Maria Mayer and Hans Jensen, who shared the
other half, were the first of the nine to be presented. A speech in
Swedish by a member of the Swedish Academy of Sciences introduced
them as a group, then each of the three, first Wigner, then Mayer, then
Jensen, was summoned to cross the stage and receive from the king's
hand the Nobel medal and diploma. It was this brief but highly conspicuous performance that had troubled Maria Mayer in advance, although she carried it out neatly enough, coming forward and down the
step to stand before the king, who was standing too, or rather towering,
for he was an exceptionally tall man and perfectly upright in spite of his
eighty-one years. She held out her right hand to grasp his, but instead
of receiving in her left hand the medal, a half pound of gold 65 millime-
ters in diameter, and the diploma, a splendid work of illuminated letter-
ing in a gold-tooled binding of blue leather, as heavy and awkward as
it was handsome, these were passed into the care of an aide who had
followed behind for that purpose. Maria Mayer's left hand and arm had
been almost completely paralyzed by a stroke three years before; the
right hand had little strength and no feeling in it. But all went well, the
handshake seemed successful, the king had smiled, Maria Mayer smiled,
then she backed away from the royal presence, up the step and onto the
stage again—a touchy feat, made more difficult by the floor-length dress;
Pearl Buck was said to have managed it in 1938 by memorizing the
pattern of the Oriental carpet during rehearsal.

Once Maria Mayer was safely onstage again among the ferns and
massed white chrysanthemums and classical statuary, her responsibilities
for the evening were at an end; she had only to listen to the speeches,
enjoy the symphonic music in between, and try by squinting past the
lights to discover where her husband was. Had she been able to see him
she would have been amazed to learn that Joe Mayer, while watching
his wife take her place near the bust of Alfred Nobel, had burst into
tears.

She remembered feeling "very small" up there on the platform, very much aware of the others who had been there before her: Planck, Einstein, Fermi, Niels Bohr. She thought especially of the physicist Max Born, who had been her teacher; she thought of her father. What would her father have said if he were still alive; what would he have felt? "He might have felt that his advice to me, 'Never become a woman!' had really come true." Her father had encouraged her to have a profession; don't just wait for some man, he used to tell her, for he had seen too many women dwindle into marriage, motherhood, baby tending and dullness. But that she would win a Nobel Prize he could not have dreamed—nobody could. A physicist who had known the Mayers in the early forties said when he heard the news, "I always thought Maria was competent. But in those years if you had asked me about her chances of winning a Nobel Prize, my answer would probably have been, 'Are you kidding?' "

She would have said the same herself. Mitchell Wilson, a novelist who was once a physicist and a student of Fermi's, had this to say about Maria and her prize: ". . . her achievement was all the more remarkable because she had done her work when she was well into her forties and she had only recently come into the field of physics from chemistry, and most of all because she was a woman."

With the playing of the Swedish national hymn the prize-giving ceremony came to a close. By limousine and bus, audience, laureates and royalty journeyed from the Concert Hall to Town Hall, where they were to banquet and later on to dance in a famous room, ornamented with a mural made of a million bits of gold-colored stone. Their entrance into the banqueting hall was to be a little ceremony in itself, for which the laureates gathered in an anteroom to await the king. Here Maria Mayer finally found her husband and smoked a cigarette; she saw, to her satisfaction, that his boiled shirt had held up well and so had his trousers, which were borrowed, or rather borrowed back, from their son Peter, to whom Joe had recently given all his evening clothes. Joe had held up well too. Although he looked, with his deeply lined face and the odd, forward-leaning angle of his upper body, like some tall, thin, weather-worn Midwesterner, a farmer perhaps or the owner of a small-town hardware store, Joseph E. Mayer was a chemist of international reputation and better known, before the Nobel Prize, than his wife. Ever since Maria's stroke he had been extremely watchful of her since she had little inclination to watch out for herself; she smoked constantly, sometimes three or four cigarettes at once. A young colleague remembered the Mayers seated side by side at a seminar in Chicago, while on the table before them a vast ashtray, with scores of butts piled in its center, was ringed by several living cigarettes Maria had started and then forgotten, all of them exuding a dense white smoke characteristic of a certain kind of low-nicotine tobacco. Maria would nudge her husband, to ask silently for a fresh cigarette, as someone in the background furtively emptied the ashtray into a wastebasket, where its burning contents met still more dead butts and the cellulose filters caught fire, so that very slowly and ethereally the slender wisps of plastic ash drifted upward from the basket. Neither the white clouds nor the plastic ash made any impression on Maria Mayer, who was intently lighting a fresh cigarette and following the subject of the seminar.

Joe Mayer was also a heavy smoker, and apparently resigned to the fact that neither of them was likely to change; instead he tried to keep Maria from overtiring herself: she could be almost asleep on her feet, yet still pushing herself, as if fatigue were a sign of failure or poor taste. When each of them had been reassured about the well-being of the other, they sat on the marble steps and chatted with Wigner and Jensen. Maria reflected later on that the brief delay, the "microsecond," as she put it, when the royalties absented themselves, might have had something to do with the tiny restrooms of the Town Hall, one- or two-seaters hardly adequate for the seven hundred guests at the banquet.

A few minutes later Maria entered the golden banqueting hall on the arm of King Gustaf Adolf. At dinner she sat beside him, vaguely troubled by the fact that she had no hearing in her left ear; suppose the king should think she was stupid? By turning her head rather sharply, however, she was able to hold up her end of the conversation, and as for the dancing, she danced well and always had, for she had been born in Germany and grew up waltzing.

The day after the prize-giving the laureates collected their checks from the Nobel Foundation and were free to go home, to resume normal life as well as possible. For many it apparently is not possible. "Of all the bizarre effects which winning the prize turns out to have on scientists, the one least often seen is heightened creativity," Mitchell Wilson wrote. And he quoted T. D. Lee, the theoretical physicist who won it in 1957 in his early thirties. " 'My God!' he said. 'What happens now to the rest of my life? What comes after this?' "

For Maria Mayer the question of "What comes after this?" was less pressing than for many, partly because she was a person of singularly gentle character, in many ways a leaner rather than the leaned-against. This trait is not usual among creative research scientists. Whether it is usual among women in that category is impossible to say, for there have been so few successful women research scientists no one has ever made any studies of their personalities. Even the two distinguished psychologists Anne Roe and Bernice Eiduson, whose pioneering studies examined scientists and their psychological world, wrote only about men, although as women in science they were naturally curious about their female colleagues.

Maria returned to La Jolla, California, put her Nobel medal in the bank vault, a gold-plated copy in a glass case in her living room, and took up daily life again—teaching, doing research, gardening, traveling, giving parties. The stroke three years earlier had slowed her walk, immobilized one arm and hand and slightly blurred her speech; never again would she be able to work as she had before, with narrowed, blinkered intensity. For many scientists, for most, the saddest result of any physical impairment would have been this loss of the ability to work really hard. But Maria seemed to have accepted it in a way peculiarly her own; it was not so much a question of the absence of self-pity, but rather a smoothing over of troubles before self-pity could even arise. In the midst of her stroke, as she lay on the floor watching a strange object thrash back and forth before her face—she learned later it had been her left hand—Maria was thinking: How terrible for Joe to have an invalid wife; I don't care so much for myself, but for him it would be terrible.

Her habit of swallowing pain and fear and resentment before they made themselves felt must have been instilled during childhood, for in large part it reflects the world where Maria Goeppert-Mayer grew up, the world of the German university. Born in 1906 in Kattowitz, Upper Silesia, she had come with her parents to the university town of Göttingen when she was four. Here her father, Friedrich Goeppert, was a professor of medicine, the sixth generation of university professor in his family. The entire educated upper middle class to which they belonged tended to approach its manifold duties and pleasures, whether civic, cultural or social, with an air of high seriousness that became in its more exaggerated form ponderous, pompous—all that is called by social commentators "Germanic." And those of the upper middle class who became professors were especially burdened by a sense of duty and privilege, for they had inherited after World War I much of the veneration reserved for Kaiser, empire and vanished aristocracy in a country where rank and status were of the first consequence.

When Maria's mother, Frau Professor Goeppert, walked into a shop every other woman in it was content to see her served first, unless there should be another frau professor present, and then other subtleties of rank and tenure must be somehow weighed. She had not always been a frau professor, however; Maria's mother had been born Maria Wolff, the eldest of six children whose father died early, leaving only a pension on which they managed to live, but meagerly. Maria Wolff became a schoolteacher specializing in French; she also gave piano lessons, and "was always invited to every big party because she could sing and play, beautifully." The teaching career came to an end with marriage, and her duties henceforth were to supervise the household, to entertain, enjoy herself and uphold the social position of a professor's wife, all of which she did most conscientiously. Far from leaving her household entirely in the care of servants, Frau Goeppert was constantly on hand and busy, an excellent and resourceful manager, a celebrated hostess. Maria remembered that at Christmas her mother always bought the tallest tree she could find, for "she couldn't *stand* not having the tallest tree. One year she bought a tree and she saw a taller one, so she took back the one she had and bought the other instead." Her composed and somewhat preoccupied face, rounded above a well-filled and matronly frame, hovers in the background of Maria's childhood photographs; both the Goepperts had hoped for several children but after a number of stillbirths they were grateful they had the one.

Maria's father had been part of a large and distinguished family; several of his brothers as well as his forebears were at one time or another university professors. Friedrich Goeppert himself, as professor of pediatrics at Göttingen and the founder of a children's clinic there, had found a calling for which his nature was perfectly suited:

> He was the kind of person whom everybody loved . . . I always had the feeling when he came into my room when I was sick, I felt better. And so many other children said that too. When he walked to the hospital in the morning, sometimes, especially after Christmas, there would be just a whole gang of children, and saying, O Herr Goeppert, I want to tell you what I got for Christmas . . . and I asked him, Who are they? And he said, I don't know. But they all, at some time, had been sick, and seen him, and they loved him. Everybody did.

She felt much closer to him than to her mother, Maria remembered. "Well, my father was more interesting, you see. He was after all a scientist."

Many of her childhood memories had to do with her father's unusual patience and his rare ability to awaken her curiosity in the world around her. She recalled, at the age of three or so, seeing a half moon and asking what it was, and being told by her father exactly what it was. "Any sensible question he would answer." When she was seven he prepared special glasses so she might watch an eclipse of the sun, and when the time came, once again everything was carefully, patiently explained. They went on science walks together, to collect fossils in the quarries, or into the country to learn all the trees and plants by name. And, "when I was a child, before I went to school, one spring he went every morning with me up on the hills and had breakfast in a little restaurant and came down again, just talking. . . . That was around Easter time, and I would find Easter eggs; there would suddenly be some Easter eggs, and I would never notice that my father had dropped them." She also remembered being told that her father often came home late at night from work and asked her mother to wake the child so he could play with her.

Of course my father always said I should have been a boy. He said, Don't grow up to be a woman, and what he meant by that was, a housewife . . . without any interests. I mean, he saw so many women who had just played with their children and had no interests whatsoever, and this he didn't like. . . . Did I think it strange for him to say such things to me? No, not at all; he could say anything to me. No, I felt flattered and decided I wasn't going to be just a woman.

No matter what the words themselves said, his entire manner was one of loving interest; he enjoyed his child's company and took pleasure in her just as she was, a blond, blue-eyed, active little girl with a round, pale face, very earnest and unguarded in expression, in her actions mischievous, adventurous, intense.

The adventurousness Herr Goeppert encouraged. In his philosophy of child raising he was apparently far ahead of his time, and while he was in some respects controversial, he had an international reputation; when Maria was herself a mother living in America, she chose her pediatricians by the simple procedure of asking if they had heard of Friedrich Goeppert's work, and whether or not they approved of it. It was one of his cardinal beliefs, for example, that "The mother is the natural enemy of the child."

He felt that mothers limited a child's freedom because they were fearful; whatever was at all risky, venturesome, daring, frightened them so that they refused to allow it, or else the fear was conveyed to the child. Thus mothers tended to stifle curiosity and inhibit enterprise. Once when Maria was eight or so, she was out by herself in the woods near home when her parents came by. "I'll show you," she called to them. "I can go to the top of that tree." But no sooner had she grasped the first branch than her father took her mother by the arm and gently led her away; had they stayed, Frau Goeppert might have cautioned Maria, or made her come down. Maria came to think of herself as a "brat," roaming everywhere, into everything, never really ill-behaved but willful and mischievous. Once she and another girl took a hearty dislike to a child they knew and spent weeks designing and building ingenious traps to catch her in, real traps, as if she were a forest animal. Many of Maria's classmates—a year or two older than she was, since Maria was always an exceptionally good student—were awed by her, and others were envious; one girl wrote a journal recording all the exploits she and Maria Goeppert had undertaken together, and saved it and showed it one day to her children.

The place the Goepperts had chosen to settle in and raise their daughter was a quiet medieval town, in a rural setting that consisted almost entirely of a great university. In the mid-nineteenth century Heinrich Heine wrote that the town of Göttingen, "renowned for its sausages and university . . . contains 999 fireplaces, sundry churches, a maternity hospital, an observatory, a university prison, and a Ratskeller, where the beer is very good." In Maria's childhood it had hardly changed; the ancient town walls, made of earth and faced with stone, were still intact, there were half-timbered houses, intricately carved, a Gothic church tower, murky student taverns where the beer was still excellent and the sausages famous, and private cars were a curiosity; until the First World War even bicycles were rare. All the houses had gardens, or so it seemed to Maria; the mathematician Hilbert, whom she thought of as "the king of Göttingen," lived in a house just below the Goepperts, and Hilbert had a garden with a blackboard running its entire length, shielded by a roof so he could walk back and forth with his students and write equations even in the rain.

As late as the 1960s there were still a few horse-drawn carts in the streets of Göttingen, and in the pleasant, tree-shaded walk around the town walls one met nursemaids with infants, professors with their eyes riveted to their papers, lovers, businessmen, schoolboys with their books in satchels on their backs and *Studenten-futter*—student-feed—in their fists: peanuts, raisins and oats mixed together and bolted by the handful. The heart of this serene, almost antique community, its chief interest and source of pride, was the Georgia Augusta University, known everywhere in the world, especially among mathematicians, as Göttingen; according to an inscription in one of the student taverns, *"Extra Gottingam non est vita"*—There is no life worth living outside Göttingen—and almost everyone who lived or studied there would have agreed. Except Heine: he wrote that "the inhabitants of Göttingen are divided into students, professors, philistines, and cattle—which four classes, however, are anything but rigorously kept apart."

Whenever she had to write a brief autobiography the adult Maria invariably included in it a phrase like the following, from *Les Prix Nobel en 1963:* "On my father's side, I am the seventh straight generation of university professor." Throughout her life she continued to be intensely proud of all the generations marching behind her in academic dress, but as a little girl she might have been somewhat burdened by such an impressive inheritance, knowing that she was an only child, who must either take her place in the academic procession or bring it to a halt. Perhaps it was nothing so clearly formed; perhaps it was only a diffuse demand for duty and high performance on the part of two affectionate parents who demanded a great deal of themselves. Such an atmosphere, where much was given in the way of interest and love, and much was expected, was usual among German families of their class. And Maria was probably a susceptible little girl, if anything can be learned from the earnest, unsmiling face in her photographs. At any rate she had headaches throughout much of her childhood, "terrible headaches, sort of consistently. One year I was only allowed to go to school for two hours a day. But my father always said, 'If you want to make yourself an invalid, you can. Don't do it.' Also, he told me, it will be better when you get older. . . . he was right, of course." She had no idea what caused the headaches, had no conscious recollection of any unspoken demands, intellectual or otherwise; as well as she could tell, she got headaches because she was the kind of child who "reacted to anything with headaches, to any cold, to any strain." And they kept her home from school, as did a collection of minor illnesses, for long stretches of time.

Apparently a childhood history of minor physical ailments that tend to isolate a child for long periods at a time is a recurring theme in the early lives of many scientists; according to Anne Roe, in *The Making of a Scientist,* the group that suffered from it most markedly was the theoretical physicists. And Bernice Eiduson, writing ten years later than Roe, found much the same thing; her scientists had been children not too different from others, some lonely and withdrawn, others aggressive and rebellious, while still others seemed quite ordinary, "except for one feature consistently mentioned throughout the interviews: periods of isolation from the customary groups with which a child might be expected to identify . . ." What is important "is that such experiences invariably led the scientists to look to their own resources for solace and amusement. What they did by themselves varied according to age and individual interest. There were collectors, tinkerers, heavy readers, those who solved mathematical puzzles. . . . But what they did seemed not so crucial for later work as the fact that they had searched for resources within themselves and become comfortable being by themselves."

The parents of these children had to be able to watch them playing alone and let them be, neither rushing to furnish company themselves nor trying to find other companions; from this, a child learns that being alone is perfectly acceptable. He may also learn it has special advantages: if one can enjoy being alone, one can rise above the longing to be amused, entertained and instructed by others. There is a certain sweetness to such independence; it is a way of conquering loneliness and the fear of loneliness, by mastering them.

But the sight of a boy playing alone and enjoying it is likely to be tolerated far better by parents than the same isolation on the part of a girl. Girls are traditionally supposed to be sociable, to please others; it is their stock in trade. Not only is solitude often considered rather odd in a girl, what she does with it may be expected to follow certain lines; the sight of a little girl tinkering or collecting, solving mathematical puzzles or impaling beetles, comparing the sizes of pebbles or watching ice crystals form might startle parents who expect to find her reading, or playing the piano, or dressing her dolls. "I probably did play with dolls," Maria recalled, "but I don't really remember it." And she learned to sew and knit and crochet at the age of five, but she never cared for it at all. Apparently she used her isolation just as a boy might have, in learning to profit from being alone and to enjoy it; her mother never discouraged her and her father applauded every instance of her curiosity. Alert to every sign of an inquiring mind and an intellectual disposition, he made it clear that this was what would please him most.

On Maria's eighth birthday Archduke Ferdinand of Austria was assassinated. The visiting, the hospitality and party giving disappeared; in the photograph albums, stern uncles in uniform, their backs straight as riding crops, replace the smiling groups assembled for family picnics. At the end of the war, when food became scarce and there was near-starvation in the cities and strict rationing even in country towns like Göttingen, Frau Goeppert's ingenuity came to the fore. "She arranged all kinds of things," Maria remembered, "which were illegal and which fed us. You see there were all these patients of my father's, who came from the country, and they had no money to pay, so they would come with sausages and things of that kind." Frau Goeppert bought three piglets, two for the infant clinic run by Herr Goeppert and fed on the leavings of the clinic rations, the third for the Goeppert household. When all three were killed there was sausage and smoked ham and pork chops; the pig's ears went into turnip soup, "and it really changed the flavor," Maria recalled. The year of the turnip soup, at the end of the war, was one of real suffering even in Göttingen, and there were many children with stomachs bloated from a diet of turnips.

Maria was in her early teens when the war ended, still going to the Hohere Tochterschule, where she was especially good at languages and mathematics. Soon the Goepperts' roomy old house filled up with company again. There were elaborate formal dinner parties for the adults, with the table laid early in the morning, "perfectly, so there was no rush and no hurry." And starting a few years later there were dances for the young people, with all the rooms thrown open, the two living rooms, the upstairs study, the bedrooms, the dining room, and flowers everywhere, flowers from the garden and from the market, flowers brought by guests. A tiny band was hired for the dancers, three or four musicians always including violin and saxophone, but the dancing continued long after the musicians had gone, for Frau Goeppert played piano until four in the morning.

By 1921 Maria had left the public elementary school to enter the Frauenstudium, a little three-year private school run by suffragettes to prepare a handful of girls for the examination that would admit them to the university. "It somehow was never discussed, but taken for granted by my parents as well as by me that I would go to the University. Yet, at that time it was not trivially easy for a woman to do so," Maria wrote. And when she had been at the Frauenstudium for a year the suffragettes lost all their money in the rapidly mounting inflation, along with the little house they owned and used as a school. There was no public institution in Göttingen to prepare girls for the university; there was in fact no alternative to the suffragettes, who promised to scrape along for one more year in borrowed quarters, but after that, they told the students, they would have to shift for themselves.

In the winter of 1922, as it happened, a brilliant young Italian named Enrico Fermi came to Göttingen to study physics with Max Born, financed by a fellowship from the Italian Ministry of Public Instruction. "In Göttingen for the first time in his life Fermi savored the taste of wealth," Laura Fermi wrote some thirty years later. "The inflation in Germany was then spiraling upward at a tremendous speed. Fermi exchanged the weekly instalments of his fellowship at an increasingly advantageous rate. . . . And he experienced the pleasures that riches can give. By the end of his seven months' stay in Göttingen, Fermi invested his savings in a brand-new bicycle for himself." During that same period Maria and her father went bicycling too, going off into the country sometimes for a week at a time, and it frequently happened that while they were away all of the money Herr Goeppert took with him became completely worthless, so that he had to wire home for more.

Maria was seventeen when the Frauenstudium finally closed its doors; her teachers suggested she might go the following year to the preparatory school for boys. But the idea of being the only girl there did not appeal to her at the time, and she told them she would try to take the fearsome Abitur, the university entrance examination, one year earlier.

"And they said, 'Well, you won't be able to do it.'

"I said, 'I will.' "

"You won't be able to do it, *and* you are too young. You won't be admitted [to the examination]!'

"I said: 'All right. I'll take my chance on that too.' And then I pulled all strings that I could to be admitted to the examination. I took mine in Hanover. There were four or five of us from our little school and there were about thirty boys. . . . And of course we were much impressed, because the boys were so much older than we were, and they seemed so mature, and they were very worried." If the boys were worried, surely the four or five girls had better reason to worry, Maria more than the others, since she had had two years of preparation instead of three.

The Abitur, covering mathematics, French, English, German, physics, history and chemistry, consisted of a week of written examination and a day of oral. Only one of the thirty boys passed, but all the girls did. As for the boy, one of the examining teachers said later, "Well, he wasn't really good, but he made the impression of an earnest young man." This same earnest young man went into physics at Göttingen, where he was a student of Hertha Sponer, a friend of Maria's. And one day Maria and Hertha Sponer walked home together. "I don't know where I got this dumbbell," Hertha Sponer said, of the earnest young man. "How did he ever pass even the Abitur?"

Maria explained how he had passed. Hertha Sponer said, "He isn't really an earnest young man, but he has such a deep voice that he gives the impression that he is."

She was now a bona fide university student, a slim, graceful blonde who came to be known as "the prettiest girl in Göttingen," with a face still almost childishly rounded and dreamy, and hardly intellectual—no gauntness, no "bones," so that she looked more like an English debutante with a fine complexion and a passion for horses than the bluestocking mathematician she meant to become. Her French teacher at the Frauenstudium had found this distressing. " 'You have such a beautiful gift for languages, why do you go into mathematics?' . . . But I never considered going into languages. What do you do with them? I mean in mathematics—mathematics I liked."

Mathematics had been, until 1920, what Göttingen was best known for—"academically speaking, the mathematical center of the world," according to one historian of science. Much of its eminence was due to Felix Klein, a mathematician who brought to Göttingen, through his interest in the practical applications of his science, a flock of small technological industries, factories making optical equipment, measuring apparatus and so forth, which were clustered outside the town walls. But while his main interest was in applied mathematics, Felix Klein also brought to Göttingen some of the most abstruse mathematicians of his day, men like Minkowski, who specialized in relativity theory, and the

Goepperts' neighbor Hilbert. It was Hilbert who once addressed an engineers' congress with the following message, meant to bridge the gap between pure mathematics and technology: "One hears a lot of talk about the hostility between scientists and engineers. I don't believe in any such thing. In fact I am quite certain it is untrue. There can't possibly be anything in it because neither side has anything to do with the other."

It was said that Hilbert suggested Max Born, a former student of his, for the chair of theoretical physics in 1921; Born himself invited James Franck as professor of experimental physics. The Goepperts already had many close friends among the mathematicians and physicists, so many that Maria had come to be regarded as a sort of universal niece by the scientific community, and the Borns and Francks soon joined their circle. Franck's daughters went to the same school as Maria; Max Born was to be Maria's mentor when she studied for her doctorate, and both men came to play important roles in her professional life. But their arrival in Göttingen had repercussions of the first importance for the university itself and for the history of science.

James Franck was the son of Jewish bankers in Hamburg, an elegant, courtly man blessed with a rare sweetness of manner. He had been an officer during the war, which was exceptional for a Jew, and had come home so sick from polyneuritis and loss of vitamins that he crawled up two flights of stairs to his bedroom in order not to ring the bell and alarm his wife. On a preliminary visit to Göttingen, Franck took a walk in the woods to quiet his mind before giving a talk at Hilbert's colloquium— "and I didn't know where I was," he recalled. "The question was how could I come in time to this colloquium? And I found a road, on that road there came a big beer transport with big horses before it. And I asked where the man was going. He said he was heading to Göttingen. 'All right, I get on with you.' And he brought me to the University. I ran down from there to Hilbert's colloquium, to the amusement of the students." In the stately world of the German university Franck was a strikingly unceremonious figure.

Max Born, a distinguished atomic physicist of forty when he came to Göttingen, was a musician, a lover of poetry, and a man of marked emotional fragility, for he wrote that he had a nervous breakdown in 1928 that kept him away from his duties for a year; Maria and others remembered Born as suffering from some kind of nervous disability off and on throughout the mid-twenties. Outwardly a cool, composed and rather formal person, more remote than Franck although far more amiable than the usual stiff German professor, Born was able to conceal his sensitivity and moodiness from all but his closest friends. When Enrico Fermi was in Göttingen with Born a few years earlier he had felt isolated, foreign, "groping in uncertainty and seeking reassurance," according to Laura Fermi. "He was hoping for a pat on the back from Professor Max Born." But Born told Maria years later, "It was I who needed the slap on the back, this brilliant young Italian disturbed me and I was depressed; I needed the slap on the back."

These two men, the gentle James Franck and the tense, volatile Max Born, brought to the University of Göttingen a shift in its center of interest; while hitherto it had been chiefly known for its mathematics, its most exciting work was to become the exploration of a new physical world, a newly discovered and invisible world—the world of the very small.

After the turn of the century the atom was believed to be filled with a fluid, electrically positive and containing within it a number of electrons—the only then-known atomic particle—that were electrically negative; the number of electrons in the atom was sufficient to cancel out the positive electricity of the fluid, since everyone could see that matter was electrically neutral. But in 1911 Ernest Rutherford, in Manchester, showed experimentally that the atom contained a dense, small, electrically positive nucleus; this discovery was followed by Niels Bohr's vision of the atom as a planetary system, with electrons orbiting that dense, small nucleus as planets orbit the sun, following fixed paths. Soon it became clear that the electrons were strictly confined to certain orbits and all other space forbidden to them; they could not come closer to the nucleus than the innermost orbit, nor could they use the space between orbits, except to jump from one "shell" or orbit to the next.

The Bohr-Rutherford atom created pandemonium within the European scientific community. How was the electron to know what orbit to take—how account for the number of electrons in each "shell"; it seemed the electron had to know where to go, where to jump from shell to shell, but this was inconceivable. The more information, mainly mathematical in character, the physicists gathered, the more it became apparent that the rules governing the everyday world and its motions, the so-called classical mechanics, did not apply to the world of the very small. A coherent system, capable of explaining the workings of the atom as clearly and predictably as Newtonian physics explained and predicted the motions of heavenly bodies, had somehow to be put together.

Physicists and mathematicians at every major center of learning in Europe, whose habit it was to work alone in settings of medieval serenity, meeting once or twice a year to talk over results in leisurely fashion, were now pulled together by the powerful fascination of the atom. In the years between the two world wars conferences, lectures, meetings, visits brought the theoreticians to Göttingen or to Copenhagen, to Munich or Cambridge to share the latest results, so that they might then scurry home to work again, tensely and feverishly, then rush off to another meeting or conference where if they were lucky Niels Bohr could be talked to or heard or argued with. Even students and professors drew together, according to one historian, for "Experience and knowledge were worth little. Old and young became comrades on this journey into the interior of matter. Both alike took pride in their common conquest of fragments of knowledge. Both showed equal modesty and bewilderment before the impenetrable." Within the space of a few years, it seemed, everyone in physics had come to know everyone else, and this birth of a true scientific community in Europe eventually took on a new and somber significance in the 1930s.

And during the twenties—the "golden twenties," as they were called in Germany—the arrival at Göttingen of the two eminent atomic physicists Franck and Born brought men like Heisenberg and Pauli and Oppenheimer and Fermi, Compton, Pauling, Dirac and Wigner; here, shuttling between Göttingen and Copenhagen, Heisenberg in his midtwenties worked out the beginnings of a quantum mechanics, based on a sophisticated mathematical theory and preserving the traditional view of matter as discrete particles. Born and a colleague of his perfected it.

A year later an Austrian, Erwin Schroedinger, worked out another mechanics using mathematical theories that viewed matter as waves. Physicists were at first astounded, for there was not a single piece of experimental evidence to support the view of matter as wave; yet both systems gave equally good results, and eventually it was seen that the two seemingly unrelated visions, the particle mechanics and the wave mechanics, were different expressions of the same reality. They are used today interchangeably.

"It became more and more clear that . . . we had stumbled upon a quite unexpected and deeply embedded layer of the secrets of Nature," Pascual Jordan wrote. The physicists who worked on atomic science during the golden twenties went about their work in a state of sometimes indescribable excitement, which they experienced with awe, with fear or with delight, according to temperament. As early as his first experiments with the atom Rutherford foresaw the possibility of fission and was grateful it was not experimentally possible. But the German physicist Nernst, somewhat later, wrote: "We may say we are living on an island of guncotton."

It was the greatest intellectual adventure of the twentieth century, this discovery of the planetary atom and the gradual composing of the laws that governed it, but outside of the very small scientific community in Europe it created little interest. The Weimar Republic had problems of its own far more pressing than any scientific questions. And in the United States, even at the universities atomic physics was mainly a rumor; Oppenheimer had to go to Göttingen in 1927 to learn theoretical physics from Max Born. He had not known until then that such a profession even existed.

Maria was still in the Frauenstudium when she had her first taste of atomic physics. The elderly mathematician Hilbert, believing that physics was much too difficult to be left to physicists, was in the habit of giving semipopular lectures once a week on the most recent atomic developments, and it was his custom, according to Maria, to invite to these lectures as guest of honor any "woman with whom he happened to be in love." On a day when he had no female guest of honor for his lecture he happened to meet his young neighbor Maria, and said,

"Won't you come?" She was very flattered, and told her parents she didn't intend to go to school that day but would go to hear Hilbert instead, "and since I was a brat they let me do it . . . and I learned a lot, and it was very interesting."

Her interest lay dormant for the next few years. Maria had entered the university as a student of mathematics, at a time when there was a sudden increase in the number of women studying mathematics. Nevertheless at Göttingen, as at every German university, women were a tiny minority; until the First World War there had been a ruling that any Göttingen professor could refuse to have a woman in his class, and the rule was occasionally invoked. By the early twenties less than a tenth of the university population was female, while in the United States, by contrast, women accounted for more than a third of all undergraduates. Still, matters had improved since the 1880s, when a German girl named Agnes Pockels almost created the field of surface physics, single-handed and in the privacy of her own kitchen. According to Dr. Florence Sabin:

There was a young girl of nineteen in a small town of north Germany with a strong bent for research, but when her brother went to the University of Göttingen she, according to the customs of her country, remained at home. Agnes Pockels had observed the streaming of currents when salts were put into solution and, by attaching a float to a balance, had found that salts increased the pull of the surface of the fluid. In other words, she had discovered surface tension. This was in 1881. She did not know whether anyone else had ever observed this phenomenon, but, through her brother, she brought her work to the attention of the Professor of Physics at Göttingen. It was, however, new and he failed to grasp its significance. For ten years she went on studying the properties of solutions quite alone in her own home. Then the renowned English physicist, Lord Rayleigh, began to publish on this subject, and so she wrote to him about her work. With a fine sense of honour he sent a translation of her letter to the English journal, *Nature*, asking that it be published. He wrote that the first part of her letter covered nearly the same ground as his own recent work and that with very "homely appliances" she had arrived at valuable results respecting the behaviour of contaminated water surfaces. It is interesting to note that it is this same "homely device" that is still used to measure surface tension. Lord Rayleigh then added that the latter part of her letter seemed to him very suggestive, raising, if it did not fully answer, many important questions. Then for a few years he arranged for the publication of all of her work in English, until the Germany of another era (1898) was proud to accept her discoveries for publication in her own language.

In Maria's day at Göttingen there was even a woman professor of mathematics, Emmy Noether, the daughter of a mathematician and herself one of the illustrious mathematicians of her day; however, Emmy Noether was not paid a regular salary, and her position had been obtained only because Hilbert fought furiously for her.

The reason for the sudden interest in mathematics among female university students in the early twenties was a newspaper article about the shortage of high school teachers of mathematics in schools for girls. There was widespread unemployment in Germany at that time, and news of the shortage gave rise to a little flock of female mathematicians, most of whom intended to qualify for the teaching certificate rather than for the Ph.D. For a while Maria thought she too might quit after qualifying for the certificate. She went to a few of the required classes, in psychology and philosophy, but the philosophy class discussed at length whether or not a dog had a surface; and suppose the dog were shaved, what became of the surface then? The psychology class was no better; Maria went to two lectures, then persuaded her teachers to say she had attended throughout, for she was often able to get around red tape with wonderful facility. In the end, she lost interest in the teaching certificate.

There were also moments when it was not even clear she would stay in mathematics. She thought for a while of going into medicine and talked it over with her father, but "my father talked me out of being a physician, because he always suffered with every child that he lost. He said, it's just . . . too hard. I mean, not too hard physically, but too hard to stand." Looking back on it, she realized later he had been right: "I think I would have been a bad physician; I am not like my father."

Although Maria may have resembled him intellectually, in character she had become increasingly like her mother. The mischievous child had grown into something of a *princesse lointaine*, a faraway, unattainable princess; she was "the prettiest girl in Göttingen," but she was also reserved, controlled, shy, extremely aloof. She found displays of emotion uncomfortable, her own emotions or those of others, so that for many people Maria was very difficult to know; like her mother she was conscientious, hard on herself, a perfectionist, and also like her mother she was generous and loyal. But the qualities Herr Goeppert was remembered for had to do with warmth and richness of emotion, with strong, perhaps eccentric convictions, passionately held; these are not likely characteristics for a mathematician or a physicist, nor were they visible in Maria's personality. For Herr Goeppert the suffering when he lost a child was too much to bear, and yet he bore it; but Maria, when she thought of becoming a doctor, had thought mainly of going into medical research —as if the suffering were not only too much to bear but too much even to contemplate.

Perhaps it was partly because of her cool, controlled aloofness that Maria found herself, at the university, making friends with men rather than with women; for a number of the girls she had known at the Frauenstudium were there, although her closer friends among them were a year behind. With men, small talk was less necessary, one could exchange ideas, discuss the work, but closeness and intimacy would not be required; even if some romantic attachment developed, and with a girl as pretty as Maria it happened often, there were ways of protecting one's innermost feelings. Besides, she liked men better. "I have to confess, I never much associated with the women. I don't know, I always was with the boys . . . and that was enjoyable, you see. . . . some of these men were very intelligent, and to keep up with them was wonderful. So I had two friends with whom I sat in all my classes on the first right-hand row, in mathematics. And the three of us competed, the three of us could always do—everything."

It was a pattern Maria stuck with throughout her university career, in a sense throughout life. For there were other women in the sciences at Göttingen and some, like Hertha Sponer, were as intelligent as any man and as challenging to keep up with. And there were little groups of women, enclaves within the larger student body where girls clung to one another for support, maximizing the sexual differences; this held no appeal for Maria. She was one of those who always preferred to sit with the boys, to eat with them, work with them and to ignore as far as possible the sexual differences.

One day in 1927 Maria met Max Born, on his way to his physics seminar. "Why don't you come along?" he asked, and she did. The seminar consisted of some twenty or thirty students who went afterward for a walk with Born: "the whole seminar—anyone who wanted to come along and go somewhere in the hills and have a rustic supper in one of the village inns," talking physics all the time. The informality of this association between lofty professor and lowly students, the intensity of their mutual interest in their subject, and the subject itself apparently fascinated Maria. She found herself increasingly tugged toward physics; mathematics began to lose its charm. "Mathematics began to seem too much like puzzle solving. Physics is puzzle solving too, but of puzzles created by nature, not by the mind of man."

During that same period she happened one day to meet Johann Von Neumann (who became one of the greatest twentieth-century mathematicians) in the hall. "I had a beginning mathematics course and he had Heisenberg's lecture. And Johann Von Neumann said to me, 'You know it's very exciting. Heisenberg tells us what he thought about last night.' " And what he thought about last night might have been his "uncertainty principle"—the impossibility of knowing, precisely and at any one time, both the position and the velocity of a given particle of matter—a concept that became basic to atomic physics, but was at first so revolutionary that Einstein recoiled from it, believing that God does not play at dice. For young people like Maria and Von Neumann to hear what Heisenberg thought of the night before was to see the future being pieced together before their eyes.

It was also in 1927, the year Maria switched from mathematics to physics, that her beloved father died, a blow for which neither Maria nor her mother was prepared. To Maria it now became a sacred obligation to complete the work for her Ph.D. Although there was no very striking resemblance between Dr. Goeppert and Max Born, perhaps Born's emotional fragility, the evidence of turbulent feelings no matter how well concealed, made it possible for Maria to find him especially sympathetic during that period. The relationship of student to mentor

—of graduate student to the professor under whom he does his dissertation—has always resembled the parental one, and the German term for mentor is Doktorvater—doctor-father. Graduate students faithfully copy minor quirks as well as basic styles from their mentor, arranging their laboratories in precisely the same fashion as his, even twenty or thirty years later. Probably no one could have taken the place of Maria's father, but having Max Born as her mentor must have made the next few years easier than they might otherwise have been. She felt for him a girlish adoration that became, in time, affectionate respect.

Early in her career as a physics student Maria made friends with a young man who sat beside her in the quantum mechanics lecture; his name was Victor Weisskopf. Viki, as everyone called him, and Maria became a part of a group of three or four students who walked together and ate together, and since Maria had to be home for dinner every day she often ate two dinners, one at home and one in town. They talked quantum mechanics, "and learned a lot by talking with each other, seeing each other's troubles and straightening them out," but they also competed with one another, especially Maria and Viki. His interest in her did not remain entirely intellectual. The Goepperts' home and the home of the mathematician Landau, where there were two attractive daughters, offered a seemingly endless round of dances and entertainments as suitably chaperoned settings for the young people's flirtations. Not everyone was admitted inside this charmed circle of Göttingen's best society; a young American physicist remembered later that he had loved Maria Goeppert from afar, and it seemed as if everyone else did too: "We were all in love with her; not that I ever said a word to her, I didn't even know she spoke beautiful English." Maria had spent several months in Cambridge, where she heard Rutherford lecture, and her English was quite good.

While Maria continued her studies in physics and a young chemist named Joseph Mayer finished the graduate work in Berkeley that would lead to a postgraduate year in Göttingen, the golden twenties of the Weimar Republic drew to an ominous close. In Göttingen, however, and especially among the physicists and mathematicians, politics was a distant and rather sordid disturbance, one they tended to ignore. When

Maria came to the United States in the spring of 1930 she was amazed at everyone's asking what she thought about Hitler; she thought hardly anything about Hitler. She rarely thought about politics at all.

Göttingen, like all German universities, was entirely state controlled; also like all German universities it was an enclave of conservatism, its professors formal, disciplined, authoritarian. "One doesn't nod to a student. One doesn't acknowledge the existence of a student," explained the Göttingen physicist Pohl, and he spoke for most of his fellows. They were professors because they were guaranteed acceptable, antiseptic and unlikely to upset any applecarts, requirements apparently unchanged since Heine complained about university proctors who must "take good care that no students duel . . . and that no new ideas, which must still remain in quarantine before Göttingen for several decades, are smuggled in by an inquisitive instructor." The winds of change that followed the First World War, sweeping away kaiser and empire and setting in motion the doomed machinery of the Weimar Republic, freed the genius of the writers, artists and playwrights associated with Weimar— Brecht, Grosz, the Bauhaus, the brilliant film makers and the surrealistic photographers who left their mark on European art between the wars —but they passed right by the university, and when Hitler came into power, fourteen years of socialism had barely ruffled its self-satisfied calm.

The physicists, however, were an exception. In 1933, shortly after the declaration of the racial laws, the new minister of education asked Hilbert if the Physics Institute at Göttingen had really suffered so much from the departure of the Jews and their friends. Hilbert said, "Suffered? No, it didn't suffer, Herr Minister. It just doesn't exist any more." For while many of the physicists at Göttingen were exceptions to the German rule that the university is a conservative arm of the establishment, often more established than the establishment, this was not because physics attracts humanists and idealists in greater number than other disciplines. It was mainly because, for reasons still little understood, physics in the twentieth century has attracted so many Jews. Max Born and James Franck were both examples of the kind of cultivated Jewish physicist who had known from birth that he would never become an "insider"; official anti-Semitism was an unwavering policy before the First World War, although in circles like Franck's social anti-Semitism had begun to fade. In the twenties and early thirties men like Szilard, Von Neumann and Teller appeared at Göttingen; "outsiders" twice over, they were self-exiled Hungarian Jews and part of what Laura Fermi called the "Hungarian mystery," the explosion of talent in many fields, but mostly in physics, from one small and unimportant country. There were physicists at the German universities and at Göttingen who were not Jews, and there were even a few who became active Nazis. Still, the cast of characters was such that the physicists formed a little island of humanism in the midst of the university.

If Max Born, an internationalist and a pacifist to the end of his life, was extremely left politically in comparison to other university professors, he was slightly to the right compared to the Weimar artists and writers and to the Jewish population in Germany as a whole. James Franck, like many of Maria's relatives, deeply loved Germany and the Germans, but he could not really trust the left and the Weimar regime; leftists were unpredictable, violent. Maria had an uncle who resigned an important government post rather than work for the Weimar Republic. Yet her people had a greater distaste for the military and the right; throughout her life Maria shrank from the sight of men in uniform, and encouraged her son to get out of ROTC long before it was the fashion for young men of conscience to do so in America.

The physicists at Göttingen, then, distrusted the left and the Weimar government (except perhaps for Born, the most liberal of all of them) and feared the right; they preferred to ignore politics altogether, since they knew from experience that politics only meant trouble—greed, manipulation, corruption. They trusted physics instead; it would never betray them. And this trust, this abiding love for their science, was one more force that isolated them from the rest of the university and from German society as a whole, for the Weimar years had seen the growth in Germany of neoromanticism, a "rampant mysticism" apparent from one end of the political spectrum to the other, born of a revulsion against materialism, reason, technology, and a hunger for spiritual renewal. Science was the natural enemy of mysticism, and the physicists were going in precisely the opposite direction from the rest of the country, where the young sang folk songs, their elders worshiped Wagner, and a longing for older, simpler, earthier values, for more emotion and less reason, was felt on every level of society.

Buried in the physics department by day, and at night among other young scientists either working or dancing, Maria was largely unaware of what went on beyond Göttingen, just as she was unaware of the full import of the fevered productivity of the Weimar artists and writers. "The excitement that characterized Weimar culture stemmed in part from exuberant creativity and experimentation; but much of it was anxiety, fear, a rising sense of doom," according to the historian Peter Gay. Some of Maria's family had begun to realize they were living on the edge of the abyss, but Maria knew nothing about it; by 1929 she was working on her dissertation under Born, and it was her primary concern.

That winter of 1928–29, the coldest Europe had seen since Napoleon took his army into Russia, Joe Mayer came from California to Göttingen on a Rockefeller grant. Premonitions of the financial disaster that was to overtake the United States had already been felt in Germany; but money had been in short supply there since the end of the war, and Joe cut a considerable swath with his Rockefeller money. He bought a car first thing—"I was a Californian; what does a Californian do without a car?"—and the second thing he bought was a supply of whiskey and gin; he was fresh from Prohibition.

He had been born in New York in 1904, the only child of an Austrian-born engineer and an American schoolteacher. Joe's mother, Kate, gave up teaching when she married; she was a brisk, capable, humorous and unusually energetic woman. When she was in her sixties in New York, Kate Mayer took male visitors to see the sights on foot and wore them out. Joe's father, who died five years before Joe came to Göttingen, had been a quiet, studious man; he studied applied mathematics at the Sorbonne, became a bridge engineer and married late—he was twenty years older than his wife. Joe remembered him as "very broadly-educated . . . and always reading; and not novels, I mean Freud, or Veblen."

Partly because his father was so much older, partly because he was by nature a rather distant person—"he didn't play baseball with me or anything like that"—Joe was closer to his mother; it was the kind of childhood family both Anne Roe and Bernice Eiduson found with amazing frequency among their scientists. Eiduson learned that almost half her subjects "did not know their fathers very well. . . . Neither the scientists who knew their fathers intimately nor the ones who knew them slightly liked them very much. Generally the fathers were described as rigid, stern, aloof, and emotionally reserved." Maria's father, of course, was none of these, and it is interesting to note that the sociologist Alice Rossi speaks of close father-daughter relationships among famous women mathematicians.

Joe and his parents lived in Montreal for a while, where his father was assistant chief engineer in the building of the Quebec Bridge, then they moved to Hollywood for his retirement. Joe had had a certain amount of asthma as a child, persisting into adulthood and sometimes leading to bronchitis or pneumonia, but he never remembered much childhood isolation, not from other kids. "At least in Montreal I was always around with a gang. . . . we lived on a dead-end street of small houses, and there were boys in every second house. . . . I was sort of tall and gangly and would lose most of the fights I'd get in." He wasn't much good at sports as a child, and his great love was a Meccano set to which he devoted much of his time and all the money he could get hold of.

Joe had always been a good student and was always going to be a scientist. "Somehow my father always talked like a scientist . . . and I had always assumed that's what one does." His last year in high school he took a chemistry class with a particularly fine teacher, and right after graduation found work as a chemist in the sugar mills, first in California, then in Utah. "We were just bench chemists, you know; you just let something in until it gets red. I mean, it was rather interesting for a high school kid, but I wouldn't want to do it more than two campaigns." All the same he was pretty proud of himself at the time, having been on his own and self-supporting, away from home for six months at the age of sixteen.

Having established his independence, Joe was ready to consider going to college; a boy who worked in Utah with him wanted to go to Cal Tech so Joe went with him, entering in January of 1920 and working straight through the summer so that he graduated in 1924, at twenty. If he had not been the outstanding student in his class, he had done quite well academically, and had also acquired some reputation as an athlete, especially in swimming; he was captain of the swim team in his senior year. Then Joe entered graduate school at Berkeley, where it was his great good fortune to work directly with the famous Gilbert Newton Lewis, one of the fathers of physical chemistry in America, whose inclination was experimental rather than theoretical during most of a half century of distinguished work. Joe's doctoral dissertation was an experimental one, hardly surprising in view of his boyhood interests:

When I was young, seventeen or so, I felt I could understand pretty much how everything worked. A car, for example; you knew how to look under the hood and fix what went wrong, you had to know. You knew how a radio worked; you could build one. But today, in spite of our having learned so much about the way the world is put together—well, I have no idea of how my Mercedes works. And the remote control device for opening the garage door—how does it work? Oh sure, I can say "radio waves," but what does that mean? I couldn't take it apart and put it back together again. My scientific friends have pointed out, well, you didn't know when you were young how everything worked, you didn't know how a cow worked. But I have a fairly good idea *now* how a cow works; whereas the world is getting full of things whose workings hardly anyone can understand or reproduce.

Newly arrived in Göttingen, where he was to work with Born and Franck, Joe would have met Maria at the university one day or other; he could hardly have kept from meeting her. But as it was he met her his first day in town, having decided before he left California that the Goepperts' house was the place to stay. A friend of Joe's had returned to Berkeley after a year in Göttingen. " 'There are two pensions,' he said, 'that the Americans live in. But . . . if you can, get a room in a private house there. The pensions, you get tired of them; besides, all the Americans live there, so you don't get to meet Germans. And in particular,' he said, 'you know there's one place where it would be lovely if you could get in . . . besides, it has the prettiest girl in Göttingen.' "

When her husband died Frau Goeppert had decided to take in boarders, a decision that was, in Göttingen, entirely unremarkable. As the university made no official provision for the housing of students, they had always taken lodgings among the townspeople, often the most cultivated and enterprising of the townspeople, who appreciated having the wide world brought into their sitting rooms. Maria never had anything to do with these transactions; all arrangements concerning the boarders, like most of the details of daily life, remained Frau Goeppert's province. But the day Joe Mayer turned up, Frau Goeppert was sick and in bed.

"So I went, and rang the doorbell and a pretty little girl came and opened the door, and I started talking my beautiful German . . . to ask whether they had a room. And dammit, she answered me in English . . . she wouldn't listen to my German."

Joe had learned his German partly from his Austrian father, and was inordinately proud of it, but Viki Weisskopf, for one, was never much impressed; Joe's German sounded pretty American to him. He was impressed by the way Joe bought the car, though; everyone was. "He went up to the counter and put all his cash on it, as if buying bread." Perhaps Weisskopf suspected Joe of an interest in Maria even at the start, but he liked him anyhow; Joe was eminently likable, according to Weisskopf, "a lanky, tall, not very worldly American." He was also quick-witted, humorous, opinionated and friendly; he had a spectacular temper, dearly loved an argument, and was good at athletics, especially the showier kind. Maria said she never paid much attention to the new boarder until one day at the municipal swimming pool, when she saw him swim.

Soon they were playing tennis together, swimming, hiking and carrying on the strenuously athletic style of courtship that was popular among young Germans of their class. And they danced together; one didn't take a girl to a dance, but found her there, perhaps by prearrangement. "There was one party we went to," Joe recalled, "and Viki Weisskopf and I both wanted to take Maria home; and Viki had been annoying me, as usual, by insisting on talking English all the time. . . . And finally I decided I was going to get even with him, and I took a coin out of my pocket, and I said, 'All right, let's flip. Heads I win, tails you lose.'

And he wasn't fast enough, you see." Maria, who stood by watching them, caught on before Weisskopf did. "I thought it was so clever." Before the summer was over they were talking about marriage; rather, Joe was.

He had fallen in love with an irresistibly pretty face, with a quick intelligence, occasionally rather competitive, with a faraway princess. Maria was a prize, a challenge, aloof and hard to know and rather intriguingly aristocratic in her tastes, while Joe was blunt, down to earth, somewhat naïve. He loved beer, for example, the beer that Göttingen was famous for and all the young people drank at parties, but Maria disdained it. Her father had gone through university without touching beer and she preferred to do the same; she drank white wine instead. Joe loved to argue, would argue about anything, on either side, in self-exciting fashion cranking up his emotions as he went and sometimes losing his temper in the process, but Maria kept herself under such stern control that she had no temper, and took no pleasure in heated argument. If she was a challenge because she was hard to know and hard to get close to, it may well be that there was added challenge in the problem of prying her loose from Göttingen, where she was deeply embedded because of her close ties to her family, her adoration of Max Born, and her dependence on her mother.

If Maria had fallen in love with Joe for the convincing reasons that he was delightful company, by nature considerate and supportive, and with the powerful added charm of being very much in love with her, she too may have had another reason; married to Joe and transported to America, she would be forced to break away from her mother. Frau Goeppert behaved like "a mother hen with an only chick," according to one old friend of Maria's; and Maria behaved like a well-brought-up German girl of good family, docile and obedient and devoted to her mother. But docility and obedience are the wrong traits for creative scientists; reluctant though Maria was to leave her mother, she may also have hoped, unconsciously, that Joe would force her to do so.

One day they drove to Karlshaven, a small town across the river Weser, with the best restaurant in the neighborhood of Göttingen. And to get there they took a one-car ferry, "just a raft, really," and asked the ferryman how late he worked, so they would know when to come back. Ten o'clock, he told them. But that night was the night they became engaged, a lengthy process that kept them so busy they realized the ferryman would be gone by the time they reached his crossing, so they went all the way around to a bridge instead. Two years later they were on that ferry again; the ferryman recognized them immediately. Where had they been that night, he demanded; he had waited till after midnight to take them across again. "We were getting engaged," they told him. Or so it seemed in retrospect. For a few weeks later, in September, Joe was once more pressing for a firm promise: "he rather energetically demanded a decision from me, and I have the impression that I engaged myself to him, so to speak," Maria wrote to Frau Goeppert that autumn while touring Italy and Switzerland with relatives; Joe and Kate Mayer were touring Switzerland too and their paths had crossed. "Deep in my heart I am not quite sure," the letter continues, "but I believe, eventually I will be sure." Her state of mind can be imagined from the fact that Maria neatly crossed out the last eight words after first changing "believe" to "hope." "It appears so terribly senseless and selfish to me, to thus run out on you. For the time being I cannot even conceive of it! Do not be sad as yet, nothing is quite certain yet. . . ."

Frau Goeppert must have become resigned at last, or if not resigned, aware that matters were out of her hands, for she soon began pointing out that Maria was spending so much time with Joe she was ignoring her dissertation. "You'd better get married," she told her daughter, "or you'll never finish up your degree." Much of the work on the dissertation problem assigned by Born, and concerning a quantum-mechanical effect in atoms, had already been done, but the work had to be organized and written up; physicists who complete all their experiments or calculations without ever writing up their results are by no means unknown. There was yet another hurdle—the examination for the degree, the first and last examination a German student takes from the time he enters university to the day he is awarded the Ph.D.

One day Maria and Joe drove in Joe's little Opel to Leyden, to visit the theoretician Ehrenfest, who spent much of his time in Göttingen and was one of its most gifted teachers, so gifted that James Franck once remarked: "I was afraid to ask him a question, because if I asked him a question, it took a terrific time. He didn't let me out of his claws, I may say, until I really understood this thing I had asked and in each detail. Sometimes I didn't want to understand each detail." Once arrived at Ehrenfest's house—an extraordinary establishment, bought out of a private income that subsequently dwindled, it had proved too costly for the Ehrenfests to maintain, and the only clock to be seen was a pocket watch hanging on the dining room wall—Ehrenfest demanded to know how Maria would write up her dissertation. Maria explained her ideas; Ehrenfest listened, then told her there was no more time to waste, she must go upstairs immediately and not come down again until the entire thesis was committed roughly to paper. Then he led her to his own study, locked the door and left her there; three hours later she had completed an outline that satisfied Ehrenfest.

Other pressures were brought to bear; Joe nudged and nagged at Maria to finish her thesis. The two of them had decided to give a dinner party the day after Christmas and neglected to mention their plan to Frau Goeppert. She was amazed when they finally told her; didn't Maria know the servants were always given that day off? What were Joe and Maria to do now, she demanded; for Maria had never really learned to cook, in spite of a long visit to her Aunt Vera a few years ago with the sole purpose of acquiring a little domesticity. They told her they'd manage all the same; the truth was, Joe was a fairly capable cook himself. Then they went out and bought a haunch of venison, larded it with bacon and set to work at the coal stove in Frau Goeppert's kitchen with the cookbook propped open before them. In the course of preparing an elaborate meal that was to reach its climax in a flaming plum pudding, Maria grew increasingly confused and frustrated, until it seemed to Joe she was on the brink of tears. Realizing that she had never before tried to work in a servantless kitchen, he told her, "If you get your Ph.D., Maria, I'll hire a maid for you, but if you don't get it, no maid." She bucked up and attacked the haunch of venison with fresh resolve.

They were married one morning a few weeks later, in mid-January, at the city hall; that afternoon there was a party at Frau Goeppert's house with the bride in a floor-length white dress. Kate Mayer, who had been touring Europe since autumn, came to the wedding, and Joe remembered her staring meditatively at a porcelain lion throughout the ceremony, looking as if she wondered what it all meant. She, Kate Mayer, a widow with an only child, had acquired a daughter-in-law, but Frau Professor Goeppert, who was also a widow with an only child, must stay behind in her vast, old-fashioned house and watch that daughter-in-law depart for an unknown country across an ocean. Kate Mayer wrote a kind and unaffected note to the Frau Professor reminding her that there would be all those long, wonderful summers to look forward to, that the children were bound to be happy together, that she would be a second mother to "your little girl," but she may have felt somewhat guilty all the same.

The week-long honeymoon they spent in Berlin, at a fashionable hotel, going to plays and visiting a flock of Maria's relatives and her old nursemaid, Tutti. On their return to Göttingen they found an empty house. "We were so terribly disappointed when we learned . . . that you already left this afternoon! And when I then found nothing but your business-like note, when I had so much counted upon an embrace, I actually burst into tears. . . . I have not seen you for a week and I do not even know whether you look well or miserable, how you stood up in all the many worries, etc., and anyway I am longing for you quite terribly. . . . at this moment I cannot possibly conceive how I should be able to do without you at the banks of the Missouri. When will you be back?" Frau Goeppert probably took herself off, on a long visit to relatives, in order to leave the young people alone in the house; it seems she had not counted on Maria's longing to talk, confide, discuss, share. Maria's letter was followed by a few lines from Joe, who was also sorry to have missed Frau Goeppert; Maria must now return to her dissertation, he added.

It was supposed to be finished by mid-February. "All we have to report," Joe wrote to Frau Goeppert the first of the month, "is work and kisses." But February fifth was Joe's birthday, and Maria emerged from her thesis writing long enough to ask her mother what she ought to do about the birthday; would Mother cable her suggestions for a birthday present, or had they better postpone the celebration altogether until

Frau Goeppert's return? Apparently a festive birthday took place without Frau Goeppert, for Joe and Maria had fresh grapefruit for breakfast the morning of the day, specially ordered from Florida by Kate Mayer, and in the evening there were twenty-six apples, each with a candle in it.

The thesis was nearing completion; forty years later Eugene Wigner was to describe it as "a masterpiece of clarity and concreteness." But now the examination approached. One of Maria's old friends, Max Delbrueck (Nobel laureate in biology in 1969) had just flunked his examination, because of the experimental part. The conservative Professor Pohl, the same Pohl who would not dream of nodding to a student, would not even acknowledge the existence of a student—Pohl was given to asking questions about classical physics, which none of the students cared about, rather than quantum physics, in which they were passionately interested. Delbrueck had Pohl on his examining committee, Pohl asked his classical questions, and Delbrueck went down in defeat. Now all those who faced examinations were shivering.

As the day came closer Maria may have reinspected her feelings about the German university system; until then, she had felt it was far better than the British. The British had to take all those examinations, she used to say, recalling her visit to Cambridge. But the Germans never wasted their time with examinations; from the time they were admitted until they were ready with their dissertation they took only one examination —the one she was facing. And therefore each student had no way of knowing from past experience how well he was likely to stand up under the barrage, how nervous he got, how each of the different professors behaved.

About Born, it was well known that he always examined a student on the subject on which he happened to be lecturing at the time. Born was lecturing on thermodynamics, a subject Maria never liked, never felt at home with. "Don't ask me anything about thermodynamics," she told Born. "I don't understand it." Born, Franck and Windaus, all three eventually Nobel laureates, were her examining committee, Franck in the place Pohl might have had. And Born asked nothing about thermodynamics, but nothing about quantum mechanics either. "Why should

I?" he said later. "I knew you knew it." Meanwhile, out in the courtyard some forty of her fellow students were waiting to hear Maria's fate. When it was over and they learned she had passed, Joe brought them all back to Frau Goeppert's for brandy; he had been sure all along she would pass, he said; he never doubted for a moment.

With Kate Mayer they were to leave Göttingen for Cherbourg and the transatlantic steamer on the twentieth of March. Frau Goeppert's doubts and fears and loneliness were kept from Joe, although not entirely from Maria; her Aunt Vera told Maria it was better to go. "I have two sons," she said. "They will stay here, and there will be a war and they will die in that war." Vera's sons did fight in the war, although they didn't die in it; they were both crippled, and another of Maria's aunts lost her two sons.

In the spring of 1930 Maria saw no reason to believe Germany would go to war, but there were other reasons it might be better to leave. Although she had always hoped to do it, it would be extremely difficult for her to become a professor in a German university, where women were a great rarity, and professors, in contrast to lesser ranks, were minor princes, usually one to a department. In America it might be easier.

Joe had been offered his first academic position as associate in chemistry at Johns Hopkins, Baltimore; therefore Maryland was what Maria must try to picture as she rode in the railway car toward Cherbourg. What she looked forward to most, she wrote to her mother, was unpacking her luggage and bringing "all the images from home" into her new existence. Once on the ship, Joe added in a postscript, she would no longer be able to change her mind and run back to Göttingen.

The crossing, second class on the SS *Europa*, was glorious; Maria strolled the decks with a slide rule in hand wondering if they would break the record of the SS *Bremen*. She played deck games and danced, longing for her mother, fearful of America, and everlastingly grateful for the sweetness of her new husband and the kindness of Kate Mayer. By April Fool's Day they were in Baltimore.

Here Maria found herself in the position of having to adapt, simultaneously, to a new husband, a new country and her new professional status, and page after page flew across the Atlantic to Frau Goeppert, beginning almost the day they disembarked and continuing for weeks. That her mother had been able to refrain from writing a single line until ten days after the young couple left was a source of amazement to Maria; she told her mother everything, waited hungrily for replies, and cabled, prepaid, when eight days had passed without a letter from Germany.

Her reception by the university was rather cool, but not utterly discouraging in view of the depression. As Maria explained to her mother, she had been offered no regular academic appointment, but she was to have a salary of a few hundred a year for helping a member of the physics department with his German correspondence. She would also have a chance to do work of her own in a little room in the science building; her name would be in the catalog, or rather the initial of her maiden name—she was to be listed simply as "G"—and the few hundred dollars would be enough for a maid when they had a place of their own. She and Joe, Maria told her mother, had decided to live in a boardinghouse for three months, because they were going to spend the summer at Michigan, at the famous summer school, and there was no point to settling down before they knew the city. Meanwhile they could save money for the car they both wanted, a successor to the "dear little Opel."

There were some disputes about this car. Joe wanted something practical but Maria wanted a convertible; "a solid-top car is no fun," she insisted.

We tried out a big Buick today. But since unfortunately I made a sad face all day long, Joe also lost his enthusiasm, is also unhappy and hence we dropped the whole idea of buying a car. This is how things stand to-day. Tomorrow it will probably look quite different.

But now I must tell you something cheerful. Yesterday afternoon in between our shopping we stopped into a charming small restaurant. Joe, with his inborn cheek, asked the waiter for a bottle of wine. But the waiter was discreet and he did not even hear it. Yet with the oysters (which are here the most inexpensive popular dish) he brought us a coffee pot and two mocha cups. Since some Americans drink coffee with their lunch we did not raise any protest. But the coffee had a funny red color and when we sampled it, there it was, delicious Chianti! That is the dry America for you!

It was a strange and difficult country altogether, Maria felt; how dull the Americans were, not even colored Easter eggs for breakfast, nothing special about Easter at all except that parade. A little girl, buying chewing gum for her penny rather than chocolate, struck Maria as "typically American." Shopping for lampshades, buying a blouse, she reported each expedition in detail to her mother, but otherwise kept her feelings about America rather severely to herself; when anyone asked how she liked it she would say, "Not so bad."

No one at Johns Hopkins, Maria told her mother, did quantum mechanics. Neither did anyone seem to feel the need for it, or to realize that in the young Mrs. Mayer, fresh from the fount of quantum mechanics, they had someone unique—with one exception: "Joe and I did quantum mechanics all afternoon and for once we quarreled relatively little. But now we are both exhausted." In later years she remembered only that Joe had been an apt and willing pupil, and Joe, forty years later, had also forgotten they ever fought about it: "Maria was always much more erudite in theory than I—I learned all the quantum mechanics I know from her."

Quantum mechanics was not entirely unknown in the States, nor was it unknown to Joe, who had spent a year with Born at Göttingen; but like most American chemists he had learned the Schroedinger system, based on the theory that matter works like waves, rather than the Born-Heisenberg system of particle mechanics. This was what Maria had learned, and was teaching him. And "a number of things that are harder, in the approach most chemists use, Maria was able to work out quickly and elegantly," according to Joe. Nevertheless, as a bride of three months engaged in teaching her husband atomic physics, Maria apparently had her hands full. Not only did Joe love to argue, he loved to argue about abstractions, ideas; certainly one would not expect a scientist to argue hotly about something personal, to lose his temper about matters close to home, for he became a scientist with a view to avoiding the personal, the emotional, whatever is closest to home. But Maria, who could enjoy animated discussion, had no liking at all for heated argument; unable to lose her temper, she would struggle against tears, then run from the room. They had fallen in love because they were so different; still, it took getting used to.

Later that month in a letter to Frau Goeppert on the vexed question of the car, Maria used the German term for "big fight," "big stink," three times with noticeable pleasure. If her mother had not received the cable Maria sent, Maria would raise a big stink in Baltimore. If Frau Goeppert's maid Rosa is not properly treated for her lung condition Frau Goeppert ought to raise a big stink, "einen furchtbaren Krach"; and as for the big stink that arose in Göttingen between two distinguished mathematicians, Maria only wished she had been there to see it. But since Maria never in her life raised a big stink about anything—even when she had considerable provocation, "I don't like to be mad" was her response—the imaginary fusses may have had their origins in the tension that rose between herself and Joe when she taught him quantum mechanics, or in the nagging ache of homesickness, or in the university's continued coolness, perhaps in all three.

By summer they had a five-seater Buick, Joe's choice, with which to drive to Michigan and the summer school. Fermi and Ehrenfest lectured there, and there Maria met Laura Fermi, on her first visit to the States. In her own way Mrs. Fermi was as puzzled by America as Maria was:

> There seemed to be total incomprehension of some instinctive human feelings in the Americans' insistence on separation of the sexes, asking husbands to stag dinner parties, leaving poor young wives to mope at home; or planning women's lunches, where the same poor wives were to find their way among strangers speaking an idiom strange in words and meanings, without the much-needed support of those pillars of strength, their husbands.

The two women met for the first time in Ann Arbor and liked each other, although they became friends only when the Fermis settled for good in America nine years later. Laura Fermi remembered Maria as "blonde and slender and . . . decidedly delicate." What Maria remembered most about the Fermis was Enrico's being, in the Italian style, very much the boss, while Laura seemed subdued, perhaps not properly appreciated. Joe's chief impression was of "a very young and pleasant little Italian, with unending good humor, and a brilliant and clear method of presenting what he has to present in terrible English."

Back in Baltimore that fall the Mayers rented a tiny row house; there was a maid now, once a week, and Maria taught herself to cook with Joe's help. She often resented the inconvenience of a servantless little house—the whole thing would have fitted into Frau Goeppert's dining room, she used to say—but in other ways life in Baltimore had become somewhat more supportable. She had begun to make friends.

Joe had an older colleague in the chemistry department named Frank Rice, and Frank had a new bride twenty years younger than he was; her name was Katherine, she had a Ph.D. in biochemistry, and she was only three months younger than Maria. The two women became best friends the instant they met. Katherine Rice was probably Maria's first close woman friend, and they must have made a rather formidable pair, both bluestockings and well aware of being far better educated than any other faculty wife; they were also aware of being attractive, young and well-dressed, for the Mayers had a modest little inheritance from Joe's father, enough to make a down payment on their first house a few years later and to keep them from the day-to-day worries about money that were the lot of most junior faculty. "We were pretty snobbish about things," Katherine Rice recalled. Once when a photographer tried to take pictures of the science professors swimming, Maria withdrew. To be photographed in a wet bathing suit, she felt, was unladylike and also unprofessional, as was a certain costume she described to her mother: "The blue skirt . . . was really too short and too small and unfit for a Ph.D."

If Katherine Rice was Maria's closest friend, her most important friendship professionally was with Karl Herzfeld. Max Born had written to him early in 1930, recommending Maria and asking, "Will you look out for her?" Nothing could have given Karl Herzfeld greater pleasure. He was a stiff, ceremonious, shy, warmhearted man, devoutly Catholic and German to the core, with no one to talk German with. A pretty, German-speaking young woman he could fuss over; a Göttingen-trained scientist to whom he could teach physical chemistry so that they could collaborate; a polished, comparatively worldly female (he was most unworldly himself, living in the dormitory and hoping one day to live in a monastery and teach at a Catholic institution) to whom he could be chivalrously devoted, was a gift from heaven. Maria in turn was pleased at the chance to collaborate with Herzfeld, to learn physical chemistry from him and from Joe. She would have been better pleased if she could have done quantum mechanics, but apparently that was not possible; for one thing there was no real interest in quantum mechanics at Hopkins at the time. It was a European, not an American, phenomenon. Experimentalists need their machines, their apparatus, but what the theorist needs is paper, pencil and a cluster of enthusiastic colleagues. There are exceptions, of course, a very few theoreticians who prefer to work in complete isolation, but most of them require one or more of their fellows to use as sounding boards, to argue, discuss, build up ideas and demolish them with. Maria took up chemistry instead.

As it happened, what she learned from Herzfeld, and even more what she learned from Joe in the way of habits and attitudes common among chemists, proved invaluable to Maria in later years. The experimental chemist is something of a plodder; he accumulates facts, data, effects. As Joe described it, Maria began to learn from him "chemistry in the sense of the facts. Most theoretical physicists take great pride in not knowing one chemical compound from another." The typical theorist looks for a single, brilliant illumination; he wants to dazzle, to make a splash. "It's not that physicists ignore facts, but there's a tendency not to look at all the different chemical elements," to overlook the facts one doesn't like. With Herzfeld Maria did theoretical physical chemistry, and it was also theoretical work she did with Joe, but Joe was an experimentalist and always had been; he had the background and tastes of a tinkerer and had put together his radio and much of his car, and it was from Joe that Maria acquired the chemist's practical approach to science.

Between Herzfeld and Joe, Maria had a fairly varied career at Hopkins, working on energy transfer on solid surfaces, behavior of hydrogen dissolved in palladium, etcetera. Her best work, and the first to bring her to the serious attention of other American scientists, had been started at Herzfeld's suggestion and was carried out after he left Hopkins; with a former student of his she investigated the physical theory of dyes.

The physicist R. W. Wood, whom Maria described to her mother as "the most clever experimentalist in the world . . . the king of Baltimore, just like Hilbert of Göttingen," had made her welcome from the beginning. August though he was, and considerably older, and of an uncertain, irritable temper, "To me he is unbelievably kind and civil, as far as that is possible for him. He even takes his pipe out of his mouth." Wood told Maria he had heard she wanted to do experiments, had seen a number of things she might be interested in and invited her to visit his office; Maria found it all rather uncanny and was convinced she would finally get on his nerves. But in view of her precarious position at the university, having so powerful a friend and ally was a good omen; meanwhile Maria, who was herself the soul of propriety and conventional good behavior, was not quite sure what to make of R. W. Wood.

"Right now he is engrossed in a murder case. He is reconstructing a bomb for the police, a bomb that was used in an attack. All he has are the debris, but his reconstruction is very successful," she told her mother.

James Franck was an old friend of Wood's, and came at his invitation to Johns Hopkins when he had to leave Germany, an invitation prompted in part by Wood's approaching retirement. Franck loved him, but this did not prevent his seeing Wood with all his contradictory traits, childlike and immensely gifted, bad-tempered, patient and humorous, as a sort of scientist-mountebank:

And of course he was a practical joker, and he made so many practical jokes that many people hated him. . . . And they always tell the story . . . that dinosaurs had the brain partly in the tail and partly in the head. Wood had the brain in his fingers. Wood has never passed an official doctor's examination. He failed absolutely mathematics. And to go beyond sines and cosines, that was already the end of his mathematics. . . . He was always three months during the summer on Long Island. He had there a little old house and there was an old stable. And his wife let him do in this old stable whatever he wanted to. And he made experiments all the time. But there he built coupled pendulae—just two strings and little hooks on it at the end, and coupled with an old spring. And studied the behavior and looked at it. And for months he has not done anything else than just studied coupled pendulae. But at the end of the three months he knew more about it than any one. . . . He had an instinct where interesting things could be. He was also to some degree crazy. Now who is not? But his craziness was that he could not differentiate between the important things and the unimportant things he did. He regarded his practical jokes—the book, "How to Tell the Birds from the Flowers"—as equally important with his physics.

Franck also said, "Give Wood a dollar and send him to the five-and-ten store, he comes back with a laboratory." And although she continued to fear her "high boss" would lose interest in her, Wood remained kind and civil to Maria; for a time she had an office next door to his, and occasionally they worked together. Once it was on experiments involving a spectroscope, which Wood put together in front of Maria's eyes out of two very old razor blades, lenses, either of quartz or of glass and damaged, a grating, and some chewing gum to stand the lenses up, all of which he found in his pockets. "And what he did with this was really wonderful," Maria said. One day she went out and bought a new lens, got fresh razor blades from Joe and made a proper spectroscope, which she presented to Wood. "What do we need with such a fancy gadget?" he demanded. Twenty years later it was still in use at Hopkins.

He was said to have whole laboratories in his pockets. Honeymooning in Yellowstone, Wood stood with his wife before what was called the Emerald Geyser, while the guide explained it was green because of the presence of algae; up came the geyser, as Wood reached into his pocket and brought out a vial of fluorescein dye, which he covertly emptied into the gushing water, soon a brilliant green. "But it's never been *that* green," the guide muttered.

He was tall and thin and looked like Mephistopheles, Maria thought. This curious constellation of qualities—the ingenious and bottomless pockets, the practical jokes, occasionally cutting, the unconventional appearance and bearing—brings to mind a number of other first-rate physicists: Richard Feynman, Nobel laureate, virtuoso performer on the bongo drums, designer of many elaborate practical jokes; Edward Teller, who created clever games for the children of his friends and could never resist a puzzle; Leo Szilard, Enrico Fermi. Laura Fermi saw three of the major figures of the Roman school of physics, Fermi, Amaldi and Rasetti, as sharing "a certain playfulness, a naïve love of jokes and silly acting that they brought into their serious work." And Einstein's biographer Ronald Clark believed that "To the end he retained a touch of clowning humor . . . an unexpected sense of the ridiculous."

All are illustrious examples of the physicist as imp, but the trait is equally noticeable among lesser lights: "Scientists generally regard the borderline between the creative and the nonsensical as a very thin one," according to Dr. Eiduson. And in his pursuit of nonsense many a physicist has been drawn to practical jokes, perhaps because there is something mildly hostile, mildly destructive in most practical jokes; their essence is that they attack established order. And the physical scientist is in the profession of destroying established order, not entirely, but one section at a time. If he is productive and creative he must overthrow one aspect of reality so as to replace it with a structure of his own. He doesn't attempt to overthrow the lot; after all, he is a scientist because he admires reality. Neither does he wish to espouse it with a whole heart, in which case he would be an engineer. Rather he keeps one corner of himself forever set apart, and in this corner stands the small boy, the infant Fermi, Feynman, Szilard or R. W. Wood, who will from time to time take a good swift shattering kick at existing reality, then put it back together again, his own way.

Frau Goeppert spent five months or so with Joe and Maria that first year, in the rented house they had begun to fill with carefully chosen, simple, modern furniture, in striking contrast to the hand-me-downs most professors lived with during the depression. All the same, only a month or two after she had gone home Maria was planning and dreaming of a long stay in Göttingen at her mother's side. This visit, when it finally took place—Born offered her a summer position in 1931— somewhat relieved her homesickness, for now she saw face to face some of the disagreeable aspects of life in Germany that she had forgotten, in her longing for "real forests. And friends. And the language." She saw old-fashioned kitchens, no ice water, every inconvenience. And the political situation in Germany, although she was still able to convince herself there was no pressing need for concern, was harder to ignore. Not until her annual visit in July of 1933 was Maria forced to see what her Aunt Vera had known three years earlier.

Maria had put off applying for American citizenship, but as the birth of her first child approached she realized she wanted this child to be born of two American parents; at the time, a two-year period of residence, rather than five years, was sufficient, and Maria became a citizen within months of learning she was pregnant. Their daughter Marianne was born in the spring of 1933; at almost precisely the same time, during a three-week period in April and May of 1933, the first racial laws of the Nazis, aimed at "cleansing the civil service," removed some two hundred university teachers from their posts. Max Born, along with many of the Göttingen physicists and mathematicians, left Germany almost immediately; James Franck hoped to remain. Like Joe Mayer and many others, he believed the Nazis would not last much longer; because Franck had been an officer during the war, and "somebody who was liked by absolutely everybody," as Maria remembered it, "everybody said, 'Franck is an exception,' even the anti-Semites. . . . He was offered, at a certain stage, early in the time of the Nazis, to have his own institute. . . . And he debated it very much, and he said, 'If I do that, the first man whom I'm getting into the institute will be Edward Teller. He's a Hungarian Jew and they have to swallow that.' "

But German refugee scholars abroad, as well as men like Rutherford and Niels Bohr, apparently had a clearer picture of what was happening in Germany than many Germans, and a number of agencies to help the exiled intellectuals sprang into being as early as May of 1933 in several European countries—France, Holland, Belgium, Switzerland, etcetera. The longest-lived of these agencies was the Academic Assistance Council in England, begun by the economist Sir William Beveridge partly at the persistent prodding of another brilliant young Hungarian, Leo Szilard. Szilard's recollections of the beginnings of the Academic Assistance Council concern his conspiracy in Vienna with a Viennese economist, Schlesinger:

So I phoned Schlesinger and suggested that he invite Beveridge to dinner. Schlesinger said no, he wouldn't invite him to dinner because Englishmen, if you invite them to dinner, get very conceited. However, he would invite him to tea. So we had tea, and in this brief get-together, Schlesinger and [the German economist] Marschak and Beveridge, it was agreed that Beveridge, when he got back to England, and when he got the most important things he had on the docket out of the way, would try to form a committee which would set itself the task of finding places for those who have to leave German universities. He suggested that I come to London and that I occasionally prod him on this, and that if I were to prod him long enough and frequently enough, he thought he would do it. Soon thereafter he left, and soon after he left, I left and went to London.

Some British professors had been regularly setting aside a fixed percentage of their salaries to support exiled German colleagues; in December of 1933 a similar scheme was suggested by two German-born Princeton physicists, in a letter in German circulated among American scientists of German birth or education. Maria Mayer and Karl Herzfeld were to act as temporary treasurers for this group until more permanent arrangements could be made. In spite of the depression, in spite of xenophobia and stringent immigration laws, artists, architects, doctors, psychiatrists as well as physicists and mathematicians began to find their way from Germany to American universities, signaling the start of what became "the greatest collection of transplanted intellect, talent and scholarship the world has ever seen," in the words of one historian. And among physicists the most valuable links in the chain of rescue were the personal contacts of the nineteen twenties, when young Americans like Oppenheimer had gone to Göttingen in search of "the black mystery of quantum mechanics," as Maria put it; or to Munich, or Berlin, with Rockefeller money; when all roads eventually led to Copenhagen, when Cal Tech, Berkeley and the Michigan summer schools brought a stream of illustrious foreign lecturers to the States. When Oppenheimer left Göttingen he went to Berkeley to share his mystery, having made friendships and alliances in Germany; just as quantum mechanics helped bring European scientists together, so it helped American and European scientists to know and depend on one another, and finally it made a life-or-death difference to some. To be offered even a temporary position at an American university after 1933, one's work had to be known, one's reputation partly established. One could not be too young—under thirty-five, say—but neither could one be too old, past fifty-five or fifty-seven, when it was considered hardly worth the trouble to rescue a scientist upon the brink of retirement and a pension.

The Mayers had always been hospitable, even in the tiny apartment they rented for their summer at Michigan; Joe liked company around him, liked the talking, the friendly drinking, the opportunity for argument. As for Maria, if she was not naturally, wholeheartedly a lover of large parties and much company, she did seem to feel that hospitality was a duty, a pleasant duty to be carried out according to certain high standards. Now hospitality became for both of them an important obligation. Streams of German visitors began to come and go from their Baltimore home, so many that in the late thirties Maria had a thank-you note from one young man describing in detail all the kindness he had received at the Mayers' hands, yet neither she nor Joe was ever able to recall his visit, not even when they met him some years later face to face. In 1934, on their annual trip to Göttingen, they found that Frau Goeppert's student boarder was a young woman physician. She was engaged to a physician who, unlike herself, was a Jew, and the law did not permit them to marry. The Mayers brought Dr. Ruth Hechler home with them to Baltimore as a domestic, since all other immigration lists were hopeless. She lived with them for two years, taking care of Marianne and studying for her state boards, until she could get a job and send for her fiancé.

For about a year after Marianne's birth, Maria did very little work in her attic office at Johns Hopkins. She spent most of her time at home, playing with the baby: "It was such an experience to have a child, such a tremendous experience!" It would have been easy to return to work with such excellent help in the house, with a husband who actively encouraged her and with the lifelong memory of a father who had implored her, "Don't become a woman!" But she was tugged from the opposite direction as well. All along Maria felt a lack of appreciation and recognition at the university—"because I was young I was cocksure of myself, I thought I was good"—yet they ignored her. She returned to work "with a vengeance," according to Herzfeld, when Marianne was a year old, yet throughout her nine years at Hopkins Maria's position hardly altered. She was never paid more than a few hundred a year, never had a place at the university in the sense of a voice, or a vote in departmental matters, and her rank was always volunteer associate. She had seen an empty office and asked if she might have it; she was refused, and given a room in the attic instead. In other words Maria was simply tolerated, in a position one sociologist describes as that of the "fringe benefit," the academic wife whose husband has a fairly secure position, so that the university considers her a captive who can be hired with no guarantees, for as little as possible, and dropped whenever it becomes expedient. All over the States, even with the eroding of so-called nepotism laws that forbid the hiring of husband and wife in the same college, or department, fringe-benefit wives are exploited by institutions large and small, public and private; women's colleges have usually given them fair treatment but now the women's colleges are disappearing. Some women are fairly comfortable with fringe positions, preferring not to commit themselves wholly to a profession. And it is entirely possible that during the Hopkins years Maria was one of them. She enjoyed her teaching and her research, and if she was discontented with her ambiguous position, she was not discontented enough to do something about it, to fight for herself or allow Joe to fight.

In 1935 James Franck came to Hopkins; invited by R. W. Wood and Herzfeld, he was at first at a loss about what kind of physics to do, since there was no money and no apparatus for the physics he had done at Göttingen. But there were plenty of trees in Baltimore and plenty of leaves, so Franck decided to investigate photosynthesis. Once Franck was established at Hopkins, a number of fine atomic physicists began coming on periodic visits, Edward Teller and George Gamow among them. There was also the Dutch physicist Gerhard Dieke, who had come to Hopkins when the Mayers did; Dieke had done atomic theory in Europe, but turned to experimental work in America. With any of these men Maria could have talked atomic physics. Yet somehow she never really thought of collaborating with Dieke; as for Teller, his visits came only once a week, and they were hurried, and anyhow he was becoming interested in nuclear physics. Maria said later, "I don't know why I didn't make more use of the opportunity." Had she wanted to badly enough, surely she would have snatched at the chances she had; and had she wanted badly enough to teach, at a proper salary and with suitable rank and tenure, she might have done so at Goucher College nearby. But somehow it seemed impractical, inconvenient.

The Mayers bought a larger house with a lovely garden; Joe came home every day for lunch, and a close friend of Maria's remembered "a plaintive remark about the difficulty of providing imaginative lunches as well as dinners." She also remembered "Maria's amusement when in an interview . . . Joe stated that a working wife with some help in the house could easily run a household, with children, in about two hours a day." It was clear to Joe that Maria, being a physicist, must do physics; he had married a fellow scientist, and he saw no reason for her to become something else, something less. What on earth, he once wondered, do couples talk about when they're not both in the same line of work? Why, he once had a student whose wife was an English major who stayed home after she got her degree; they did nothing but fight.

One reason Joe Mayer wanted his wife to work was that he loved science; he could not conceive of anyone else's not loving it. Perhaps another reason was that, like so many scientists, he felt some faint pangs of guilt about this love. Science, until quite recently, has demanded that one work at it time-and-a-half, which scientists are only too eager to do since they are happiest when working. Still, many suspect that their wives and children, or other aspects of their lives or selves, are being cheated. Therefore they must justify their happiness at working so hard: they do it to serve society, perhaps. Or they are underpaid, but happy to be underpaid, and by scrimping along on inadequate salaries they punish themselves for enjoying total immersion in their work.

By being married to a fellow scientist as passionately dedicated as he was, Joe could have avoided many distractions, avoided, for example, coming home from work and being treated to a long and detailed description of what his children did during the day. Of course the baby was a "tremendous experience," as Maria put it. But that anything on earth could continue to be more exciting than science might have seemed incredible to Joe; if he encouraged Maria's return to work with a vengeance, it was partly, no doubt, for the fun of having her to work with, partly for the pleasure of seeing her career flourish, and partly because it proved what he knew to be the truth—that science was the "tremendous experience," while babies wore out with time.

Even without Joe's active encouragement Maria would probably have been lured slowly but surely into wholehearted engagement with her profession. Whether she could have succeeded without his encouragement is another matter. Science is a difficult profession; it has, more than many others, its periods of depression and self-doubt. A man must go on with his work nevertheless, for the money is needed to support his family, and besides, he has been brought up in the belief that a man works, that there is no alternative. A woman scientist in such a situation does have an alternative, however; she can throw up her hands, stay home with the family, or continue working but in lower gear, confining herself to teaching, perhaps, or puttering away at unimportant research. She may regret it later on, but later on will be too late. When Maria was tempted to throw up her hands she had Joe to keep her from making a permanent posture of it.

In dealing with research scientists and their feelings about their work, one comes inevitably to the question: Why does the scientist love science so much? To ask this of a scientist is to hear, within minutes, the answer: "It's fun; we love it because it's fun." And if one wants to know in what way it's fun he might explain that it's fun to learn, to understand, to satisfy one's curiosity. But this pertains to one aspect of science only—to the learning part, the part of science that has already been done; if you are satisfied only with learning and understanding you are not a scientist but a student of science, although perhaps a most sophisticated one. For upper-level research scientists like the Mayers the fun lies in the other part, in discovering "what no one else knew the day before yesterday, even if it's trivial," as Joe Mayer has it. Surely scientific research has its drudgeries, defeats, long stretches of boredom and routine, yet it seems universal among those engaged in original research, from the merest postdoctoral fellow to men of Nobel caliber, that they tend to describe their feelings about their work in such vivid terms that everything else in life—everything—sounds pale beside it.

"I know if I ever had to stay home because a child was sick, I did it, and hated it," Maria once said. Once, she recalled, she stayed with Willard Libby and his family when the Libby twins were very small, and felt so sorry for Mrs. Libby, having to be home all the time with two small, chattering children. "The men went away, and there she was.

. . . How could she stand it?" Edward Teller came by that day and took Maria out for lunch, and she was so relieved to be with him and talking science that she was amazed when he told her at the end of the meal that she had been speaking German all along. Yet Maria was an affectionate and conscientious mother, who thoroughly enjoyed her first baby and was almost overcome with joy at the arrival of the second. Katherine Rice remembered having been amazed to see, when Peter was born in 1938, how desperately Maria had wanted a son, and feeling somewhat baffled by her adoration of the second child.

In speaking of those personality traits that tend to be common among research scientists, Bernice Eiduson frequently uses the words "emotional constriction" and "control." By constriction she means not a lessened intensity of emotion, such as the stereotype that would have us believe scientists are emotionless, but rather that there is a narrowness of emotional experience, an absence of wide and varied emotional involvements and of intense personal relationships. Instead emotion is channeled into work; intense relationships with others usually center around work, around colleagues or rivals or students. And passion—jealousy, fear, aspiration, yearning—is also channeled into work. Like a river forced by steep, rocky banks into a narrow bed, the scientist's passions cut deep.

His greatest sorrows as well as his greatest rewards come from his work; the migraine headaches, for example, follow committee meetings rather than fights with his wife. For the scientist—who has chosen to identify himself with physical reality, the same trustworthy, likable, predictable physical reality that he learned to trust and be curious about in the isolated periods of his childhood—finds "wisdom in things," in the apt phrase of the biophysicist George Wald. But in people, including himself, he finds what is unpredictable and undependable and refuses to be controlled. Make no mistake about it, the physicist feels as if he controls matter. He knows better, yet the delicious illusion of being enmeshed with it, of having invented parts of it, is there all the same. Polycarp Kusch said of his colleague I. I. Rabi that Rabi rode around the nucleus seated on electrons; Rutherford was described by the physicist George Gamow as an old woodcarver like Gepetto, in Disney's

Pinocchio, engaged in making nuclei which he painted "red for the positively charged particles and green for the negative ones." And the students of Niels Bohr, most of whom became eminent physicists, often spoke of "the atom that Bohr built."

"While some scientists primarily perceive science as rational, others see it, even with its emphasis on the structured and logical, as 'irrational,' " Dr. Eiduson points out. In order to do anything of importance in scientific research one must be to some degree intuitive, open to the irrational within one's self, for intuition directs the leap toward the unknown in science as surely as in painting, poetry, architecture, music. Yet the scientist went into science in order not to have to deal with the irrational, the primitive, impulsive and chaotic; as Einstein said, he wished to free himself from "the chains of the merely personal, from an existence which is dominated by wishes, hopes and primitive feelings." Perhaps we can look at scientific research as a way of safely doing both, of putting one's emotional life under the rational control that comes from becoming matter—from being a bit of the atom and riding around the nucleus in orderly fashion—while at the same time one can remain in touch with that rich, creative and frightening aspect of the self that provides intuition.

If this is a fair picture, if a life in science meets such contradictory needs and impulses, it seems understandable that Joe Mayer believed there could be no better life, and that when his wife's interest in it flagged, he urged her on. Both of them hoped their children would be scientists, yet they felt no need to persuade or allure them into science, for one had only to be exposed to it to realize it was more wonderful than anything else.

One day in 1937 a cable from Göttingen warned Maria that her mother was dying; the steamer *Bremen* was due to sail from Manhattan that very night, at midnight, and Joe, who belonged to a Germania Club in Baltimore, persuaded a fellow member, the Baltimore agent of the steamship line, to arrange for a ticket and for a supply of cash to meet Maria at the dock. The train got her into Manhattan at midnight, and the ship waited an hour until she was safely on board. In Göttingen, as she went about the sad duty of closing up the house and selling whatever she could bear to part with, Maria met an old friend of hers, a woman physician who had been a student of her father's and had treated Marianne several times during her long visits with her German grandmother. Now Dr. Maria Stein was desperate; she could no longer remain in Germany because of the racial laws, had stayed too long already, planned to go to Scotland and wondered about America. "If you ever need me, don't hesitate to tell me," Maria said. Then she returned to Baltimore with quantities of the Dresden china her mother had loved.

A year later Peter was born. During much of her pregnancy Maria had felt large and clumsy; she disliked going onto the campus that way and felt ungainly moving about in a laboratory. She and Joe had been giving a joint seminar on statistical mechanics, a branch of physics concerning the laws that govern assemblies of molecules. The idea occurred to one or the other of them that they might write a textbook on the subject, and they bought a Corona portable and set to work, with Maria doing the typing. They thought of it at the time as a short-term project, something for Maria to do while she was pregnant. But *Statistical Mechanics* took two years to write; one of them would write a chapter and the other would write it over, so that it acquired in the end the virtues of binocular vision, having been written and rewritten by a chemist and a physicist.

A pretty southern girl who was a graduate student of Joe's during that period remembered how happy they all were then; their days were "exciting, full and always stimulating. . . . we regularly took two or three afternoons off a week, to hike or ride horseback or the like. . . . they treated ideas as a game—to be played whenever possible but not to the exclusion of living the good life and enjoying one's friends." And a student of Maria's at Hopkins once wrote to ask her how she managed to live so graciously on an academic salary; Maria told him the secret was in living beyond your means. Another student remarked on the stylish way the Mayers tackled Prohibition: "Others may have been content with bathtub gin, but Joe and Maria, using an old washing machine, perfect for crushing grapes, made wine." But in spite of the great delight of having an infant son, in spite of good friends and well-used leisure, in spite of the book, the garden and the parties, the years just before and after Peter's birth left a bitter taste with Maria. When she was still pregnant, Joe had been fired.

He was an associate professor, at most institutions a tenured rank, but Hopkins did not consider associate professors as tenured. Still, he had been there seven years, and the right to automatic tenure after such a length of time was even then being championed by the American Association of University Professors. "I have no doubt that the AAUP would have considered the case, as they were trying to get the six or seven year rule on tenure through, but I did not look forward to being a 'cause,' " Joe said later. Besides, he had two job offers almost immediately, each at twice the Hopkins salary, one from Chicago, one from Columbia. Ignoring the two-year period before the firing was to take effect, he resigned on the spot and took the Columbia offer. But Maria felt hurt, guilty, baffled; she suffered for every indignity inflicted on Joe —"Joe had an incredibly rotten time the last year at Hopkins; it shouldn't happen to anyone!" Katherine Rice felt—and in addition, Maria believed it must somehow have been her fault, or partly her fault, and she suffered for that as well.

Hopkins had gone through a change of administration, money was tight; Herzfeld had already left, James Franck was about to leave for Chicago, and the university that could not hold onto a Nobel laureate like Franck was clearly lacking in something other than money. Still Maria burned; she could not bear for Joe to be fired, she hated feeling she had been to blame. Finally, she recalled, she told herself, "The hell with it, I will enjoy myself. And I did." She enjoyed herself by playing bridge for hours on end.

Just how realistic she was in feeling herself to blame is hard to judge; neither Herzfeld nor Franck had been fired, only shoved and edged out. It seems clear that many mistakes were made at Hopkins during that period, but Joe's being fired suggests a certain animus aimed directly at him. Joe thought later it was possible that the dean of physical sciences, a "he-man geologist," hated women. Maria felt she was a certain amount of trouble all along, her needs always somehow having to be fitted in; even though she accepted her lack of status and her tiny salary without too much grumbling and strongly discouraged Joe and others from fighting on her behalf, it often happened that they fought anyhow, and the results, according to Maria, were sometimes damaging.

Herzfeld apparently agreed with Maria that she might have been indirectly the cause of Joe's being fired, and as Maria's colleague and supporter he felt he was also involved, for "there was . . . an antifeminine bias among some faculty in the department and perhaps the feeling that three Germans—Maria, Franck and I—were too many. Parallel to that were complaints by some students against Joe's lectures in chemistry, as too 'modern'; Joe, who is an excellent teacher, had required of his students the understanding of modern physics that is today essential for the chemist." He had been teaching quantum mechanics according to Born; he had also become increasingly interested in theoretical work, partly because of Maria's influence.

Joe Mayer was probably the only one of those concerned who found his own firing of limited interest. With the manuscript of *Statistical Mechanics* under his arm he turned to Columbia and the future, neither regretful nor visibly injured in his self-esteem.

What the immediate future held for the Mayers they had seen, imperfectly and with awe, shortly before they left Hopkins for New York. On January 26, 1939, Niels Bohr and Enrico Fermi opened a conference on theoretical physics in Washington, D.C., at which Bohr announced the discovery, by Hahn and Strassman, in Germany at the close of 1938, of what seemed to be nuclear fission, resulting from the bombardment of uranium with neutrons. Bohr was deeply concerned about the threat of war in Europe; when the Fermis had met him at the pier only days before, Laura Fermi found him "stooped like a man carrying a burden. His gaze, troubled and insecure, shifted from the one to the other of us, but stopped on none." He was also concerned with what nuclear fission meant; it was considered highly probable that the fission process released secondary neutrons, and if these could be used to split other uranium nuclei, which would in turn free other neutrons, great quantities of energy might be generated. The island of guncotton described by Nernst at Göttingen was beginning to shift and quake in prophetic fashion.

Before the Washington meeting was over Joe and Maria drove hurriedly back to Hopkins with their friend Robert Fowler, who hoped to duplicate the results of the Hahn-Strassman experiment; physicists from all over the country were doing the same that January, and the *Physical Review* for February 15 carried accounts of corroborating experiments at the University of California, the Carnegie Institution and Johns Hopkins.

When Bohr had been welcomed at the dock by the Fermis, they were themselves very recent arrivals; Laura and Enrico Fermi and their two children had left Italy the preceding November to claim Fermi's Nobel Prize in Stockholm, and then continued to the States, for Mrs. Fermi was a Jew, and Italy had recently begun to copy German racial laws. They had taken an apartment in Manhattan near Columbia, where Fermi had a professorship, and Laura Fermi tried to fit herself into her new life; this she managed in part by thinking of the area directly around Columbia as a village, one of many small, friendly little villages into which the city of New York was divided.

One day her husband told her, " 'Several of my colleagues live in a town called Leonia. It is in New Jersey, just across the George Washington Bridge, on the other side of the Palisades. Let's go see what it looks like.' It was February, and an icy-cold afternoon. As we got off the bus at the stop-light in Leonia, a gust of wind blew in our faces and blinded us. We did not know where to go." They decided to visit the Harold Ureys.

"The Ureys were in their large living-room and had a fire going. Our visit was a success. . . . Dr. Urey talked at length to us, in his serious, slightly professorial tone, about Leonia and its excellent public schools, about the advantages of living in a middle-class town where one's children may have all that other children have. . . . By the following summer we were the happy owners of a house on the Palisades, with a large lawn, a small pond, and a lot of dampness in the basement." Their lawn puzzled them until they discovered it consisted solely of crabgrass. To Leonia that autumn also came the Mayers, Joe, Maria, Marianne and the infant Peter; they had never thought of living anywhere else, for it was clear to Maria that one could not live in a city with two small children. The Mayers and the Fermis had already become friends during the course of the summer, having met at an ocean resort in New Jersey called Sunset Rock. The Mayers had rented a cottage, the Fermis came along after a while and wanted to rent a cottage too, but the owner of the resort was suspicious of them, having a low opinion of "Eye-talians," and the Mayers, to whom hospitality was a law, invited the four Fermis to share their cottage. Now that they were friends and neighbors in Leonia, the Fermis and the Mayers became fellow conspirators. The Fermis had lived under fascism for years, and knew how insidiously it could begin; the Mayers were well-informed through Maria's relatives of the progress of nazism in Germany. Home-grown fascism was what both couples most feared—fascism in America, the result of Hitler's inevitable victory in Europe, and the rise of the German Bunds supported by European fascists. That Hitler would win seemed incontestable, for one could not ignore his easy and persistent victories since the European war began. As Laura Fermi remembered it:

The Mayers and the Fermis determined to leave the United States together if nazism should become established in this country. During the many evenings spent with the Mayers between the fall of France and America's entry into the war, we made plans together. Between a philological argument on the origin of some English word and a piece of advice on gardening that the Mayers passed down to the Fermis, we prepared to become modern Robinson Crusoes in some faraway desert island.

We made plans as soundly conceived in the theory, as carefully worked out in all details, as might be expected from a group which included two theoretical physicists and a practical, American-raised chemist.

Joe Mayer was to be our sea captain, a role in which he was not excessively experienced. Enrico's knowledge of currents, tides and stars, would help. His delight at the prospect of experimenting with compass and sextant was encouraging. Yet Joe felt we should practice navigation in the Florida waters at the first opportunity.

Meanwhile, there was much we could do. Maria Mayer and Enrico could consult and determine what part of our civilization was worth saving. Accordingly, Maria could collect the best-suited books. Enrico, the descendant of farmers, could study the agricultural problems of our refuge. It was my task to see that our colony would not go naked in years to come. I might decide on cotton seed and spinning wheels or on bolts of cloth. It did not matter, so long as everyone was clothed. A few scientifically selected persons would be invited to join our expedition: we ought to have a doctor; we ought to have children of such age, sex, and heredity that they could later marry ours and people the island.

What island we would make ours was still to be determined. In a war in which the United States would in all likelihood participate on the side against Germany, the Atlantic Ocean was out of the question. The Pacific Ocean is sown with islands. In the temperate zone between the Hawaiians and the Philippines there were numberless islets large enough for us. We would search for a desert island among them. We could not foresee Pearl Harbor, and we could not foresee the Japanese!

Fermi, along with Leo Szilard, had begun in 1939 a long-drawn-out attempt to persuade the government to do some research into what came to be known as the "uranium problem," but for a long time their efforts had little or no result; science and government in the States had never had much to say to each other, and the first attempts at conversation were frustrating. An adviser to the Navy, after hearing Fermi describe the possibilities of uranium fission, telephoned a physicist who worked at the Carnegie Institution to ask, "Who is this man Fermi? What kind of a man is he? Is he a Fascist or what? What is he?"

At home in Leonia, Laura Fermi was concerned with earthier matters not unlike the problems that had faced Maria Mayer nine years before. Instead of several well-trained servants she had only the nursemaid they brought from Italy, now transformed into a general houseworker. It took their combined talents to cook in an American household, with Laura Fermi holding the cookbook, translating quantities into metric measures and interpreting directions on cans. Mrs. Fermi had never before seen dry-cleaning shops, and she sponged, brushed and steamed Enrico's suits herself; she had never before seen a supermarket and was terrified of them. Maria Mayer, to whom supermarkets were still a comparative novelty, began making shopping trips once a month to a neighboring New Jersey town, for the sake of the budget, and Laura Fermi went with her.

Once the two women made a bargain; the Mayers loved gardening and landscaping, but Laura knew nothing about it. Maria, on the other hand, hated to sew, "so I volunteered to do her mending in exchange for lessons in gardening. I don't remember how long the pact was observed: I certainly did not do much mending for the Mayer family. I vaguely remember them moving soil and stones in their back-yard and re-landscaping it completely. In spite of her frail looks, Maria was very strong."

The Fermis also had trouble with the language during their first years in this country, for Enrico had learned his English from scientific papers and Laura got hers from British novels; when their daughter Nella began coming home from grade school and making fun of the way they spoke, the Fermis turned to Alice Kimball, the wife of a Columbia chemistry professor. The Kimballs, like the Fermis, became Joe and Maria's close friends in Leonia; in some ways Alice was for Maria the prop and support and confidante Katherine Rice had been. As a teacher of English for the Fermis she proved to be resourceful; she had them read aloud from "Hiawatha," whose rhythms seemed to Alice uniquely American. Alice Kimball was the first American employer of Dr. Maria Stein, the German doctor from Göttingen who had studied with Maria's father and left Germany in 1937; remembering Maria's promise to her, Dr. Stein now turned to the Mayers for help after an unsatisfactory few years in Scotland, and they were able to bring her to the States in 1940. Dr. Stein lived with the Mayers for a year while learning English, supporting herself meanwhile with elaborate crochetwork such as place mats that were bought in quantities by the Columbia wives, and going out as a baby nurse. The Kimballs' first baby was her first patient.

Statistical Mechanics, by Mayer & Mayer, was ready for publication. But there was a difficulty, as Harold Urey pointed out, connected with the title page. The name Joseph Edward Mayer was to be followed by the title "Associate Professor Chemistry, Columbia University." After Maria Goeppert-Mayer—what? Columbia had never offered her a position, and Maria had gone there with none of the cocksureness she claimed she brought to Hopkins, the self-assurance of youth; nevertheless she had hoped for something. Nothing was forthcoming, not even office space of her own, although they did offer Maria "someone else's office. . . . It was awkward, I could not use it." Harold Urey brought the matter up at a meeting of the chemistry department; perhaps some sort of honorary appointment could be made for this Dr. Maria Mayer, if only for the sake of the book. . . . Silence.

In the end Urey assigned Maria to do some lecturing to chemistry students so that "Lecturer in Chemistry, Columbia University," could be written under her name on the title page. The book became a classic in its field. According to one theoretical physicist, a student of Fermi's who was later a friend of Maria's, "it made Joe Mayer's reputation." It had little effect on Maria's reputation, however. As Joe realized later, most people, emphatically including the powers-that-be at Columbia, took for granted that the book was almost entirely Joe's work, that Maria had been a sort of editorial assistant, her position as coauthor representing mainly conjugal affection.

Laura Fermi remembered Maria, during those years, as not working, or else not working very much; in the sense of passionate involvement with her work, she was indeed not working. But even had she been impassioned, and stubborn, she might not have made a dent on the physics or chemistry departments at Columbia University where, since the early thirties, the distinguished anthropologist Ruth Benedict had been balancing her impressive reputation and her negligible rank, which seriously limited her power to help her graduate students as they deserved. It was only just before Ruth Benedict's death in 1948 that she was awarded a full professorship—"long and strenuously resisted on the grounds of sex," as Margaret Mead points out. Ruth Benedict was then one of the foremost American anthropologists; Maria Mayer, when she came to Columbia in 1939, was in her early thirties, looked ten years younger, and except for the excellent paper on the physical theory of dyes and the new textbook, had nothing to offer Columbia that would mitigate the irreparable fact of her sex.

In September of 1939, when France and England declared war on Germany, less than a year had passed since the Hahn-Strassman work on fission. Leo Szilard and Fermi had continued their efforts, sporadic, and not very optimistic on Fermi's part, to find official support for an investigation into the "possibility that uranium might be used as an explosive that would liberate a million times as much energy per pound as any known explosive. My own feeling is that the probabilities are against this . . ." as George Pegram of Columbia wrote to Admiral Hooper and the Navy in the spring of 1939. Szilard was hopeful, however; it was his nature to be hopeful. By the summer of 1939 he and

Eugene Wigner, also a Hungarian and like Szilard an exile, were confer-
ring with Einstein in Princeton. "The three men decided that they
would prepare a letter to President Roosevelt and that Einstein would
sign it, being by far the most prominent of all the scientists in the
United States. By the time the letter was ready, its content carefully
planned and thoroughly discussed by several physicists, Einstein had
gone for a rest at a remote place near Peconic on Long Island. A car
was needed to reach him, and Szilard, who does not drive, engaged the
help of a third Hungarian-born physicist, his young friend Edward
Teller. It was August 2, 1939." So reads Laura Fermi's account of the
letter that launched the Advisory Committee on Uranium.

Like the vast effort that followed it, the earliest stages of the attempt
to make a chain reaction are studded with the names of the exiles Hitler
made. The work of Bohr and Rutherford a generation earlier had proceeded in a perfectly natural way, unhurried except by the urgency of
intellectual excitement, to fission. That the discovery of fission then took
place quite literally on the eve of a world war; that the German racial
policies had almost emptied continental Europe of that very type of
being, at once audacious and orderly, rational and irrational, a rebel
eager to destroy and to hold fast to reality—in a word, the theoretical
physicist, so often for mysterious reasons in the twentieth century a Jew,
if not a Hungarian as well—these must be accounted coincidences.
Moving and strange coincidences, they nevertheless have their lighter
side: Victor Weisskopf remembered with what difficulty he, still an
Austrian citizen but working for the American government, got permission from American authorities to attend a special conference with three
British experts, when joint Anglo-American atomic efforts began. The
British experts turned out to be Peierls, Simon and Halban—three
Central European Jews, exiled by Hitler.

On December 6, 1941—a day before Pearl Harbor—America decided, in earnest and persuaded in part by the success of some British
investigations, to try to build an atomic weapon. Enrico Fermi, officially
an enemy alien, began making mysterious trips to Chicago, from which
he returned with fever and a touch of bronchitis; these trips culminated
in his removal the following spring to the University of Chicago. Laura

Fermi stayed behind in Leonia so that her children might finish the school year. She had no idea what her husband was supposed to be doing in Chicago. "Enrico walked to work every morning. Not to the physics building, nor simply to the 'lab,' but to the 'Met. Lab.,' the Metallurgical Laboratory. Everything was top secret there. I was told one single secret: there were no metallurgists at the Metallurgical Laboratory. Even this piece of information was not to be divulged."

But neither had she known about the nature of his work at Columbia; Fermi had been trying to see if a self-sustaining chain reaction was experimentally, as well as theoretically, possible. Maria had worked with Enrico's group from time to time during the three years he was at Columbia; now, with Fermi already in Chicago, where he was to build the first atomic pile, and Laura preparing to join him, Maria acquired from the Fermis a long-lived memento of the Leonia days—their first American car. "It was an old Dodge," Laura Fermi recalled, "whose original owners were old people who used it only to drive to church." The day after Pearl Harbor Maria had been offered her first real American job, a half-time teaching position at Sarah Lawrence College in Bronxville, New York. She was to start work almost immediately, and she needed a car of her own.

Maria began teaching at Sarah Lawrence abruptly, with no opportunity to prepare what she would teach; one day there was the job offer, and the request that she come there within a week and explain to a group of deans how she would go about teaching. When Maria turned up at Sarah Lawrence she told them, "You ought to put together a course that unifies all the sciences—astronomy, chemistry, physics. You really ought to have a man to do this—I don't know if I can do such a thing."

The deans told her by all means to go ahead, and within days Maria was teaching a unified science course of her own creation to a roomful of girls. She had never, since high school days, been in a classroom filled only with girls, and most of them were engaged in knitting. Then they began to be troubled because what they were learning refused to fit into categories. What are we supposed to be doing here? they asked Dr. Mayer. Is it physics or chemistry or what? "It's science," she told them.

Almost as soon as Maria began teaching at Sarah Lawrence, Joe was hired to work at the Aberdeen Proving Grounds in Maryland, investigating conventional weapons. He spent five days a week there, a sixth at Columbia and Sundays at home; this arrangement was hard on the children, and hard on Maria, who had never really liked Leonia or their house—it was cheap and badly built and didn't heat well, she felt, and worse than that, Joe was practically never in it. Looking back on that period, she said she had felt "actively miserable" all the time he was gone, and the single day he was home took on a feverishly festive air. But Joe, for all that he missed his wife and children, adapted well to the demands the war made on him; he was an adventurer, he said, without the dangers. At Aberdeen the guns were going all the time, so that one had a terrific sense of urgency, yet no one was shot at; this curious situation, as if he were an actor in a war movie, followed Joe Mayer to the Pacific toward the end of the war, and left him with a rueful awareness that he was finding it all damned exciting.

Later that spring Maria had a second job offer, this time from Harold Urey, who wanted her to join a secret research group at Columbia, engaged in separating the isotope uranium-235 from the much more abundant uranium-238; U-235 was readily fissionable, U-238 was not. The secret research group became the SAM project a year or so later —the initials standing for the code name Substitute Alloy Materials— and Urey became its director of research. Maria found this second opportunity bewildering; she had had reservations about leaving the children for her teaching job at Sarah Lawrence, for in case of illness there was no way to get home from Bronxville in a hurry; in Baltimore their house had been within walking distance of the university. Peter was still very young and subject to a succession of colds and minor ailments. And Joe was almost living in Maryland, so that the prospect of depriving them of mother as well as father seemed alarming. Still, it was flattering to be wanted as a scientist, in her own right, not merely as an appendage of Joe's—to be given a chance to do research and get paid for it, actually paid for it.

Maria told Urey she would work for him half-time; definitely not on Saturdays, although everyone else did, for she wanted that time for the children. And if anything happened, if one of them took sick, she would insist on staying home. Urey had always held Maria in high esteem, and accepted her terms; Marianne remembered the time her mother told her she would be gone every day during the week and they would be cared for by a nursemaid, for "she would be happier when she was home if she worked more, and we'd all be better off." The nursemaid was an English girl, well-educated and reliable, who had been stranded in the States by the war. Joe and Maria felt that she made all the difference, that they could now safely leave the children in her hands, that she would be as affectionate as she was sensible. And sensible she clearly was; Alice Kimball remembered her resourcefulness and dependability whenever Peter was sick. But the children disliked her. They felt she was severe, unsympathetic, bossy—qualities that were especially hard on the Mayer children because their mother had always been exceptionally permissive, perhaps out of loyalty to Dr. Goeppert's philosophy. A stiff British nanny was rather a shock after their mother and the succession of warmhearted, uneducated German maids.

But they never mentioned any of this to Maria, for she was engaged in helping win the war, the war America was fighting not against Germany, or the German people, but against Hitler. The distinction had been very carefully made for the two children, who repeated it to their friends: their mother, as well as their father, was doing something for the war, and it was not against the German people. The neighborhood children, as Peter recalled, were pretty skeptical about these fine points. Surely the war was against the Germans, Peter's mother even had a German accent, and Peter himself was suspect, for he was an awkward child, easy to tease, and sick so much of the time.

Maria worried about him; whenever he had a slight fever she worried. Her husband very sensibly told her to throw away the thermometer, but this she could not do. She worried, she reassured herself on the score of the English governess—"an educated person, you see, so we felt quite sure that the children are in hands that are all right"—and she kept to herself her increasing fears connected with the secret research project. Suppose they should find some efficient way of separating uranium isotopes, and suppose an atomic weapon should really be the result: what if the war were still going on and they used this weapon against Germany? For while she believed they were fighting Hitler rather than the German people, there was no way a bomb could single him out; her fears for her native country and people were only partly relieved by D-day and the allied invasion of the Continent. She kept track of the invading armies by marking their progress on a large wall map, but every pin she put in place stabbed a familiar town or river.

The SAM job was not half-time after all, not in practice. "There were always things that came up; you were supposed to write a report with someone else, who gave it to you at the last minute—and it was lousy. You had to write it over, then, write a decent report." Several times she stumbled home at the end of a long Saturday and dropped to sleep on the enclosed porch, where Joe found her when he returned from Aberdeen on his Sunday off.

"Urey usually assigned me not to the main line of research of the laboratory, but to side issues, for instance to the investigation of the possibility of separating isotopes by photochemical reactions. This was nice, clean physics although it did not help in the separation of isotopes." It had become increasingly clear that the way to separate U-235 was by a gaseous diffusion process, a process Maria never worked on. Nevertheless, she was extremely successful at SAM; for one thing, the job itself expanded quite independently of Maria, in fact the entire SAM project ballooned, and where she had originally had two or three scientists working under her, she now had twenty. The other factor was that she worked hard, was utterly conscientious, and found she loved having responsibility. Deprived, until then, of most of the satisfactions that ought to accompany hard work—money, recognition, approval—she now had them all. Whereas before only Joe and a few colleagues told her she was doing well, "here I was suddenly taken seriously, considered a good scientist." And she came to feel that it was at Columbia, during her years with SAM, that she finally quit being a fringe-benefit faculty wife and became a true professional. "It was the beginning of myself standing on my own two feet as a scientist, not leaning on Joe."

It seems to have been during this same period that a series of physical ailments, apparently unrelated, began to splutter and explode like tiny time bombs; there was a gall bladder operation, followed by pneumonia, that kept her hospitalized for months; Harold Urey brought Maria some work to do in the hospital to keep up her spirits and to be sure her salary would continue. There was a thyroid operation, within a year; and by the end of the war Maria was taking a substitute for hydrochloric acid, since it seemed she no longer manufactured her own.

Around the summer of 1944 two graduate students of Edward Teller's came to work with Maria. It was Teller's habit then, and for the rest of his life, never to do a paper alone—only once, he said, did he do anything all by himself, and it was his worst piece of work. Now he had become interested in properties of matter at extremely high temperatures, in connection with his work at Los Alamos; he had the two students ready to do their dissertations, and he had caught Maria's interest in the matter. All that remained was to find an arrangement whereby work along such classified lines might be done outside Los Alamos, for Maria had explained she would not leave Leonia, the children and Joe. One of the students, Harris Mayer (no relation to Joe), had already met Joe when he went to his office several years before to get permission to take the statistical mechanics course. "I opened his office door, and there were three boys, who turned out to be Joe Mayer and two students. Joe was about forty then, and he looked awfully young. He had blond hair, a California complexion, and he didn't own an overcoat." Harris Mayer found Maria, like Joe, amazingly youthful; she looked like a girl to him, and it was difficult to think of her as a mother. Another thing that made it difficult was Maria's reluctance to talk about her children, for Harris, who had been raised in the belief that it is good manners to inquire of every mother how her children are, never seemed to get any response beyond a brief acknowledgment. No doubt to discuss her children at length would have been, for Maria, the same as making small talk; it was something she did not do.

To get the thesis project started it was necessary to have a meeting with a security officer; accordingly Maria and Teller went to an office in Washington, D.C., where they were treated to a security lecture. The security officer explained to Maria that by giving away seemingly unimportant pieces of information one may disclose more than what had been intended. For example, he said, one cannot keep secret that there is a factory at Hanford and that there is work going on at the Metallurgical Laboratory in Chicago. What must be kept secret is the connection between the two.

But that there was secret work being done at Hanford was a revelation to Maria; as she and Teller left the building he told her he hoped he would never commit such a breach of security as that officer had just made.

In February of 1945 Joe was sent to the Pacific for several months to see how the men trained at Aberdeen were using their weapons; Maria decided she might as well go to Los Alamos in his absence, leaving the children in Leonia with the nursemaid. Laura Fermi and her children had been living in Los Alamos since the summer of 1944; like most of the Los Alamos wives, she knew nothing about the project, no more than she had known two years earlier what was done at the Met. Lab. With the Mayers, it was Maria who knew and Joe who speculated. Joe's ignorance, of course, was not like Laura's, since Joe knew the work at SAM had been somehow connected with the development of a weapon based on uranium fission—every scientist in America knew that; besides, Joe had been invited to work on this secret weapon in its earliest stages, and refused, because he couldn't take it seriously. What Joe Mayer did not know was that in December 1942 Fermi's crew at the Met. Lab. had successfully operated the world's first atomic pile; Arthur Compton phoned the news to Conant, at Harvard, with the memorable phrase, "The Italian navigator has just landed in the new world." Neither did Joe know that atomic weapons were being assembled at Hanford and Oak Ridge. He had been convinced from the start that an atomic weapon could not be developed in less than twenty or thirty years. "I'm working on this war, you're working on the next," was his comment to Maria when the subject came up.

She was finding it an increasingly painful secret to keep. Unlike most of the other scientists of German birth or education who worked on the bomb, Maria had left her country voluntarily; she loved Germany and the German people, and hoped that Hitler—a monstrous aberration who managed somehow to hold an entire nation captive—would be defeated with as little destruction as possible. By contrast, many of the other German scientists had mixed feelings about the country that had exiled them, and may well have felt that Hitler was not unique, that he had found thousands of little Hitlers to carry out his commands. Maria was also haunted by a fear that the Germans were working along similar lines, and were already close to success; in this she shared the beliefs of most American scientists in the bomb project:

Their reasoning was logical to the point of simplicity. It must be remembered that many of them had had at least part of their scientific education at German universities, and some of the foreign-born scientists all of their education. They had a natural and, in large measure, a justified admiration for German science. . . . Since the Germans had started their uranium research about two years before us, we figured they must be at least two years ahead of us. They might not have the bomb yet, but they must have had chain reacting piles going for several years. It followed that they must have fearful quantities of artificial radioactive materials available. How simple it would be for them to poison the water and food supplies of our large cities with chemically non-detectable substances and sow death wholesale among us by dreadful invisible radiations.

The fear was so real that the scientists were even sure of the place and the date of Hitler's supposed radioactive attack. The Germans must know, they thought, that Chicago was at that time the heart of our atom bomb research. Hitler, loving dramatic action, would choose Christmas Day to drop radioactive materials on that city. Some of the men on the project were so worried they sent their families to the country. The military authorities were informed and the fear spread. I heard rumors that scientific instruments were set up around Chicago to detect the radioactivity if and when the Germans attacked.

It was then and there that our atom bomb project became a "race" with Germany.

This is the account given by the physicist Samuel Goudsmit, who led the first spy mission into Germany on the heels of the Allied invasion forces, to learn just how sophisticated the German atomic effort really was. He discovered it amounted to practically nothing, that the Germans were still talking of a "uranium problem." Niels Bohr could have told him as much; Bohr had already gone to Winston Churchill with the message that the Germans had no atomic bomb and never would have, but Churchill was convinced Bohr had been duped. "Don't send me any more long-haired scientists," he was supposed to have said.

Like most American scientists, then, Maria believed a bomb must be developed by the Allies before the Germans made one, but she was probably one of the few who was also afraid the Allies would succeed in time to use the bomb against Germany—clearly an emotional bind. The bomb itself had begun to trouble her. Max Born, in Scotland, had refused to take any part in the British atomic project; in Chicago James Franck was one of the first to draw back in fear and apprehension from the vision of nuclear war in June of 1945, when he and six other Chicago scientists asked the secretary of war to refrain from atomic bombardment of Japan, and to substitute a demonstration of the new weapon before representatives of the United Nations, on an uninhabited island. Franck and Born were the heroes of Maria's youth, and it is not surprising that she should come to conclusions similar to theirs. The conquest of the atom, seen by the scientists of the forties as a fascinating, an irresistible puzzle—"technically sweet," in Oppenheimer's words—was no less fascinating to Maria; but it was also a source of much internal conflict, rooted in the loves and loyalties of the past. Joe would have understood her feelings and sympathized without sharing them to the same degree, but Maria was unable to tell him anything, nor was there anyone else she could turn to.

On V-E day Maria was in Leonia alone, for Joe was still in the Pacific. A big party had been planned for all the Columbia people, but to celebrate the victory seemed impossible to Maria; she could have celebrated peace, but victory implied a rejoicing in the defeat of people she loved, people who had suffered while she was safe, who might be suffering still. She decided to stay at home with the children. Late that day Alice Kimball telephoned and told Maria to come to them. "We will not celebrate the victory either," Alice said, so Maria went to the Kimballs', and they heard *Die Meistersinger* on the radio, and Teller happened to be in town and he came too.

If there was no longer a German enemy to use the bomb against, the bomb itself was nearing completion, and the whole intricate, far-flung effort to produce it was poised on the brink of success, demanding to be tested. Lacking the German enemy there was still a Japanese enemy, and almost everyone who had been engaged in the race with German science shifted mental gears accordingly; it now seemed clear that the bomb must be finished in order to avoid a land invasion of Japan. When Maria was in Los Alamos shortly after V-E day, this was what all the scientists talked about, the forthcoming secret tests of the weapon they had been working on so long and with such passionate dedication.

In Los Alamos, as always, Maria worked with Teller, a great pleasure for her because she found in him one of the world's finest teachers, not in the classroom perhaps, but person to person. This time she was housed in a women's dormitory, where a sign clearly stated that no men were permitted after ten o'clock, except for husbands. Yet every morning the place echoed with the sound of boots. When Maria mentioned this anomaly to Laura Fermi, Laura was incensed, and saw to it that Maria had a little house of her own, a charming place full of someone's collection of Navajo rugs. Maria was so comfortable there she thought of staying on in order to see the first tests of the bomb at Alamogordo in mid-July. That way she could meet Joe in Albuquerque on his way home from the Pacific, and they could go East together. But then she realized she had better leave for Leonia at the end of June; meeting Joe in New Mexico, and choking down the secret of the world's first atomic explosion, was something she could not bear to contemplate.

Joe came home somewhat earlier than expected and Maria met him in Albuquerque after all; they returned together to Leonia and the children, and only a few days later Maria went to Columbia, where Harold Urey stopped in to see her. He had been trying all day, he said, to reach General Groves in Los Alamos by phone, but he couldn't get Groves; he couldn't get anyone there. "What do you conclude from this?" Urey asked Maria, with significantly lifted eyebrows. The two of them were the only people at Columbia who knew the first bomb test was scheduled for mid-July, and Maria said she concluded just what he concluded. It was July sixteenth, the Day of Trinity.

Then, with Marianne and Peter, the Mayers went to Nantucket for their first family vacation since the war began. They rented a little cottage and spent their days swimming and hunting for clams, which the Mayer family did in serious and methodical fashion, two of them walking one way, two the other way, then exchanging paths so that each pair could get the clams the other missed. They were walking on the beach one day in August when a neighbor ran up to Joe and asked, "Did you have anything to do with the atomic bomb, Professor Mayer?" She had just heard the news of Hiroshima on the radio. The children were prodded to walk on ahead, the neighbor left, and Maria was able at long last to tell Joe everything, or almost everything; even while she was speaking he found it hard to believe. Peter, who was seven, kept on hanging back, suspecting that whatever his parents were talking about with such intensity was something he wanted to hear, but Marianne pulled him away.

During the war Maria had had only one letter from her German family, a series of "vital statistics," sent through the Red Cross; now news began to filter through. There had been losses, some of them tragic, but Göttingen itself had been declared a hospital city and was almost untouched, so she had much to be grateful for, as she scoured the closets for outgrown and outworn clothing to send to an aunt who was caring for refugees from Silesia. So much was sent, there seemed to be such a frantic outpouring of clothing and money and CARE packages, that Marianne wondered if her mother felt somehow guilty—perhaps because she had not been in Germany to share the fate of her relatives. Marianne offered to use her own money to send clothing and food to a German girl her own age, and Maria thought it was a wonderful idea. One day Joe drove home from Aberdeen in the car he had always left there to use during his work week, and the thought suddenly came to Maria: He's not going back! Life is worth living again! Peacetime, with all its perplexities, was upon them.

The SAM job no longer existed; Maria returned to her half-time teaching at Sarah Lawrence. She would have time now for the children. Throughout the war she had suffered from a nagging feeling that she was neglecting them, a feeling considerably reinforced by Peter's doing badly in school. He had trouble with language, especially learning to read; Marianne, who had gone to nursery school speaking only German because of the German maids, learned English in no time and was a beautiful reader, but awkward, gangly Peter seemed to learn nothing. She would be able to read to him now, perhaps that would help. The wartime separations had been hard on Marianne as well. Her father had been gone so much of the time that she felt out of touch with him, and was by nature too reserved to make demands on his attention now that he was home again. She also felt cut off from her mother; day after day Marianne had run home from school full of the day's excitements, remembering as she flung herself into the house that there was only the maid to tell them to. By evening, when her mother had come home, the day's excitements had lost their edge. She sometimes felt she knew the mothers of some of her friends better than she knew her own. Although Marianne at twelve was an exceptionally shy child, quiet, well-behaved, eager not to give trouble, she did make one attempt at putting family affairs on a more intimate footing. She told her mother one day that she was sick of hearing science talked about all the time, and Maria made a household rule on the spot: no shop-talk during the cocktail hour or at dinner. It was a rule she conscientiously tried to observe from then on.

Maria's position at Columbia was as vague as ever. The chemistry department had always held a weekly seminar, after which everyone went out to dinner; Maria used to go with Joe and the Kimballs, and when Joe was in Aberdeen the two women went alone. Once someone from the chemistry department phoned to tell Maria that while she would be welcome at the seminar it was felt that her presence and Alice's, at dinner, was awkward. Maria, who was deeply hurt, never again went to either the seminar or the dinner, nor did she allow Joe to raise hell about it, as he wanted to do. Such incidents naturally colored her feelings about Columbia, as did her long-standing dislike of Leonia. "It was a suburb. I don't like suburbs. The women all talked about their babies and the men talked science." Just as at Göttingen, Maria sat with the men. It was something a number of her friends remarked on, her continuing difficulty in making close friendships with women, her preference for substantial conversation rather than small talk.

There was another advantage to sitting with the men: they enjoyed her being there and they showed it. Among the chemists and physicists in the Mayers' circle, one saw the same people at parties one had seen at work, and usually talked about the same things. It wasn't a matter of talking shop, but rather of talking about what was most "fun," and in the company one was happiest with. For the camaraderie among fellow scientists is an especially strong tie; they are bound together not only by similar interests but by similar temperaments. To those who believe science is the best possible way of life it is natural to conclude that scientists are the best possible company, and having to "socialize," to avoid shop talk and enjoy oneself in a particular way, can be the opposite of relaxing. Yet at parties the pressure is there, a pressure exerted by hostesses or other women guests—to mix, to join the ladies, to forget the lab.

When Maria "sat with the men" they could continue to discuss what was "fun," and with the added pleasure of a woman's presence. A former student of Maria's remembered that in the forties Fermi and Teller used to hold forth when Maria was with them, and "one felt this was a performance for Maria, because she could listen in a most attractive way." She could listen, she could understand, she could contribute, and if she was not Fermi's equal, who was? Nevertheless, some of the women she knew resented Maria's social behavior; when the Mayers left Leonia in 1946 a member of a women's club there wrote an angry letter to a local paper, complaining that Maria never took any part in civic life.

If the end of the war meant, for Maria, a fresh start with Peter and Marianne as well as an end to the interest, the generous salary and the status of her SAM job, where she had been an equal among equals thanks to the government's refusal to discriminate against women, the war's end meant something different to Joe and his colleagues. Joe had been working hard on weapons problems and enjoying it; Harold Urey had been working hard on uranium and the bomb effort, and loathed every minute of it. Each of them had the same desire now, a desire shared by Fermi, by Teller, by all the splendid constellation of scientists Arthur Compton had gathered at the Met. Lab.: they were champing at the bit, avid to take up their scientific careers again and return to unclassified research and university teaching.

In mid-July 1945, only a few days after the secret Alamogordo tests, three representatives of the University of Chicago had gone to Los Alamos, or rather, close to it, since security regulations did not permit them within the gates; on the terrace of a hilltop home in Santa Fe they ate a lunch of sandwiches brought from Los Alamos by Fermi and a few colleagues, and discussed a plan to set up a group of basic research institutes at the University of Chicago. Physicists, chemists, biologists, engineers who had worked together at the Met. Lab. could remain together; the institutes were to be a meeting ground for science and industry, allied to the University of Chicago, which was then under the imaginative leadership of Robert Hutchins. Shortly after the war ended, Teller, Urey and Joe Mayer were all offered jobs at Chicago. Urey was the first to accept.

He had thought for a while of settling in the Pacific Northwest, the gateway to the Orient and the future, it seemed to him; but Urey had made a trip to the University of Washington, in Seattle, and described to its president, a physicist by training, his plans for a group of research institutes there. "He didn't know what I was talking about—he wanted to make me a dean!" Urey told the Mayers with scorn when he got back to Leonia. On the way home he had stopped at Chicago and spoken to Hutchins, and he knew now that was where he wanted to go. Teller decided he too would go to Chicago. But Joe and Maria thought they ought to visit the place before they made up their minds; Teller told them his telegram would probably arrive in Chicago when they did.

In Chicago Joe was offered a full professorship; he would also be a member of the Institute for Nuclear Studies. Fermi and Franck, Urey and Teller would be there, and the offer was irresistible. Then, when Joe told the Chicago people he was ready to accept, they turned to Maria: "We have been thinking for a long time of giving you an offer, but we knew you could never come without Joe. Now he is coming, and you too." She had been unprepared for such an offer, for any offer at all. She was to be an associate professor at the university and a member of the Institute for Nuclear Studies. There was no salary, however, not even a nominal one, because of the university's religiously observed nepotism clause that forbade the hiring of husband and wife even in different departments. Maria never really resented the nepotism rule, or perhaps it was that the people responsible, the people she had reason to resent, were a distant and impalpable "they," while the men she worked with and saw every day valued and respected her. "I was received in the nicest manner.... The institute ... gave me a beautiful office." Still, she found it a source of much pleasure and some amusement when, in 1959, she and Joe were both invited to the University of California and Chicago forgot the nepotism rule and offered her a salary. She was in her early fifties then; it was to take some twenty years for the academic world to see its way clear to paying Maria Mayer for her services.

Having decided to accept the positions at Chicago, Joe and Maria were taken aback at learning from Dean Bartky that Teller wasn't coming after all. How could that be? they asked. He had just told them he sent a telegram of acceptance. But Bartky showed them Teller's telegram: CAN NOT DECIDE TO COME TO CHICAGO. . . . Could even a mercurial Hungarian have changed his mind so fast? Perhaps, Joe said, it was meant to read CAN NOW DECIDE . . .

Bartky said, "Go tell your friend Teller to send me a telegram with a single word on it, either yes, or else no."

Back home in Leonia, Maria phoned the Kimballs and asked them over for a drink. When they got there she told them with great pride, "We are *both* going to Chicago." They left Leonia in February of 1946, in high spirits and with few regrets; Maria was radiant with energy, ready to succeed everywhere now that she had a real position with a fine university. An experimental school for faculty children was attached to the university, and she felt hopeful that Peter's reading problems, in the hands of competent professionals, would be conquered at last.

Then the Tellers, Mayers and Ureys set about house hunting with the understanding that all their leads would be pooled, for there was a serious postwar housing shortage in Chicago, as well as considerable prejudice against minorities or foreign accents. Joe and Maria rented a huge white elephant of a house with five bathrooms, and this became their base of operations; here for several weeks the Tellers stayed with them, and so did one of Teller's graduate students, his wife and year-old baby. Presiding over the kitchen was the latest in the long series of European expatriates for whom the Mayers' home was a gateway to America.

Teller's student, Boris Jacobsohn, his wife and baby occupied one large bedroom; Mrs. Jacobsohn became alarmed when Maria insisted on carting the baby's crib around till she found the right spot for it, for in her eagerness to spare the younger woman extra exertion, she seemed to forget about sparing herself. One night Mrs. Jacobsohn sat in the bedroom while her infant daughter stood up in the crib and Teller and Jacobsohn discussed, in the exuberant style that was Teller's specialty, some aspect of their work; Teller spoke while gesturing and striding from one end of the room to the other, and when he reached the crib he punctuated whatever he was saying by extending an open hand in the direction of the baby—it was well known that Teller adored babies. But the hand, carried by its own momentum, continued downward until it cupped the baby's head, somewhat forcefully, Mrs. Jacobsohn felt; then Teller wheeled and strode in the opposite direction as the mother tried to calculate how much punctuation her child could endure without injury. She dared not say a word to Teller, although she did her best to catch her husband's eye. He saw nothing; he was deep in physics. Meanwhile Mrs. Teller had prepared for bed and hoped to induce her husband to join her, for the Tellers, who had one little boy, badly wanted a second child. In a floating negligee Mrs. Teller appeared at intervals at the bedroom door to call to her husband, "Edward, it is time for bed," but Teller heard nothing, since he too was deep in physics. Less than a year after the visit to the Mayers the Tellers had a baby girl, but to Mrs. Teller and Mrs. Jacobsohn it was clear, that night, that one cannot hope to interrupt a conversation between physicists with trifling family matters.

One day there was news of a promising house on the South Side; the Tellers drove out to see it, but when they got there Mici Teller refused even to get out of the car. The Mayers went all the same, noticing first the rotting little side porch that was all the Tellers had looked at. They climbed out of the car and pressed their faces against a dirty window and saw an octagonal room, perhaps a dining room, with handmade Dutch tiles on the fireplace. Inside was a great oak staircase, five bathrooms, six fireplaces, high ceilings everywhere; outside, room for several gardens. They bought it. Like the decision to come to Chicago, the house never ceased to give Maria pleasure. It seemed to smile on all their ventures, just as the university with its affectionate welcome seemed to smile on her desire to return to physics, to theoretical nuclear physics —that's what everyone had become interested in nowadays.

And Peter flourished in Chicago. He would not go to the university's private school, he told his mother, and stubbornly stuck to it. He went to the public school, as he wished, and gradually his reading difficulties disappeared. It seemed he was bright, perhaps even remarkably bright, although as tall, skinny and awkward as ever. He and Marianne fought continually, or so it seemed to Maria; it left her at a loss, for she herself had no way of dealing with ugly feelings like the anger and jealousy the children seemed to be expressing. Joe was no help; he never seemed much interested in the children's problems at that time, perhaps because he had been away from them for so long, perhaps because, like so many men, he found young children less interesting than older ones. When Peter and Marianne were in their teens, science, politics and the objective world became grounds of common interest with their father, subjects for family discussion or for the long and passionate disputes that Joe always found so delightful.

He had always been an arguer, a man who dearly loved disputation and would even take the wrong side of an argument for the pleasure of it. His famous temper, infrequent but dramatic, had been known to erupt in the midst of a discussion of urban renewal or the rise of Tito. Marianne remembers how often her father would contradict any political statement she or Peter made, and follow it up with a challenge. "But how can you take that point of view?" they would demand. "You don't believe it, do you?" "Certainly not," he would tell them, "but if you believe in your side you ought to be able to argue it." When Marianne was in college, she brought a friend home for the weekend along with the friend's fiancé, and Joe spent the weekend disputing every statement the young man made, keeping him up late at night in the process. When they had gone, Marianne told her father it was awful of him to do that to a guest. "Best weekend I've had in years," Joe retorted.

Once the war was over, like most of his colleagues Joe looked forward to the chance to do science again. He had already made important contributions to the theories of liquids and solutions, as well as to the quantum mechanics of atoms and molecules. There had also been a subtle shift in his approach to science, for Joe was by now a theoretical chemist rather than an experimental one, and the change, which had taken place gradually and partly because of Maria, was so complete that those of his colleagues who had not known him before the Chicago days were often unaware he had not always been a theoretician. He was, and always had been, a teacher of exceptional talent. "With infinite patience, he considers and rephrases an idea until the kernel has been separated from the shell," according to a former student, when the American Chemical Society gave Joe a national award for his teaching in 1969. Another student described him as having "passionate feelings about science." All these qualities, as well as a dry wit and the ability to think on his feet, found expression in one of Joe's most memorable undertakings at the University of Chicago, the weekly science seminars.

The Institute for Nuclear Studies did not confine itself to studies of the nucleus, neither did it have a building of its own, but was scattered throughout the campus wherever its members happened to be working on chemistry or physics. To keep the institute together and keep each member informed about what the others were doing, a seminar was suggested; someone said Joe ought to run it. Joe said that was fine with him, but he wanted it completely informal, there wasn't to be any appointed speaker or fixed subject, but "anybody who has anything to say, he'll talk about it." For as long as he liked, or until effectively interrupted; for five minutes or twenty.

Joe belittled his own contribution to the institute seminars; it was like running a Quaker meeting, he maintained; all he did was keep track of whose turn it was to interrupt. But there was more to it than that. Academic seminars are usually strongly colored by the personality of the seminar leader, and this is especially apparent during the question periods. Some scientists—very few, however—are men of the most delicate tact. Niels Bohr is probably the immortal example. When he found himself unable to make any sense out of a talk, unable to see any merit or interest in it no matter how hard he tried, Bohr assured the speaker it was most interesting. At the opposite pole was Wolfgang Pauli, once Born's assistant at Göttingen and one of the most brilliant of the atomic physicists; Pauli was often witty, devastating and cruel. A seminar leader is in a fine position to expose pretentious nonsense or ignorance, or to pounce on the occasional errors of capable men, all under the guise of objective inquiry. As for Joe Mayer, he was described as a hard man, a driving man, but never a destructive one, and he kept the Chicago seminars sharp and lively and argumentative, like himself.

There was another secret to the success of the science seminars at Chicago, namely the men who took part in them. Someone remembered that "Being with them was like sitting in on a conversation of the angels," and much of the brilliance of this angelic horde radiated from Fermi, who had gathered about him an extraordinary group of graduate students, Lee and Yang and Goldberger among them. At the seminars Fermi and Teller "argued and discussed and shouted and built on each other's thoughts," Maria recalled. A number of Nobel Prize-winning discoveries were first tentatively described there, and in time the reputation of these meetings became so lustrous that they acquired almost legendary status, and, like legends, had attributed to them events that could not possibly have taken place at the science seminars.

At home, in their handsome old house on the South Side, Joe and Maria found that the third-floor billiard room, once a ballroom, had a balcony originally meant for an orchestra but now used as a glassed-in porch. Joe added shelves at window level and copper trays for watering orchids, so that it became a makeshift greenhouse. Turning their attention out of doors, they planted vegetables, berries and flowers, in beds of rich loam on top of sand; their soil was a foot above that in the neighbors' gardens, and Maria enjoyed the neighborhood mystification over why everything seemed to grow better for the Mayers. And at the university, she set herself the task of learning nuclear theory.

According to Laura Fermi, physicists found themselves in a strange situation at the end of the war:

They had "harnessed nuclear energy," as the popular saying goes, but they knew little what the nucleus was like. Nuclei performed meekly at men's will, they split in two, they released the energy that was inside them. Nuclei were willing to do this very fast and to cause an atomic explosion, or slowly, in a controlled chain reaction. But they had not given up the secret of their structure.

This is what the physicists claimed. But all scientists are greedy persons, who want to learn more and more, who are never satisfied with the state of their knowledge. The truth is that quite a few facts were known about nuclei: that they are made of protons and neutrons; that these are held together by very great forces; that these forces are different from any known so far. But the nature of nuclear forces escaped the physicists; it was a challenging riddle.

To the solution of this riddle the efforts of the Chicago scientists were bent; a giant cyclotron was constructed there, the "biggest of all gadgets that Fermi had ever seen," and at the Argonne there was to be a nuclear reactor. It was here, at the Argonne National Laboratory established shortly after the Mayers' arrival, that Maria was enabled to earn a half-time salary, for the director, Robert G. Sachs, was a former student of hers, a theoretician who thoroughly respected Maria's abilities and considered himself fortunate in being able not only to hire her, but to pay her. Maria did most of her learning in nuclear theory at the Argonne. For she had come to Chicago with "very little knowledge of Nuclear Physics! It took me some time to find my way in this, for me, new field. But in the atmosphere of Chicago, it was rather easy to learn nuclear physics." Not from books—"I mean I never looked at a book. I read books occasionally, but I didn't sit down with a book and learn it"—but by a kind of absorption process that took place at the small weekly seminars held at the Argonne. The first few times Maria went she understood nothing. After that, "I went to those seminars and asked two questions after each one. And no more than two. And I'd better assimilate the answer to those two questions." She felt she didn't care to take a chance on their becoming impatient with her, just as she had feared that her "high boss," R. W. Wood, might lose interest in her; ebullient self-confidence was not Maria's strong point in those days.

The two questions were usually addressed to Edward Teller; outside of the seminars Maria spoke with Teller and Fermi whenever she could, for it was the quickest and most natural way to learn nuclear physics. Laura Fermi remembered Maria in those days as being different from the companionable Maria she had gone shopping with and offered to sew for, before the war: "My impression is that faculty wives like me did no longer have easy access to Maria Mayer, because she was always talking to the men and had a too technical conversation."

If the field was new to her, it was not completely new, for Maria had written two papers on nuclear theory in the thirties; nevertheless almost all her work at Hopkins had been concerned with physical chemistry, and her SAM work had taught her nothing about the nucleus. Many of the people at Chicago had been immersed in the nucleus since before the war, as Teller had, and a whole jargon had grown up during the war years, in common use among the nuclear physicists but quite strange to Maria. Joe remembered her telling him after one Argonne seminar that someone had said something about a thimble. Everyone else apparently knew what it was, but Maria had to devote one of her two questions to this mysterious thimble. "The thimble is a hole in the reactor—but what the hell did that mean to Maria?"

When she had been at Chicago about a year, Teller came to Maria with an idea that fascinated him, a theory about the origin of the elements; as always, he wanted someone to work with him, to serve as audience and sounding board. He also wanted someone to do the involved mathematics, an aspect of theoretical physics in which Maria was especially adept, and she welcomed the chance, for working with Teller was both instructive and exciting. His theory itself was in line with beliefs current at the time, that most of the elements had been formed when the universe was very young, perhaps as part of a Creation process, a belief that has since been discarded. As Teller wrote later, "Our theory continues to appear to me as something amusing, but unfortunately, neither she nor I believe in it any more. . . . It is now believed that the elements have been mostly formed in supernova explosions and have been accumulating through the ages." In other words, Creation—element-building—has been a continuing process.

Work began. Teller had several other projects in hand for which he was equally enthusiastic, so that it was only at intervals that he could give his full attention to Creation. Soon both Teller and Maria began to be struck by the fact that a few elements—tin, for example, and lead —were more abundant than their theory, or any other theory they could imagine at the time, explained. This they discussed at length, wandering in and out of each other's offices to complain, "This nucleus we will never be able to fit—this nucleus won't fit our theory, and that false it can't be!" For an element to be extremely abundant meant it had a very stable nucleus; the unstable ones were subject to radioactive decay, in the course of which they became other elements. And why were those particular nuclei, the lead and the tin and the others, so remarkably stable?

Teller went out of town, leaving Maria to ponder the abundant elements and their nuclei by herself, a good thing, she felt later on, for in Teller's presence she tended to be silent—he was so quick, so dazzling, and she was so much the apprentice. It was while Teller was away at Los Alamos that she decided to inspect all the information they had about these elements and their nuclei, quite calmly and systematically, "and then it fell out that in these nuclei either the number of protons or the number of neutrons were very special." More "special" numbers were to turn up later, but at the time those Maria found were 82 and 50; all the abundant nuclei had either 82 or 50 neutrons—those nuclear particles that have weight but no charge—or else 82 or 50 protons, the positively charged nuclear particles that tell what element an atom is.

Teller was still absent, so Maria discussed these curious facts with several other colleagues, and once when Hans Bethe happened to overhear he said, "You know Elsasser, some years ago, did something like that. You'd better look it up." She did so; Elsasser was someone she knew from Göttingen, and the paper he had written in 1933 on the stability of certain elements was pretty much forgotten. Far more was known about nuclei in 1948 than had been available to Elsasser; still, Maria found it reassuring that someone else had tried to find meaning in the regular occurrence of certain numbers connected with the nucleus.

She told Teller all about it when he got back, but he was only moderately interested. "My own interest was much too strongly focused on the origin of elements to pay much attention to the magic numbers," he said later. For the mysterious neutron and proton numbers soon became known as "magic numbers," a term almost everyone thought Maria herself had invented; she used the words herself, even in her scientific papers, where austere language is the tradition. She liked the phrase and thought it captured the spirit of mystery attached to her numbers. But apparently it had been Eugene Wigner who first called the numbers of the stable nuclei "magic numbers" to show it was all charming nonsense; he told her so in 1963 when they were in Stockholm together.

Encouraged by Elsasser's work, Maria began to look through papers published during the past few years, searching for further examples of stable nuclei. Meanwhile Teller lost whatever interest he had in them, becoming more and more deeply committed to work on nuclear weapons; much of his former playfulness seemed to have disappeared, perhaps as part of a change in outlook and style brought about by the war. Marianne used to speak of "Leonia Teller," who invented nonsense games for her and Peter to play, one of them involving deadly aim with spitballs, and "Chicago Teller," who was all business. Maria took her questions mainly to Fermi then; the magic numbers continued to interest him. To the original two, 50 and 82, she had added others, so that there was now a total of seven: 2, 8, 20, 28, 50, 82, 126. Any element with a magic number's worth either of protons or of neutrons was extremely stable, and as the numbers had increased to seven, so had the mystery deepened.

Month after month Maria spent much of her working day with the numbers, either discussing them with Fermi—"Of course in those discussions I learned a great deal, a great deal!"—or collecting and studying data from nuclear experimentalists, men who worked with cyclotrons or nuclear reactors, observing the nucleus under bombardment. And over and over again their accounts proved to be studded with the exact same numbers, those stubborn witnesses to some sort of nuclear order no one had yet imagined. The experimentalists themselves offered no explanation for the nuclear numbers they passed on to Maria; it was a theorist's job to fool with numbers and work up explanations. And so far as Maria could tell, no theorist was much interested except for herself and Fermi. When she came home in the evenings, to the hallowed cocktail hour that was supposed to be a leisurely, stress-free pause at five o'clock, when parents and children were to gather and refresh themselves and not talk one word of science, she would find the children waiting expectantly with juice glasses in hand. Instead of subsiding into her chair, sipping her martini or Old Fashioned and listening to the children's accounts of their day, Maria unloaded onto Joe's lap everything she had learned and thought and read about at work, every example of the persistence of her baffling numbers, meanwhile filling the air with the dense white smoke of her special cigarettes and gulping her drink. The children waited for an opening; Marianne especially, quiet and well-behaved but bursting with concealed impatience, thought it was like wartime all over again, only worse, because her mother was far more excited. As for Joe, he had been interested in Maria's magic numbers from the start; with his chemist's taste for facts and phenomena, he listened, nodded, encouraged, telling Maria never mind if it doesn't make sense. Keep on accumulating numbers—for even though there is no explanation, even though they are magic, uncomfortable to theorists, who require explanations rather than facts, they are real. Magic, yet real.

Maria was working full-time now, half-time at the Argonne with a half-time salary, and half-time at the university and the institute, without a salary, unable, in spite of her best intentions, to put her work out of her head when she came home. She no longer found either the time or the opportunity for the kind of close friendship she once had with Katherine Rice or Alice Kimball, nor did she have the emotional energy that must be devoted to such friendships; her emotional energy went into her work. Nevertheless, hospitality was deeply ingrained in the Mayers, and with a certain amount of reshuffling, exchanging many small parties for a few large ones, they were able to continue in their previous pattern. Great backyard cookouts for Joe's students, at which Joe broiled the steaks—filling Laura Fermi with admiration, for who could imagine Enrico Fermi broiling steaks?—were a regular event. The Mayers played duplicate bridge every two weeks or so with the Willard Libbys and others, and there were many informal parties where charades, "murder," mental telepathy and similar games, to which Fermi was notoriously addicted, formed the chief entertainment. If Maria had few close women friends in Chicago, she seemed in general more comfortable with the women than she used to be; they didn't talk about babies the way they had in Leonia, she said, perhaps because they were older, or had different interests, and in any case the men and the women stayed together at parties. And it was during the Chicago years that the custom began of a New Year's Eve party at the Mayers', a custom that snowballed—for once you've asked someone, Maria believed, how can you not ask him the next year and the next? By the end of the fifties over a hundred guests were coming to the Mayers' on New Year's Eve, some from abroad. Every room of the three-story brick house was thrown open; there were flowers, orchids from the hothouse, dancing in the balcony of the third-floor billiard room and singing in the library. It was the closest they could come to Göttingen.

Christmas was another occasion when work was put aside, perhaps forcibly, and Maria gave herself over to nostalgic pleasures; at first she and Joe had continued the German custom of lighting the Christmas tree only with candles of pure beeswax, but they later added electric lights as a sop to modernity. Otherwise Christmas was celebrated in the style of Maria's childhood, and Marianne recalled that her mother "never left the house during Christmas week, except to shop. She always cooked lentil soup for Christmas Eve and on Christmas Day we had roast goose with red cabbage."

The garden and the "greenhouse" continued to be Maria's chief hobby and artistic joy; at the university she was unusually conscientious in relation to her students, and to the endless committee work so many of her colleagues griped about, escaping if they could. Unpaid, Maria did it anyway. Otherwise she was almost constantly preoccupied with her numbers. "I never got rid of thinking, what are they? They lived with me for a year." Several of her colleagues were openly skeptical of this continued interest, especially as Maria had begun to consider a shell model of the nucleus, vaguely similar to the accepted model of the planetary atom. Shell models had been around since the early 1930s, and had been worked on by a number of physicists including Bethe, Feenberg and Wigner; it all came to nothing, however, and Wigner in particular considered shell theories a waste of time. One did not lightly overlook the beliefs of a man of Eugene Wigner's stature, but as it happened Maria was not completely familiar with Wigner's conclusions.

Why did the persistence of the magic numbers suggest to Maria a shell model? The generally accepted model of the nucleus was that of a drop, in which the protons and neutrons jittered about, held in place by terrific forces of unknown origin. This drop model, originated by Niels Bohr, was considered unsatisfying; most theorists expected it would eventually be replaced by a more accurate and revealing model, but meanwhile it was all there was, they used it for lack of anything better, and in high energy physics it proved to be quite productive. A shell model kept intruding itself into Maria's mind because the magic numbers reminded her, just as they had reminded Feenberg, Wigner, Bethe and the others, of certain magically stable numbers in ordinary atomic physics.

The atom is seen as a little planetary system, with electrons orbiting the nucleus as planets orbit the sun. In certain elements, the bands— or shells—of orbiting electrons are so tightly bound to the nucleus that they do not easily enter into chemical combination with other elements, by losing or gaining electrons. Helium, neon, argon, krypton and xenon, all gases, are the elements whose electrons are so bound, and as a reward for their trustworthy behavior physicists call them the "five noble gases." Each of them has a number by which it is known in the table of elements, the number indicating how many protons are in its nucleus, which is the same as the number of electrons composing its planetary system; the five noble gases may be said to have "magic numbers" of electrons.

It was natural, therefore, that those who worked on shell models of the nucleus in the thirties wondered if the repeated occurrence of certain stable numbers of nuclear particles might have a similar meaning. Perhaps there were also shells of the protons and neutrons that formed the nucleus, held in place by a kind of averaging-out of all the forces they themselves generated, and the protons and neutrons orbited within the nucleus in those certain shells, but not in the spaces in between. Some of these shells might be terrifically stable—therefore those nuclei would be abundant in nature, resistant to the breaking down that would transform them into other elements. It was this nucleus—a good deal like an onion, so that Pauli began to call her "the Madonna of the Onion"—that Maria had been pursuing.

Fascinated by her magic numbers, encouraged by Fermi and largely ignorant of Wigner's arguments against shell models, Maria wrote a paper in April of 1948, putting forth a shell theory of her own; it appeared in *Physical Review* in the course of the summer. She used the phrase "magic numbers" in it repeatedly, and it caught a certain amount of attention, mostly among those who had worked on shell models before. But the paper had nothing more to offer than what Maria had worked out so far, observations about the occurrence of the magic numbers bolstered by vast amounts of new and recent information from experimentalists working with cyclotrons and reactors. There were no really fresh illuminations, no new theories, just more facts.

Two physicists who had already worked on shell models—Wigner and David Inglis—had given some thought to a phenomenon called spin-orbit coupling, and then rejected it as unimportant. Spin-orbit coupling occurs in the atomic model and can be visualized quite readily as Maria once pictured it for Marianne. They were huddled before a fireplace one winter morning when all the radiators were cold because there had been no oil deliveries; everyone had been up late the night before, at a party where there was dancing, and a few Germans called for a waltz. And when Marianne said to her mother, "What is spin-orbit coupling? I've never been able to understand it," Maria recalled the party, the dancing, the waltz, and offered the following:

Think of a roomful of waltzers. Suppose they go round the room in circles, each circle enclosed within another, just as the electrons circle the nucleus, each shell enclosed within a larger one. Then imagine that in each shell or circle you can fit twice as many dancers by having one pair go clockwise, the other counterclockwise (forget that at some point they will meet and crash; electrons don't have that problem). Then add one more variation: all the dancers are spinning round and round like tops as they circle the room, each pair both spinning and orbiting. But only some of those that orbit counterclockwise are spinning counterclockwise; the others are orbiting counterclockwise but spinning clockwise. The same is true of those that are dancing around clockwise—some spin clockwise, others spin counterclockwise.

So do the electrons. And there is a certain difference in the energy an electron needs to spin one way as compared to spinning the other way. "Everybody who has ever danced the fast waltz knows that it's easier to dance one way around than the other," as Maria put it. But the difference, with electrons, is not very great, and physicists refer to it in patronizing fashion as "fine structure." Wigner and Inglis had both considered the possibility that the same sort of effect might take place in the nucleus, but they found it useful only when considering the light nuclei—for heavy nuclei the effect petered out. Apparently David Inglis had wondered in passing about the possibility that the effect was a strong one in nuclei—that there might be a very great energy difference between the particles spinning round one way as compared to the other; he had scribbled a question to himself along those lines in the margin of one of his papers. But it made no sense, after all, there was no evidence for it, and like a sensible theorist he ignored it; when shell model theories were swept away, spin-orbit coupling went with them.

One day Maria and Fermi were in her office talking shell model as usual; Fermi's office was much larger than Maria's, but it was a place she tried to avoid, for Fermi could not bear smoking while Maria found it difficult to endure even ten or fifteen minutes without a cigarette. In his office good manners required that she forgo her cigarettes, but in her own she felt free to smoke unceasingly since Fermi might leave when he wished. Nothing more had come of all their many hours of talk than Maria's one paper, although Fermi had generated several ideas he meant to work on when he got around to them. He never did get around to them, and Maria never remembered what those papers were going to be about, "because I then got so excited it wiped everything out." Someone had knocked on the door; a head had appeared in the doorway to say that Professor Fermi was wanted on the phone in his office, and as Fermi rose to leave he finished the sentence he had just begun. "What about spin-orbit coupling?" he asked Maria, as he headed for the doorway.

Maria said, "Yes, Enrico, that's the solution."

"How can you know?" Fermi asked. And then he left to attend to his phone call. Maria had taken up pencil and paper and started calculating as if the spin-orbit coupling existed and was very strong—as if it mattered considerably in which direction the nuclear particles twirled as they orbited. The shells—the possible paths the particles could travel in —snapped apart and rearranged themselves now that extra paths had become possible, and everywhere the magic numbers tumbled out; the numbers occurred wherever a shell was most tightly bound in place.

But it had happened in her mind even before she saw it on the paper, an awesome process that Maria would never forget; and before it happened in her mind, she felt it almost bodily: the feeling she had then was what made the day of the Nobel Prize an anticlimax. James Franck once said that the way he could tell a new idea was really important was the feeling of terror that seized him; the mathematician Norbert Wiener wrote about the pain of an unresolved mathematical discord. And Robert Wilson, a distinguished nuclear experimentalist, described at length the aspect of terror in his creative insights in an interview in *The Way of the Scientist*, by the editors of *Science and Technology:*

. . . the real kicks come, of course, when you have . . . filled yourself with a particular problem, and—you know—you have a great desire to have some clarity in it. You go through this long, hard period of filling yourself up with as much information as you can. You just sort of feel it all rumbling around inside of you, not particularly at a conscious level. Then—it can happen at any time —you begin to feel a solution, a resolution, bubbling up to your consciousness. At the same time you begin to get very excited, tremendously elated—pervaded by a fantastic sense of joy. . . .

But there's an aspect of terror too in these moments of creativity. You must come pretty close to—can you call it the life force? Being shaken out from your normal experience enhances your awareness of mortality. . . . I think there's something universal about the experience of something coming from your subconscious almost fully formed. It's like throwing up when you're sick.

Maria had no recollection of pain, of awe or terror, but the intensity of her feeling was related to theirs. It was something she couldn't describe, but it wiped everything else out of her mind.

She worked all the rest of that day, and toward evening she "floated home." Joe was out of town, and "that evening . . . I was invited somewhere. Bill Libby picked me up to take me there. We were an hour late because I had to tell him—he didn't understand it at all, but I just had to tell somebody." Joe came home a day or so later, and as soon as Maria saw him she said, "Joe, the magic numbers are explained."

He said, "Who did it?"

Maria told him who did it, and how she did it. Joe was immediately struck by its rightness and simplicity, Maria recalled, for it was "straightforward, with no assumptions, no changed assumptions." He said, "You must publish immediately."

But there were certain complications, or Maria felt there were. She had seen preprints of papers by two of the physicists, Nordheim and Feenberg, who had done shell model work before. Perhaps their new papers were inspired by her "magic number" paper, perhaps not. Still, she had been sent their work before publication, and hers, her spin-orbit paper, as yet unwritten, would be competing with theirs. I'll wait, she told Joe. I'll write to the editors of *Physical Review* and ask when those papers will come out, and send them something that I will ask them to print at the same time. I must not take advantage because I saw their preprints.

Joe said that was nonsense. Courtesy to colleagues was one thing; this was being overpunctilious. It didn't even make sense; why not write it up immediately and let *Physical Review* hold up publication if they felt there was any question of competition; that way the date it was received would appear with the paper and her priority would then be clearly established. For Joe could not help being aware that this sudden spurt of interest in shell models made it not unlikely that someone else, perhaps even someone building on Maria's already published work, would hit on a similar solution to the problem. And the longer she waited the likelier this became.

Maria admitted the good sense of his remarks but she elected to wait all the same. In answer to her inquiry, *Physical Review* said that the papers of Nordheim and Feenberg would appear in the June 1949 issue, and in view of the multiplicity of shell model systems suddenly being advanced, would she please explain hers in a brief letter that could be printed with similar brief letters from Feenberg and Nordheim, in order to show how the three theories differed? This letter Maria duly wrote in February; it was indeed brief. It was skimpy; it was not likely to convince anyone, except a physicist like Maria who had lived with the data for months, and its publication was delayed until June, as she had requested.

During the next few months Joe repeatedly teased and prodded her about when she would write up her theory, really write it up. It was not precisely a theory, since that would mean there was proof along theoretical lines; it was an insight, a vision, theoretical in nature and based on an intuitive belief in spin-orbit coupling, whose existence has since been proved, by others. At the time, however, Maria had no proof; she had felt, thought and calculated what would take place in the nucleus if there were strong spin-orbit coupling and she did so against the backdrop of all the experimental data she had spent months piling up and meticulously analyzing. But that was as far as she could go.

Perhaps she suspected she was going too far. Perhaps that accounted for the many months she hung fire while Joe continued to needle her, as only he, with his dramatic temper and his "passionate feelings" about science, could needle. "For God's sake, write it up!" Marianne heard him yelling one day in an angry voice. "You have to write it up—you have to do it right now!" He would have spoken almost as angrily to a student or junior colleague who had developed a brilliant new idea, then found excuses for failing to publish it; what else does a scientist do to advance both his career and the progress of science but publish, and as soon as possible? Yet here was Maria, whose abilities had for so many years been taken far too lightly by others, suddenly in possession of a striking and invaluable vision, hiding it away out of quixotic modesty.

Even Edward Teller wondered about the delay; he too suspected Maria of modesty. And if she had continued modestly holding back, the shell model nucleus would have been proclaimed to the world from another quarter entirely, from the University of Heidelberg, in fact, "and my work would have meant experience, not the Nobel Prize," as Maria told a reporter once. Thanks in large part to Joe's persistence, by December of 1949 Maria had written two full-length papers for *Physical Review*, setting forth in detail the shell model system and the experimental data to back it up. These two papers, published side by side in April 1950, were enough to convince both Nordheim and Feenberg of the rightness of Maria's insight, whereas the little letter had meant nothing to them.

One wonders just how unreasonable her modesty was. Lawrence Wilets, a nuclear theorist familiar with the history of the shell model, believes "it took nerve—it took unmitigated nerve to propose such a model with no real theoretical justification." Many theoreticians would have had the nerve; a strong competitive spirit and buoyant confidence in one's work are honorable traits in science, but it is not really strange that Maria lacked them at the time. She was a newcomer to the field, having returned to physics after an absence of many years; she was not used to raising her voice in the councils of her peers, where for so long she had been ignored or patronized. And she was by nature gentle, albeit stubborn, better suited to repeating the truth in a small voice than to trumpeting it forth. Time, and success, must have strengthened her confidence in herself to some degree, for one of Maria's students remembered her telling him, when someone published a paper based on mistaken assumptions, "Let's hurry and publish ours before G——discovers his error!"

She might have been more hesitant still but for the all-important fact that Fermi agreed with her; Maria explained it to him the morning after that meeting in her office, and "after a week, when I had written up the other consequences carefully, Fermi was no longer skeptical. He even taught it in his class in nuclear physics."

"Of course you must publish," Fermi told her.

Maria said, "I think we should publish together—you have helped me so much."

Fermi said, "No. Because, you see, I am a famous man. If I put my name on it, it will always be attributed to me—and it is really not my work, it is yours."

A short while later he asked if she would explain her theory, and Nordheim's and Feenberg's competing shell model systems, at the institute seminar, the celebrated seminar Joe ran along the lines of a Quaker meeting. Maria did so, and such was the climate and fame of Joe's seminars that the story came into being that Fermi had asked his question, "What about spin-orbit coupling?" in the middle of the meeting, and that Maria had created her shell model system on the spot, with Fermi's words still echoing in the air.

But if Fermi was convinced, skepticism remained in other quarters;

one day Maria spoke at Princeton, where Oppenheimer was colloquium master. Her voice was whispery, as always, the German accent competing with the British one. She was nervous and shy and she chain-smoked as usual; turning to the blackboard, she took up a piece of chalk and became confused as to which was chalk and which was cigarette. A young theorist who heard her lecture found it hard to take seriously. "I might accept it more readily if she didn't always call them 'magic numbers,' " he said to himself. "It sounds like hocus-pocus, numerology. Why not stable numbers? That you could take seriously."

One person who did not need much convincing was Weisskopf, the Mayers' old friend from Göttingen. He had seen the brief little letter even before it was published, and instantly approved. "You know," he told Maria, "it must be right—because I have a letter that was sent to me by Hans Jensen, in Heidelberg. He has the same system. If Jensen says it too, it must be right." Weisskopf had received Jensen's letter by mail with the request that it be sent on to *Physical Review;* it had already been submitted to the German publication *Natur,* and rejected. So Jensen's letter was delayed, between the first submission and the time it took to go to Weisskopf; and Maria's letter was also delayed, delayed in the writing and delayed for months at *Physical Review,* by her request. Although Jensen's letter was published one month earlier than Maria's, it was taken as self-evident that they had been conceived at the same time.

But if Maria had not developed the two long papers that she finished in December, the theory might have come to be regarded as Jensen's alone, for it takes more than a brief and sketchy letter to establish full priority. And Jensen had not wasted time, as Maria had, after the letter; in July he and two colleagues published two papers in *Natur,* developing the shell model in detail. Jensen's claim to the shell model was therefore in impeccable order. Joe knew about it, by way of Weisskopf, and it must have strengthened the feeling he had had from the start, that each month Maria delayed publication lessened her chances for priority.

This news—that a well-respected Heidelberg physicist had come up with a shell model based on spin-orbit coupling at the same time she had —gave rise in Maria to a number of feelings, ranging from annoyance and resentment—how much better to have been first, and the only one! —to satisfaction—it is sure to be accepted now, sure to be right, if we both came to it independently. Many scientists have had the experience of learning, as Darwin did, that someone halfway round the world has duplicated many years' worth of work, when it was too late to speed it up, withdraw, reroute. Bitterness and spoiled lives sometimes result. But Maria was fortunate on several counts; she had not invested years, only one year. And her nature was one that strongly desired to smooth over differences before they ever arose. In no time she had convinced herself that this was a stroke of luck. She looked forward to meeting Hans Jensen, was prepared to like him, to work with him; they had, after all, shared something unique—the experience all scientists pursue, and only some can have undiluted. If science is fun, as they all insist it is, the moment of intuitive discovery is the dip in the roller coaster—the break in the roller coaster, rather, the split second when the rider hurtles across the rails and becomes aware that the steel beneath him has disappeared and he is skidding across an abyss.

Bernice Eiduson refers to the "paranoid leap," a phrase she borrows from the philosopher Kierkegaard, who thus describes the really creative ideas, "for they are antithetical to everything we know, everything realistic, every way in which we are accustomed to thinking about something." Eiduson's description of the paranoid leap, the alliance between craziness and stability that underlies creativity in science, is illuminating:

Because such "crazy" thinking takes one out of the reality sphere, one has to be a fairly well stabilized and integrated person, not to be threatened by thinking in bizarre ways, when controls are at a minimum, and letting one's unconscious take over. One can only think crazily enough to produce something really revolutionary or original when he has some strongly entrenched thinking styles on which he can rely and to which he can come home. Without these, the dangers to personality organization are very great, and so frightening that it would be unlikely that one could let his mind go to the fantastic proportions and distortions that are necessary to come up with a unique idea.

People like Fermi, Bohr, Pauli, Heisenberg, had crossed the abyss a number of times; moreover, they had dangled at its edges for weeks, even months. If we picture Bohr, as his students pictured him, putting the atom together bit by bit, all the time he spent doing it he stood balanced over the abyss. Once the planetary atom had been composed it became part of reality, but while it was in the process of creation there was only nothingness, a nothingness Bohr had to be able to tolerate, to enjoy, to desire, or he would never permit himself another creative idea.

But Maria Mayer, in 1948, was in her early forties. There was no reason to believe she would ever again ride that roller coaster, although she might circle around nothingness and stick her feet in it from time to time; she was deeply grateful for what had already been granted her, and may have felt in this a bond between herself and the unknown Jensen. Certainly she was not all open-handed generosity, eager to let anyone who wished take part in her discovery; once Fermi had gracefully drawn back from her first offer she saw no need to repeat it. As for Joe, who had encouraged her from the very first suspicions of the magic numbers, his style of thinking influenced Maria in a number of subtle ways; for example, it is most unusual that a theoretical physicist should also accumulate and analyze the experimental data that backs up his theories, yet Maria had done so, partly because she learned from Joe to respect experimental data. Jensen did what most theorists do—he left all that to two colleagues. Joe happened to meet one of them in Germany in 1949, and he told Maria later the man had no particular interest in the shell model theory, and did not even seem to understand it. Nevertheless, Joe felt that his position in connection with Maria's shell model work was strictly defined; he was teacher, audience, father confessor, but he was not a collaborator. There were times, Joe recalled, when he had felt himself drawn into the work, ready to succumb to his interest in it and become a partner. Yet he felt unmistakably that Maria was letting him know: Hands off, this is mine. He kept to his original role, therefore, finding satisfaction in the thought that no one would be able to imagine now that Maria was riding on his coattails.

It was during this same period, the late forties, that Joe Mayer had an amusing encounter. The psychologist Anne Roe had secured a grant from the U.S. Public Health Service for a psychological study of scientists; she planned to work with sixty-four eminent men, roughly divided among biologists, social scientists and physical scientists. When it came time to select the physical scientists from those names Dr. Roe's judges had given her, she found them markedly skittish. There were far more refusals from physicists than from scientists in the other categories, and many of those who agreed to meet her had first devoted a good deal of effort to checking her credentials. Not only were physicists skittish and skeptical; in another part of the study they were sometimes scornfully uncooperative, forgetting to post the notices Dr. Roe had sent them. But when she asked Joe to be one of her eminent subjects, he was quite willing.

It wasn't that Joe Mayer had a higher opinion of psychology than his colleagues; like so many physicists and chemists he tended to be suspicious of a discipline that was not precisely a science, yet called itself a science. Many physicists, especially theoreticians, are further put off by the fact that as a group they are brighter—that is, they test higher for IQ—than any other scientists; and since it is almost invariably true of physicists and chemists that they value intellect over all other qualities, they often find it hard to take psychologists seriously. They will say, for example: How am I to let someone tamper with my mind when he's nowhere as bright as myself or my colleagues? They are similarly distrustful of all forms of psychotherapy, since it is the very opposite of intellectual, giving priority to the emotional rather than the cerebral. Dr. Roe's conclusion was that physicists suffered more from "free anxiety"—a chronic, generalized and unfocused anxiety, that attaches to almost any situation—than the other scientists.

But Joe had learned that Anne Roe's husband was George Gaylord Simpson, a geologist of international reputation; if her own science was suspect, her husband's was not. He also found when he met her that Dr. Roe was a charming woman. Joe therefore decided in her favor, and was duly interviewed, tested and immortalized in the classic four-year study; he said he was never really able to decide which of the more than twenty physical scientists, hidden behind made-up names, was himself, but he rather enjoyed the whole project.

Early in 1949 Joe was invited to an international meeting in Florence, one of the first of the large-scale postwar scientific conferences; it was to take place that summer, and he arranged to go north later on to Göttingen. Maria wanted desperately to go with him, mainly out of a longing to see Germany again, but also because she would have liked a chance to meet Hans Jensen. They had begun a friendly and sympathetic exchange of letters that spring, with Jensen gallantly referring to "your theory" while Maria spoke of "our theory"; once, when she became dejected by continued skepticism about the shell model, Jensen tried to cheer her up with, "You have convinced Fermi, and I have convinced Heisenberg—what more do we want?"

But Maria had no official invitation to the conference, given by the International Union of Pure and Applied Physics and devoted to statistics and thermodynamics; therefore her fare to Europe would not be paid for, as Joe's was. The visit to Germany was to be brief, just a few days sandwiched in among a number of commitments already fixed for that summer; it seemed extravagant, a self-indulgence Maria could not justify to herself. She stayed at home, and hung on Joe's letters instead.

He told her about giving a speech in the famous Mathematical Library, which had been built with Rockefeller money and was the pride of Göttingen, housing what was probably the finest collection of its kind in Europe. The windows were all broken and the books gone, through no one's fault—they had been stored in a salt mine for safety during the war, and an accidental explosion destroyed everything. Looking at the broken windows, seeing the empty shelves, Joe found he had more to say than he could manage; his eyes filled and his face streamed with tears. Later on he met a number of people who were already teaching Maria's shell model system; and he heard about some Russian scientists who had been utterly baffled by it, having translated the word "shell" as "grenade."

Maria resolved to find some way of returning to Germany herself: "it was in a sense terrible to go back, but I felt I had to, and before too long." She "wanted to see it, even when it might have been bad, I wanted to see it." Fortunately the State Department was looking for people with scientific training to visit German universities and tell them which projects to back, whom to trust; a friend at Chicago suggested the Mayers, and interviews began early in 1950, to be followed by streams of red tape that continued until two days before they were ready to leave, at the end of summer.

Joe and Maria reached Germany in late August; the first place they visited was Frankfurt. It was a hot day when they arrived, and in downtown Frankfurt the Mayers were aware of a stench that seemed to rise from the pavement under their feet. What is this smell? Maria asked Joe. He said he had smelled it before; in Corregidor. Frankfurt had been saturation-bombed toward the end of the war, and during one bombing the asphalt caught fire so that "everyone who was downtown that day is downtown still," Joe told Maria. It was a prophetic start for the three months they were to spend in Germany, where day after day, in a familiar and beloved setting, they came upon the frightening and incomprehensible past. Their reactions were somewhat different; to Joe, the indiscriminate bombing of civilians was stupid, chiefly because it was inefficient, and he had been very bitterly against it all along. "We had the data in Aberdeen in super secret files. German production had increased in spite of the bombing. It was no worse than other things done in the war but it was *not* an efficient way to win a war!" Maria found her feelings harder to put into words; there had of course been an attack on England's life . . . if more effort had been put into a landing, sooner . . . but it was necessary to accept . . . "I was only glad it was over," she said later. "I felt no anger." In fact she was unable to remember what she did feel at the time—perhaps because all strong emotion had been as dutifully repressed as the terror she failed to feel later in the midst of her stroke.

Everyone in Germany seemed to be looking backward, recounting their losses or cataloguing their complaints against the American or British occupation forces; except in Berlin, Americans were disliked by the population in general. But the German scientists, Maria believed, felt differently. Most of them had welcomed the Americans and were amazed at the restrictions placed on them by the occupation. "They were not permitted to have Geiger counters, for example. The Germans said, 'We do not want to cheat. We cheated under Hitler. We do not want to cheat our friends.'

"One could only guess, read between the lines, guess that there were many scientists who were in internal exile." A woman Maria knew, a Berliner, told them she used to see the trains taking the children to Auschwitz, "and she always made a point to go to these trains, and give some toys to these children which were going," so there were ordinary citizens as well as scientists who had been in internal exile. Yet Maria felt they were rare. Again, her observations were different from Joe's, for Joe believed there were many ordinary citizens who were totally unaware of the extermination camps, while Maria felt this was impossible, that one could only have remained unaware by refusing to know.

When they returned to the States several of the European-born scientists asked Maria if she had seen Heisenberg; she had not. Heisenberg's name, unspoken, seemed to be on everyone's lips in the German universities, but the Mayers had gone as official representatives of the State Department, and except for those who knew them personally, they were treated as visitors, cordially but at arm's length. Maria "had a feeling" about Heisenberg, who had remained in Germany, the guardian of German science, as he put it, and the chief of its atomic effort, which had amounted to so little. Other German scientists, Otto Hahn, for example, the codiscoverer of fission, had also remained in Germany, but Hahn's behavior was not Heisenberg's. Hahn had been persistently and openly contemptuous of the Nazis, while Heisenberg's tacit support of the regime disappointed all those who knew and loved him as a young man at Göttingen, boyish, athletic, bursting with the juices of life. "But nobody would say anything against Heisenberg," Maria recalled. "Somebody asked me when I came back, 'Did you feel that you could shake hands with him?' I said, I wanted to shake hands with everybody, I felt I would behave towards Heisenberg as if I knew nothing about . . . In fact, we didn't really know anything, we just had a feeling."

In 1951 Maria was able to return to Germany again, briefly and by herself, and this time unofficially. She had been elected a member of the Heidelberg Academy of Sciences, perhaps at the request of Hans Jensen, whom she had met the previous year. Maria was invited to Heidelberg and afterward she and Jensen and several other German scientists, were invited by Bohr to Copenhagen. She looked forward intensely to this short visit, and one of the German scientists who greeted her when she first arrived said, "This year you are again one of us." Now the others spoke freely to her; many were quite open in their resentment of Heisenberg. By the time they reached Copenhagen, what Maria had suspected a year earlier became perfectly evident—there were two camps among the German scientists. Heisenberg, von Weizsäcker (whose father was undersecretary of state in Hitler's cabinet) and one other man formed one party; Jensen, Kopferman, Houtermans were among the other party. "What I remember is that always von Weizsäcker and Heisenberg were together. For instance, we went on an excursion, to some castle. Our group was with some Danes, some Dutch people—and those three were always alone." But if the war had strained the bonds of friendship among physicists, it had not broken them; old ties were reasserted, and Heisenberg's isolation eventually became a thing of the past.

From Jensen, that summer, Maria heard a remarkable story. Early in the war, before Niels Bohr was smuggled out of Sweden by the British in 1943, "Jensen went in the name of many others to Copenhagen to talk to Bohr . . . to get Bohr's—he said 'absolution'—for taking money from the German government to work with; and they got that 'absolution.' And they promised Bohr they would tell him everything they could find out. And they did that. That's treason, you know. They kept Bohr *exactly* informed about everything they could find out." That was how Bohr knew what the Nazi atomic effort amounted to, although Churchill could not believe him, nor could the Americans.

Now that Maria was able to talk to Jensen at length and informally, she found she liked him as much as she had expected to, and the idea of a collaboration, which he had earlier suggested, seemed appealing; Hans Jensen was easy, relaxed, entirely without ceremony, dressed in unfashionable clothes that rarely matched. He had something of the quality the British call "cheekiness," a certain irreverence that had taken the form, during the war, of smuggling a number of Jews out of Germany, as well as reporting scientific progress to Bohr, while his outward behavior was proper and circumspect. Although the rest of their party lived in the quarters provided in Copenhagen by Bohr's institute, Jensen stayed in the home of one of the men he had helped to leave Germany, a Jewish businessman who had finally settled in Denmark and prospered.

Jensen told Maria later that one of the reasons he suggested they write a book exploring the implications of their shell model was the Nobel Prize. It was not likely they could win it as matters stood, for it would have to be split in a curious way, a way it had never been split before, among Maria, Jensen and Jensen's two colleagues, who had gathered the experimental data. The idea of the prize, which is rarely far from the outermost edges of a physicist's mind when really promising work is under way, had somehow not occurred to Maria. It had occurred to Jensen, though, and it had also occurred to Joe.

In the fall of 1951 there was to be an international scientific meeting in Chicago; Maria returned from Europe to be told she need have nothing to do, no entertaining whatever in connection with it. Still, she and Joe decided they could not let others take the entire burden, and they resolved to give a cocktail party in their garden every afternoon for four days running, then provided themselves with 288 chemical beakers —100-cubic-centimeter lipless beakers—as cocktail glasses. The beakers stayed with them, diminishing in number over the years until by 1970 only seven were left, but Joe and Maria continued to use the seven; they seemed to be ideal cocktail glasses for scientists.

Before the international conference that fall, the institute at Chicago had met to decide who would be invited; Maria was of course a member of the Institute for Nuclear Studies, but a nonvoting member; even in Chicago, where she had always felt warmly welcomed and appreciated, such details cropped up from time to time to remind her that she was, after all, a faculty wife, unpaid by either the institute or the university. Nevertheless she had gone to the meeting, voteless but not voiceless, to insist that Hans Jensen be invited to the conference. The book on which they hoped to collaborate could only be written if a series of long visits in the States could be arranged for Jensen; certainly Maria couldn't go to Germany for long stretches of time. Even if she wanted to, Joe would object. Therefore Jensen, who had no domestic ties, would have to come to the Chicago meeting, and once he was there other visits, lectureships, appointments would surely open up.

When she had spoken in favor of Jensen, Maria had also brought up the names of other German scientists she hoped to see invited, and her curious position at the institute struck its director, Samuel Allison; at a meeting a week later he proposed that Maria be made a regular member, attending meetings and voting like the others. Joe promptly got up to leave the room so that his presence might not influence the decision, but before he reached the door she had been unanimously voted in. Hans Jensen was duly invited, he came to Chicago, and invitations from several universities followed—Wisconsin, Princeton, Cal Tech. Nevertheless the book did not leap to life. Jensen and Maria continued to admire each other, continued to agree on almost every matter of importance, so that their goodwill was somewhat exaggerated by their friends. Gamow wrote: "When they met to compare their results, they found that they both were born on the same day of the same year, and so they became very good friends," but in fact Maria was a year older than Jensen and their birthdays were several days apart. But it was quite true that their eyeglasses were so much alike that whenever Maria forgot hers, Jensen offered his.

The difficulty had to do with a difference in their work habits; Maria was always methodical, conscientious, orderly, prepared to do what was expected of her at almost any cost. Jensen put things off until the last possible moment, then worked like fury in the hope of catching up; each probably admired the opposite quality in the other, but progress slowed to a crawl. A mutual friend of theirs reported that he visited Maria after seeing Jensen in Berkeley, and Maria's first breathless words were, "Is he working on it? Has he done anything yet?" But if the book was not being written, the dedication was already complete. Jensen had carefully composed the following: "To our most patient and most constructive critic Joseph E. Mayer." For from the beginning of what proved to be a four-year project Joe acted as moderator, both critic and audience: "I knew enough about it to be able to understand everything that was clear," and what was not clear he had no trouble spotting; it was whatever he could not understand.

In 1953 Joe and Maria had the chance to make a trip around the world, beginning with a visit to Japan at the invitation of the International Union for Pure and Applied Physics. Marianne was already at Ripon College, a small coeducational school where her shyness and reserve showed signs of melting; she was a biology major, her enthusiasm for the subject somewhat moderate, perhaps, but further study might change that. Peter was fifteen, and he was to spend part of the time living with the Libbys, and part at camp. He was still rather gawky, a tall, skinny boy with an extraordinary appetite. Lorlei Libby remembered that while he was with them their compost heap caught fire, and Peter raced after it with the water hose, and kept on racing, triumphantly brandishing the hose, even after it had broken off from the spigot. This bit of news, and others relating to the health of Peter's dog, who underwent surgery for ear trouble, were duly relayed to Joe and Maria, and their letters home described their progress from Japan to Hong Kong to India, Israel and Europe.

The visit to Hiroshima had worried Maria; she was relieved when she learned they would be there for only one day:

It is very pleasant that they can't accommodate us in Hiroshima and we live out here [on a nearby island]. Our experiences in the city of Hiroshima were not very pleasant. Incidentally, the city is completely rebuilt. You would have no idea that it was destroyed, if you did not know. Except, they have left one damaged building intentionally unrepaired, probably just in order to photograph American tourists in front of it. . . . last night newspaper reporters appeared with a woman writer and a man who was a victim of the blast. We eliminated the newspapermen, but talked with the others. The man had badly burned hands and showed us his burned back. Today we heard that he could have gotten all that repaired at any time within the last years. Then we saw the same man, in front of the carefully preserved ruin selling atomic bomb souvenirs. A huge picture of his burned back hung on the stand.

Even the one day at Hiroshima was more than Maria cared to spend; just as she had erased the anger she might justifiably have felt at the fire bombing of Frankfurt, so, in Hiroshima, she wished all the pain and ugliness whisked out of sight and made smooth again. "When you decide to feel good about things, you can," she once said, and "One has quite a bit of control over one's emotions!"

They returned from the European part of their trip to hear some tragic news in Chicago. Fermi had been in Italy, where he learned that Italian food no longer agreed with him. He was quite sick, had taken sick while still abroad, had gone to a hospital in Chicago where an X ray was made, nothing was found, and he was told to return in four weeks. But then the chief physician at that hospital came back from his vacation and looked at the X rays; an exploratory operation was ordered. They learned eventually that there was a widespread cancer and nothing could be done. "He endured it," Maria said, "with the greatest grace you can imagine."

At first Fermi hoped to dictate a book. His wife had recently written one, a biography of Fermi and the bomb project called *Atoms in the Family*. But then Fermi realized he hadn't the strength to write, even with a secretary. He took great pleasure in the success of Laura's book, however; during the last week of his life it was on the best-seller list. Fermi had just been awarded a prize by the Atomic Energy Commission that later became known as the Fermi Award, America's most important scientific prize, and he told Maria and Frieda Urey how proud he was of Laura's success. "Prouder of her book than of anything I accomplished in my life-time," Maria remembered him saying. But Frieda remembered it differently: "Fermi said he was prouder of Laura's success than of his AEC prize," which seems much the likelier version. To Maria it was terribly important that Fermi, whom she so admired, should come at last to a realization of his wife as a person with projects of her own, someone who could succeed or fail quite apart from himself.

"I have a feeling he willed himself to die," Maria said. "You see the Marshalls were going to have the cyclotron for a week. And they saw him before that. And they said, we'll come back on Sunday of next week and tell you what we have found. And Fermi said, send the news up to St. Peter. He was dead by that time."

In 1955 the book at long last was completed, although Jensen had never mended his working habits and it was clear he had written somewhat less than half. In a rush of contrition he told the Mayers, "We won't even put my name on it!" They told him that was out of the question, but Maria did accept without further argument his offer that her name be put before his, out of alphabetical order. To Joe, these discussions about the authorship of the book provided a certain amount of amusement, aware as he had always been that many people credited him with all the work on *Statistical Mechanics* and believed that whatever other work Maria had done, she had done only because he helped her. Now there would undoubtedly be many who would say the shell model book was chiefly Jensen's. As it happened, some people said the shell model work was mainly Jensen's, while others believed it was mainly Fermi's. "Whenever a man and a woman collaborate, the lion's share of the credit is sure to go to the man," Joe said, as it had when the Curies collaborated, and when Lise Meitner worked with Otto Hahn.

Once the book was published, having firmly established the Mayer-Jensen nucleus as the most significant advance in nuclear physics since the war, both the Mayers began to notice that whenever Jensen visited them in the fall, while the Nobel Committee was meeting in Stockholm, he seemed "fidgety." Joe began to get fidgety just from watching him. Frieda Urey, leaving one year for a long vacation in Europe, told Maria, "We'll see you in Stockholm." It was a possibility Maria tried hard not to take seriously, although Joe rather enjoyed the prospect.

Both children were hovering on the brink of adulthood; Marianne, ready to graduate from college now, had switched her major from biology to German, and declared she would never work full-time once she had children, for she didn't want them to confide their hopes and joys to a nursemaid. She meant to marry and become a "woman," in the sense her grandfather Goeppert had used that word to young Maria. From this they had reason to conclude that she was managing to find her own goals and definitions, not entirely at variance with those her parents had selected for her, yet uniquely her own. Peter had entered Cal Tech and expected to major in physics. So Maria's work had prospered, the children were flourishing, and life should have been good—yet it wasn't. Chicago was no longer the wonderful place it used to be; with Fermi's death, both Joe and Maria felt that everything had gone dull and lusterless, and even the institute seminars were not the same. Maria's health had not improved; on her fiftieth birthday, quite without warning, she lost most of the hearing in one ear. Several of Maria's lifelong friends remarked on a change that seemed to take place in her spirits during the mid-1950s; they found her harder to reach, more aloof than ever. Perhaps her physical health was at the root of it, perhaps it worried her, although Maria never seemed to take it seriously and never took care of herself except in the most minimal way. She might have been mourning the passage of time, the end of the most productive years of her life. Fermi's death was one reminder of mortality, and James Franck, a very old man but a beloved one, had had a series of heart attacks. He was the last link to Maria's childhood and Göttingen, one more proof that time is inexorable.

"After one of his heart attacks he wasn't supposed to have visitors, but then his daughter called me," Maria remembered, "and said 'He'd like to see you.'"

That visit was a revelation. The peace with which Franck said, "Well, all right if I die, so what. I have had a wonderful life. I have had two wonderful wives." No mention about the trouble he has gone through in Göttingen. That was wiped out, he was thinking only of the pleasant things in life, and how "he had gotten more recognition than he had deserved. He was really not a good physicist, but he had gotten a tremendous amount of recognition and this was after all gratifying . . . although he did not deserve it"—a completely peaceful attitude. They told him he should not do any more science. He said, "This I will not do, I will walk a little slower and all that, but they cannot tell me not to think about science."

Franck's declaration that he "was really not a good physicist," but was given a tremendous amount of recognition he did not deserve, was of course a statement Maria disagreed with; it was an expression of the rare sweetness and humility of the man.

In 1959 there came the promise of a fresh start—the offer of two full professorships, one for Joe Mayer in chemistry, one for Maria Mayer in physics, at the new San Diego campus of the University of California, and within twenty-four hours the University of Chicago trustees offered Maria a full professor's salary, in the hope of keeping her there. But they decided against staying, and turned toward California and La Jolla. The Ureys were already there and it was said to be beautiful, by the ocean, gardens everywhere, and, as Frieda pointed out, they would be helping to build up a new place. Before they could leave, however, a family matter had to be attended to, for Marianne, who had refused to become a scientist, was nevertheless preparing to embrace science. She had managed to fall in love, to get herself engaged and ready to be married in a way precisely calculated to give the greatest pleasure to her parents, for the boy she loved was Donat Wentzel, an astrophysicist whose father was a physicist and an old friend of the Mayers. Maria planned a beautiful wedding, and went to work on the orchids in her hothouse— all twenty of the plants were coaxed into bloom in time for the reception. "There were at least four sprays on each plant and twenty-five flowers on each spray," Marianne recalled. "It was really something."

Then they began the difficult task of dismembering the Chicago household and moving West. For Maria especially it was a sad business, no matter how beautiful La Jolla would be, no matter what honors and dignities awaited her there. The moving job seemed endless. Maria found that it was hard work physically as well as mentally, and once they were in La Jolla, in a spacious and handsome modern house whose front faced the ocean while in the patio a semitropical garden framed a swimming pool, somehow no one seemed to realize just how tired she was, no one offered to help her put her books away.

It was in October, only a few weeks after their arrival, that Maria had the stroke. By Christmas she was out of the hospital and home again, stubbornly, persistently resolved that Joe's life would not be different. Her own life would necessarily be different, however; she was no longer so mobile, and she tired easily, although she fought against showing it. At forty she had looked like a girl and exuded vitality; in her middle fifties, although nature had dealt harshly with her, she continued to demand a great deal of herself. A young colleague of hers remembers that a year or so after the stroke, Maria had dinner at his house; when the other guests had left the table he stood behind her chair waiting for her to rise, and when she was ready, he pulled out her chair, only then realizing she had not been ready at all, but meant to shift position before she stood up. Maria crashed to the bare wood floor, and as he stooped to help her up, blazing with fear and guilt, he was amazed that her first words to him were, "It's all right—no one saw."

Each autumn, when scientists on both sides of the Atlantic speculated anew about who would receive that year's Nobel Prize, Mayer and

Jensen's names always came up. In 1953 a Hamburg newspaper had printed the mistaken report that Jensen had won, and by the early sixties he had given up hope; even Joe's buoyant faith had started to waver. On November 5, 1963, the Mayers were awakened by the telephone at four in the morning, the operator asking for Dr. Maria Mayer to take a call from Stockholm. "But I don't know anyone in Stockholm!" she said as she reached for the telephone; Joe, who had answered it, ran from the darkened bedroom to put a bottle of champagne on ice. It was a Swedish newsman reporting that Mayer and Jensen had just been awarded the Nobel Prize.

"I really don't know what to say. Is it really true? I still can't believe it's true," Maria cried. And then, "Oh, how wonderful! I've always wanted to meet a king." In Heidelberg, Hans Jensen's first reaction had been complete disbelief. He thought it was a joke, insisting, "I have had previous experience with this kind of nonsense." But as soon as he had been convinced, he announced that he was "proud and happy and very, very glad," and emphasized the fact that he had done his earliest shell model work with two colleagues, the experimentalists Haxel and Suess; they were not included in the later work, but he wanted to make sure their contribution would be remembered.

Joe and Maria drank their champagne, had a breakfast of bacon and eggs on the patio, telephoned Peter and Marianne, and received the formal announcement of Maria's award in the shape of a telegram from the Nobel Foundation. For the next forty-eight hours their home was under siege. "La Jolla Mother Wins Nobel Prize," announced a local newspaper, completely nonplussed. The telephone rang without respite; everyone called, including Laura Fermi, who felt "somewhat surprised that she seemed really pleased to receive my congratulations. She and I had traveled different paths and were no longer close friends but I suppose she was still grateful for Fermi's 'chance remark.' " Maria was in a state of high excitement, delighted to hear from everyone who wished her well but also terribly tired, overwhelmed by what was still an unforeseen and stunning honor, even a bit confused—for a friend who telephoned to congratulate her was startled by Maria's inquiring, as soon as he gave his name, about the health of his little girl, who had

had a minor infection a few days earlier; he had almost forgotten about it, but Maria assumed he was calling to give her news of the child's progress. Frieda Urey realized how dazed Maria was and offered to help her shop for the trip to Sweden, choosing a green brocade gown for the Nobel ceremony and three cocktail dresses. Maria had her old gray Persian lamb coat remade, but it failed to come in time; she called the furrier and told him she needed the coat, she was going away, but nothing happened. She called again, saying she had to catch a plane for Stockholm within days. "Stockholm," cried the furrier. "You're *that* Mrs. Mayer. I thought it was just some lady going to San Francisco for the weekend."

Until the very last moment Joe and Maria tried to persuade Peter to come to Stockholm for the ceremonies. But Peter had switched from physics to economics when he entered graduate school in Berkeley, a decision that came as a mild surprise to Joe and a disappointment to Maria. "If only Joe had discussed it more with him," she said later. Like Marianne, Peter was beginning to find his own goals without turning entirely away from those of his parents, and economics seemed to him to have human values as well as stern mathematical underpinning, while physics had no human values at all. He knew how badly his mother wanted him to come to Sweden, but felt it would be impossible, that his position there would be that of a child and he was not yet old enough to support such a position with grace. He declined, and his trousers went instead.

Someone warned Joe that Nobel week would be exhausting for Maria, and he used part of the two weeks that remained before they must show up in Sweden to give her a short vacation in Denmark. Arriving in Stockholm, they were taken to a suite at the Grand Hotel opposite the palace, where their rooms were filled with flowers from friends on both sides of the ocean; Max Born, bursting with pride in his former pupil, had not only sent flowers but released to the newspapers an accurate account of her life, hoping to correct some of the errors he claimed to have seen and referring to the young Maria as "pretty, elegant, a high-spirited young lady traveling in the best Göttingen society." Born had retired from the University of Edinburgh in 1953, and returned with his wife to Göttingen, where he wrote his memoirs, played piano, and translated into English the humorous works of his favorite nineteenth-century poet.

Nobel week takes place during the shortest and therefore the darkest week of the year, when daylight lasts two or three hours; wherever the Mayers went they were told by the Swedes, "The wonderful thing about the Nobel ceremony is that it gives us something to look forward to." At the hotel one morning the maids came in wearing crowns studded with lighted candles in honor of Santa Lucia Day, inserted into the darkest part of the year to keep up Scandinavian spirits. Street lights were on all day long, and the city was "flagged," displaying everywhere the national flags of each of the laureates. And another, unexpectedly festive note was the transformation of Hans Jensen, who had always before dressed in the most casual manner, regardless of fashion; he had gone to a really good tailor, ordered a wardrobe for Nobel week, and arrived in Stockholm beautifully dressed, almost a dandy.

Everything about Nobel week and Stockholm had, for Maria, a fairy-tale quality, the sense of an unattainable dream attained, and a certain curious aftertaste, bittersweet and possibly characteristic of the unattainable when it is finally pinned down. According to Mitchell Wilson, a few years later: " 'To my surprise, winning the prize wasn't half as exciting as doing the work itself,' she said to me with some perplexity. *That* was the fun—seeing it work out!' Even the memory of the lack of elation seemed to sadden her." But Joe's enjoyment of Nobel week was fuller; he had wept when he saw Maria take her place onstage, partly out of pride and partly out of the sense of drama that makes some people weep at weddings. Seeing one's wife enshrined in a pantheon might bring any man to tears.

Was he ever jealous—did he never experience the least regret that he had not persuaded Maria to share the work with him so that they could have taken twin places in the scientific pantheon? Joe's answer to that was, No, not really. "I have had some little triumphs of my own," he adds; what better assurance that he could enjoy Maria's triumph without reservation? Joe had been awarded at various times the Chandler medal by Columbia University; the Kirkwood medal by Yale University; the

Debye Award by the American Chemical Society; the Gilbert Newton Lewis medal by the California section of the American Chemical Society, among others, and was to become in 1973 President of the American Physical Society, a singular honor for a chemist.

At home again, Maria worked at research and teaching, contributed to the further development of the Mayer-Jensen nucleus, and followed its evolution as it changed from an onion to a cigar, at least in the heavy nuclei. She gardened a little, having learned to her delight that the orchids that needed a greenhouse in Chicago flourished out of doors in La Jolla; she still entertained. On Joe's sixtieth birthday, only months after their return from Stockholm, twenty-four guests were invited to a stately dinner of chateaubriand and pommes soufflées, created by the cook the Mayers had brought with them from Chicago, and served with the full complement of silver, crystal and damask, the whole having been planned, shopped for and supervised by Maria.

Joe's work in theoretical chemistry had become increasingly abstruse and philosophical, but as a teacher and seminar leader he had not changed since the Chicago days; one of his former students recalled his method as "an exciting, at times a frightening, experience, and a great way to learn." By the late 1960s Peter had become an assistant professor of economics, and therefore the eighth generation of university professor in the family. And Marianne was now the mother of a little girl with whom she stayed home, as she had always intended. The child's chatter drove her up the wall, she said, and it was entirely the right decision for her all the same. Once her daughter was in school, Marianne meant to return to work, but to some part-time job that would always allow her to be home when her child came home. It was a decision she had reached along with her husband, for they both felt their lives would be more satisfying if she had something besides household trivia and a little girl's daily schedule to discuss with him at night. What she did not want was a profession, an engrossing, demanding profession.

Joe felt "they were both fine people, Peter and Marianne." Like her husband, Maria was thoroughly pleased with her children, yet she remained somewhat puzzled by them, puzzled as to why Peter had given up science, and why Marianne never wanted serious work of her own

—"perhaps because her husband never expected it." She herself could not have continued in science without Joe's encouragement, she said, and she might well have been right: if it is hard to think of Maria Mayer without science, it is impossible to think of her without Joe; one cannot picture her as a woman alone, entirely devoted to physics like Lise Meitner, or the widowed Marie Curie. Maria Mayer died in February of 1972, having been spared the necessity of living on without her husband, and concerned to the last about burdening him with an invalid wife.

As to why there are so few women in physics—in any of the sciences —Maria herself had no idea; she never had a woman graduate student of her own, and saw how few there were at any of the universities where she worked, perhaps one a year. It's just not something girls are used to thinking about, she believed; they want to do what they have seen their mothers do, keep house, that kind of thing. Yet Maria's mother kept house, and Maria wanted something different; Marianne had the model of Maria before her yet turned away from science. Both the daughters of Katherine Rice, Maria's friend at Johns Hopkins who was first a biochemist, then a psychiatrist, had the model of a scientist mother, yet each of them made it known quite early that she would never have a career in science or in anything else; like Marianne, they meant to become housewives and they did.

The psychiatrist Erik Erikson, in examining the differences between the ways girls and boys think, has advanced with the greatest delicacy the possibility that there are differences not necessarily caused by environment. Differences, for example, relating to the way children are inclined to perceive the world—"the girls emphasized inner and the boys outer space." Each sex, Erikson suggests, is strongly influenced by the body, by the structure of bone and muscle within which it lives; and the tone of the muscular system as well as the entire arrangement and purpose of the body is clearly different, known to be different, from birth. "The question is, what *is* really surprising about this?" he asks. Some women have found it surprising all the same; at a conference on women and the scientific professions a gifted young woman biologist asked, "Should we perhaps conclude that women might be set to work on the interior of the atom—but not on a subject like the emission of radioactivity? Then perhaps Marie Curie might not have made her discoveries."

The insights offered by Erikson and many others who agree with him go a long way toward explaining the scarcity of women in the scientific professions. For example, it is believed that women look for relationships, intellectually; that they pay particular attention to the context, to the whole picture, while men try to find a single, simple unity—in other words that men are analytic, women holistic. And as Margaret Mead points out: "Almost the whole of the intellectual apparatus with which college students are expected to operate was devised by men. . . . the imagery and figures of speech that are most meaningful for males are opaque and difficult, like a strange tongue, to the girls." Furthermore, if the most creative scientists have been to some degree rebels and imps, tearing down part of the existing structure to replace it with one of their own, it is not strange that there have been few women in their ranks, for women have usually been so brought up that the rebel in them is not cherished; there is even some question as to whether this too might not be biological, whether a biological awareness of the need for physical stability might not be experienced by women so that creative destruction holds less appeal for them. It is interesting to note, here, that Maria Mayer's father held a different philosophy, encouraging adventure and risk-taking in his daughter, and believing that the mother, who is sensible and cautious, is her child's natural enemy.

According to the sociologist Jessie Bernard, "most male scientists would rather be known for being first than for being modest. This is less likely to be the case with women. . . . If . . . acceptance of new ideas is difficult when they are presented by aggressive, ambitious, competitive men, it is even more difficult when they are presented by women, whom we are not accustomed to seeing in the idea-man or instrumental role. We are simply not used to looking for innovation and originality from women." Such reservations might have been going through Maria Mayer's unconscious mind when she should have been writing her long shell model papers; such reservations may go through the minds of women students of the sciences early in their careers, when they must make long-term decisions about how hard to work, how high to aim—whether they mean to teach or do research, to do research as part of a large team or in a more individual way, to choose the daring problem or the routine one.

The subject of daring—risk-taking—is one that must enter into any examination of women and achievement, for to achieve greatly one must always risk greatly. But this is especially true in science, or has been especially true until the quite recent past. Women tend to draw back from risk-taking; when they are daring, it is more likely to be for the sake of others than for the competitive, self-fulfilling drives, the drives that power science. The following passage by the racing driver Stirling Moss has to do with the difference between women drivers and men, but it captures some of the essential difference between women scientists and men:

I do think that no woman could become a truly great racing driver. . . . I don't believe that lack of physical strength, ability to hold the car, that sort of thing, keeps women from driving as well as men. My sister Pat, for example, certainly has ample physical energy to do three hundred miles flat out in a Grand Prix car. I doubt that Pat would even have to go into her reserve. It isn't lack of strength. It's just that women are almost never *personally* competitive. . . . In rallying . . . there are women who are very good indeed; there are women who will beat all but the top men, and beat them easily. But rallying is running against the clock, and women do that sort of thing very well. Also, rallying makes much of minute detail, and women are good at that, too. . . . But women will not compete, as the Spanish say, *mano a mano*, hand to hand. They will not go into really brutal competition with another person; they will not, or they cannot, as a rule, reach the highest plane of the competitive urge, where a man will say: "Right, now I've had enough of hanging about, now I'll have a go, now we're going to separate the men from the boys here." No, they won't do that. Mind, I'm not saying that's wrong, or a bad thing, I'm just saying that's the way it is. When someone says that if women ran the governments of the world there'd be no wars, no argument comes from *my* corner of the room. It's probably true.

Scientists, although competitive, are certainly less so than racing drivers, but if we discount that part of Moss's explanation, or partly discount it, and take his general meaning to be that women drivers who are very, very good fail to beat the best men because they will not ultimately give it all they've got—and sometimes more than they've got —the picture is fairly accurate. Men drivers reach a point where they drive to win if it kills them; women don't. Men scientists, dedicated, competitive, immersed in work they consider more exciting, more important than any other aspect of their lives, have often behaved like racing drivers, willing to pay any price for achievement. If they are hard on themselves in the process, hard on others such as their wives and children, it has all been for science, an idealized and glorious goal transcending any one individual life. And one reason scientists idealize Science, it has been suggested, is in order that they may pursue their work without feeling selfish about it: it's not for oneself, they say in effect, but for that which is greater, more beautiful, longer living, purer than the self.

But women have been reluctant to pay the price demanded for greatness in science. Therefore the best women have done better than all but the very best men, but the best men are the ones who become the hero figures—and all scientists are hero worshipers—so that young women who might have entered scientific careers have had few models of their own sex to inspire them.

Perhaps this is about to change. Joe Mayer thinks it will; he is by nature an optimist and in any case prejudiced in favor of women scientists, so one wonders how objective he is. Perhaps there is also some wishful thinking in his conclusions, since Joe has had a number of women graduate students, and enjoyed every minute of it. "He is . . . one of the few people who really believes women have a place in science and has often protected girl graduate students from the prejudices of his misogynist colleagues," according to a former student of Joe's. His prejudices aside, Joe Mayer believes that women in science are becoming increasingly acceptable to men, not only to men professors but to husbands and prospective husbands. And he may be right. For in the years following the Second World War, a series of changes in how science is done have been remarked by a number of observers. Research has grown increasingly costly and more intricate, and the more intricate the equipment the larger the team required to run it, so that much of the research in, for example, high energy nuclear physics is done by great teams rather than one, two or three individuals. This teamwork science causes a certain amount of consternation among the older scientists, brought up to honor the dedicated, individualistic approach. They speak scornfully of the "gentleman scientist" who works from nine to five, and then turns to other interests, to literature, music, art. He takes the cultivation of his hobbies or avocations seriously, and deliberately takes time away from his work for his other pursuits, which are means in themselves, not, as they were to earlier generations, ways of refreshing the mind and spirit so that one could return to the one true mistress, Science.

"Undeniably . . . the technical community itself lost something when it got rich. Sciences which were once little enclaves of noble monomania are diluted with competent men building honorable conventional careers," according to the editors of *Science and Technology*. But if we are already witnessing the decline of the noble monomania that was scientific research at its most creative, perhaps we will be rewarded by a world in which there will be increasing opportunity for women, who have been unwilling to give themselves utterly and wholly to science, but have been willing, indeed eager for honorable careers.

But Maria Mayer's career took place in another context; her teachers were the men who created the atom and found out its laws, and she herself belonged to the first generation that followed them, when physics demanded complete devotion. Her success remains, in a sense, mysterious. For Maria was almost always a part-time scientist; she started working full-time on research during her Chicago years, when she was learning nuclear physics and returning to physics from chemistry—yet even this is extraordinary, for a physicist rarely leaves his field in the hope of returning, partly because there is too much to be relearned, partly because the emotional tone has been damaged, one has spread oneself thin, and how can all the forces be refocused over again? Much of this is myth, of course, yet scientists are firm believers in the mythology of science, and Maria had as her heroes men who had worked time-and-a-half, all their lives, at physics—men like James Franck, who would not stop thinking about physics even if it endangered his life.

Nevertheless, when she returned to work in a much-altered field after an absence of many years, Maria Mayer achieved a singular success in a short time, and against great odds; apparently it was also something of a mystery to Maria, who said much of it was due to having Joe for a husband. In Stockholm, as she waited on the platform to receive her medal, she thought of her father, and of Max Born. These three, father, teacher and husband, were the men who had loved and encouraged her, each in his own individual way, expecting the best, ready to be disappointed with anything less. Maria Mayer's final secret may be that she wanted so badly to give what she thought they wanted.

Notes

Introduction

page

xiv Graves quote: Robert Graves, *The Greek Myths* (Harmondsworth, England: 1955), p. 18. See also Mary Jane Sherfey, M. D., "A Theory on Female Sexuality" in *Sisterhood Is Powerful* by Robin Morgan (New York: Random House, 1970), p. 220.

xvi The wife of a Nobel laureate: Frieda Urey.

Margaret Sanger

Excerpts from material in the Sophia Smith Collection have not been footnoted.

3 "That beast of a man": Emily Taft Douglas, *Margaret Sanger: Pioneer of the Future* (New York: Holt, Rinehart & Winston, 1970), p. 16.

3 "passing through Corning at night": Lawrence Lader, *The Margaret Sanger Story and the Fight for Birth Control* (Garden City, L.I.: Doubleday, 1955), p. 16.

4 Margaret once told a friend: private communication.

4 "Though never very strong": Margaret Sanger, *My Fight for Birth Control* (New York: Farrar & Rinehart, 1931), p. 10.

5 "Every day, even when going to work": Margaret Sanger, *Margaret Sanger: An Autobiography* (New York: W. W. Norton, 1938), p. 16.

5   Her mother's carrying the responsibilities of the family: Sanger, *My Fight*, p. 11.

5   "The fathers of the small families": Sanger, *Autobiography*, p. 28.

5   "We, the children of poorer parents": Sanger, *My Fight*, p. 9.

5   "My father must have realized": *ibid.*, p. 19.

6   "blind, imperious, driving": Margaret Sanger, *Happiness in Marriage* (New York: Blue Ribbon Books, 1926), p. 39.

6   "The only memory I have": Sanger, *My Fight*, p. 11.

6   The "two Me's": Sanger, *Autobiography*, p. 25.

7   Need to be alone; "cosmic forces": Douglas, *op. cit.*, p. 250.

8   "monster father": Sanger, *My Fight*, p. 29.

10   "He took care of me": Sanger, *Autobiography*, pp. 61–62.

11   "I know one charming young man": Sanger, *Happiness*, p. 229.

11   Hoppe quotes: private communication.

11   One astute observer: private communication.

12   "You go ahead and finish": Sanger, *Autobiography*, p. 66.

13   "Adolescence of the Twentieth Century": Max Eastman, *Enjoyment of Living* (New York: Harper & Row, 1948), p. 423.

14   "some of the nicest girls": Sanger, *Autobiography*, p. 45.

14   Eastman quote: Eastman, *op. cit.*, p. 523.

14   "the Madonna type": Mabel Dodge Luhan, *Movers and Shakers* (New York: Harcourt, Brace, 1936), p. 69.

15   Kennedy quote: David M. Kennedy, *Birth Control in America: The Career of Margaret Sanger* (New Haven: Yale University Press, 1970), p. 12.

18   Douglas quote about Peggy: Douglas, *op. cit.*, p. 37.

18   "three lovely, healthy children": Sanger, *My Fight*, p. 58.

18   "Peggy, the most independent": *ibid.*, p. 20.

19   "Ignorance and neglect": *ibid.*, p. 48.

19   "They claimed my thoughts": *ibid.*, p. 50.

20   "a kindly man": Sanger, *Autobiography*, p. 91.

20   "As I stood there": *ibid.*, p. 92.

21   Kennedy quote: Kennedy, *op. cit.*, pp. 17–18.

22   "The pursuit of my quest": Sanger, *Autobiography*, p. 94.

22   "with the proprietor": *ibid.*, p. 216.

23   "I wanted to bind": Sanger, *My Fight*, p. 58.

23 Bill Haywood quotes: *ibid.*, p. 60.
24 "together with the savings": Sanger, *My Fight*, p. 63.
24 "After I had obtained": *ibid.*, p. 73.
25 "I knew something must": Sanger, *Autobiography*, p. 106.
25 For contents of *The Woman Rebel* see: Mary Ware Dennett, *Birth Control Laws* (New York: F. H. Hitchcock, 1926), pp. 168–169.
26 "I have no apologies": Sanger, *My Fight*, p. 80.
26 "extraordinary results": Sanger, *Autobiography*, p. 111.
29 "a mutual and satisfied": Kennedy, *op. cit.*, p. 25.
29 "Upon the complete realization": Sanger, *Happiness*, p. 119.
30 Visit of two federal agents: Sanger, *Autobiography*, p. 115.
30 "I had had no notice": Sanger, *ibid.*, p. 117.
31 "I wanted no one to influence": Sanger, *My Fight*, p. 93.
32 "compelled me to leave": Sanger, *Autobiography*, p. 120.
33 "on the appointed afternoon": Kennedy, *op. cit.*, p. 28.
35 "and we sat down before the humming flame": Sanger, *Autobiography*, p. 134.
35 "I had rarely known": Havelock Ellis, *My Life: Autobiography of Havelock Ellis* (Boston: Houghton Mifflin, 1939), p. 520.
35 "I have begun this new year": Arthur Calder-Marshall, *The Sage of Sex, A Life of Havelock Ellis* (New York: G. P. Putnam's Sons, 1959), p. 198.
35 Today this manic depression: *ibid.*, p. 125.
36 "for I had no prejudices": Ellis, *op. cit.*, pp. 309–310.
37 "That this new friendship": *ibid.*, p. 521.
38 "I am never reconciled": *ibid.*, p. 631.
39 "Ellis has been called": Sanger, *Autobiography*, pp. 140–141.
39 "what Christians called God": Calder-Marshall, *op. cit.*, p. 73.
40 "Although the Dutch League": Sanger, *Autobiography*, p. 148.
41 Bill's letter to Margaret, from the Sophia Smith Collection, appears in considerably more sedate form in Lader, *op. cit.*, pp. 80–81, and in *My Fight*, pp. 120–121.
43 "five hundred short extracts": Lader, *op. cit.*, p. 80.
44 Kennedy quote: Kennedy, *op. cit.*, p. 34.
44 "with lights dimmed": Sanger, *My Fight*, p. 122.
44 "a queer sense of presentiment": *ibid.*, p. 122.

44   "It seemed strange to be greeted": Sanger, *Autobiography*, p. 180.

46   "inability to work with others": Preface to *Margaret Sanger: An Autobiography* (Elmsford, N.Y.: Maxwell Reprint Co., 1970), p. ix.

46   "Emma Goldman . . . belatedly": Sanger, *Autobiography*, p. 207.

47   "As I looked over the situation": Sanger, *My Fight*, p. 126.

47   The account of Peggy's death: Sanger, *Autobiography*, p. 181.

48   "This fresh contact": Sanger, *My Fight*, p. 128.

48   "the far off voices"; "as the ideas I have sought": *ibid.*, pp. 130–131.

48   Quote from *New York Sun: ibid.*, p. 138.

49   "All my friends regarded": Sanger, *Autobiography*, p. 190.

51   John Haynes Holmes quote: Douglas, *op. cit.*, p. 116.

52   "I decided to open": Sanger, *Autobiography*, pp. 211–212.

52   "a quiet, intense young woman": Douglas, *op. cit.*, p. 100.

52   "a hive of futile"; "open a birth control clinic": Sanger, *My Fight*, pp. 153–154.

53   Mabel Dodge quote: Luhan, *op. cit.*, pp. 69–71.

54   "Would the women come?": Sanger, *Autobiography*, p. 216.

54   "lead to the repeal of all laws": Lader, *op. cit.*, p. 117.

54   "It makes little difference": Sanger, *My Fight*, p. 165.

55   "thin and emaciated": Sanger, *Autobiography*, p. 233.

56   "for reflection"; "Behind them at the upper windows": *ibid.*, pp. 250–251.

57   Hoppe quote: private communication.

58   "Desire is generated in the pursuit": Sanger, *Happiness*, p. 60.

58   "impressive result of our imprisonment": Sanger, *My Fight*, p. 189.

59   "the mothers of the child laborers": *ibid.*, pp. 190–191.

60   "At times the homesickness": Sanger, *Autobiography*, p. 266.

62   "From 1920 on": *ibid.*, p. 272.

63   Lader quote about Wantley: Lader, *op. cit.*, p. 160.

66   "what particularly aroused me": Sanger, *My Fight*, p. 219.

66   "The seventh child": *ibid.*, p. 221.

67   Dennet quote: Dennett, *op. cit.*, p. 201.

67   Webb quote: Beatrice Webb, *Our Partnership* (New York: Long-
     mans, Green, 1948), p. 360.
67   "An army of star writers": Sanger, *My Fight*, pp. 244–245.
68   Birth control as a magical cure: Peter Fryer, *The Birth Controllers*
     (New York: Stein & Day, 1966), p. 216.
68   "Some lives drift": Sanger, *My Fight*, p. 3.
70   Douglas quote: Douglas, *op. cit.*, p. 187.
74   One of the most popular and long-lived books: Hannah Mayer
     Stone and Abraham Stone, *A Marriage Manual: A Practical
     Guidebook to Sex and Marriage* (New York: Simon &
     Schuster, 1935).
76   "Side by side with the clinic": Sanger, *Autobiography*, p. 369.
76   "He was in a frivolously": Sanger, *My Fight*, p. 285.
77   In later years Huxley remembered: tape-recorded interview with
     Sir Julian Huxley conducted by Martha Stuart; files of Planned
     Parenthood.
77   "If you could hear the way he speaks": Françoise Delisle, *Friend-
     ship's Odyssey* (London: William Heinemann, 1946), p. 362.
77   "was embarking on having two lovers": *ibid.*, p. 366.
77   "I know what a poor sort": *ibid.*, p. 370.
78   "It had been a great occasion": Sanger, *My Fight*, pp. 293–294.
83   "Well, we'll just cross these off": Sanger, *Autobiography*, p. 385.
84   "The whole company rose": Lader, *op. cit.*, p. 245.
86   "To me, this cause": Sanger, *My Fight*, pp. 330–331.
88   "the telephone in my apartment": Sanger, *Autobiography*,
     p. 402.
89   a profile of Margaret: Helena Huntington Smith, "They Were
     Eleven," *The New Yorker*, July 25, 1930.
93   "the whole subject"; "if I were the Creator": Dennet, *op. cit.*,
     p. 178.
93   "and tell him how many children": Lader, *op. cit.*, p. 273.
93   Kennedy quote: Kennedy, *op. cit.*, p. 267.
94   Coughlin quote: Douglas, *op. cit.*, p. 219.
95   "For the first time the Senate": Sanger, *Autobiography*, pp. 426–
     427.
96   "to see for myself": Sanger, *Autobiography*, p. 433.

97   "I rushed up from Washington": *ibid.*, p. 433.

97   "the demands of history": Lader, *op. cit.*, p. 283.

101   "would be of tremendous value"; "after listening to him": Sanger, *Autobiography*, p. 470.

104   "and had added that a doctor": *ibid.*, p. 427.

104   Dickinson telegram: Kennedy, *op. cit.*, p. 217.

105   "those whose interest it is": *ibid.*, p. 257.

106   Ernst quote: tape-recorded interview conducted by Martha Stuart; files of Planned Parenthood.

110   Margaret onstage at New Delhi: *ibid.*

111   Rock quotes: *ibid.*

Edna St. Vincent Millay

Material from *Letters of Edna St. Vincent Millay* has not been footnoted, except for those few passages the reader might not readily identify as originating in the letters. Excerpts from Millay's poems have not been footnoted; whether quoted or named, they will be found in *Collected Poems*, with the exception of the five sonnets, "From a Town in a State of Siege," which appear in *Huntsman, What Quarry?*

118   Millay describes her father's departure: Alan Ross Macdougall, *Letters of Edna St. Vincent Millay* (New York: Harper & Row, 1952), p. 176.

118   Cora Millay quotes: Elizabeth Breuer, "Mother of Poets," *Pictorial Review*, March 1930.

119   Cora Millay quotes: *ibid.*

120   Dell quote: Floyd Dell, *Homecoming: An Autobiography* (New York: Farrar & Rinehart, 1933), p. 305.

122   Wilson quote: Edmund Wilson, *The Shores of Light: A Literary Chronicle of the Twenties and Thirties* (New York: Farrar, Straus, 1952), p. 686.

123   Cora Millay quote: Breuer, *op. cit.*

124 Wilson quote, "a little old woman with spectacles": *Shores*, p. 760.

124 A girlhood friend of the Millays': Ethel Knight Fisher, "Edna St. Vincent Millay's Youth," *St. Nicholas Magazine*, September 1936 and October 1936.

125 Edmund Wilson remarked on: *Shores*, p. 755.

126 Langner quote: Lawrence Langner, *The Magic Curtain* (New York: E. P. Dutton, 1951), p. 121.

127 "And before she had finally gone": Edmund Wilson, *I Thought of Daisy* (New York: Charles Scribner's Sons, 1929), p. 59. Set in the Greenwich Village of the twenties and autobiographical in character, *I Thought of Daisy* describes a woman poet closely modeled on Edna Millay—so closely that I have taken her as a faithful portrait, although this was not Wilson's precise intention. He refers to the novel and Edna's part in it in *The Shores of Light*, p. 790. He had sent her a copy of the manuscript: "I thought that she had been offended by a character that was partly derived from her," and adds that she was not offended at all, but "had made careful and copious notes and had good-naturedly undertaken to re-write in what she thought a more appropriate vein the speeches assigned to the character partly based on herself."

127 "mediocre manuscripts": Macdougall, *op. cit.*, p. 17.

129 Wilson quote: *Shores*, p. 758.

129 For an exploration of the psychoanalytic view of claustrophobia see Bertram D. Lewin, "Claustrophobia," *Psychoanalytic Quarterly*, vol. 3, 1935. On page 227: "The psychoanalysis of numerous dreams and of neurotic claustrophobia explains the fear of being buried alive as the transformation into dread of the wish to return to the womb."

130 Yeats quote: Miriam Gurko, *Restless Spirit: The Life of Edna St. Vincent Millay* (New York: Thomas Y. Crowell Co., 1962), p. 43.

130 Orrick Johns quote: Macdougall, *op. cit.*, p. 18.

131 Rittenhouse quote: Jessie B. Rittenhouse, *My House of Life* (Boston: Houghton Mifflin, 1934), p. 252.

132   Ficke-Bynner letter, Macdougall, *op. cit.*, p. 18.

133   MacCracken, "poets at college": Jean Gould, *The Poet and Her Book: A Biography of Edna St. Vincent Millay* (New York: Dodd, Mead, 1969), p. 53.

133   "I know my work has not been very good yet": Florence G. Jenney, "As I Remember Her," *Russell Sage College Alumnae Quarterly,* Winter 1951.

134   Song and drama at Vassar: Henry Noble MacCracken, *The Hickory Limb* (New York: Charles Scribner's Sons, 1950), pp. 76–77.

134   Haight quotes: Elizabeth H. Haight, "Vincent at Vassar," *Vassar Alumnae Magazine,* May 1951.

135   Haight on May Day incident and petition: *ibid.*

138   "hardly large enough": Floyd Dell, "Edna St. Vincent Millay," *The Literary Spotlight* (New York: George H. Doran, 1924), p. 87.

139   Cowley quote: Malcolm Cowley, *Exile's Return* (New York: Viking Press, 1951), p. 72.

139   Cowley quote: *ibid.*, p. 69.

141   Dell quotes: Floyd Dell, "My Friend Edna St. Vincent Millay," *Mark Twain Journal,* 12 (Spring 1964).

141   Dell as Millay's first lover: see Ficke's sonnet "Questioning a Lady," *Selected Poems* (New York: George H. Doran, 1926); see also Norman A. Brittin, *Edna St. Vincent Millay* (New York: Twayne Publishers, 1967), p. 39.

142   Wilson quote: *Shores,* p. 759.

142   "There began for us": Dell, "My Friend Edna St. Vincent Millay."

142   Ficke poem: "Questioning a Lady."

143   Haight quote: Haight, *op. cit.*

144   Ficke poem: "Fantasy for a Charming Friend," *Selected Poems.*

145   Langner quote: Langner, *op. cit.*, p. 110.

146   "I find myself suddenly famous": Rittenhouse, *op. cit.*, p. 254.

147   Rittenhouse quote: *ibid.*, p. 253.

147   "some bright batik": Wilson, *Shores,* p. 748.

147 Wilson on Millay's intensity and neurotic character: *ibid.*, p. 756.

148 "There was something of awful drama": *ibid.*, p. 752.

148 "I'm the druggist": Wilson, *I Thought of Daisy*, p. 63.

149 Millay's preoccupation with death: *ibid.*, p. 64.

150 Sheean quote: Vincent Sheean, *The Indigo Bunting: A Memoir of Edna St. Vincent Millay* (New York: Harper & Row, 1951), p. 109.

150 "I remarked that her ex-admirers": Wilson, *Shores*, p. 769.

158 Untermeyer quote: Harriet Monroe, *A Poet's Life* (New York: Macmillan, 1938), p. 394.

159 "a little schoolgirlish": Max Eastman, *Great Companions: Critical Memoirs of Some Famous Friends* (New York: Farrar, Straus and Cudahy, 1959), p. 78.

159 One biographer: Gould, *op. cit.*, pp. 156–157.

160 Dell quote: *Homecoming*, p. 308.

162 Popular novel: Newton Stevens, *An American Suffragette* (New York: W. Rickey & Co., 1911).

162 FPA quote: Franklin P. Adams, *The Diary of Our Own Samuel Pepys* (New York: Simon & Schuster, 1935), p. 72.

162 Eastman's first meeting with Boissevain: Max Eastman, *Enjoyment of Living* (New York: Harper & Row, 1948), pp. 521–522.

163 For an account of the *cause célèbre* and the last days of Inez Milholland see: Frank Marshall White, "Where There Are Women There's a Way," *Good Housekeeping*, August 1918.

163 Inez Milholland's last words: Eastman, *Enjoyment of Living*, p. 572.

164 Eastman on Boissevain's "deals": Max Eastman, *Love and Revolution* (New York: Random House, 1964), p. 80.

164 "a strain of something feminine": Eastman, *Enjoyment*, p. 521.

164 "With no particular talent": Wilson, *Shores*, p. 771.

166 "I would rather have the right": Dell, *Homecoming*, p. 303.

167 Max Eastman once said: from an interview with Eastman at Martha's Vineyard in 1968, a few months before his death.

168 The story of the may baskets: from an interview with Leonie Adams in Seattle, 1969.

168 FPA quote: Adams, *op. cit.*, p. 520.

169 Boissevain's account of housekeeping arrangements at Steepletop: Alan Ross Macdougall, "Husband of a Genius," *Delineator*, October 1934.

169 "nursed her like a mother": Dell, *Homecoming*, p. 308.

169 Eastman said another time: Eastman interview.

171 Millay's first biographer: Elizabeth Atkins, *Edna St. Vincent Millay and Her Times* (Chicago: the University of Chicago Press, 1936), p. 200.

171 Boissevain to Macdougall: "Husband of a Genius."

173 "hotel for birds": Sheean, *op. cit.*, p. 6.

174 Boissevain described by Alyse Gregory, the wife of Powys: *Letters of Llewelyn Powys* (London: John Lane, The Bodley Head, 1943), p. 33.

176 Eastman's account of the cocktail party: Eastman, *Great Companions*, p. 90.

178 Quote from the *Musical Observer:* Mary F. Watkins, "Operatic Events of the Past Month," *The Musical Observer*, April 1927.

178 "Mr. Taylor himself could be observed": *ibid.*

178 When the final curtain went down: *ibid.*

179 "But if we must have opera": *ibid.*

179 The visit at the Vanderbilt Hotel: Wilson, *Shores*, p. 772.

180 Deems Taylor quote: "Edna St. Vincent Millay, 1892–1950," *Commemorative Tributes of the American Academy of Arts and Letters, 1942–1951* (New York, 1951), p. 106.

180 Wilson's visit to Steepletop: *Shores*, pp. 775–776.

181 Wilson's second visit a year later: *Shores*, p. 777.

182 Ficke poem: *op. cit.*

182 Boissevain to Macdougall: "Husband of a Genius."

183 Wilson on Millay's being childless: *Shores*, p. 778.

183 Norma Millay on her sister's being childless: from an interview with Norma Millay, Steepletop, the fall of 1968.

183 "when she had apparently spent weeks": Wilson, *Shores*, p. 778.

185 For Millay's role in the Sacco-Vanzetti demonstrations see: Gurko, *op. cit.*, pp. 178–187.

186 Boissevain described by Alyse Gregory: Powys, *op. cit.*, p. 33.

187 Boissevain's quote, marriage as an adventure: Macdougall, "Husband of a Genius."

187 Eastman on the Boissevains' drinking: *Great Companions*, pp. 102–103.

188 Millay on housekeeping: Elizabeth Breuer, "Edna St. Vincent Millay," *Pictorial Review*, November 1931.

189 Eastman thought perhaps: Max Eastman, "A Passing Fashion," *The Nation*, December 5, 1928, p. 628.

191 Humphries quote: Rolfe Humphries, "Miss Millay as Artist," *The Nation*, December 20, 1941.

192 A contemporary critic: Genevieve Taggard, "A Woman's Anatomy of Love," *New York Herald Tribune Books*, April 19, 1931.

193 Wilson on "Fatal Interview": *Shores*, p. 779.

193 Boissevain on monogamous marriage: Macdougall, "Husband of a Genius."

194 when Harper, many years later: Macdougal, *Letters*, p. 348.

194 Wilson quote: *Shores*, p. 774.

195 For an extended discussion of psychoanalytic theories involving the sea, water, etc., see Sandor Ferenczi, M.D., *Thalassa: A Theory of Genitality*, (New York: W. W. Norton, 1969. Originally copyright by the Psychoanalytic Quarterly, Inc., 1938). See especially p. 48.

195 Boissevain to Gene Saxton: undated letter in Norma Millay's files at Harper & Row.

196 Jenney quote: *op. cit.*

198 Boissevain to Saxton: October 31, 1934, in Norma Millay's files at Harper & Row.

201 Boissevain to Saxton: undated, in Norma Millay's files at Harper & Row.

201 Telegram, Millay to Saxton: March 17, 1936, Norma Millay's files at Harper & Row.

201 Boissevain to Saxton: undated, Norma Millay's files at Harper & Row.

203 Boissevain to Alyse Gregory: Macdougall, *Letters*, p. 282.

205 "a true conscientious objector": Grace Hamilton King, "The Development of the Social Consciousness of Edna St. Vincent Millay as Manifested in Her Poetry" (New York: New York University, 1943). Unpublished Ph.D. dissertation.

205 She told a reporter: Brittin, *op. cit.*, p. 139.

205 A friendly critic: Thomas Caldecott Chubb, "Shelley Grown Old," *North American Review,* Spring 1938.

208 Eastman quote: *Great Companions,* p. 102.

208 Sinclair quotes: Upton Sinclair, *A Cup of Fury* (New York: Channel Press, 1956), p. 90.

210 "Miss Millay, who has been ill": *New York Herald Tribune,* October 25, 1939, p. 11.

211 "After I am dead and gone": King, *op. cit.*

212 Wilson quote: *Shores,* p. 779.

214 In 1940 she wrote a poem: "The President with a Candidate's Face," *New York Herald Tribune,* November 3, 1940, sec. II, p. 1.

214 Sheean quote: *op. cit.*, p. 59.

215 Untermeyer quote: Jean Starr Untermeyer, *Private Collection* (New York: Alfred A. Knopf, 1965), p. 72.

217 Sheean quote: *op. cit.*, pp. 35–36.

219 "just like the old days": Sheean, *op. cit.*, p. 11.

220 The Wilsons' visit to Steepletop: Wilson, *Shores,* pp. 784–788.

221 Dorothy Thompson's visit to Steepletop: Gould, *op. cit.*, p. 272.

221 "the room became so charged": Wilson, *Shores,* pp. 787–788.

222 Canfield quote: Cass Canfield, *The Publishing Experience* (Philadelphia: University of Pennsylvania Press, 1969), p. 10.

223 She told Mary Herron: Macdougall, *Letters,* p. 368.

224 Norma believed: Introduction to *Collected Lyrics of Edna St. Vincent Millay* (New York: Washington Square Press, 1959), p. xii.

224 Ciardi quote: "Edna St. Vincent Millay: A Figure of Passionate Living," *Saturday Review,* November 11, 1950.

226 Ficke poem: *The Secret and Other Poems* (New York: Doubleday Doran, 1936).

Maria Goeppert-Mayer

Much of the material for the Mayer section came from my interviews with Joseph and Maria Mayer, and is not footnoted, nor are excerpts from Maria's unpublished letters to her mother.

233 A physicist who had known the Mayers: private communication.

233 Wilson quote: Mitchell Wilson, "How Nobel Prize-Winners Get That Way: Science Laureates," *Atlantic Monthly*, December 1969.

235 Wilson quote: *ibid.*

239 Heine quote: Heinrich Heine, *The Sea and The Hills* (Boston: Chapman & Grimes, 1946), pp. 19–20.

239 Heine quote: *ibid.*, p. 21.

240 The group that suffered from it: Anne Roe, *The Making of a Scientist* (New York: Dodd, Mead, 1952), p. 87.

240 Eiduson quotes: Bernice Eiduson, *Scientists: Their Psychological World* (New York: Basic Books, 1962), pp. 47–50.

242 "It somehow was never discussed": *Les Prix Nobel en 1963* (Stockholm: The Nobel Foundation, 1964).

243 Fermi quote: Laura Fermi, *Atoms in the Family* (Chicago: University of Chicago Press, 1954), p. 31.

243 The Abitur: tape-recorded interview with Maria Mayer conducted by Thomas S. Kuhn, February 1962. Archive for History of Quantum Physics, American Philosophical Society Library.

244 "academically speaking": Barbara Lovett Cline, *The Questioners: Physicists and the Quantum Theory* (New York: Thomas Y. Crowell, 1965), p. 176.

245 Hilbert quote: Robert Jungk, *Brighter Than a Thousand Suns* (New York: Harcourt, Brace, 1958), p. 14.

245 Franck goes to Hilbert's colloquium: tape-recorded interview with James Franck and Hertha Sponer conducted by Thomas S. Kuhn and Maria Mayer, July 1962. Archive for History of Quantum Physics, American Philosophical Society Library.

246 Fermi quote: Fermi, *op. cit.*, p. 31.

247 "Experience and knowledge": Jungk, *op. cit.*, p. 18.

248 Jordan quote: Jungk, *op. cit.*, p. 9.

248 Nernst quote: Jungk, *op. cit.*, p. 8.

249 Sabin quote: Jessie Bernard, *Academic Women* (University Park: Pennsylvania State University Press, 1964), pp. 306–307.

250 Emmy Noether's position at Göttingen: see "Men of Modern Mathematics: A history chart of mathematics from 1000 to 1900," produced for IBM by the office of Charles Eames; biographies and mathematical notes by Ray Redheffer. Redheffer's statement about Noether was corroborated in a private communication to me by Hel Braun, Department of Mathematics, University of Hamburg.

253 Weisskopf quote: private communication.

253 A young American physicist: private communication.

254 Pohl quote: tape-recorded interview with Maria Mayer conducted by Thomas S. Kuhn, February 1962, *op. cit.*

254 Heine quote: *op. cit.*, p. 23.

254 Hilbert quote: William H. Cropper, *The Quantum Physicists* (London, Toronto, New York: Oxford University Press, 1970), p. 113.

255 Fermi quote: Laura Fermi, *Illustrious Immigrants: The Intellectual Migration from Europe, 1930/41* (Chicago: University of Chicago Press, 1968), p. 53.

256 Gay quote: Donald Fleming and Bernard Bailyn, editors, *The Intellectual Migration: Europe and America, 1930–1960* (Cambridge, Mass.: Harvard University Press, Belknap Press, 1969), p. 12.

257 Eiduson quote: Eiduson, *op. cit.*, p. 22.

257 Alice Rossi speaks: Jacquelyn A. Mattfield and Carol Van Aken, eds., *Women and the Scientific Professions* (Cambridge, Mass.: MIT Press, 1965), p. 92.

259 Weisskopf quote: private communication.

262 Franck on Ehrenfest: tape-recorded interview with James Franck and Hertha Sponer, conducted by Thomas S. Kuhn, 1962, *op. cit.*

263 "at the banks of the Missouri": her destination, Baltimore, is nowhere near the Missouri River.

264 Wigner on Maria's thesis: see *Physics Today*, May 1972, p. 72.

266 To spend the summer at Michigan: "The annual University of

Michigan summer school for theoretical physics was one of the special attractions for Europeans and Americans," according to Charles Weiner, "Physics in the Great Depression," *Physics Today*, October 1970. Begun in 1927, it was part of a "conscious effort to strengthen physics departments and . . . produced a unique and vigorous physics enterprise in the U.S."

268   Fermi quote: Fermi, *Atoms*, pp. 80–81.

268   Laura Fermi remembered Maria: Fermi, *Illustrious Immigrants*, p. 204.

269   Rice quote: private communication.

271   Franck on R. W. Wood: tape-recorded interview with James Franck conducted by Thomas S. Kuhn, July 1962, *op. cit.*

272   Honeymooning in Yellowstone: there are innumerable R. W. Wood stories current among physicists; many can be found in William Seabrook, *Dr. Wood* (New York: Harcourt, Brace, 1941). This particular anecdote came to me by way of the Mayers and appears also in Seabrook, pp. 47–48.

272   Fermi quote: Fermi, *Atoms*, p. 45.

273   Clark quote: Ronald W. Clark, *Einstein: The Life and Times* (New York: World, 1972), p. 3.

273   Eiduson quote: Eiduson, *op. cit.*, p. 134.

274   Szilard quote: Fleming and Bailyn, *op. cit.*, pp. 97–98.

275   "the greatest collection": Fleming and Bailyn, *op. cit.*, p. 12.

277   "fringe benefit": Bernard, *op. cit.*, p. 102.

278   "a plaintive remark": private communication.

280   "emotional constriction": Eiduson, *op. cit.*, pp. 93–97.

280   Wald quote: from an address entitled "The Human Enterprise" given July 1, 1970, at the Seattle Center Playhouse.

280   Kusch quote: this statement was made by Kusch in a colloquium at the Physics Department, University of Washington, February 25, 1965.

280   Gamow quote: *Mr. Tompkins Explores the Atom* (New York: MacMillan, 1945), p. 42.

281   "the atom that Bohr built": see the poem by Peierls in Cline, *op. cit.*, p. 88.

281   Eiduson quote: Eiduson, *op. cit.*, p. 102.

281   Einstein quote: Cline, *op. cit.*, p. 73.

282 Quotes from former students: private communications.

283 Rice quote: private communication.

284 Herzfeld quotes: private communication.

284 Fermi on Bohr's arrival: Fermi, *Atoms*, p. 154.

285 Fermi on Leonia: *ibid.*, p. 145.

286 Fermi on the Mayers: *ibid.*, pp. 170–171.

287 "Who is this man Fermi?": Fleming and Bailyn, *op. cit.*, p. 114.

287 "so I volunteered to do her mending": Fermi, private communication.

289 Mead quote: Margaret Mead, *An Anthropologist at Work: The Writings of Ruth Benedict* (Boston: Houghton, Mifflin, 1959), p. 429.

289 Pegram quote: Fermi, *Atoms*, p. 162.

290 The letter to Roosevelt: *ibid.*, p. 165.

290 Weisskopf remembered: Jungk, *op. cit.*, p. 113.

291 Fermi quote: Fermi, *Atoms*, p. 176.

291 "It was an old Dodge": Fermi, private communication.

293 Marianne remembered: Mary Harrington Hall, "An American Mother and the Nobel Prize—A Cinderella Story in Science," *McCall's*, July 1964.

295 Harris Mayer quote: private communication.

296 "The Italian navigator": Marjorie Johnston, ed., *The Cosmos of Arthur Holly Compton* (New York: Alfred A. Knopf, 1967), p. 248. Compton was Chairman of the Physics Department, University of Chicago, and Director of the U.S. Government's Plutonium Research Project. James B. Conant, President of Harvard, was Chairman of the National Defense Research Committee.

297 Goudsmit quote: Samuel Goudsmit, *Alsos* (New York: H. Schuman, 1947), pp. 7–8.

297 Bohr and Churchill: told me by Maria Mayer. A similar statement describes the American reaction to Bohr's report in Goudsmit, *op. cit.*, p. 178.

298 In Chicago James Franck: that Franck's proposal included mention of the embryo United Nations is not generally known even among scientists. See Alice Kimball Smith, *A Peril and a Hope:*

The Scientists' Movement in America: 1945–47 (Chicago: University of Chicago Press, 1965), Appendix B.

299   The Day of Trinity: Trinity was the code name for this first test of the bomb, a name apparently chosen by Oppenheimer because "It was just something suggested to me by John Donne's sonnets, which I happened to be reading at the time," according to Nuel Pharr Davis, *Lawrence and Oppenheimer* (New York: Simon & Schuster, 1968), p. 225.

302   "one felt this was a performance": Harris Mayer, private communication.

304   The Tellers and the Jacobsohns: Ruth Jacobsohn, private communication.

308   "a conversation of the angels": Hall, *op. cit.*

308   Fermi quote: *Atoms*, p. 263.

309   Fermi quote: private communication.

310   Teller quote: private communication.

311   Teller quote: private communication.

314   "never left the house": Hall, *op. cit.*

316   Wigner and Inglis: this description of the status of shell model and magic numbers comes from discussions with the Mayers and with Lawrence Wilets; David Inglis, of the University of Massachusetts, feels it would be more accurate to point out that there was some continuing interest in the shell model during the war, but only so far as the light nuclei were concerned, "while heavy nuclei remained mysterious."

318   James Franck once said: Jungk, *op. cit.*, p. 17.

318   Norbert Wiener wrote: Norbert Wiener, *I Am a Mathematician* (New York: Doubleday, 1956), p. 86.

318   Wilson quote: Robert Colburn, ed., *The Way of the Scientist,* by the Editors of *Science and Technology* (New York: Simon & Schuster, 1967), pp. 51–54.

319   She had seen preprints of papers: Robert G. Sachs of the Enrico Fermi Institute points out that the work of Eugene Feenberg, Washington University at St. Louis, aiming at an explanation of the magic numbers by a shell model, was an especially

valuable stimulus to Maria, for his "wrong" answers helped put
her on the track of the right answer.

321   Wilets quote: private communication.

321   One of Maria's students: private communication.

322   "I might accept it more readily": Wilets, private communication.

323   the "paranoid leap": Eiduson, *op. cit.*, p. 125.

325   Theoretical physicists brighter: see Roe, *op. cit.*, pp. 162 and 165
for verbal, spatial intelligence tests.

325   "free anxiety": Roe, *op. cit.*, p. 221.

329   Compare Maria's feelings about Heisenberg with those of Szilard, *The Way of the Scientist*, p. 24. Szilard felt that Heisenberg and other German scientists of great ability "got so little
pleasure out of contemplating giving a bomb to Hitler" that
they never really tried. Goudsmit, in *Alsos*, was skeptical of
this point of view.

331   Gamow quote: George Gamow, *Biography of Physics* (New York:
Harper & Row, 1961), p. 301.

333   Frieda Urey quote: private communication.

335   Maria Mayer on Franck: tape-recorded interview with Maria
Mayer conducted by Thomas S. Kuhn, *op. cit.*

337   In Heidelberg Hans Jensen's first reaction: *The New York Times*,
November 6, 1963.

337   Fermi quote: private communication.

339   Wilson quote: Wilson, *op. cit.*

341   Erikson quote: Mattfield and Van Aken, *op. cit.*, p. 31.

342   Mead quote: Bernard, *op. cit.*, p. 284.

342   Bernard quote: Bernard, *op. cit.*, p. 174.

343   Moss quote: Stirling Moss and K. W. Purdy, "Speed and
Women," excerpts from *All But My Life*, *Atlantic Monthly*,
October 1963.

345   "Undeniably . . . the technical community": Colburn, *op. cit.*,
p. 17.

Bibliography

Margaret Sanger

For the life of Margaret Sanger I have used her own works, *My Fight for Birth Control*, and the later *Margaret Sanger: An Autobiography*, and the Sanger material in the Sophia Smith Collection. Among the supplementary readings listed below, David M. Kennedy's scholarly *Birth Control in America: The Career of Margaret Sanger*, and Peter Fryer's *The Birth Controllers*, of which one chapter is devoted to Sanger, are especially valuable. Lawrence Lader's *The Margaret Sanger Story and the Fight for Birth Control* was written during her lifetime, and with her approval and collaboration.

Calder-Marshall, Arthur. *The Sage of Sex, A Life of Havelock Ellis*. New York: G. P. Putnam's Sons, 1959.

Dennett, Mary Ware. *Birth Control Laws*. New York: Frederick H. Hitchcock, 1926.

Ditzion, Sidney. *Marriage, Morals, and Sex in America*. New York: Bookman Associates, 1953.

Douglas, Emily Taft. *Margaret Sanger: Pioneer of the Future*. New York: Holt, Rinehart & Winston, 1970.

Drinnon, Richard. *Rebel in Paradise: A Biography of Emma Goldman*. Chicago: University of Chicago Press, 1961.

Duvall, Elizabeth S. *Hear Me for My Cause: Selected Letters of Margaret Sanger*, 1926–1927. Northampton: Smith College Press, 1967.

Eastman, Max. *Enjoyment of Living*. New York: Harper & Row, 1948.

Ellis, Havelock. *My Life: Autobiography of Havelock Ellis.* Boston: Houghton Mifflin, 1939.

Fryer, Peter. *The Birth Controllers.* New York: Stein & Day, 1966.

Goldman, Emma. *Living My Life.* New York: Alfred A. Knopf, 1931.

Kennedy, David M. *Birth Control in America: The Career of Margaret Sanger.* New Haven and London: Yale University Press, 1970.

Lader, Lawrence. *The Margaret Sanger Story and the Fight for Birth Control.* Garden City, L. I.: Doubleday, 1955.

Luhan, Mabel Dodge. *Movers and Shakers.* New York: Harcourt, Brace, 1936.

Sanger, Margaret. *Happiness in Marriage.* New York: Blue Ribbon Books, 1926.

———. *Margaret Sanger: An Autobiography.* New York: W. W. Norton, 1938.

———. *My Fight for Birth Control.* New York: Farrar & Rinehart, 1931.

Edna St. Vincent Millay

Any biographical study of Edna St. Vincent Millay must begin with her works and published letters. I have not included a complete bibliography of her own writings, however, since most readers will find the *Collected Poems* sufficient; those dramatic works discussed in the Millay section are also listed here. For better bibliographical information the works of Brittin and Gurko, both excellent studies of the life and poetry, should be consulted.

Collected Poems. New York: Harper & Row, 1956.

Aria da Capo. In *Twenty-five Best Plays of the Modern American Theatre,* edited by John Gassner. New York: Crown, 1949.

Conversation at Midnight. New York: Harper & Row, 1937.

The Lamp and the Bell. New York: Frank Shay, 1921.

Letters of Edna St. Vincent Millay. Edited by Alan Ross Macdougall. New York: Harper & Row, 1952.

Adams, Franklin P. *The Diary of Our Own Samuel Pepys.* New York: Simon & Schuster, 1935.

Atkins, Elizabeth. *Edna St. Vincent Millay and Her Times.* Chicago: University of Chicago Press, 1936.

Breuer, Elizabeth. "Edna St. Vincent Millay." *Pictorial Review,* November 1931.

————. "Mother of Poets." *Pictorial Review,* March 1930.

Brittin, Norman A. *Edna St. Vincent Millay.* U.S. Authors Series. New York: Twayne Publishers, 1967.

Cowley, Malcolm. *Exile's Return.* New York: Viking Press, 1951.

Dell, Floyd. *Homecoming: An Autobiography.* New York: Farrar & Rinehart, 1933.

Deutsch, Helen, and Hanau, Stella. *The Provincetown.* New York: Farrar & Rinehart, 1931.

Eastman, Max. *Enjoyment of Living.* New York: Harper & Row, 1948.

————. *Great Companions: Critical Memoirs of Some Famous Friends.* New York: Farrar, Straus & Cudahy, 1959.

————. *Love and Revolution.* New York: Random House, 1964.

Ficke, Arthur Davison. *Selected Poems.* New York: George H. Doran, 1926.

Gould, Jean. *The Poet and Her Book: A Biography of Edna St. Vincent Millay.* New York: Dodd, Mead, 1969.

Gurko, Miriam. *Restless Spirit: The Life of Edna St. Vincent Millay.* New York: Thomas Y. Crowell, 1962.

Haight, Elizabeth Hazelton. "Vincent at Steepletop." *Vassar Alumnae Magazine,* February 1957.

————. "Vincent at Vassar." *Vassar Alumnae Magazine,* May 1951.

King, Grace Hamilton. "The Development of the Social Consciousness of Edna St. Vincent Millay as Manifested in Her Poetry." Ph.D. dissertation, New York University, 1943.

Langner, Lawrence. *The Magic Curtain.* New York: E. P. Dutton, 1951.

MacCracken, Henry Noble. *The Hickory Limb.* New York: Charles Scribner's Sons, 1950.

Macdougall, Alan Ross. "Husband of a Genius." *Delineator,* October 1934.

Munson, Gorham. *Penobscot, Down East Paradise.* Philadelphia: J. B. Lippincott, 1959.

Powys, Llewelyn. *The Letters of Llewelyn Powys.* Edited by Louis Wilkinson. London: John Lane The Bodley Head, 1943.

Sheean, Vincent. *The Indigo Bunting: A Memoir of Edna St. Vincent Millay.* New York: Harper & Row, 1951.

Van Doren, Carl. *Three Worlds.* New York: Harper & Row, 1936.

Ware, Caroline. *Greenwich Village 1920–1930.* Boston: Houghton Mifflin, 1935.

Wilson, Edmund. *I Thought of Daisy.* New York: Charles Scribner's Sons, 1929.

———. *The Shores of Light: A Literary Chronicle of the Twenties and Thirties.* New York: Farrar, Straus, 1952.

Maria Goeppert-Mayer

Bernard, Jessie. *Academic Women.* University Park: Pennsylvania State University Press, 1964.

Born, Max. "Recollections of Max Born." *Bulletin of the Atomic Scientists,* Sept., Oct., Nov., 1965.

Cline, Barbara Lovett. *The Questioners: Physicists and the Quantum Theory.* New York: Thomas Y. Crowell, 1965.

Colburn, Robert, ed. *The Way of the Scientist,* by the Editors of *Science and Technology.* New York: Simon & Schuster, 1967.

Cropper, William H. *The Quantum Physicists.* London, Toronto, New York: Oxford University Press, 1970.

Eiduson, Bernice. *Scientists: Their Psychological World.* New York: Basic Books, 1962.

Fermi, Laura. *Atoms in the Family.* Chicago: University of Chicago Press, 1954.

———. *Illustrious Immigrants: The Intellectual Migration from Europe, 1930/41.* Chicago: University of Chicago Press, 1968.

Fleming, Donald, and Bailyn, Bernard, eds. *The Intellectual Migration: Europe and America, 1930–1960.* Cambridge, Mass: Harvard University Press, Belknap Press, 1969.

Forman, Paul. "Environment and Practice of Atomic Physics in Weimar Germany." Ph.D. dissertation, Berkeley, 1967. Ann Arbor: University Microfilms, 1968.

Gay, Peter. *Weimar Culture.* New York: Harper & Row, 1968.

Goudsmit, Samuel. *Alsos.* New York: H. Schuman, 1947.

Hall, Mary Harrington. "An American Mother and the Nobel Prize—A Cinderella Story in Science." *McCall's,* July 1964.

———. "The Nobel Genius." *San Diego Magazine,* August 1964.

Heine, Heinrich. *The Sea and The Hills.* Boston: Chapman & Grimes, 1946.

Hewlett, Richard G., and Anderson, Oscar E., Jr. *The New World, 1939/1946.* University Park: Pennsylvania State University Press, 1962.

Jungk, Robert. *Brighter Than a Thousand Suns.* New York: Harcourt, Brace, 1958.

Les Prix Nobel en 1963. Stockholm: The Nobel Foundation, 1964.

Mattfield, Jacquelyn A., and Van Aken, Carol, eds. *Women and the Scientific Professions.* Cambridge, Mass.: MIT Press, 1965.

Mayer, Maria Goeppert. "The Structure of the Nucleus." *Scientific American,* March 1951.

Roe, Anne. *The Making of a Scientist.* New York: Dodd, Mead, 1953.

Wallace, Irving. *The Prize.* New York: Simon & Schuster, 1961.

Wiener, Norbert. *Ex-Prodigy: My Childhood and Youth.* Cambridge, Mass.: MIT Press, 1964.

Wilson, Mitchell. "How Nobel Prize-Winners Get That Way: Science Laureates." *Atlantic Monthly,* December 1969.

Index

About the Author

Joan Dash was born in Brooklyn, New York, and educated at Barnard College. She always intended to be a writer, and after graduating in 1946 worked for various magazines and trade papers while her husband, J. Gregory Dash, earned his doctorate in physics at Columbia University. Not until the family moved to Los Alamos, New Mexico, and the company of three young a children and an isolated small community surrounded by southwestern desert drove her to it, did Mrs. Dash begin writing short stories. Nothing reached print, however, until after a Guggenheim year in Cambridge, England. Back in Los Alamos, she began selling articles to the woman's page of the *Manchester Guardian*, and then—both fiction and non-fiction—to a variety of publications: *Seventeen, Gourmet, The Minnesota Review, The Michigan Quarterly Review,* among others.

An article in *Mademoiselle* in the late 1960s, which discussed the marriages of gifted women, led to *A Life of One's Own.* The Dashes were now living in Seattle, Washington, the three children were nearly grown, and, having long wondered why she was not writing a book, she stopped wondering and began working.

73 10 9 8 7 6 5 4 3 2 1

DATE DUE